国内外经典教材辅导系列·英语类

《美国文学简史》
笔记和考研真题详解

主编：圣才考研网
www.100xuexi.com

中国石化出版社

内　容　提　要

本书是英美文学经典教材《美国文学简史》(第3、4版)(常耀信主编)的学习辅导书。全书完全遵循该教材的章目编排，共分26章，每章由两部分组成：第一部分为复习笔记(中英文对照)，总结本章的重点难点；第二部分是考研真题与典型题详解，精选名校经典考研真题及相关习题，并提供了详细的参考答案。

圣才考研网(www.100xuexi.com)提供常耀信《美国文学简史》辅导方案【视频课程、电子书、题库】。购书即可享受大礼包增值服务【本书电子书(电脑版、手机版)+全国名校真题汇编电子书】。手机扫码(本书封底)领取本书大礼包。

图书在版编目(CIP)数据

《美国文学简史》笔记和考研真题详解/圣才考研网主编.—北京:中国石化出版社,2023.7
(国内外经典教材辅导系列·英语类)
ISBN 978-7-5114-7204-5

Ⅰ.①美… Ⅱ.①圣… Ⅲ.①英语-研究生-入学考试-自学参考资料②文学史-美国-研究生-入学考试-自学参考资料 Ⅳ.①H310.421②I712.09

中国国家版本馆CIP数据核字(2023)第142648号

中国石化出版社出版发行

地址:北京市东城区安定门外大街58号
邮编:100011　电话:(010)57512500
发行部电话:(010)57512575
http://www.sinopec-press.com
E-mail:press@sinopec.com
武汉市盛宏源印务有限公司印刷
全国各地新华书店经销

*

787×1092毫米16开本16.75印张407千字
2023年8月第1版　2023年8月第1次印刷
定价:62.00元

序　言

我国各大院校一般都把国内外通用的权威教科书作为本科生和研究生学习专业课程的参考教材，这些教材甚至被很多考试(特别是硕士和博士入学考试)和培训项目作为指定参考书。为了帮助读者更好地学习专业课，我们有针对性地编著了一套与国内外教材配套的复习资料，并提供配套的名师讲堂和题库。

《美国文学简史》(第3、4版)(常耀信主编)一直被用作高等院校英语专业美国文学教材，被许多院校指定为英语专业考研必读书和学术研究参考书。作为该教材的学习辅导书，本书具有以下几个方面的特点：

1. 梳理章节脉络，剖析核心考点。每章的复习笔记以该教材为主并结合其他教材对本章的脉络框架进行梳理，并参考了国内名校名师讲授该教材的课堂笔记，因此，本书的内容基本涵盖了教材的核心考点。

2. 中英双语对照，凸显难点要点。本书章节笔记采用了中英文对照的形式，强化对重要难点知识的理解和运用。

3. 精选考研真题，补充难点习题。本书精选名校近年考研真题及相关习题，并提供答案和详解。所选真题和习题基本体现了各个章节的考点和难点，但又不完全局限于教材内容，是对教材内容极好的补充。

与本书相配套，圣才考研网提供常耀信《美国文学简史》网授精讲班、电子书、题库。

购书即可享受大礼包增值服务【本书电子书(电脑版、手机版)+全国名校真题汇编电子书】。手机扫码(本书封底)领取本书大礼包。

圣才考研网(www.100xuexi.com)是圣才学习网旗下的考研考博专业网站，提供考研公共课和全国500所院校考研考博专业课辅导【一对一辅导、网授精讲班等】、电子书、题库、全套资料(历年真题及答案、笔记讲义等)、国内外经典教材名师讲堂、考研教辅图书等。

考研辅导：kaoyan.100xuexi.com(圣才考研网)
资格考试：www.100xuexi.com(圣才学习网)

圣才学习网编辑部

目　录

第 1 章　殖民地时期的美国

1.1　复习笔记

I. American Puritanism

The British began to immigrate to North America in the first half of the 17th century. The first permanent English settlement in North America was established at Jamestown, Virginia in 1607. In 1620, the ship Mayflower carried about one hundred Pilgrims and arrived at Plymouth, Massachusetts. In pursuit of religious ideals and for many other reasons, many Puritans immigrated to the United States. The Puritanism they believed in later took root in the New World and had a profound impact on American thought and American literature.

1. Doctrines of Puritanism

The Puritans believed in the doctrine of predestination put forward by the theologian John Calvin, including original sin, complete depravity, and limited redemption.

2. The influence of Puritanism on American literature

(1) The idealism of Puritan had exerted a great influence on American writers.

Overall, American literature, at least white American literature, is based on the myth of the Garden of Eden in the Bible. To a large extent, it is a literary form of pious idealism as the legacy of American Puritanism. The Puritans longed to live in perfect order. With great courage, they hope to establish a new Garden of Eden in the United States so that they can finally live an ideal life. Encouraged by this sense of mission, they were very optimistic in the face of difficulties and obstacles. These have become important nourishment for the production and development of American literature. Optimism is embodied in the works of many American writers.

Ⅰ. 美国清教主义

英国向北美的移民活动开始于17世纪上半叶。英国于1607年在北美建立了第一个永久性海外殖民区：弗吉尼亚州的詹姆斯敦。1620年“五月花”号载运100余名移民抵达马萨诸塞州的普利茅斯。很多美国早期的移民是清教徒，他们出于宗教理想等多种原因来到美国。他们信奉的清教主义后来在新大陆生根发芽，并对美国思想和美国文学产生了根深蒂固的影响。

1. 清教主义的教义

清教徒信奉神学家约翰·加尔文宣扬的预设定论，原罪，彻底的堕落，有限制的救赎等神学主张。

2. 清教主义对美国文学的影响

(1) 清教徒的理想主义对美国作家的文学创作产生了深远的影响。

从总体来看，美国文学——至少是白人的美国文学——是建筑在《圣经》伊甸园神话基础上的文学。在很大程度上，它是美国清教主义遗产，是体现虔诚理想主义的一种文学形式。清教徒梦想着生活在一种完善的秩序之下，怀着勇气和希望在美国建立新的伊甸园，以使得他们能最终过上理想的生活。在这种使命感的鼓舞下，他们面对艰难险阻却充满乐观主义情绪。这些都成为美国文学产生和发展的重要滋养。乐观主义体现在许多美国作家的作品里。

(2) American Puritans' metaphorical way of observing things led to the emergence of symbolism, which is typical in American literature. Puritan theology and Puritan literary practice are the main reasons for the development of native symbolism in the United States. To the pious Puritans, the reality of the world is just the symbol of God. All phenomena in life are part and concrete manifestation of God's intention. It is easy to spot this symbolic process which often occurred in Puritan thinking. Over time, this process became part of the cultural traditions on which the American people and writers grew up. Symbolism is commonly used by Jonathan Edwards, Emerson, Hawthorne, and Melville. This unique way of observing the world by the Puritans is a basic component of their education	**(2)美国清教徒观察事物的形象视角催生了具有典型美国文学特点的象征主义。** 清教神学和清教徒的文学实践是美国本土象征主义发展的主要原因。在虔诚的清教徒看来，现实的大千世界都只是上帝的象征而已。生活中的一切现象都是上帝意图的组成部分和具体表现。这种象征过程常见于清教徒思维中。随着时间的推移，象征主义便成为美国人民和作家赖以成长的文化传统的一部分。象征主义是乔纳森·爱德华兹，爱默生，霍桑，麦尔维尔等著名美国作家常用的技巧。清教徒这种独特的观察世界的方式是他们所受教育的一个基本构成部分。
(3) In terms of the writing skills, the conciseness of Puritan works also profoundly affected American literature. Puritan writers show a fresh, concise, and direct writing style. Their simple and elegant rhetoric often stems from the direct influence of the Bible. Their works have left a lasting influence on American literature.	**(3)在写作技巧方面，清教徒作品的朴实无华也深刻地影响了美国文学。** 清教徒作家的写作风格是语言清新、简单、直接；修辞简朴、诚挚，带有《圣经》直接影响下的高贵气质。这些都给美国文学留下了持久的印迹。
Ⅱ. Overview of the colonial literature American literature grew out of humble origins. Diaries, histories, journals, letters, commonplace books, travel books, and sermons. In short, personal literature in its various forms, occupied a major position in the literature of the early colonial period.	**Ⅱ. 殖民地文学简介** 美国文学由很多粗糙的文体发展而来。日记、稗史、札记、书信、备忘录、游记及布道文稿等在内的各种形式的私人文字，在早期殖民时期的文学中占据着主要地位。
1. Major writers of the colonial period **(1) John Smith (1580 –1631)** Captain John Smith was one of the founders of the colony Jamestown, Virginia. His writing about North America became the source of information about the New World for later settlers. In *The General History of Virginia*, he wrote about his capture by the Indians and his rescue by the famous Indian Princess, Pocahontas. Another thing he wrote about that became historically important was his description of the fertile and vast new continent in his *A Description of New England*.	**1. 殖民地时期主要作家** **(1) 约翰·斯密斯** 约翰·斯密斯上校是弗吉尼亚州詹姆斯敦殖民地的建立者之一。他的作品中有关北美的叙述成为后来移民了解北美新大陆的信息来源。 约翰·史密斯在《弗吉尼亚通史》中讲述了他被印第安人俘虏及被著名的印第安公主郎波克杭特丝营救的故事。 他的另一部具有重大历史意义的作品是《新英格兰概览》，其中描述了肥沃且广袤的美洲新大陆。

(2) William Bradford (1590 –1657)

In 1620 William Bradford led the Mayflower endeavor and became the first governor of the Plymouth Plantation with his group of pilgrim fathers.

His major work is *Of Plymouth Plantation.*

(2) 威廉姆 · 布雷福德

在1620年威廉姆 · 布雷福德率领清教徒前辈移民乘“五月花”号到达美洲，他后来成为普利茅斯的首任总督。

他的主要作品是《普利茅斯开发史》。

(3) John Winthrop (1588 –1649)

John Winthrop was the first governor of the Massachusetts Bay colony.

In his famous speech *A Model of Christian Charity* he states that “we must consider that we shall be as a city upon a hill, the eyes of all people are upon us.”

The two major poets in the colonial period were Anne Bradstreet and Edward Taylor.

(3) 约翰 · 温思罗普

约翰 · 温思罗普是马萨诸塞湾殖民地的首任总督。

在其著名演说《基督教博爱的典范》中他说到“我们将成为山巅之城，全世界人民的眼光都在注视着我们。”

殖民时期的两大诗人是安 · 布雷兹特里特和爱德华 · 泰勒。

(4) Anne Bradstreet (1612 –1672)

Anne Bradstreet was known as the “Tenth Muse” who appeared in America.

① Major works

The Tenth Muse Lately Sprung Up in America
Contemplations
“Upon the Burning of Our House”
“To My Dear and Loving Husband”
“In Reference to Her Children”
“The Flesh and the Spirit”
“As Weary Pilgrim”

② Analysis of her major works

◆“Contemplations (9)”

When the poet heard the grasshopper and cricket sing, she thought of this as their praising of their Creator and searched her own soul accordingly. This poem typically shows the way Puritans perceive the physical world.

◆“The Flesh and the Spirit”

This poem depicts two sisters arguing about their values. What “flesh” represents is the seductive power of secular materials. The “spirit” tries to persuade the “flesh” to believe in the divine majesty of God. The twin sisters are evidently integral parts of one Puritan mind.

(4) 安 · 布雷德斯特里特

她被称作在美国出现的“第十个缪斯”。

①主要作品

《美洲最近出现的第十位缪斯》
《沉思录》
《写在我家失火之际》
《献给我亲爱的丈夫》
《关于她的孩子们》
《灵与肉》
《疲惫的朝圣者》

②主要作品分析

◆《沉思录》第九首

当诗人听到蝈蝈和蛐蛐同时鸣叫，她感到这是它们对上帝恩惠的赞扬。她由此开始反思自己。这首诗突出地表现出清教徒形象地观察世界的方式。

◆《灵与肉》

这首诗描述了两姐妹的争论。“肉”所代表的是世俗的物质的诱惑力。而“灵”则试图说服“肉”相信上帝的神圣伟大。两姐妹代表了一个清教徒的完整思想。

(5) Edward Taylor(1642 –1729) Edward Taylor was a Puritan poet, concerned about how his images spoke for God. **① Analysis of major works** ◆"Huswifery" This poem indicates that the poet saw religious significance in a simple daily incident like a housewife spinning. The spinning wheel, the distaff, the flyers, the spool, the reel and the yarn have all acquired a metaphysical significance in the symbolic, Puritan eyes of the poet. ◆"Upon a Spider Catching a Fly" The poet sees the spider as a symbol of Hell. Obviously, Taylor believes in God and thinks that God can save people who have made mistakes, even the guilty, from the dark trap of hell.	**(5)爱德华·泰勒** 爱德华·泰勒是个清教徒诗人，他的诗歌形象主要为上帝辩护。 **①主要作品分析** ◆《家务》 这首诗中，诗人赋予了家庭主妇纺织这一普通的日常事件强烈的宗教意味。在诗人这个清教徒的眼里，纺车、线杆、梭子、线筒及线卷，这些意象都具有抽象的意义。 ◆《蜘蛛捕蝇有感》 诗人把蜘蛛视作是地狱的象征。显然，泰勒信仰上帝，认为上帝能把犯错之人，甚至是有罪之人从地狱的邪恶圈套里拯救出来。
(6) Thomas Paine (1737 –1809) Thomas Paine was born in England and came to America in 1774. His life was one of continual, unswerving fight for the rights of man. He was a major influence in the American Revolution. **① Major works** *Common Sense* *The American Crisis* "The Times that Try Men's Souls" *The Rights of Man* *The Age of Reason* **②Analysis of his major works** ◆*Common Sense* *Common Sense* criticized the British monarchy and promoted the development of the upcoming struggle to overthrow colonial rule. Paine asserted that only by following the call of human intuition, common sense, and conscience, the crisis faced by the North American colonies could be resolved. This pamphlet was popular in the colonies. It promoted the legalization of independence and also encouraged the American people in their painful struggle. ◆*The American Crisis* *The American Crisis* is made up of 16 pamphlets written between 1776 and 1783. The first pamphlet "The Times that Try Men's Souls" came out at one of the darkest moments of the revolution. "The harder the struggle, the more glorious the triumph," when Washington had it read to the troops, it proved a heartening stimulus, a spurring excitement to further action with hope and confidence.	**(6)托马斯·潘恩** 托马斯·潘恩出生于英国，于1774年来到美国。他的一生堪称为人的权利而坚持不懈、努力奋斗的一生。他是美国独立革命时期最有影响力的人物之一。 **①主要作品** 《常识》 《美国危机》 《考验人的灵魂的时代》 《人的权利》 《理性的时代》 **②主要作品分析** ◆《常识》 《常识》抨击了英国的君主制，推动了即将到来的推翻殖民统治的斗争的发展。潘恩认为只有听从人的直觉、常识和良心的召唤，北美殖民地面临的危机才能得以解决。这个小册子在殖民地受到热捧，它宣扬了独立的合法化，也鼓励了痛苦斗争中的美国人民。 ◆《美国危机》 《美国危机》由16篇写于1776年至1783年的小册子组成。其中第一篇《考验人的灵魂的时代》写于美国独立战争最灰暗的时刻。"战斗越艰苦，胜利越光荣，"当华盛顿把这篇文章念给士兵听时，它宛如一剂兴奋剂，鼓舞军民满怀信心和希望勇往直前。

(7) Philip Freneau

Philip Freneau's great position in the history of American literature is reflected in many aspects. He dedicated his poetry creation ability to the country's struggle for independence. His poems praised the justice of the people and exposed the atrocities of the British colonists. In addition, he is also one of the prominent representatives of initiating American literary nationalism. Freneau was the first to give up imitating English poems and directly observe and describe everything around him. He admired the style and features of the American land and Indian civilization.

① Major works

"The Wild Honey Suckle"

"The Dying Indian: Tomo Chequi"

"The Indian Burying Ground"

② Analysis of major work

◆"The Wild Honey Suckle"

In this poem, the lyric beauty, the heartfelt pathos, and the multiple emotional responses and echoes that the sight described are simply amazing. Here we can see the poet enjoys the beauty that the American landscape is capable of offering. This poem is an indication of the poet's dedication to American subject matter.

(8) Charles Brockden Brown

His works embody obvious Gothic characteristics. He realized that his inspiration was rooted in his own land, and he attached great importance to describing the character's inner world. His works had a significant impact on later American writing.

◆Major works

"Edgar Huntly"

"Ormond"

"Arthur Mervyn"

"Wieland"

(7)菲利普·弗瑞诺

菲利普·弗瑞诺美国文学史上的重要地位体现在很多方面。他把自己的诗歌创作才能奉献给了国家的独立斗争事业，其诗歌歌颂了人民的正义事业，揭露了英国殖民者的暴行。除此之外，他还是开创美国文学民族主义的突出代表之一。弗瑞诺率先摆脱模仿英国诗作的影子，直接观察和描写四周的一切。他崇尚描写美洲大地的风貌和印第安文明。

①主要作品

《野生的金银花》

《奄奄一息的印第安人：托姆·柴吉》

《印第安人墓地》

②主要作品分析

◆《野生的金银花》

这首诗旋律优美，伤感之情动人心扉，其中描写的景色引发复杂的情感激荡和共鸣。诗人尽情享受着美国土地的美丽风景。该诗体现了诗人致力于描写美国本土的题材。

(8)查尔斯·布罗克登·布朗

他的作品体现出明显的哥特式特征。他意识到自己的灵感植根于自己的土地。他非常重视对人物内心世界的描述。他对后来的美国写作产生了不小的影响。

◆主要作品

《埃德加·亨特利》

《奥蒙德》

《亚瑟·默文》

《维兰德》

1.2 考研真题与典型题详解

I. Fill in the blanks.

1. The term "Puritan" was applied to those settlers who originally were devout members of the Church of ________.

2. The most enduring shaping influence in American thought and American literature was ________.
3. Hard work, thrift, piety and sobriety, these were the ________ values that dominated much of the early American writing.
4. Many Puritans wrote verse, but the works of two writers, Anne Bradstreet and ________, rose to the level of real poetry.
5. *The Tenth Muse Lately Sprung Up in America* is a collection of poems composed by ________.
6. On January 10, 1776, Thomas Paine's famous pamphlet ________ appeared.
7. Except *Common Sense*, Paine's the other two famous works were ________ and ________.
8. Thomas Paine's second most important work ________ was an impassioned plea against hereditary monarchy.
9. Thomas Paine, with his natural gift for pamphleteering and rebellion, was appropriately born into an age of ________.
10. Philip Freneau was noteworthy first because of the nature of his poems. They were truly American and very patriotic. In this respect, he reflected the spirit of his age. Therefore, he has been called the "________ of American Poetry".

Ⅱ. Multiple Choice

1. Anne Bradstreet was a Puritan poet. Her poems made such a stir in England that she became known as the "________" who appeared in America.（北二外 2016 研）
   A. Ninth Muse　B. Tenth Muse　C. Best Muse　D. First Muse
2. The first permanent English settlement in North America was established at ________.（北二外 2009 研）
   A. Jamestown　B. New York　C. Boston　D. Concord
3. The first settlers who became the founding fathers of the American nation were quite a few of them ________.（北二外 2008 研）
   A. Quakers.　B. Anglicans　C. Catholics　D. Puritans.
4. It is a critical commonplace now that American literature is based on a myth, that is, ________.（北二外 2008 研）
   A. the ancient Greek myth of Zeus
   B. the British myth of the Saint Grail
   C. the Biblical myth of the Garden of Eden
   D. the legend of the Sleepy Hollow
5. The common thread throughout American literature has been the emphasis on the ________.
   A. Revolutionism　B. Reason　C. Individualism　D. Rationalism
6. The ship "________" carried about one hundred Pilgrims and took 66 days to beat its way across the Atlantic. In December of 1620, it put the Pilgrims ashore at Plymouth, Massachusetts.
   A. Sunflower　B. Armada　C. Mayflower　D. Titanic
7. The English colonies in North America rose in arms against their parent country and the Continental Congress adopted ________ in 1776.
   A. the Declaration of Independence　B. the Sugar Act

C. the Stamp Act D. the Mayflower Compact

8. What style did the seventeenth century American poets adapt to the subject matter confronted in a strangely new environment?

A. The style of their own.

B. The style mixed with English and American elements.

C. The style mixed with native-American and British tradition.

D. The style of established European poets.

9. Anne Bradstreet was a Puritan poet. Her poems made such a stir in England that she became known as the ________ who appeared in America.

A. Ninth Muse B. Tenth Muse C. Best Muse D. First Muse

10. It was not until January 1776 that a widely heard public voice demanded complete separation from England. The voice was that of ________, whose pamphlet *Common Sense*, with its heated language, increased the growing demand for separation.

A. Thomas Paine B. Thomas Jefferson

C. George Washington D. Patrick Henry

11. Which is not connected with Thomas Paine?

A. *Common Sense.* B. *The American Crisis.*

C. *The Rights of Man.* D. *The Autobiography.*

12. "These are the times that try men's souls", these words were once read to Washington's troops and did much to spur excitement to further action with hope and confidence. Who is the author of these words?

A. Benjamin Franklin. B. Thomas Paine.

C. Thomas Jefferson. D. George Washington.

13. Which work is written by Freneau?

A. *The Rights of Man.* B. *The Wild Honey Suckle.*

C. *Poor Richard's Almanac.* D. *The Day of Doom.*

Ⅲ. Explain the following term.

1. American Puritanism (南开大学 2008 研)

Ⅳ. Read the following quotations and answer the questions.

Passage 1

I heard the merry grasshopper then sing,
The black-clad cricket bear a second part;
They kept one tune and played on the same string.
Seeming to glory in their little art.
Small creatures abject thus their voices raise,
And in their kind resound their Maker's praise,
Whilst I, as mute, can warble forth no higher lays?

Questions:

(1) This is the ninth of the "Contemplations" written by an early American woman writer. What is her name?

(2) Make a brief comment on this short poem.

Passage 2

Huswifery

Make me, O Lord, thy spinning wheel complete.
Thy holy word my distaff make for me.
Make mine affections thy swift flyers neat,
And make my soul thy holy spool to be.
My conversation make to be thy reel, and reel,
the yam thereon spun of thy wheel.

Questions:

(1) Identify the poet of this poem.

(2) Make a brief comment on this poem.

Passage 3

These are the times that try men's souls: The summer soldier and the sunshine patriot will in this crisis, shrink from the service of their country; but he that stands it now deserves the love and thanks of man and woman. Tyranny, like hell, is not easily conquered; yet we have this consolation with us, that the harder the conflict, the more glorious the triumph. What we obtain too cheap, we esteem too lightly: This dearness only that gives everything its value. Heaven knows how to put a proper price upon its goods.

Questions:

(1) Which book is this passage taken from?

(2) Who is the author of this book?

(3) Whom is the author praising? Whom is the author criticizing?

(4) What do you think of the language used in the book?

Passage 4

From morning suns and evening dews
At first thy little being came:
If nothing once, you nothing lose,
For when you die you are the same:
The space between, is but an hour,
The frail duration of a flower.

Questions:

(1) Who is the writer of these verses?

(2) What is the title of this poem?

(3) Give a brief comment on this poem.

V. Short answer questions

1. Who was Anne Bradstreet? What were her literary achievements?

2. What are the basic Calvinist tenets? (国际关系学院 2007 研)

VI. Essay question

1. What is the significance of American Puritanism in American literature?

参考答案及解析

I. Fill in the blanks.

1. England

（清教徒(Puritan)，是指要求清除英国国教 Church of England 中天主教残余的改革派。其字词于 16 世纪 60 年代开始使用，源于拉丁文的 Purus，意为“清洁”。）

2. American Puritanism

（美国文化源于清教文化，由清教徒移民时传入北美。美国主流价值观都可以追溯到殖民地时期一统天下的清教主义，并且清教思想对美国文学有着根深蒂固的影响。）

3. Puritan

（清教主义，起源于英国，在北美殖民地得以实践与发展。清教徒强调艰苦奋斗、勤俭节约、虔诚和淡泊。这些价值观也影响了早期的美国文学。）

4. Edward Taylor

（美国殖民时期最著名的诗人是安·布雷兹特里特和爱德华·泰勒。）

5. Anne Bradstreet

（安·布雷兹特里特是美国殖民时期著名的诗人。其代表作是诗集《最近在北美出现的第十位缪斯》(*The Tenth Muse Late Sprung up in America*)。）

6. *Common Sense*

（1776 年美国独立的风潮开始，托马斯·潘恩支持美国独立，反对英国的殖民专政，撰写了他的成名小册子《常识》，为美国从英国殖民中独立出来辩论，批评英国国王残暴无能，认为独立后的美国应该建立共和国。）

7. *The Rights of Man*, *The Age of Reason*

（潘恩著名的作品包括，《常识》《人的权利》《理性的时代》。）

8. *The Rights of Man*

（1791 年 3 月，托马斯·潘恩在伦敦出版《人权论》，激烈抨击埃德蒙·伯克(Edmund Burke，1729—1797)的《法国革命感言录》(*Reflections on the Revolution in France*)(1790)。《人权论》的可贵之处还在于，它冲破了当时笼罩于整个西方思想界对英国君主立宪政体的迷信，深入骨髓地批判了这一政体，给当时还处于摸索状态的法国革命指明了共和主义的崭新方向。）

9. Revolution

（潘恩是美国独立革命时期著名的作家之一。）

10. Father

（菲利普·弗瑞诺是开启美国民主主义的突出代表之一，他被称为“美国诗歌之父。”）

Ⅱ. Multiple Choice

1. B　安·布雷兹特里特，清教徒诗人，1630 年从英国来到新大陆马萨诸塞湾殖民地，以《第十个缪斯在美国出现》闻名。
2. A　詹姆斯敦是英国人在北美的第一个永久定居地。
3. D　早期来到北美的殖民者有不少是清教徒，因而殖民时期的文学深受清教思想影响。
4. C　由于深受清教主义的影响，美国文学——至少是美国的白人文学——是建立在《圣经》伊甸园神话基础上的文学。

5. C 美国价值观的核心是个人主义，因而，个人主义也成为贯穿美国文学史的主线。

6. C 1620 年 100 多名清教徒前辈乘坐“五月花”号船到达美国马萨诸塞州的普利茅斯。

7. A 1776 年 13 个英属北美殖民地奋起反击英国的殖民统治，并且 1776 年 7 月 4 日，大陆会议通过了一份由托马斯·杰弗逊起草的《独立宣言》(*Declaration of Independence*)。

8. D 17 世纪美国诗人大多沿袭英国诗歌的风格。

9. B 安·布雷兹特里特被誉为“美国出现的第十个缪斯”。

10. A 潘恩的《常识》号召美国摆脱英国的统治。

11. D 《自传》是本杰明·富兰克林的代表作，其余三项都是潘恩的主要作品。

12. B “这是考验人的灵魂的时刻”，这句话选自潘恩的《美国危机》。

13. B 《野生的金银花》是弗瑞诺最具代表性的作品。

Ⅲ. Explain the following term.

1. The word Puritanism is originally used to refer to the theology advocated by a party within the Church of England. The term Puritanism is also used in a broader sense to refer to the attitudes and values considered characteristic of the Puritans. It has been employed to denote a rigid moralism, or the condemnation of innocent pleasure, or religious narrowness adhered by the early New England Puritans. The American Puritanism as a cultural heritage exerted great influence over American moral values. And this Puritan influence over American Romanticism was conspicuously noticeable. In addition, a preoccupation with the Calvinistic view of original sin and the mystery of evil marked the works by such famous writers as Hawthorne and Melville.

Ⅳ. Read the following quotations and answer the questions.

Passage 1

(1) Anne Bradstreet.

(2) This short poem offers the reader an insight into the mentality of the early Puritan pioneering into a new world. When the poet heard the grasshopper and the cricket sing, she thought of this as the praise to their creator and searched her own soul accordingly. It is evident that she saw something metaphysical inhering in the physical, a mode of perception which was singularly Puritan.

Passage 2

(1) Edward Taylor.

(2) The poem indicates that the poet saw religious significance in a simple daily incident like a housewife spinning. In his symbolic Puritan eyes, the spinning wheels, luggage racks, flyers, spools, reels and yarn all have certain metaphorical meanings.

Passage 3

(1) *The American Crisis*

(2) Thomas Paine

(3) Paine is praising those who stand “it”, it referring to “the service of their country”. In the meantime, Paine is criticizing those who shrink from the service of their country in this crisis.

(4) The language is plain, impressive and forceful. Paine himself once said that his purpose as a writer was to use plain language to make those who can scarcely read understand.

Passage 4

(1) Philip Freneau.

(2) "The Wild Honey suckle".

(3) Here Freneau offers a version of an abundant America with potential for providing a good life for all. The poem is also an indication of his dedication to American subject matter as he examined peculiarly American characteristics of the countryside.

V. Short answer questions

1. Anne Bradstreet (1612 ~ 1672) is one of the most important figures in the history of American Literature. She is considered by many to be the first American poet, and her first collection of poems, *The Tenth Muse Lately Sprung Up in America*, *By a Gentlewoman of Those Parts*, was the first book written by a woman to be published in the United States. Mrs. Bradstreet's works also serve as a document of the struggles of a Puritan wife against the hardships of New England colonial life.

2. Calvinist theology is sometimes identified with the five points of Calvinism, also called the doctrines of grace. In English, the five points are sometimes referred to by the acronym TULIP, which means Total Inherited Depravity, Unconditional Election, Limited Atonement, Irresistible Grace and Perseverance of the Saints England colonial life.

VI. Essay question

1. The settlement of the North American continent by the English began in the early part of the 17th century. Many early American immigrants were Puritans, and they came to the United States for a variety of reasons. The Puritanism they believed in later took root in the New World and had a profound impact on American thought and American literature.

The American Puritans were idealists, believing that the Church should be restored to the "Purity" and religion was a matter of primary importance. They accepted the doctrine of predestination, original sin, total depravity and limited atonement. Overall, American literature, at least white American literature, is based on the myth of the Garden of Eden in the Bible. With great courage, they hope to establish a new Garden of Eden in the United States so that they can finally live an ideal life. Encouraged by this sense of mission, they were very optimistic in the face of difficulties and obstacles. These have become important nourishment for the production and development of American literature. Optimism is embodied in the works of many American writers, such as Emerson, Whitman, etc.

Puritan theology and Puritan literary practice are the main reasons for the development of native symbolism in the United States. To the pious Puritans, the reality of the world is just the symbol of God. All phenomena in life are part and concrete manifestation of God's intention. It is easy to spot this symbolic process which often occurred in Puritan thinking. Over time, this process became part of the cultural traditions on which the American people and writers grew up. Symbolism is commonly used by Jonathan Edwards, Emerson, Hawthorne, and Melville. This unique way of observing the world by the Puritans is a basic component of their education

Regarding the technique, simplicity characterizes the Puritan style of writing. The style is fresh, simple and direct; the rhetoric is plain and honest, without a touch of nobility often traceable to the direct influence of the Bible. All this has left an indelible imprint on American writing. Thus, American Puritanism has been, by and large, a healthy legacy to the Americans.

第2章 爱德华兹·富兰克林·克里夫古尔

2.1 复习笔记

American critic Van Wyck Brooks, when commenting on the 18th century America and American character, noted that Jonathan Edwards and Benjamin Franklin together represent the 18th century. American Puritan tradition is characterized by both religious piety and dispassionate pragmatism Jonathan Edwards represents the former and Franklin the latter. Both men were devout Puritans.	美国评论家范·威克·布鲁克斯在评述到18世纪美国及美国人性格时指出：乔纳森·爱德华兹和本杰明·富兰克林两人是18世纪的杰出代表。决定美国人性格的清教主义传统具有宗教虔诚和冷静务实两个特点；乔纳森·爱德华兹代表前者，富兰克林代表后者。两人都是虔诚的清教徒。
I. Jonathan Edwards (1703 – 1758)	**I. 乔纳森·爱德华兹**
1. Life	**1. 生平**
Born into an extremely religious family, Edwards entered Yale College at the age of 13 and received his master's degree in 1723. He later became a pastor in the suburb of Northampton, Massachusetts. In his sermons he focused on describing the awesome power of God, the fall of man, and the need for man to communicate with the Holy Spirit and to receive God's favor. He was one of the key figures in the emergence and development of the Great Awakening movement in North America. He became famous not only in North America, but also in Europe.	爱德华兹出生于一个宗教气息极其浓郁的家庭里。13岁，他进入耶鲁大学学习，于1723年获得硕士学位。后来他成为马萨诸塞州北安普敦郊区的牧师。他在布道时着重讲述上帝的威力、人的堕落以及人与圣灵的交流、接受上帝恩惠的必要性等。他是促进北美"大觉醒"运动发生和发展的关键人物之一。他不仅扬名北美，而且饮誉欧洲。
2. Ideas	**2. 思想**
(1) He was the first modern American and the country's last medieval man.	**(1) 他是美国第一位具有现代思想的哲学家，美国最后一位思想依旧停留在中世纪的神学家。**
His works reveal the modern consciousness of the man. He was influenced to no small extent by Newton's mechanical view of the universe and the Lockean thesis. He tried to reconcile Puritan ideas with the new rationalism of Lock and Newton.	他的作品显示出他思想的强烈现代意识。他深受牛顿机械宇宙观和洛克哲学思想的影响。他竭力调和清教思想和洛克、牛顿的理性主义。
His works also show his mentality as a medievalist. He loved to walk alone in the woods, having a pleasant conversation with Christ, with his body and mind deeply placed in the surroundings of God. This is what is called "the communion of the soul with God". This communication comes from a heartfelt "conversion" rather than from rational considerations.	他的作品也显示出他作为一个中世纪人的心态。他喜欢在林中独自漫步，和基督愉快的交谈，身心都深置于上帝的包围中。这就是所谓"灵魂与上帝的交流"，这种交流由发自内心"皈依"而来而不是出于理性的考虑。

(2) He was a good deal of a transcendentalist. His personal narrative can be seen as his spiritual autobiography. He believed that God is everywhere. God manifests himself through nature and man, who is both a part of God and therefore divine. His work "*The Shape of Sacred Things*" is considered to be the forerunner of the transcendentalist nature symbolism in the 19th century. And his Puritan mysticism is fully and clearly stated in the writings of Ralph Waldo Emerson in the 19th century.	**(2) 他在很大程度上是一位超验主义者。** 他的个人叙事可以看作是他的精神自白。 他认为上帝无处不在。上帝通过自然界和人类来体现自己，人既是上帝的一部分，因此也是神圣的。 其作品《神圣事物的形影》堪称19世纪超验主义自然象征论的先导。而他的清教神秘主义在19世纪爱默生的著作中得到了全面而明确的陈述。
3. Major works *The Freedom of the Will* *The Great Doctrine of Original Sin Defended* *The Nature of True Virtue* "Sinners in the Hands of an Angry God" "Personal Narrative" *Images or Shadows of Divine Things*	**3. 主要作品** 《自由的意志》 《伟大的基督教教义的原罪说辩》 《真正美德的本质》 《发怒的上帝手中的罪人》 《自述》 《神圣事物的形影》
Ⅱ. Benjamin Franklin (1706 – 1790) Being a rare genius in human history, Franklin was a "Jack-of-all-trades"—printer, postmaster, almanac maker, essayist, scientist, orator, statesman, philosopher, political economist, ambassador.	**Ⅱ. 本杰明 · 富兰克林** 富兰克林是人类历史上少有的天才。他博学多才，有很多身份：出版家、邮政总长、历书作者、散文家、科学家、演说家、政治家、哲学家、政治经济学家、大使、业务员等等，是个万事通。
1. Life Franklin was born into a poor family of candle makers. He was very industrious. At the age of 16, he began publishing critical articles under the pseudonym "*Silence Dogood*", and at the age of 17, he fled to Philadelphia to make a living, where he later became a publisher. He helped establish the University of Pennsylvania's predecessors, the Medical College of Pennsylvania and the North American Philosophical Society. He was also a renowned scientist of his time. He was one of the founding fathers of the United States because he signed the Declaration of Independence, the Treaty of Alliance with France, the Treaty of Peace with England and the U. S. Constitution. Franklin's literary stature is largely due to two of his literary achievements, namely, *Poor Richard's Almanac* and *The Autobiography*.	**1. 生平** 富兰克林出生于一个贫穷的蜡烛制造匠家庭。他非常勤奋好学。16岁时开始以笔名"静行善"发表评论文章。17岁时只身逃往费城谋生，后成为出版商。他协助建立了宾夕法尼亚大学的前身——宾夕法尼亚医学院和北美哲学学会。他也是当时著名的科学家。他还签署过《独立宣言》、《美法同盟条约》、《英美和平条约》和《美国宪法》，是美国的缔造者之一。富兰克林在文学上的地位主要由他的两项文学成就奠定，即《穷查理历书》和《富兰克林自传》这两部作品。
2. Analysis of major works ◆*Poor Richard's Almanac* Franklin first issued *Poor Richard's Almanac* in 1732 and it continued to be issued for 25 years. The almanac contains poetry,	**2. 主要作品分析** ◆《穷查理历书》 富兰克林于1732年首次发行《穷查理历书》，这本历书持续发行

prose, and many idiomatic sayings that soon became household words, many of which became mottos for people in the world. Many of his aphorisms come from other writers. But he enriched them with his own humorous wisdom, which makes *Poor Richard's Almanac* entertaining and educational.

◆ *The Autobiography*

(1) *The Autobiography* is one of the finest works of autobiographical literature. It is a concise and extremely engaging account of Franklin's leap from poverty and humility to wealth and fame. It is a faithful account of the glorious career of America's first self-made man. The whole book consists of four parts, written in different periods.

(2) *The Autobiography* is, first and foremost, a Puritan document because it records the Puritans' self-reflection and self-improvement. It is also the best illustration of the Puritan moral principle that in order to be successful, one must be hardworking, simple, and prudent.

(3) *The Autobiography* amply illustrates that Franklin was the voice of the American Enlightenment in the 18th century. He represented that in America, man is essentially good and free, with the God-given inalienable right to freedom and the pursuit of happiness. The book celebrates the realization of the American dream by telling the story of success through self-reliance.

(4) The style of *The Autobiography* reflects the simple, straightforward and concise style of the Puritans.

Ⅲ. Hector St. John de Crevecoeur (1735 – 1813)

Crevecoeur was a French settler. His famous work is *Letters from an American Farmer*.

◆ **Analysis of *Letters from an American Farmer***

Crevecoeur wrote back to Europe about the nature and significance of the new nation of the United States to help the world understand it better. *Letters from an American Farmer* contains 12 letters. The first eight letters illustrate the pride of being an American. However, from the 9th letter onward, the author's tone begins to become subdued. He realized that the new world also had slavery, greed, violence, famine, and disease, which were thought to be found only in the old world of Europe. A pessimistic tone lingers in *Letters from an American Farmer*. It reflects the author's disillusionment.

长达25年。书中有诗歌，散文，以及许多成语箴言。这些成语箴言很快便家喻户晓，成为许多人为人处世的座右铭。他的许多格言来源于别的作家，但是他充分运用自己的幽默智慧简化丰富了这些格言，这使得《穷查理历书》寓教于乐。

◆《自传》

(1)《自传》是自传体文学中的上乘佳作。它简明而引人入胜地叙述了富兰克林由穷苦卑微而跃至富有、闻名的故事。它忠实地记录了美国第一位自力更生者光辉灿烂的职业生涯。全书由四部分组成，分别写于不同时期。

(2)《自传》首先是一本清教文献。它记录了清教徒的自我反省和自我完善。它也是清教道德原则的最好诠释，为了取得成功，人必须勤劳、简朴、谨慎。

(3)《自传》充分说明了富兰克林是18世纪美国启蒙运动的代言人。他体现了在美国，人本质是善良自由的，拥有上帝赋予的不可剥夺的自由及追求幸福的权力。该书通过讲述自力更生而获取成功的故事，歌颂了美国梦的实现。

(4)《自传》的文体体现出清教徒朴素、直爽、简洁的风格。

Ⅲ. 克里夫古尔

克里夫古尔是法国移民。其著名作品是《来自一个美国农夫的信》。

◆**《来自一个美国农夫的信》作品分析**

克里夫古尔写信向欧洲介绍美国这个新国家的性质和意义，以帮助世界了解美国。《来自一个美国农夫的信》包括12封信。前8封信流露出作为美国人自豪的心情。然而，从第9封信开始，作者的语调开始变得低沉。他意识到美国也存在着被认为只有欧洲旧世界才有的各种罪恶——奴隶制、贪婪、暴力、饥荒和疾病。《来自一个美国农夫的信》中萦绕着悲观主义的基调，体现了幻灭的情绪。

2.2 考研真题与典型题详解

I. Fill in the blanks.

1. In his __________ Benjamin Franklin creates the image of a boy's rise from __________ to riches and demonstrates his belief that the new world of America was a land of opportunities which might be met through hard work and wise management.（天津外国语学院 2008 研）
2. If we say Jonathan Edwards represents the upper levels of the American mind, __________ represents the lower levels.
3. Before his death, __________ had gained a position as America's first systematic philosopher.
4. Jonathan Edwards' work *Images or Shadows of Divine Things* anticipated the nature symbolism of __________ in the 19th century.
5. Franklin's claim to a place in literature rests chiefly on his __________ and __________.
6. Benjamin Franklin's best writing is found in his masterpiece __________.
7. Franklin was the epitome of the __________, the versatile, practical embodiment of national man in the 18th century.
8. Eighteen-century America experienced an age of __________, of __________, and __________ like England and Europe.

Ⅱ. Multiple Choice

1. The first symbol of self-made American man is __________.（北二外 2009 研）

   A. George Washington　B. Washington Irving
   C. Thomas Jefferson　D. Benjamin Franklin
2. At the Reason and Revolution Period, Americans were influenced by the European movement called the __________.

   A. Charitist Movement　B. Romanticist Movement
   C. Enlightenment Movement　D. Modernist Movement
3. In American literature, the eighteenth century was the age of the Enlightenment. __________ was the dominant spirit.

   A. Humanism　B. Rationalism　C. Revolution　D. Evolution
4. Jonathan Edwards' best and most representative sermon was __________.

   A. *A True Sight of Sin*　B. *Sinners in the Hands of an Angry God*
   C. *A Model of Christian Charity*　D. *God's Determinations*
5. The secular ideals of the American Enlightenment were exemplified in the life and career of __________.

   A. Thomas Hood　B. Benjamin Franklin
   C. Thomas Jefferson　D. George Washington
6. From 1732 to 1758, Benjamin Franklin wrote and published his famous __________, an annal collection of proverbs.

   A. *The Autobiography*　B. *Poor Richard's Almanac*
   C. *Common Sense*　D. *The General Magazine*

Ⅲ. Explain the following term.

1. the literary form of autobiography (北二外 2008 研)

Ⅳ. Essay questions

1. Analyze *The Autobiography of Benjamin Franklin*.
2. Analysis of *The Poor Richard's Almanac*.

参考答案及解析

I. Fill in the blanks.

1. *Autobiography*, poor

（富兰克林在《自传》中讲述了其白手起家、自力更生的故事，平凡却生动的讲述表明他坚信通过努力就能实现美国梦。）

2. Benjamin Franklin

（美国文学评论家范·威克·布鲁克斯(Van Wyck Brooks)在《美国的成年》(*America's Coming Age*)中指出乔纳森·爱德华兹和本杰明·富兰克林是美国 18 世纪的两位重要的哲学家，他们是不同层次思想的代表。）

3. Jonathan Edwards

（乔纳森·爱德华兹(1703 – 1758)是美国"大觉醒"(the"Great Awakening")的领军人物，他生前赢得了"美国第一位系统的哲学家"称号。其著名作品是《意志自由》(*Freedom of the Will*)。）

4. Transcendentalism

（乔纳森·爱德华兹的作品《神灵的形影》(*Images or Shadows of Divine Things*)对 19 世纪的超验主义对象征主义的运用产生了很大的影响。）

5. *Poor Richard's Almanac*, *Autobiography*

（富兰克林在文学上的地位主要取决于《穷查理历书》和《自传》。）

6. *The Autobiography of Benjamin Franklin*

（本杰明·富兰克林文学上最大的成就体现在他的作品《本杰明·富兰克林自传》上。该书以平易的文风叙述了富兰克林艰苦创业、自学成才、坚持不懈的奋斗历程。）

7. Enlightenment

（富兰克林是启蒙思想的缩影，是 18 世纪理性的代表。）

8. enlightenment, reason, order

（18 世纪的美国处于启蒙、理想、秩序的时代。）

Ⅱ. Multiple Choice

1. D　富兰克林是第一个自力更生、白手起家的美国人的标志。
2. C　欧洲的启蒙运动对美国理性和独立革命时期产生了深远影响。
3. B　启蒙运动通常是指在 18 世纪初至 1789 年法国大革命间的一个新思维不断涌现的时代，与理性主义等一起构成一个较长的文化运动时期，所以法国启蒙运动时期被称为"理性时代"。18 世纪的美国同样受到启蒙思想而影响，因而理性主义是这个时期美国文学的主导思想。
4. B　美国神学家乔纳森·爱德华兹最具代表性的布道是《愤怒的上帝手中之罪人》(*Sinners in the Hands of an Angry God*)。

5. B 作为美国财富和智慧的象征，美国人民把富兰克林的头像印在100美元纸钞的正面。200多年来，这位智者的思想一直被那些希望拥有美德并过上富足生活的人们所遵循和实践着。他的个人生活和职业生涯代表了美国启蒙运动中世俗化的理想。

6. B 《穷理查历书》(*Poor Richard's Almanac*)它是由美国资本主义精神最完美的代表——本杰明·富兰克林所写。该出版物从1732年至1758年不断出现。它幽默、睿智、形式奇特，通篇贯彻着人类的智慧精华，书中的名言警句与人生箴言即使在现在看来也具有很积极的作用。

Ⅲ. Explain the following term.

1. the literary form of autobiography: An autobiography is a person's description of his or her life. It is usually written in narrative form. An autobiography presents life events from the author's point of view and offers insights into the author's own ideas and beliefs. Benjamin Franklin and his work *Autobiography* is the representative of autobiography.

Ⅳ. Essay questions

1. The book is probably the first of its kind in literature. It is the simple yet immensely fascinating record of a man rising to wealth and fame from a state of poverty and obscurity in which he was born, the faithful account of the colorful career of America's first self-made man. The book contains four parts, written at different times.

   It is, first of all, a Puritan document. It is Puritan because it is a record of self-examination and self-improvement. It is also a convincing illustration of the Puritan ethic that in order to get on in the world, one has to be industrial, frugal, and prudent.

   It is also an eloquent elucidation of the fact that Franklin was spokesman for the new order of the eighteenth-century enlightenment, and that he represented in America all its ideas, that man is basically good and free by nature, endowed by God with certain inalienable rights of liberty and the pursuit of happiness. Through telling a success story of self-reliance, the book celebrates, in fact, the fulfillment of the American dream.

   The style of the book is the pattern of Puritan simplicity, directness, and concision. The lucidity of the narrative, the absence of ornaments in wording and complex, involved structures in syntax, and the Puritan abhorrence of paradox are all well graphically demonstrated here and in the whole of the book. Taken as a whole, it is safe to say that the book is an exemplary illustration of the American style of writing.

2. Benjamin Franklin created a character, Poor Richard, in whose name the work appeared, and whose real existence was debated humorously and seriously. For almost a quarter of a century, he kept publishing Poor Richard's Almanac, expanding its literary part to the intense delight of its readers.

   Apart from poems and essays, he managed to put in a good many adages, and commonsense witticisms which became household words and many mottos of the most typical kind. He did not always write the maxims himself. He borrowed from others and made good use of his own wit and wisdom to simplify and enrich their axiom. There are many similar statements filling almanac, and taught as much as amused. The practical wisdom of Franklin shone forth rays of grandeur from its pages.

第3章 美国浪漫主义·欧文·库柏

3.1 复习笔记

I. Overview of American Romanticism

The Romantic period in American literature stretches from the end of the eighteenth century through the outbreak of the Civil War and was an important stage in the history of American literature.

1. Background

(1) A vibrant, new America was hungry for new forms of literary expression. The political independence, the economic boom, the buoyant national mood and the upward spirit of the times contributed to the outbreak of romantic feelings. The literary environment has provided a wide space for literary creation. Various magazines have sprung up in great numbers, facilitating the development of literature.

(2) Foreign ideas and cultural influences inspired the spread of Romanticism in America. The Romantic movement that spread across England and Europe in the early 19th century played a decisive role in the rise of American Romantic literature.

(3) First, "the spirit of the place" was radically new and alien. The American national experience of "pioneering" into the west served as the rich material for American literature. Second, American Romanticism was influenced by the cultural heritage that is American Puritanism. Third, the "newness" of the Americans as a nation propelled American writers to write their own New World.

2. Characteristics

(1) From its inception, American Romantic literature has had its own unique attributes. It is the product of the fusion of several American factors. It expresses "a genuinely new experience" and contains "a strange quality".

(2) Due to domestic and foreign factors, American Romanticism has both imitative and independently creative characteristics.

I. 美国浪漫主义简介

美国文学中的浪漫主义时期开始于18世纪末，到南北战争爆发为止，是美国文学史上的重要阶段。

1. 背景

(1) 生机勃勃、开创新生活的美国渴望有新的文学表达形式。政治的独立、经济的腾飞、乐观的民族情绪以及时代的上进精神促进了浪漫主义情感的爆发。文学环境为文学创作提供了广阔的空间。各种杂志如雨后春笋出现，促进了文学的发展。

(2) 外国思想和文化影响激发了美国浪漫主义思潮的蔓延。19世纪初波及英国和欧洲的浪漫主义运动对美国浪漫主义文学的兴起发挥了决定性的作用。

(3) 首先是"地方精神"的极端新异性。美国西部开拓的民族经历为美国文学提供了丰富的素材。其次，美国浪漫主义受到美国清教主义这一文化遗产的影响。此外，美国人民对美国国家的崭新意识推动了美国作家去书写他们自己的新世界。

2. 特点

(1) 美国浪漫主义文学自一开始便具有其独特的属性。它是美国因素融为一体的产物。它所表达的是"一种真正的新的经历"，包含着"一种陌生的特质"。

(2) 由于国内外因素的影响，美国浪漫主义既有模仿，也有独立创造的特性。

Ⅱ. Washington Irving (1783 –1859) **1. Life** Born in New York to a wealthy merchant family, Irving was a keen reader from an early age and began writing poetry, prose and plays as a teenager. His first novel, *A History of New York*, was a great success. *The Sketch Book*, has brought him international fame. In 1826 Irving was sent to Spain as a diplomatic attaché, and from 1829 to 1832 he served as secretary of the U. S. Embassy in London. He lived most of his later years at his residence on the Hudson River. He was unmarried for life and died in 1859. **2. His literary contribution** Irving made a unique contribution to American literature, pioneering many of the precedents in the history of American literature. (1) He was the first American writer of imaginative literature to achieve international fame. (2) He is known as the "father of American literature". The short story as a genre of American literature probably originated from Irving's *The Sketch Book*. The book also symbolizes the beginning of American Romantic literature. **3. Literary career** Irving's literary career can be roughly divided into two important periods. The first period spanned from the publication of his debut work to 1832. The second period stretched over the rest of his life. (1) In the first period, Irving mainly depicted English or European themes. He sought values in the past and in the traditions of the old world. (2) The second period saw Irving discovering a whole new spirit of nationalism in American feeling, art and literature. **4. Writing style** Irving was a masterful stylist. His gentility, urbanity, and pleasantness are all fully reflected in his style of writing. (1) First of all, he tries to avoid being preachy. His aim is to amuse and entertain.	**Ⅱ. 华盛顿 · 欧文** **1. 生平** 欧文生于纽约一个富商的家庭，自幼酷爱读书，少年时代便开始写诗歌、散文和戏剧。他的第一部小说《纽约外史》获得很大成功。《见闻札记》使他获得国际声誉。1826 年欧文作为外交随员被派往西班牙。1829 年至 1832 年他任美国驻伦敦大使馆秘书。他晚年大部分时间生活在哈德逊河畔的住所。他终身未婚，死于 1859 年。 **2. 文学贡献** 欧文对美国文学有着独特的贡献，他开创了美国文学史上的许多先河。 （1）他是第一个获得国际声誉的美国虚构文学作家。 （2）他被称为"美国文学之父"。短篇小说作为美国文学的一种类型可能源于欧文的《见闻札记》。该书也象征着美国浪漫主义文学的开始。 **3. 文学生涯** 欧文的文学生涯大致可分为两个重要的时期。第一个时期从其处女作的发表到 1832 年。第二个时期跨越他的余生。 （1）第一个时期欧文主要描写英国或欧洲主题。他在过去和旧世界里的传统中寻求价值。 （2）第二个时期欧文在美国式的情感和文艺作品中发掘出了全新的民族主义精神。 **4. 写作风格** 欧文是一位精湛的文体家。他的雅人深致、文质彬彬及和颜悦色在他的文风里都能找到充分的反映。 （1）首先，他尽量避免说教。他创作的目的在于让人赏心悦目。

(2) He is good at setting the atmosphere of the stories, which largely makes up for the thin plot. (3) His characters are so well drawn that reading them is like hearing their voices and seeing their people. (4) Humor is woven into his literary texture. (5) He is noted for his musical language and consummate workmanship. At times, he was renowned as "the American Goldsmith". **5. Major works** *A History of New York* *The Sketch Book* "The Authors Account of Himself" "Rip Van Winkle" "The Legend of Sleepy Hollow" *The history of Life and Voyages of Christopher Columbus* *A Chronicle of the Conquest of Granada* *Life of Goldsmith* *Life of Washington* *The Crayon Miscellany* "A Tour on the Prairies" "Astoria" *Adventures of Captain Bonneville* **6. Analysis of major works** ◆"Rip Van Winkle" The story reflects the author's conservative attitude. Before the war life was leisurely and peaceful. After the war, however, there were political party battles and the pace of life increased. This story demonstrates Irving's position that change and revolution disrupt the natural order of life and seems to show his reservations about a modern democratic America. ◆"The Legend of Sleepy Hollow" The creation of prototypes is one of Irving's high attainments. Ichabod is the representative of the New Englander who is through with power, the city slicker of the village, a destructive force that wants to commit fraud. He was finally driven out of the village where he did not belong, so the small village returned to peace and quiet. Brom Bones, on the other hand, is a Huckleberry-esque village boy, rude, energetic and self-supporting on the frontier. The battle between Ichabod and	(2) 他擅长烘托故事气氛，这很大程度上弥补了情节单薄这一不足。 (3) 他的人物刻画得惟妙惟肖，读后如闻其声，如见其人。 (4) 幽默构成了他文本的肌理。 (5) 其作品语言富有音乐性且完成度高。有时，他被称作"美国的戈德史密斯"。 **5. 主要作品** 《纽约外史》 《见闻札记》 《作者自述》 《瑞普·凡·温克尔》 《睡谷的传说》 《哥伦布传》 《征服格拉纳达》 《哥尔斯密传》 《华盛顿传》 《克瑞恩文集》 《大草原之旅》 《阿斯托里亚》 《博纳维尔船长历险记》 **6. 主要作品分析** ◆《瑞普·凡·温克尔》 故事反映了作者保守的态度。战前生活悠闲、平和。战后却出现政党之争，生活节奏加快。这个故事表明了欧文的立场，即变革和革命打乱了生活的自然秩序，表明他对现代民主的美国持有保留的态度。 ◆《睡谷的传说》 创造原型是欧文的造诣之一。伊卡包德是通权达变的新英格兰人的代表，他是村子里的城市滑头，一种欲行欺诈的破坏性力量。他最后被赶出本不属于他的村庄，于是小村子又恢复平静祥和。布鲁姆则是哈克·贝恩式村野之夫，粗鲁、精力充沛，在边疆自食其力。伊卡包德和布鲁姆的情场之争又可以看

Brom's love affairs can again be seen as a competition between two ethnic groups under specific historical conditions.

The writing style of the story also represents Irving's highest level.

作是特定历史条件下两个种族群体之间的竞争。

该故事的写作风格也代表了欧文的最高水准。

Ⅲ. James Fenimore Cooper (1789 – 1851)

Ⅲ. 詹姆斯·费尼莫·库柏

1. Life

Cooper was born in New Jersey to a wealthy family that owned large tracts of land. Cooper entered Yale University at the age of 14 and was later expelled for misconduct. He then went to sea as a sailor for five years. At the age of 20, he inherited a large inheritance from his father and later began writing. His second novel, *The Spy*, was a huge success. Over the next 30 years, he produced more than 30 works, including 11 nautical novels. *Leatherstocking Tales* made him famous during his lifetime and still has a large readership today.

1. 生平

库柏出生于新泽西州一个富有家庭，家里拥有大片土地。库柏14岁进入耶鲁大学学习，后来因行为不端被开除。于是他出海做水手长达5年之久。20岁时他继承了父亲的巨额遗产，后来开始写作。他的第二本小说《间谍》获得巨大成功。接下来的30年，他又创作了30余部作品，其中包括11部航海小说。《皮裹腿故事集》使他生前闻名遐迩，至今仍拥有大量读者。

2. Literary contribution

Cooper was one of the first writers to depict the Westward Movement.

Cooper's importance in American literature is reflected in the fact that he created a myth about the formative stages of American nation. In his novels, Cooper comes to realize that on the western frontier, social activity is governed by two conflicting principles, and Cooper's greatness lies in the fact that he points out that one is morally right and the other is practically inevitable. This is where the contradiction in Cooper's thinking lies. He promotes both social order and the ideal of closeness to nature and freedom.

Facing the problem of "poverty of materials" in America, Cooper claimed that the American writers were responsible for discovering new sources of fiction. He drew material from American history and those which nourished European literature and contributed to introduce the "Western" tradition into American literature.

2. 文学贡献

库柏是首批描写西进运动的作家之一。

库柏在美国文坛的重要地位体现在他创造了一个关于美国国家形成阶段的神话。在其小说中，库柏逐渐意识到在西部边疆，社会活动受到两种相互矛盾的原则的制约，库柏的伟大之处在于，他指出其中一种在道义上是正确的，另外一种则在实际上是无法避免的。这也是库柏思想上的矛盾所在。他既推崇社会秩序，又崇尚亲近自然、无拘无束的理想境界。

面对美国本土文学素材缺乏的问题，库柏认为美国作家有责任为小说挖掘新资源。他从美国历史，从滋养欧洲文学的源头活水中发掘素材，为将西方传统引介到美国文学中去做出了贡献。

3. Writing style

(1) Cooper specializes in fictional plots. His plots are sometimes too bizarre, but his stories are fascinating.

(2) The landscape under his pen is magnificent, quite like the style of Walter Scott's novels.

3. 写作风格

(1) 库柏擅长虚构情节。其情节虽有时过于离奇，但是他的故事十分引人入胜。

(2) 其笔下风景波澜壮阔，颇有司各特小说之风。

(3) He is very focused on connecting different scenes. He had never been to the frontier or lived with the Indians, yet he produced five epic masterpieces about them, which is a testament to Cooper's extremely fertile imagination. His Indians were among the first Indians to appear in American fiction, and they were perhaps the first "noble savages".

(4) His style of writing is also flawed. His characterization is dull and lacks credibility, and the use of language, especially dialect, is not authentic.

4. Major works

The Spy
Leatherstocking Tales
The Pioneers (1823)
The Last of the Mohicans (1826)
The Prairie (1827)
The Pathfinder (1840)
The Deerslayer (1841)

5. Analysis of major work

◆*Leatherstocking Tales*

(1) *Leatherstocking Tales* is a series of five tales about the life of American settlers. The protagonist Natty Bumppo is a mythic figure. When he first appears, we see a real frontiersman, a man of flesh and blood in the virgin forests of North America. But as the story moves on, he does so gathering more and more of the halo of a legendary and mythic nature around him. He becomes a type, a representation of a nation struggling to be born, progressing from old age to rebirth and youth. The protagonist in *Leatherstocking Tales* goes from the old to the golden age of youth. This is the true American myth.

(2) *The Pioneers, or The Sources of the Susquehanna* is the first published novel of *Leatherstocking Tales*. The novel is historically significant in that it was probably the first true frontier novel in the history of American literature. The story revolves around the conflict between Leatherstocking and Judge Temple. Leatherstocking advocates free and unrestrained jungle life, while Judge Temple believes that without law and order, man would be reduced to a savage. Bambo stands for the

(3)他很注重联系不同的场景。他从未去过边疆，也没有跟印第安人生活在一起过，但是他却创作了五部关于他们的史诗般巨作。这充分证明了库柏想象力极其丰富。他笔下的印第安人是美国小说中最早出现的印第安人之一，他们或许也是首批"高贵的野蛮人"。

(4)他的文体也有缺陷。他的人物刻画呆板，缺乏可信度，语言尤其是方言的使用并不纯正。

4. 主要作品

《间谍》
《皮裹腿故事集》
《拓荒者》
《最后的莫西干人》
《草原》
《探路者》
《猎鹿人》

5. 主要作品分析

◆《皮裹腿故事集》

(1)《皮裹腿故事集》由五部描写美国西部移民生活的系列小说组成。主人公纳蒂·班波的形象颇具神话色彩。刚出场时，他是一位有血有肉、实实在在的活跃在北美丛林里的拓荒者形象。随着故事的不断深入，他的神话和传说成分愈渐增强。他成为一个典型，代表着整个国家努力从暮年走向重生、走向青春。皮裹腿系列小说主人公从暮年到青年黄金时代。这是真正的美国神话。

(2)《拓荒者》是《皮裹腿故事集》中最早发表的一部。该小说的重大历史意义在于，它是美国文学史上首部真正意义上的边疆小说。故事围绕皮裹腿和坦普尔法官之间的矛盾展开。皮裹腿崇尚自由自在、无拘无束的丛林生活，而坦普尔法官则认为没有法律和秩序人就会沦为野蛮人。班波代表了博爱、亲近自然、无拘无束的理想，是道

ideals of fraternity, closeness to nature, and freedom, representing the morally right, while Judge Temple symbolizes law and civilization and embodies "the practically inevitable" aspect. Together, they built the Wild West into a civilized place, hence plural form is used in the title *The Pioneers*.	义上正确的一方。坦普尔法官象征着法律和文明，体现了"实际上势不可挡的"一方。他们一起把西部荒野建成了文明的地方，因而标题《拓荒者》使用了复数形式。

3.2 考研真题与典型题详解

I. Fill in the blanks.

1. "The Legend of Sleepy Hollow" was written by __________. (大连外国语学院 2008 研)
2. Ichabod Crane, the schoolmaster, is a character in the short story __________ collected in *The Sketch Book*. (首师大 2008 研)
3. The Romantic period in the American literary history covers the time between the end of the __________ century to the outbreak of the __________ . It started with the publication of Irving's __________ and ended with Whitman's __________ . This period is also called __________ .
4. In the early nineteenth century, Washington Irving wrote __________ which became the first work by an American writer to win financial success on both sides of the Atlantic.
5. __________ was regarded as the first great prose stylist of American romanticism.
6. __________ was regarded as Father of the American short stories.
7. In Washington Irving's work __________ appeared the first modern short stories and the first great American juvenile literature.
8. Washington Irving also wrote two biographies, one is *The Life of Oliver Goldsmith*, and the other is __________ .
9. James Fenimore Cooper's novel __________ was a rousing tale about espionage against the British during the Revolutionary War.
10. The central figure in the *Leatherstocking Tales* is __________, who goes by the various names of Leatherstocking, Deerslayer, Pathfinder and Hawkeye.
11. In *The Pioneers*, __________ represents the ideal American, living a virtuous and free life in God's world.
12. In 1823 James Fenimore Cooper wrote *The Pioneers*, the first of the five novels that make up __________. The remaining four books: *The last of Mohicans* (1826), *The Prairie* (1827), *The Pathfinder* (1840), and *The Deerslayer* (1841), continue the story of Natty Bumppo, one of the most famous characters in American fiction.

II. Multiple Choice

1. Which is NOT a main focus of the American Romantic Movement in general? (大连外国语学院 2008 研)

   A. A return to eastern philosophy.

   B. A deep and spiritual respect for nature and natural laws.

   C. The introduction of self-salvation as opposed to salvation through Christ.

D. A demand for progress and productivity.

2. Which ONE of the following concepts is related to the understanding of American Romanticism? (四川大学2007研)

A. Survival of the fittest B. indifference of the universe

C. exaltation of emotion over reason D. the human beast

3. Which of the following words does not describe the features of Irving's writings? (天津外国语学院2009研)

A. decorum B. humor C. musicality D. imagination

4. The following selection is taken from __________. (大连外国语学院2007研)

A. *The Cask of Amontillado* B. *The Legend of Sleepy Hollow*

C. *A Rose for Emily* D. *Babylon Revisited*

In the bosom of one of those spacious coves which indent the eastern shore of the Hudson, at that broad expansion of the river denominated by the ancient Dutch navigators the Tappan Zee, and where they always prudently shortened sail and implored the protection of St. Nicholas when they crossed, there lies a small market town or rural port, which by some is called Greensburgh, but which is more generally and properly known by the name of Tarry Town.

5. Which ONE of the following is the author of *The Leather-Stocking Tales*? (四川大学2008研)

A. Henry David Thoreau B. Washington Irving

C. Edgar Allan Poe D. James Fenimore Cooper

6. James Fenimore Cooper's novel __________ is the first to reveal the west and Native Americans' life in a passionate way. (北二外2007研)

A. *Go Down, Moses* B. *The Last of the Mohicans*

C. *Winesburg, Ohio* D. *O, Pioneers!*

7. Washington Irving's social conservation and literary for the past is revealed, to some extent, in his famous story, __________.

A. "The Legend of Sleepy Hollow" B. "Rip Van Winkle"

C. "The Custom-House" D. "The Birthmark"

8. It is on his __________ that Washington Irving's fame mainly rested.

A. tales about America B. early poetry

C. childhood recollections D. sketches about his European tours

Ⅲ. Explain the following term.

1. American Romanticism (四川大学2007研；北航2008研)

Ⅳ. Read the following quotations and answer the questions.

Passage 1

"There was, as usual, a crowd of folk about the door, but none that Rip recollected. The very character of the people seemed changed. There was a busy, bustling, disputatious tome about it, instead of the accustomed phlegm and drowsy tranquility. He looked in vain for the sage Nicholas Vedder…"

Questions:

(1) From which work is this passage taken?

(2) How do you understand this selection?

Passage 2

"From the listless repose of the place, and the peculiar character of it sin habitants, who are descendants from the original Dutch settlers, this sequestered glen has long been known by the name of SLEEPY HOLLOW, and its rustic lads are called the Sleepy Hollow Boys throughout all the neighboring country. Drowsy, dreamy influence seems to hang over the land, and to pervade the very atmosphere. Some say that the place was bewitched by a high German doctor, during the early days of the settlement; others, that an old Indian chief, the product or wizard of his tribe, held his powwows there before the country was discovered by Master Hendrick Hudson."

Questions:

(1) Who is the writer of this short story from which the passage is taken?

(2) What is the title of this short story?

(3) Give a definition of "short story".

Passage 3

"Arms and the clarion for the battle, but the song of thanksgiving to the victory!" answered the liberated David. "Friend," he added, thrusting forth his lean, delicate hand forwards Hawkeye, in kindness, while his eyes twinkled and grew moist, "I thank thee the hairs of my head still grow where they were first rooted by Providence for, though those of other men may be more glossy and curling, I have ever found mine own well suited to the brain they shelter. That I did not join myself to the battle, was less owing to disinclination, than to the bonds of the heathen. Valiant and skilful hast thou proved thyself in the conflict, and I hereby thank thee, before proceeding to discharge other and more important duties, because thou hast proved thyself well worthy of a Christian's praise."…

Questions:

(1) This novel was written by the first American novelist. What is his name?

(2) What is the name of the novel?

(3) The central figure in this novel appeared in this passage. It is __________.

V. Short answer questions

1. Make an introductory comment on James Fenimore Cooper's frontier saga *The Leather Stocking Tales*. (四川大学 2009 研)
2. In American literature history, the Romantic Period, during which many famous writers and their masterpieces came into being, played an important role. Washington Irving, Nathaniel Hawthorne and Walt Whitman, etc, all of whom are not ignored by us. According to their writings, discuss the features of American literature in this period.

VI. Essay questions

1. Discuss the fiction written by American High Romantics with specific reference to one work. (大连外国语学院 2007 研)
2. What is the relationship between American Romanticism and European Romanticism?
3. What's Washington Irving's main contribution to American Literature?
4. Analyze *The Legend of Sleepy Hollow*.

参考答案及解析

I. Fill in the blanks.

1. Washington Irving

   (短篇小说《睡谷的传说》(“The Legend of Sleepy Hollow”)，是华盛顿·欧文的代表作《见闻札记》(*The Sketch Book*)中最著名的两篇故事中的一篇。另一篇是《瑞普·凡·温克尔》(“Rip Van Winkle”。)

2. “The Legend of Sleepy Hollow”.

   (Ichabod Crane 是一个小学校长，欧文的《睡谷的传说》中的人物。)

3. 18th，Civil War；*The Sketch Book*；*Leaves of Grass*；the American Renaissance

   (美国浪漫主义时期开始于十八世纪末，到内战爆发为止，是美国文学史上最重要的时期。华盛顿·欧文出版的《见闻札记》标志着美国浪漫主义文学的开端，惠特曼的《草叶集》是浪漫主义时期文学的压卷之作。浪漫主义时期的文学是美国文学的繁荣时期，所以也称为“美国的文艺复兴”。)

4. *The Sketch Book*

   (美国作家华盛顿·欧文被英国作家萨克雷称为“新世界文坛送往旧世界的第一使节”。《见闻札记》被当时的英国评论界誉为“美国富有想象力的第一部真正杰作”，它“组成了它所属的那个民族文学的新时代”。)

5. Washington Irving

   (华盛顿·欧文是美国著名作家，他被誉为美国第一位浪漫主义散文文体作家。)

6. Washington Irving

   (华盛顿·欧文被誉为“美国短篇小说之父”。)

7. *The Sketch Book*

   (华盛顿·欧文的作品《见闻札记》(*The Sketch Book*)是现代文学史上第一部短篇小说集和美国第一部伟大的青少年文学读物。)

8. *Life of Washington*

   (华盛顿·欧文撰写了两部传记：《哥德史密斯传》(*The Life of Oliver Goldsmith*)和《华盛顿传》(*Life of Washington*)。)

9. *The Spy*

   (詹姆斯·费尼莫尔·库柏(James Fenimore Cooper)认为他的小说《间谍》(*The Spy*)“应当是一部纯粹美国式的以爱国为主题的书”。)

10. Natty Bumppo

    (《皮裹腿故事集》是美国作家詹姆斯·费尼莫尔·库柏的系列小说。该故事集中的主要人物是 Natty Bumppo。在不同的故事中他有皮裹腿、杀鹿者、探路人及鹰眼等别名。)

11. Natty Bumppo

    (在詹姆斯·费尼莫尔·库柏的小说《拓荒者》(*The Pioneers*)中，主人公 Natty Bumppo 正直善良，向往无拘无束的生活，是理想美国人的化身。)

12. *The Leatherstocking Tales*

    (《皮裹腿故事集》包括《拓荒者》《最后的莫西干人》《草原》《探路者》和《猎鹿人》五部小说。)

Ⅱ. Multiple Choice

1. D 美国的浪漫主义运动崇尚大自然的力量，提倡自我拯救。其中以爱默生为代表的一批作家，吸收了东方哲学的智慧，融合了欧洲神秘先验论思想，形成了超验主义。
2. C 浪漫主义把情感置于理性之上。其余三个选项都是达尔文主义的观点。
3. A 华盛顿·欧文的作品具有幽默风趣的笔调，活跃而优雅的写作风格，富于幻想的浪漫色彩，其作品富有音乐性且技艺娴熟，A 项“端庄稳重”不是其写作特点。
4. B 题中片段选自美国著名小说家 Washington Irving《睡谷的传说》(“The Legend of Sleepy Hollow”)。此段文章交代了故事的背景。文章大意为：哈德逊河东岸有很多宽阔的小河湾，在一个河湾的深处，很久之前荷兰航海家们曾占领水域，并在那里小心地靠岸，寻求圣尼古拉斯的保护。现在，那里有个小镇，或者农村的港口，有些人叫它格林斯堡，而更多人叫它泰瑞镇。
5. D James Fenimore Cooper(库柏)，美国早期作家，*The Leather-Stocking Tales*(《皮裹腿故事集》)是他的经典之作。
6. B 《最后的莫西干人》是库柏《皮裹腿故事集》五部曲之一，描写的是美国西部边疆和美洲土著印第安人的生活。选项 A《去吧，摩西》的作者是 William Faulkner(威廉·福克纳)；选项 C《小城畸人》的作者是 Sherwood Anderson(舍伍德·安德森)；选项 D 的作者是女作家 Willa Cather(薇拉·凯瑟)。
7. B 《瑞普·凡·温克尔》在一定程度上反映了欧文的保守思想。
8. A 欧文的声望主要体现在关于美国的小说上。

Ⅲ. Explain the following term.

1. American Romanticism: American Romanticism is the name sometimes given to a flourishing of distinctively American literature in the period form the end of the 18th century throngh the outbreak of the Civil War. American Romanticism is represented by works of Ralph Waldo Emerson, H. D. Thoreau, Nathaniel Hawthorne, Herman Melville, and Walt Whitman. They share certain general characteristics: moral enthusiasm, faith in individualism and intuition.

Ⅳ. Read the following quotations and answer the questions.

Passage 1

(1) This passage is taken from Washington Irving's “Rip Van Winkle”.

(2) It shows the change that Rip sees as he enters the village after the 20-year sleep and the destructive effect of the change. It also reveals, to some extent, the conservative attitude of its author.

Passage 2

(1) Washington Irving

(2) “The Legend of Sleepy Hollow”

(3) The short story in a short prose novel can usually be read in one sitting. It generally contains the six elements of a novel: characterization, setting, theme, plot, point of view, and style.

Passage 3

(1) James Fenimore Cooper

(2) *The Last of the Mohicans*

(3) Hawkeye

V. Short answer questions

1. *The Leather Stocking Tales* is a series of novels by American writer James Fenimore Cooper. Natty Bumppo is the protagonist of the series. Although his parents were white, he grew up with the Indians and became an almost fearless warrior, proficient with many weapons, one of which was the long gun. Out of respect for his forest home and its inhabitants, he hunts only what he needs to survive. He lives by the rule, "One shot, one kill." when he has to fire. He and his Mohican "brother" Chingachgook championed goodness and tried to stop the constant conflict between the Mohicans and Hurons. He is known as "Deerslayer" in *The Deerslayer*, "Hawkeye" and "La Longue Carabine" in *The Last of the Mohicans*, "Pathfinder" in *The Pathfinder*, "Leatherstocking" in *The Pioneers*, and "the trapper" in *The Prairie*. These novels tell the major events in the life of Natty Bumppo (1740 – 1806).
2. The whole nation had a strong sense of optimism and the mood of "feeling good", giving birth to the spectacular outburst of romantic feelings. The English counterpart, especially the cultural heritage, exerted a stimulating impact on the writings of the young nation. Taking foreign influence into consideration, the great works of American writers still carried typically American romanticist color. The young nation had brought forth its own Philosophy, Transcendentalism, stressing man's capacity of knowing truth intuitively, and of attaining knowledge transcending the reach of the senses.

VI. Essay questions

1. American Romanticism was influenced by its English and European counterparts since it was originated from those places. But when it came to the high romanticism, American Romanticism exhibited from the outset distinct features of its own.

   The first was its puritan heritage and rejection of Puritanism. It was more moralizing, edifying more than mere entertainment. Sex and love, for example, are subjects American authors were particularly carefully approaching. The way in which Hawthorne wrote *The Scarlet Letter* suggests that American Romanticism adapted itself to American Puritanism. It takes eloquently about the effect of the adultery on the people rather than the sin itself. Hester Prynne uses her whole life to get out of the shadow of the sin while Dimmesdale dies at last under the pressure of puritan. Hawthorne criticizes the Puritanism, keeping skeptical of religion authority.

   The second feature of fiction of High Romantics is its emphasis on psychological description. *The Scarlet Letter* employs many psychological activities to reveal directly the thoughts of characters and the psychological conflicts to develop the theme.

   The third feature is that it explores the dark side of society and human nature. At that time, the society was under the control of Puritanism and human nature was tortured. Whereas Hester is able to reconstruct her life and win a moral victory, Dimmesdale undergoes the tragic experience of physical and spiritual disintegration. Though the scarlet letter refers to Adultery, Angel, Able, A may also represent Adamic, or prehistoric, an archetypal vice suggestive of "original sin". This reveals another feature of this period fiction, which is symbolism. Besides, there are other symbols like the Meteor, Pearl, and the Rosebush Next to the Prison Door.
2. American Romanticism had much in common with European Romanticism: In response to the En-

lightenment and its emphasis on reason, Romanticism emphasized the emotional, imaginative, and subjective approaches.

European, and especially British, literary masters inspired the emergence of New World writers. American Romanticism also arose from a common cultural heritage, and was to some extent a continuation and development of English Romanticism.

Despite the great European influence, the typical works of American Romanticism have a strong American character. American writers illustrate their unique personalities in their works, growing up in the land of their homeland. The content of the American Romantic period was original and diverse. American writers also developed a number of new forms of fiction or poetry.

They also placed an increasing emphasis on the free expression of emotions and displayed an increasing attention to the psychic states of their characters. The strong tendency to exalt the individual and common man was another focus of the movement.

3. Washington Irving's contribution to American literature is unique in more ways than one. He did a number of things which have been regarded as the first of their kind in America.

He was the first American writer of imaginative literature to gain international fame. When he returned home in 1832, he was acclaimed as the one American author whom people in Europe knew about, and the Americans took as a sign that American literature was emerging as an independent entity. To say that he was father of American literature is not much exaggeration.

The short story as a genre in American literature probably began with Irving's *The Sketch Book*, a collection of essays, sketches, and tales, of which the most famous and frequently anthologized are "Rip Van Winkle" and "The Legend of Sleepy Hollow". The book touched the American imagination and foreshadowed the coming of Hawthorne, Melville, and Poe, in whose hands the short story attained a degree of perfection as a literary tradition. It also marked the beginning of American Romanticism. The Gothic, the supernatural, and the longing for the good old days which some of its pieces clearly exhibit, are Romantic enough in subject if not exactly in style, for Irving wrote in the neoclassical tradition of Joseph Addison and Oliver Goldsmith. Looking at a picture of Irving surrounded by his nieces, one does sometimes think of the old man, benign and pleasant and refined, as the uncle of American authors.

4. Washington Irving's short story *The Legend of Sleepy Hollow* is about the memorable event of an apparently headless horseman throwing his head at his rival in love, and the memorable character of Ichabod Crane with his mixture of shrewdness, credulity, self-assertiveness and cowardice.

The creation of archetypes is a particularly subtle feat of Irving's consummate craftsmanship. We may see in Ichabod Crane a precocious, effete New Englander, shrewd, commercial, a city-slicker, who is rather an interloper, a somewhat destructive force, and who comes along to swindle the villagers. His book learning turns on him, and he is driven away from where he does not belong, so that the serene village remains permanently good and happy. Brom Bones, on the other hand, is of a Huck Finn-type of country bumpkin, rough, vigorous, boisterous but inwardly very good, a frontier type put out there to shift for himself. Thus the rivalry in love between Ichabod and Brom, viewed in this way, suddenly assumes the dimensions of two ethical groups locked in a kind of historic contest.

As to the style of the piece, it represents Irving at his best. The association between a certain local and the inward movement of a character, the emotional loading of almost every line of the story, their effect on the five senses of the reader whose attention is so fully engaged and who feels so much involved in what is happening—all these have placed this and other Irving stories among the best of American short stories.

第4章　新英格兰超验主义·爱默生·梭罗

4.1　复习笔记

In 1836, Emerson's *Nature* came out, which shocked the American cultural and intellectual circles like thunder on the ground. *Nature* pushed American Romanticism into a new stage, namely its climax—the stage of New England Transcendentalism.	1836年爱默生的《论自然》问世，它如平地惊雷，震撼了美国文化思想界。《论自然》把美国浪漫主义推向了一个新的阶段，即它的高潮阶段——英格兰超验主义阶段。
I. New England Transcendentalism	**I. 新英格兰超验主义**
In the 1830s and 1840s, some New Englanders were extremely dissatisfied with the prevailing materialism at the time, so they gathered together to form an informal Transcendentalist Club to discuss literature, philosophy, trends in national life and so on. They published the journal, *The Dial*, to express and promote their ideas to the world. There are about thirty men and a few women in the club, including Emerson, Thoreau, Bronson Alcott and Margaret Fuller, most of whom are teachers or priests, who criticized the creed of Boston businessmen and the coldness and rigidity of Unitarianism rationalism. "Transcendentalism" is not a native American word. It is a Kantian philosophical term. As Emerson said, it means "any thought that belongs to the category of intuitive consciousness."	19世纪三、四十年代一些新英格兰人对当时盛行的物质主义极其不满，他们聚集在一起组成非正式的"超验主义俱乐部"，讨论文学、哲学及国家生活的形势趋向。他们出版专刊《日晷》向世人宣传他们的主张。俱乐部成员约有三十几个男性和几个女性。其中包括爱默生、梭罗、阿尔科特及富勒等人。他们多为教师或牧师。他们针砭波士顿商人的信条，抨击唯一神论理性主义的冷酷、古板。"超验主义"一词并非美国本土词汇，它是个康德哲学词汇。如爱默生所说，它表示"任何属于直觉意识范畴的思想"。
1. Major features	**1. 主要特征**
(1) Transcendentalists emphasized the spirit, or the Oversoul, and believed that this was the most important factor of existence in the universe. The Oversoul was an omnipresent, omnipotent force that promoted goodness and was the foundation and the belonging of all things. This is a totally new worldview. It opposed the 18th century mechanical concept of the universe, the development of America in the direction of mechanization and capitalism, and the trend of Americans indulging in secular matters at the cost of their spiritual life.	(1) 超验主义者强调精神，或超灵，认为这是宇宙间至为重要的存在因素。超灵是一种无所不容、无所不在、扬善抑恶的力量，是万物之本、万物之所属。这是一种新的世界观。它反对18世纪的机械宇宙观，反对美国朝着机械化、资本主义化的方向发展，反对美国人沉湎于世俗事务而忽略精神生活的世风。
(2) Transcendentalists emphasized the importance of the individual. They believed that the individual was the most	(2) 超验主义者强调个人的重要性。他们认为个人是社会的最重

important component of society. The ideal person was a self-reliant man. The individual soul communed with the Oversoul and thus possessed divinity. This new view of individuals and their importance reflected new evaluations of people. It opposed the complete degeneration of Calvinism and the dehumanization in the rising stage of capitalism. It emphasized the significance of regaining the lost individuality.

要的组成因素。理想的人是自立自强的人。个人灵魂与超灵交流，因而具有神性。这种关于人及其重要性的新观点反映出对人的新评价。它反对加尔文教义中的彻底的堕落，反对资本主义上升阶段的非人性化现象。它强调人恢复自身业已失去的个性的重要意义。

(3) Transcendentalists looked at nature from a new perspective, believing that the natural world was a symbol of the Oversoul or God. Everything in nature was symbolic, and the physical world was the embodiment of the spiritual world. This in turn strengthened the tradition of symbolism in American literature.

(3) 超验主义者以全新的目光看待自然，认为自然界是超灵或上帝的象征。自然界万物皆具有象征性，现实世界是精神世界的体现。这又加强了美国文学中象征主义的传统。

2. Sources

2. 理论来源

New England Transcendentalism was the product of the fusion of various foreign and domestic elements.

(1) Idealistic philosophy of Germany and France.

(2) Oriental mysticism.

(3) American Puritanism.

新英格兰超验主义是国外和国内各种因素融合的产物。

(1) 法国和德国的唯心主义。

(2) 东方神秘主义。

(3) 美国清教主义。

Ⅱ. Ralph Waldo Emerson (1803 – 1882)

Ⅱ. 拉尔夫·瓦尔多·爱默生

1. Life

1. 生平

Emerson was born in the home of a prominent pastor in New England. The family was in decline when he was young. He used to study at Harvard University. Later, he accepted the doctrine of Unitarianism and became a Unitarian minister in the Second Church of Boston. But soon, he resigned because he disagreed with some of the traditional rituals of Unitarianism. He was influenced by European Romanticism when travelling in Europe. After returning to America, he formed an informal "Transcendentalism Club" with friends and edited the Transcendentalist journal, *The Dial*, to explain and spread Transcendentalism. He was the most outstanding spokesperson of New England Transcendentalism. He was considered to be one of the two to three top writers in the United States during his lifetime, and the most influential philosopher and writer of his time. He was the prophet of that era and had varying degrees of influence on writers such as Thoreau, Whitman, and Hawthorne. Authors of the 20th century including Robert Frost and Wallace Stevens were also indebted to his philosophy.

爱默生生于新英格兰一个显赫牧师之家。幼年时家道中落。他曾在哈佛大学就读。后接受唯一教教义，并成为波士顿第二礼拜堂唯一教牧师。不久，因对该教一些古板仪式持异议而辞职。赴欧洲旅行时受到欧洲浪漫主义的影响。回国后跟朋友结成非正式的“超验主义俱乐部”，编辑超验主义专刊《日晷》，阐释和传播超验主义思想。他是新英格兰超验主义最杰出的代言人。他生前被认为是美国最顶尖的两到三个作家之一，是同时代最富影响力的哲学家和文豪。他是那个时代的先知，对梭罗、惠特曼、霍桑等作家产生了不同程度的影响。20世纪的作家如罗伯特·弗罗斯特、华莱士·史蒂文斯也受到其哲学的影响。

2. Analysis of major works

◆*Nature*

(1) Published in 1836, Nature is usually considered as the Bible of New England Transcendentalism.

(2) In this book, Emerson emphasizes that the Oversoul is everywhere. He believes that the universe consists of nature and human souls, and nature is the purest and can sanctify people's morality. He also advocates that people should directly experience the ubiquitous God in nature through intuition.

(3) The divine God exists in the soul of man, so man is also divine. The divinity of man becomes a favorite topic of Emerson's speeches and writings. Everyone should think that the world belongs to him, and that the world exists only for him. The idea Emerson wants to convey is self-reliance, which, at a deeper level, is a reflection of the rising spirit of that times.

(4) Nature is a symbol of God, and it coordinates the relationship between man and God. Emerson's view of nature implicates that the world around man is symbolic.

(5) Emerson's symbolic perception of nature also had a significant effect on his aesthetics. Emerson's poet has insight into the divine unity of the Universe by intuition, and has the ability to express the feelings of contact with nature to his fellowmen. True poetry and true art should lead to moral purification, organic unity and higher reality.

◆*The American Scholar*

The American Scholar has been hailed as "America's Declaration of Intellectual Independence." Emerson believed that Americans should stop imitating and importing foreign literature. Instead, they should portray the United States here and now. He called on American writers to create and portray the American land in a way unique to Americans. The importance of Emerson in the history of American cultural thought is that he embodies the desire and effort of America in a formative phase to have its own unique identity.

2. 主要作品分析

◆《论自然》

(1)《论自然》发表于1836年，它通常被认为是新英格兰超验主义的圣经。

(2) 在这本书中，爱默生强调超灵无处不在。他认为宇宙由自然和人类灵魂组成。自然是最纯洁无暇的，能够圣化人的道德。他还倡导人们通过直觉直接体验自然界无处不在的上帝。

(3) 神圣的上帝存在于人的灵魂之中，因而人也是神圣的。人的神性成为爱默生演讲和写作挚爱的话题。每个人都应认为世界是属于他的，世界只为他而存在。爱默生要传达的思想是“自助”。在深层次上讲，“自助”是时代上升精神的反映。

(4) 自然是上帝的象征，它协调人和上帝的关系。爱默生关于自然的观点表明，人类周遭的世界具有象征意义。

(5)爱默生对自然的象征性感知也深刻影响了他的美学。爱默生的诗人能够通过直觉洞察宇宙神圣的统一性，并有能力把与自然交流的感受传达给他的同类。真正的诗歌和艺术应当能够净化道德，并将人引向有机统一和更高的实在。

◆《美国学者》

《美国学者》被誉为“美国思想文化领域的独立宣言”。

爱默生认为美国人应停止模仿和引进外国文学，转而描绘此时此地的美国。他号召美国作家以美国人独有的方式进行创作、描绘美国大地。爱默生在美国文化思想史上的重要性在于他体现了处于上升阶段的美国渴望拥有自己的独特身份并愿为之努力奋斗。

Ⅲ. Henry David Thoreau (1817 –1862)

1. Life

Thoreau was a famous New England Transcendentalist. He was a good friend of Emerson, 14 years younger than Emerson. He was born in Concord, Massachusetts, entering Harvard University at the age of 17. After graduating from Harvard, he became friends with Emerson and began to accept Emerson's ideas. He was susceptible to Oriental influences such as Hinduism and Confucianism. In 1845, he moved into a small wooden house on the shore of Walden Pond and lived a simple and reclusive life for more than two years. During this period, he went to nearby villages from time to time, and once he was detained overnight for refusing to pay taxes. This inspired him to write the famous political essay, "Civil Disobedience". After returning to Concord, Thoreau wrote the famous *Walden* based on the more than two years of life experience in Walden Pond.

In the history of American literature, there were three great 19th-century writers who remained in obscurity and only won fame in the 20th century, namely Thoreau, Herman Melville and Emily Dickinson. Thoreau is now considered an important American writer in the 19th century. His influence extends beyond America. In 1969, Thoreau's statue was placed in the Hall of Fame in New York.

2. Major Works

A Week On the Concord and Merrimack Rivers

Walden

Civil Disobedience

A Plea for John Brown

3. Analysis of major works

◆ *Walden*

Thoreau's work Walden is a masterpiece of Transcendentalism. It faithfully recorded Thoreau's reflections when he communicated with nature alone. It shows that Thoreau not only accepted Emerson's Transcendentalism philosophy, but also further clarified the pantheistic characteristics of nature. Walden is all-encompassing and can be interpreted from various aspects.

(1) It is a book about self-culture and human perfectibility. Thoreau believes that the most important thing in life is to be

Ⅲ. 亨利·大卫·梭罗

1. 生平

梭罗是著名的新英格兰超验主义者。他是爱默生的好友，比爱默生小 14 岁。他出生于马萨诸塞州的康科德镇。17 岁时进入哈佛大学学习。大学毕业后跟爱默生成为好友并开始接受了爱默生的思想。他也受到过东方思想如印度教和儒学的影响。1845 年他搬进瓦尔登湖畔的一座小木屋，过了两年多简朴的隐居生活。这期间他不时去附近的村子，一次他因拒绝交税而被拘留了一夜。这激发他写成了著名的政论文《非暴力反抗》。回到康科德后，梭罗根据两年多在瓦尔登湖的生活经历写成了著名的《瓦尔登湖》。

在美国文学史上生前默默无名，在20 世纪才赢得盛名的 19 世纪伟大作家有三位，即梭罗、梅尔维尔和艾米丽·迪金森。现在，梭罗被认为是 19 世纪重要的美国作家。他的影响力超出了美国。1969 年，梭罗的塑像被竖立在纽约的"名人馆"里。

2. 主要作品

《康科德和梅里马科河上的一周》

《瓦尔登湖》

《论公民的不服从权利》

《为约翰·布朗请命》

3. 主要作品分析

◆《瓦尔登湖》

梭罗的代表作《瓦尔登湖》是一部超验主义巨作。它忠实地记录了梭罗独自与自然界交流时的反思。它表明梭罗不仅接受了爱默生的超验主义哲学，而且进一步亲身实践阐明自然界的泛神特性。《瓦尔登湖》包罗万象，可以从多种角度去解读。

(1) 它是一本关于人的自我教育和人的自我完善的书。梭罗认为

self-sufficient and strive to achieve spiritual perfection. Thoreau is hailed as the forerunner of individualism in the history of American literature. (2) Thoreau lashed out at modern civilization in the book. He believes that modern civilized life makes people lose their humanity and place people in a spiritual predicament. (3) In addition, the book shows that Thoreau wants the people of his country to get rid of complacency. He records how he reduces his personal needs as much as possible on Walden Pond. He believes that spiritual wealth is true wealth. Human spirit may not help people to become prosperous, but it helps people to make real progress in the process of self-improvement. (4) Thoreau went to live in the forest to experiment with a new way of life for himself and his compatriots. He was reborn when he came out of the forest, and his whole appearance was completely renewed. Regeneration is one of the most crucial themes in *Walden* and determines its structure.	生活中最重要的事情是自给自足，努力实现精神上的完美。梭罗被誉为美国文学史上个人主义的先驱。 （2）该书中梭罗猛烈抨击了现代文明。他认为现代文明生活使人失去了人性，将人置于精神上的困境。 （3）此外，该书表明梭罗希望国人摆脱自鸣得意、沾沾自喜的情绪。他记录了自己在瓦尔登湖上尽量将个人需求降到最低的情况。他认为精神上的富有才是真正的富有。人的精神或许不能帮助人飞黄腾达，却有助于人在自我完善的过程中取得真正的进步。 （4）梭罗去森林居住目的是为自己和同胞们实验一种新的生活方式。他从林中出来时获得了重生，整个人面貌焕然一新。重生成为《瓦尔登湖》中最关键的主题之一，并且决定了该书的结构框架。

4.2 考研真题与典型题详解

I. Fill in the blanks.

1. Ralph W. Emerson believes in the concept of the __________. It is the __________ within which every man's particular being is contained and made one with all other.（国际关系学院 2009 研）
2. Ralph Waldo Emerson wrote __________, which has been called "the Manifesto of American Transcendentalism," and __________, which has been regarded as America's "Declaration of Intellectual Independence."（南开大学 2007 研）
3. In 1836, a little book came out which made a tremendous impact on the intellectual life of America. It was entitled *Nature* by __________.
4. The great work __________ not only demonstrates Emersonian ideas of self-reliance but also develops and tests Emerson's own transcendental philosophy.
5. Ralph Waldo Emerson's truest disciple, the man who put into practice many of Emerson's theories, was __________.
6. A superb book entitled __________ came out of Henry David Thoreau's two year experiment at Walden Pond.
7. From Henry David Thoreau's Concord jail experience came his famous essay __________.

II. Multiple Choice

1. American renaissance started from __________.（北二外 2009 研）

A. Pragmatism B. utilitarian

C. New England transcendentalism D. the age of Realism

2. Which one of the following statements is applicable to the understanding of Transcendentalism? (四川大学 2008 研)

A. It is strongly influenced by social Darwinism.

B. Belief in individualism, independence of mind, and self-reliance.

C. Man has no free-will.

D. It holds that determinism governs everything.

3. Ralph Waldo Emerson's __________ is regarded as the "Declaration of Intellectual Independence". (北二外 2008 研；首师大 2009 研)

A. *Nature* B. *The Conduct of Life*

C. *Representative Men* D. "The American Scholar"

4. Point out the work that was written by Henry David Thoreau. __________(四川大学 2009 研)

A. *The Fall of the House of Usher* B. *The Rise of Silas Lapham*

C. *Walden* D. "The Legend of Sleepy Hollow"

5. "The universe is composed of Nature and the soul... Spirit is present every where". This is the voice of the book *Nature* written by Emerson, which pushed American Romanticism into a new phase, the phase of New England __________.

A. Romanticism B. Transcendentalism

C. Naturalism D. Symbolism

6. There is a good reason to state that New England Transcendentalism was actually __________ on the Puritan soil.

A. Romanticism B. Puritanism C. Mysticism D. Unitarianism

7. Transcendentalists recognized __________ as the "highest power of the soul".

A. intuition B. logic

C. data of the senses D. thinking

8. Transcendentalist doctrines found their greatest literary advocates in __________ and Henry David Thoreau.

A. Thomas Jefferson B. Ralph Waldo Emerson

C. Philip Freneau D. Oversoul

Ⅲ. Explain the following terms.

1. Transcendentalism (贵州大学 2023 研；北二外 2010 研；北航 2010 研；南开大学 2008 研)

2. Ralph Waldo Emerson (北航 2007 研)

3. Oversoul (武汉大学 2008 年)

4. self-reliance (北二外 2009 研)

Ⅳ. Read the following quotations and answer the questions.

Passage 1

To go into solitude, a man needs to retire as much from his chamber as from society. I am not solitary whilst I read and write, though nobody is with me. But if a man would be alone, let him look at the stars. The rays that come from those heavenly worlds, will separate between him and vulgar things. One might think the atmosphere was made transparent with this design, to give man, in the heavenly bodies, the perpetual presence of the sublime. Seen in the streets of cities, how great they are! If the stars should appear one night in a thousand years, how would men believe and adore; and preserve for many generations the remembrance of the city of God which had been shown! But every night come out these preachers of beauty, and light the universe with their admonishing smile.

Questions:

(1) This paragraph is taken from a famous essay. What is the name of the essay?

(2) Who is the author?

(3) What does the author say would happen if the stars appeared one night in a thousand years?

(4) Give a peculiar term to cover the author's belief.

Passage 2

Standing on the bare ground—my head bathed by the blithe air and uplifted in to infinite space—all mean egotism vanishes. I become a transparent eyeball; I am nothing; I see all; the currents of the Universal Being circulate through me; I am part or particle of God.

Questions:

(1) Which work is this selection taken from?

(2) How do you understand the philosophical ideas in these words?

Passage 3

There's a time in every man's education when he arrives at the conviction that envy is ignorance; that imitation is suicide; that he must take himself for better, for worse, as his portion... Trust thyself; every heart vibrates to that iron string.

Whoso would be a man must be a nonconformist.

Questions:

(1) This selection is selected from an essay. What is the title of that?

(2) Who is the author of the essay?

(3) According to the selection, what do you think the author believes in?

V. Short answer questions

1. Which of Emerson's works is called "America's intellectual Declaration of independence"?（国际关系学院2007研）
2. Emerson states: "Let a man then know his worth, and keep things under his feet." This indicates the author's belief in real virtue. Please make comments on this line.（南京大学2009研）
3. What is the major thematic concern of *Walden*?（国际关系学院2007研）

VI. Essay question

1. Analyze Ralph Waldo Emerson's theory of Transcendentalism with the analysis of Nature.

参考答案及解析

I. Fill in the blanks.

1. Transcendentalism; Oversoul

（爱默生信奉超验主义，在他看来，超灵为人所共有，每个人的思想存在于超灵之中，人能以直觉官能与之交融。)

2. *Nature*；“The American Scholar”

(爱默生的《论自然》被称为“美国超验主义的宣言”，其《美国学者》则被誉为美国知识分子的独立宣言。)

3. Ralph Waldo Emerson

(拉尔夫·瓦尔多·爱默生(Ralph Waldo Emerson，1803 - 1882)美国散文作家、思想家、诗人。1836 年出版处女作《论自然》(*Nature*)。《论自然》的发表为美国思想界吹来一股清风，一扫机械主义自然观的乌烟瘴气。)

4. *Walden*

(梭罗的代表作《瓦尔登湖》表明梭罗不仅接受了爱默生的超然主义哲学，而且进一步亲身实践阐明自然界的泛神特性。)

5. Henry David Thoreau

(亨利·戴维·梭罗(Henry David Thoreau)是美国作家、哲学家，他最著名的作品为著名散文集《瓦尔登湖》和论文《论公民的不服从权利》。梭罗是爱默生最忠实的追随者并且将爱默生的许多理论付诸了实践。)

6. *Walden*

(《瓦尔登湖》(*Walden*)出版于 1854 年，梭罗在书中详尽地描述了他在瓦尔登湖湖畔一片再生林中度过两年零两月的生活以及期间他的许多思考。)

7. *Civil Disobedience*

(在瓦尔登湖生活期间，梭罗因为反对黑奴制拒交“人头税”而被捕入狱。友人替他代交了税款保其出狱，但这一亲身体验却激发他写成了著名的政论《抵制国民政府》(*Resistance to Civil Government*，后改名为《论公民的不服从权利》(*Civil Disobedience*)。)

Ⅱ. Multiple Choice

1. C　美国的文艺复兴，又称为新英格兰文艺复兴，源于新英格兰超验主义。
2. B　超验主义肯定人的神圣性，主张人能超越感觉和理性而直接认识真理，“相信你自己”，是超验主义者的座右铭。
3. D　“The American Scholar”(《论美国学者》)是爱默生在哈佛大学的一篇演讲词，爱默生在演说中主张建立独立的民族文化与文学，吹起了美国文化独立的号角。
4. C　梭罗是美国超验主义作家之一，其代表作是 *Walden*(《瓦尔登湖》)。选项 A《厄舍古屋的倒塌》是 Edgar Allan Poe(爱伦·坡)的作品；选项 B《塞拉斯·拉帕姆的发迹》是 William Dean Howells(豪威尔斯)的小说；选项 D《睡谷的传说》的作者是 Washington Irving(华盛顿·欧文)。
5. B　《论自然》(*Nature*)是爱默生的第 1 部重要哲学著作，最初发表于 1836 年。它集超验主义思想之大成，有新英格兰超验主义宣言的美称。《论自然》中强调精神，或超灵，认为这是宇宙至为重要的存在因素。超灵是一种无所不容、无所不在、扬善抑恶的力量，是万物之本、万物之所属，它存在于人和自然界内。
6. A　新英格兰超验主义深受清教思想的影响，由于清教主义自身积极性与消极性共存的复杂性，超验主义者对清教的态度也是复杂的。认同、接受与怀疑、超越共存，他们一方面肯定了清教思想与价值，另一方面又批判了清教社会对人的精神的负面影响。
7. A　超验主义者将直觉作为“心灵最伟大的力量”。

8. B 美国超验主义(American Transcendentalism)是美国的一个重要思潮，它兴起于十九世纪三十年代的新英格兰地区。它是与拉尔夫·沃尔多·爱默生以及梭罗相关的一种文学和哲学运动，宣称存在一种理想的精神实体，超越于经验和科学之处，通过直觉得以把握。

Ⅲ. Explain the following terms.

1. Transcendentalism: Transcendentalism is a New England movement, which flourished from about 1835 to 1860. It had its roots in romanticism and in post-Kantian idealism by which Coleridge was influenced. It had a considerable influence on American art and literature. Basically religious, it emphasized the role and importance of the individual conscience, and the value of intuition in matters of moral guidance and inspiration. The actual term was coined by opponents of the movement, but accepted by its members. The group of people was also social reformers. Some of the members, besides Emerson, were famous, including Bronson Alcott, Henry David Thoreau and Nathaniel Hawthorne.
2. Ralph Waldo Emerson: Ralph Waldo Emerson (1803 – 1882) was an American essayist, philosopher, and poet, best remembered for leading the Transcendentalist movement of the mid 19th century. He gradually moved away from the religious and social beliefs of his contemporaries, formulating and expressing the philosophy of Transcendentalism in his 1836 essay, *Nature*. As a result of this ground breaking work, he gave a speech entitled "The American Scholar" in 1837, which Oliver Wendell Holmes, Sr. considered to be America's "Intellectual Declaration of Independence".
3. Oversoul: "The Oversoul" is an essay by Ralph Waldo Emerson, first published in 1841. For Emerson, the term denotes a supreme underlying unity which transcends duality or plurality, much in keeping with the philosophy of Advaita Vedanta. Over-soul has more recently come to be used by Eastern philosophers such as Meher Baba and others as the closest English language equivalent of the Vedic concept of Paramatman. The term is used frequently in discussion of Eastern metaphysics and has also entered western vernacular. In this context, the term "Oversoul" is understood as the collective indivisible Soul, of which all individual souls or identities are included.
4. self-reliance: "Self-Reliance" is an essay written by American Transcendentalist philosopher and essayist, Ralph Waldo Emerson. It contains the most solid statement of one of Emerson's repeating themes, the need for each individual to avoid conformity and false consistency, and follow his or her own instincts and ideas. Emerson's ideas are considered a reaction as a commercial identity; he calls for a return to individual identity.

Ⅳ. Read the following quotations and answer the questions.

Passage 1

(1) *Nature*

(2) Ralph Waldo Emerson

(3) Then, the men cannot believe and adore the God, cannot preserve the remembrance of the city of God which had been shown.

(4) Transcendentalism

Passage 2

(1) *Nature*

(2) He regards nature as the purest, and the most sanctifying moral influence on man, and advocates a direct intuition of a spiritual and immanent God in nature. In this connection, Emerson's emotional experiences are exemplary in more than one ways. Now this is a moment of "conversation" when one feels completely merged with the outside world, when one has completely sunk into nature and become one with it, and when the soul has gone beyond the physical limits of the body to share the omniscience of the Oversoul. In a word, the soul has completely transcended the limits of individuality and become part of the Oversoul. Emerson sees spirit pervading everywhere, not only in the soul of man, but behind nature, throughout nature.

Passage 3

(1) "Self-Reliance"

(2) Ralph Waldo Emerson

(3) He believed above all the individualism, independence of mind, and self-reliance.

V. Short answer questions

1. "The American Scholar" is called "America's intellectual Declaration of independence". It was a speech given by Ralph Waldo Emerson on August 31, 1837 to the Phi Beta Kappa Society in Harvard. He was invited to speak in recognition of his groundbreaking work *Nature*, published a year earlier, in which he established a new way for America's fledgling society to regard the world. Sixty years after declaring independence, American culture was still heavily influenced by Europe, and Emerson, for possibly the first time in the country's history, provided a visionary philosophical framework for escaping "from under its iron lids" and building a new, distinctly American cultural identity.
2. This line is a representation of Emerson's transcendental ideas that the individual is the most important of all and an individual should know about his own worth and give full play to his worth. If man relies upon himself, cultivates himself and brings about the divine in himself, he can hopefully become better and more perfect. He tries to convince people that doing things based on their knowledge of their worth is a perfect way to develop and improve themselves. Each man should determine his own existence. Men should and could be self-reliant. Self-reliance is also an expression of the hope that man can become the best person he could hope to be.
3. *Walden* is informed by American Transcendentalism, a philosophy developed by Thoreau's friend and spiritual mentor Ralph Waldo Emerson. It emphasizes the importance of solitude, contemplation, and closeness to nature in transcending the "desperate" existence that, he argues, is the lot of most people. Thoreau was putting into practice the Transcendentalist belief that one can best transcend normality and experience the Ideal, or the Divine, through nature.

Ⅵ. Essay question

1. Emerson was the leading New England Transcendentalist. His *Nature* is usually regarded as the Bible of New England Transcendentalism. In *Nature* Emerson affected a most articulate synthesis of the Transcendentalist views.

One major element of his philosophy is his firm belief in the transcendence of the "Over-soul". He states in *Nature* "the universe is composed of Nature and the Soul." He sees the world as phenomenal, and emphasizes the need for idealism, for idealism sees the world in God. He regards nature as the purest, and the most sanctifying moral influence on man, and advocates a direct intuition of a spiritual and immanent God in nature. In this connection, Emerson's emotional experiences are exemplary in more than one way.

Emerson holds that the individual, not the crowd, is the most important of all. If man depends upon himself, cultivates himself, and brings out the divine in himself, he can hope to become better and even perfect. He tries to convince people that the possibilities for man to develop and improve himself are infinite. Men should and could be self-reliant.

In Emerson's Transcendentalist eyes, nature was, to him as to his Puritan forebears, emblematic of God. It mediates between man and God, and its voice leads to higher truth. In a word, "Nature is the symbol of spirit." That is probably why he called his first philosophical work *Nature* rather than anything else. To him nature is a wholesome moral influence on man and his character. A natural implication of Emerson's view on nature is that the world around is symbolic.

第5章 霍桑·麦尔维尔

5.1 复习笔记

I. Nathaniel Hawthorne (1804 – 1864)

1. Life

Hawthorne was born in Salem, Massachusetts. Some of his ancestors were men of prominence in the Puritan theocracy. One of his ancestors was a colonial magistrate, notorious for his part in the persecution of the Quakers, and another was a judge at the Salem Witchcraft Trial in 1692. As his family fortune declined, Hawthorn was intensely conscious of the wrongdoing of his ancestors and this evil nature of humanity.

2. Ideas

(1) Hawthorne is seen as "a black romantic" writing the irrational, the demonic and the gothic. Viewing evil as the inherent human nature, he was haunted by a sense of sin and evil in life. In almost every book he wrote, Hawthorne discussed sin, evil and guilt.

(2) He rejected the Transcendentalists' transparent optimism about human nature and science. He holds a complicated attitude towards Puritanism.

(3) Tragedies occur as sin or evil can be passed from generation to generation. Hawthorne believed people can be educated when sin gets its punishment.

(4) He believed that romance was the predestined form of American narrative. He took a great interest in history and antiquity, which nourished his mind.

3. Writing style

(1) His literary style features ambiguity and romanticism in the American literary history. Hawthorne's ambiguity is a noticeable feature of his art. It can be seen in the narrative technique of multiple views employed in the last part of his masterpiece *The Scarlet Letter*.

I. 纳撒尼尔·霍桑

1. 生平

霍桑出生于马萨诸塞州的萨勒姆镇，他的祖先们是17世纪新英格兰清教神权统治中的显赫人物。他的一位祖先是殖民地行政官，因参与迫害贵格党人而臭名昭著。另一位祖先则是1692年萨勒姆审巫案的法官。随着家族渐渐走向没落，霍桑强烈地意识到他的祖先曾犯下的错误和人性的邪恶。

2. 思想

(1)霍桑被视为“黑色浪漫主义”的代表，他的作品常触及非理性的和邪恶的力量，并带有哥特式风格。他认为罪恶是人性的一部分，一生被罪恶感萦绕。几乎他的每一部作品都涉及到了罪行、邪恶与悔恨。

(2)他反对超验主义者对人性和科学抱着纯粹乐观的态度，对清教持有两面性的复杂态度。

(3)原罪与恶行会代代相传并导致悲剧。但霍桑相信惩罚罪恶能对人们起到教化作用。

(4)他认为传奇是美国小说叙事注定的形式。他对历史和文物古迹有浓厚的兴趣，认为它们可以滋养思想的成长

3. 写作风格

(1)霍桑的是一位思想矛盾、写作手法娴熟的美国浪漫主义作家。矛盾性是霍桑写作艺术的一个显著特征，在他的代表作《红字》的最后一部分作家运用了多重视角的写作技巧。

(2) Anatomist of "the interior of the heart", Hawthorne is an expert at psychoanalysis and exploration of human nature. His works are full of mental activities.

(3) Hawthorne is a master of symbolism and allegory to reveal and attack the crushing blows of reality, which he took from the Puritan tradition and bequeathed to American literature in a revivified form. The symbol can be found everywhere in his writing, and especially in his masterpiece, *The Scarlet Letter*.

4. Influence

Hawthorne exerted great influence on his successors. He was accorded due recognition by his contemporary James Russell Lowell in the latter's *A Fable for Critics*. He changed Herman Melville's original scheme for his *Moby Dick*. Hawthorne's fiction sets examples for novel-writing practice of writers like William Dean Howells. In the 20th century, William Faulkner and some Gothic novelists clearly showed their indebtedness to him.

5. Major works

The Scarlet Letter
Twice-told Tales
Mosses from an Old Manse
The House of the Seven Gables
The Blithedale Romance
The Marble Faun
"Young Goodman Brown"
"The Minister's Black Veil"
"Rappaccini's Daughter"

6. Analysis of his major works

◆*The Scarlet Letter*

(1) Theme-Centering on the universality of guilt, the novel explores the complexities and ambiguities of man's choices. Hawthorne does not simply describe a story of love or sin, instead he focuses on the ethical and psychological effects or consequences of the sin on common people and main characters in particular. In this way, he presented to readers the tension between society and individuals. To Hawthorne, everybody is potentially a sinner, and great moral courage is necessary for the improvement of human nature. Meanwhile, Hawthorne reveals the double sides of Puritanism in the portrayal of the priest Mr. Wilson. His accusation of Dimmesdale and Hester shows the persecution of Puritanism on people betraying its doctrine,

(2)他善于探究人的复杂心理，是人物内心的剖析师。他的作品有着丰富的心理活动描写。

(3)寓言是对现实沉重的打击，象征主义则是揭露和抨击的武器。霍桑是象征主义和寓言大师，他继承了清教的传统并将此文学遗产传给美国文学界的后人。象征手法在他的作品中随处可见，尤其是他的代表作《红字》中。

4. 影响

霍桑的影响可谓深远。詹姆斯·拉塞尔·洛威尔在《写给批评家的寓言》的末了给予他以应有的认可。他改变了赫尔曼·麦尔维尔创作《白鲸》的最初意图。威廉·迪安·豪威尔斯等作家将霍桑的作品作为他们小说创作的基准。在20世纪，威廉姆·福克纳和一些哥特式小说家对他也怀感恩之情。

5. 主要作品

《红字》
《重讲一遍的故事》
《古屋青苔》
《带有七个尖角阁的房子》
《福谷传奇》
《玉石雕像》
《好小伙子布朗》
《牧师的黑面纱》
《拉普奇尼博士的女儿》

6. 主要作品分析

◆《红字》

(1) 主题——这部小说展现了罪恶的普遍性并探究了人们面临选择时的复杂与矛盾心理。霍桑无意去讲述一个关于爱情或罪恶的故事，而是关注于罪恶感带给普通人或一些主要角色在道德和心理方面的影响，从而展示了社会与个人之间的紧张状况。对于霍桑来讲，每个人都是潜在的罪人，道义上的勇气对人性的改善是必不可少的。同时，霍桑通过塑造牧师威尔森的形象揭示了清教的两面性。威尔森对丁梅斯戴尔和海斯特通奸的指责表现了清教对违反其教规的人的压迫，

while his charitable admonition on Pearl's behalf shows the benevolence of Puritanism.

(2) Symbolism-Hawthorne describes Hester as an aristocratic and sensitive young woman who faces her execution with dignity and courage. When she is released, she does not flee the community but supports herself and her child by doing fancy needlework, taking care of her child and helping the sick and the poor. She wins the admiration and love of her fellow villagers again. So, The Scarlet Letter is a hymn on the moral growth of the woman. The scarlet letter at first indicates Adultery, a token of shame. Then it changes to Able, symbolizing genuine sympathy and help she offers to her fellow villagers. In the end, A appearing in the sky signifies Angel.

而他的劝诫又是为了珠儿的未来考虑，体现出清教仁爱的一面。

(2)象征主义——霍桑将海斯特描绘成一位仪态高贵并善感的年轻女子，从容勇敢地面对判决。当她获释后，她并没有逃离社区。她靠做精美的针线活自力更生养活孩子，将爱奉献给自己的孩子并帮助老弱病残，重新赢得了同乡人的赞美和爱戴。因此，《红字》就是一曲歌颂海斯特道德成长的赞歌。红字最初是羞耻的象征，是“通奸”；然后因为她对同乡人真诚的同情和帮助使得红字的意义变为“能干”；最后，红字A出现在天空中，意味着“天使”。

◆"Young Goodman Brown"

A young man named Goodman Brown, despite the advice of his newlywed wife, left his village and entered the forest. In the forest, Brown encountered a gathering hosted by a demon, with respected elders from the village, other villagers, and even his seemingly innocent wife participating. At the end of the story, Brown felt hopeless and lost confidence in life. He lost his faith and believed that everyone was guilty until he died.

◆《好小伙子布朗》

《好小伙子布朗》讲述的是一位名为古德曼·布朗的年轻人，不顾新婚妻子的劝阻，离开他的村庄，步入了象征邪恶的森林。在森林中，布朗撞见了恶魔主持的邪恶聚会，参与者有村中受尊敬的长者，村民，甚至还有他看似纯洁的妻子。故事的结尾布朗郁郁寡欢，对生活失去信心，失去信仰，认为大家都是有罪的，直到死去。

Ⅱ. Herman Melville (1819 – 1891)

1. Life

Melville is an American novelist, short story writer, and poet of the American Renaissance period. He had a humble educational background and began to work after dropping school. There are three things that influenced his life: being a sailor, his marriage and his friendship with Hawthorne. His experiences and adventures on the sea furnished him with abundant material for fiction. Melville had to do hackwork for the money so that he could keep his wife's extravagant style. Melville saw from Hawthorne's works an unusual understanding of evil and blackness at the core of American life. Melville revised the original design of his masterpiece *Moby Dick* after the two great minds met, and the novel was rewritten into a world classic today.

Ⅱ. 赫尔曼·麦尔维尔

1. 生平

麦尔维尔是美国文艺复兴时期著名的小说家和诗人。他接受的教育有限，辍学之后即开始工作。影响他一生的事件有三：出海，他的婚姻及其与霍桑的友谊。他在海上的经历和冒险为他的小说创作提供了丰富的素材。婚后，麦尔维尔不得不创作劣质作品以满足妻子的奢华生活。麦尔维尔认为霍桑理解美国社会之恶与黑暗的视角不同寻常。当两个人相会后，麦尔维尔的代表作《白鲸》的创作意图发生了重大改变。改写后的作品成为当今世界的文学经典。

2. Major works

Redburn

Typee

Omoo

Moby Dick

Mardi

White Jacket

Pierre

Billy Budd

The Confidence Man

Clarel

3. Analysis of major work

◆*Moby Dick*

(1) *Moby Dick* embodied Melville's bleak view of the American world in which he lived. For characters in the novel, they have no god or purpose. The loss of faith and the sense of futility and meaninglessness which feature western modern life were expressed in Melville's *Moby Dick* so well that the twentieth century has found it both fascinating and great.

(2) One of the major themes of this novel is isolation, which exists between man and man, man and society, and man and nature in the time when Melville lived. Melville also criticizes New England Transcendentalism for its emphasis on individualism and Oversoul. Another theme of this novel is "rejection and quest".

(3) Symbolism is another feature of the novel. The voyage itself is a metaphor for "search and discovery" and indicates the desire for the ultimate truth of experience. Moby Dick is the most conspicuous symbol in the novel and scholars have many interpretations of him. It is viewed as a symbol of evil, goodness, or both. Its whiteness is a paradoxical color, signifying death and corruption as well as purity, innocence, and youth. It represents the unfathomable final mystery of the universe.

(4) Melville manages to achieve the effect of ambiguity through employing the narrative technique of multiple view of his narratives. He tends to write periodic sentences. He has been praised for his rich rhythmical prose and poetic power.

2. 主要作品

《莱德伯恩》

《泰比》

《奥姆》

《白鲸》

《玛地》

《白外套》

《皮埃尔》

《比利巴德》

《骗子》

《克拉勒尔》

3. 主要作品分析

◆《白鲸》

(1)《白鲸》代表了麦尔维尔对他所生活的时代悲凉的世界观。对于小说中的人物来说，他们不信上帝，也没什么目标。西方现代生活中信仰的丢失、无用感及无意义感等淋漓尽致地表现在梅尔维尔的这部作品中，因此 20 世纪读者认为这部作品伟大且引人入胜。

(2) 该小说的主题是疏离。疏离体现于麦尔维尔生活时代的不同层面，如人与人之间，人与社会之间，以及人与自然之间。麦尔维尔同时对新英格兰超验主义过度强调个人主义和超灵进行了批判。该小说的另外一个主题是拒绝与追寻。

(3) 该小说富有象征意义。航行本身是探索和发现，寻求最终真相的隐喻。莫比·迪克是全书中最明显的象征，它可以有多种解释。有人认为它代表邪恶，有人认为它代表了善良，也有人认为它二者兼有。它的白色是自相矛盾的颜色，既代表了死亡和腐朽，又代表了纯洁、天真和青春。它代表宇宙深不可测的最终奥秘。

(4) 麦尔维尔通过运用多重视角的叙事技巧以实现文本的模糊性。他倾向于写掉尾句。他富有韵律的散文体和文笔的诗意得到了大众的赞美。

5.2 考研真题与典型题详解

I. Fill in the blanks.

1. Pearl is a character in ________ written by ________.(大连外国语学院 2007 研)
2. As a reflection of Hester Prynne's moral development, the ________ symbolically undergoes a gradual and imperceptible change from"________" to"able" and last to"angel". (天津外国语学院 2008 研)
3. Tashtego, Daggoo and Queequeg are the three main harpooners in the novel ________.(首师大 2008 研)
4. The way in which ________ wrote *The Scarlet Letter* suggests that American Romanticism adapted itself to American puritan moralism.
5. Hester Prynne is the heroine in Hawthorne's novel ________.
6. ________ is famous for writing stories about the sea and the islands of the Southern Pacific. In his masterpiece ________, he tells a story of a whaling voyage which is set a symbolic account of the conflict between man and his fate.
7. ________ is the narrator in *Moby Dick*.

Ⅱ. Multiple Choice

1. The most influential novelist in Romantic period is ________.(北二外 2009 研)
   A. Nathaniel Hawthorne　　B. Edgar Allan Poe
   C. Emily Dickinson　　D. Fenimore Cooper
2. In ________, Captain Ahab is obsessed with the revenge on a whale which sheared off his leg on a previous voyage, and his crazy chasing of it eventually brings death to all on board the whaler except Ishmael, who survives to tell the tale.(天津外国语学院 2007 研)
   A. *Typee*　　B. *White Jacket*　　C. *Moby Dick*　　D. *Billy Budd*
3. ________ is the most ambivalent writer in the American literary history.
   A. Nathaniel Hawthorne　　B. Walt Whitman
   C. Ralph Waldo Emerson　　D. Mark Twain
4. The finest example of Nathaniel Hawthorne's symbolism is the recreation of Puritan Boston in ________.
   A. *The Scarlet Letter*　　B. *Young Goodman Brown*
   C. *The Marble Faun*　　D. *The Ambitious Guest*
5. "There is evil in every human heart, which may remain latent, perhaps, through the whole life; but circumstances may rouse it to activity." The thought is reflected in ________.
   A. Nathaniel Hawthorne's *Young Goodman Brown*
   B. Mark Twain's *The Adventures of Huckleberry Finn*
   C. Walt Whitman's *Leaves of Grass*
   D. Herman Melville's *Moby Dick*
6. ________ is an appalling fictional version of Nathaniel Hawthorne's belief that "the wrong doing of one generation lives into the successive ones" and that evil will come out of evil though it may take many generations to happen.

A. *The Marble Faun*
B. *The House of Seven Gables*
C. *The Blithedale Romance*
D. *Young Goodman Brown*

7. Which is not Nathaniel Hawthorne's long novel?
A. *The Marble Faun*
B. *The Blithedale Romance*
C. *The House of Seven Gables*
D. *Dr. Heidegger's Experiment*

8. In *Moby Dick*, the voyage symbolizes ___________.
A. the microcosm of human society
B. a search for truth
C. the unknown world
D. nature

Ⅲ. Read the following quotations and answer the questions.

Passage 1（北航 2009 研）

Young Goodman Brown came forth at sunset into the street at Salem village: but put his head back after crossing threshold, to exchange a parting kiss with his wife. And Faith, as the wife was aptly named, thrust her own pretty head into the street, letting the wind play with the pink ribbons on her cap while she called to Goodman Brown.

Questions:

(1) This passage is taken from "Young Goodman Brown", who is the author?

(2) What is the symbolic meaning of "pink ribbons"?

(3) What is a symbol in literature?

Passage 2（北航 2007 研）

"Who is that man, Hester?" gasped Mr. Dimmesdale, overcome with terror. "I shiver at him! Dost thou know the man? I hate him, Hester!"

She remembered her oath, and was silent.

"I tell thee, my soul shivers at him," muttered the minister again. "Who is he? Who is he? Canst thou do nothing for me? I have a nameless horror of the man."

"Minister," said little Pearl. "I can tell thee who he is!"

"Quickly, then, child!" said the minister, bending his ear close to her lips. "Quickly! —and as low as thou canst whisper."

Pearl mumbled something into his ear, that sounded, indeed, like human language, but was only such gibberish as children may be heard amusing themselves with, by the hour together At all events, if it involved any secret information in regard to old Roger Chillingworth, it was in a tongue unknown to the erudite clergyman, and did but increase the bewilderment of his mind. The elvish child then laughed aloud.

"Dost thou mock me now?" said the minister.

"Thou wast not bold! —thou wast not true!" answered the child.

"Thou wouldst not promise to lake my hand, and mother's hand, tomorrow noontide!"

Questions:

(1) Which fiction is this excerpt from?

(2) Who is the author? What are the major artistic features of the author?

(3) Try to comment on the irony in this excerpt.

Passage 3

Hester Prynne's term of confinement was now at an end. Her prison-door was thrown open, and she came forth into sunshine which falling on all alike, seemed, to her sick and morbid heart, as if meant for no other purpose than to reveal the scarlet letter on her breast. Perhaps there was a more real torture in her first unattended footsteps from the threshold of the prison, than even in the procession and spectacle that have been described, where she was made the common infamy, at which all mankind was summoned to point its finger. Then, she was supported by an unnatural tension of the nerves, and by all the combative energy of her character, which enabled her to convert the scene into a kind of lurid triumph.

Questions:

(1) Which novel is this selection taken from?

(2) What is the name of the novelist?

(3) What do you think is the symbolic meaning of the scarlet letter on Hester's breast?

Ⅳ. Short answer questions

1. Give some different explanations of the symbolic meaning of "A" in *The Scarlet Letter* by Hawthorne. (人大 2006 研；南京大学 2008 研)
2. What does the white whale in *Moby Dick* symbolize? Why do you think so? (国际关系学院 2007 研)
3. *Moby-Dick* features several seemingly insane characters. How does insanity relate to this story? How do these characters contrast with one another? (北航 2009 研)
4. Discuss the allegory and symbolism in *Young Goodman Brown*.

V. Essay questions

1. Due to his family background and his understanding of human nature, Nathaniel Hawthorne seems to be haunted by a sense of sin and evil in life. Explain his "black" vision in *The Scarlet Letter*. (天津外国语学院 2007 研)
2. Make a comment on Herman Melville's novel *Moby Dick*. (四川大学 2008 研)
3. *Moby Dick* by Herman Melville is one of the few books in American literature that has produced an exciting effect upon readers. Try to discuss the symbolism in the book.

参考答案及解析

I. Fill in the blanks.

1. *The Scarlet Letter*, Nathaniel Hawthorne

   (Pearl 是美国作家 Nathaniel Hawthorne 小说《红字》中的人物。)
2. scarlet letter A, adultery

   (霍桑的小说《红字》中海斯特·白兰经历了道德的洗礼，红字 A 的含义也逐渐由"通奸"转变为"能干"以至后来的"天使")
3. *Moby Dick*

   (这三个人是《莫比·狄克》里的捕鲸手。)
4. Nathaniel Hawthorne

   (纳撒尼尔·霍桑的小说《红字》暗示了美国浪漫主义遵循美国清教伦理道德。)

5. *The Scarlet Letter*

（海斯特·白兰是霍桑小说《红字》中的女主人公。）

6. Herman Melville；*Moby Dick*

（赫尔曼·麦尔维尔因写南太平洋的大海和岛屿的故事而著名。他的代表作《白鲸》讲述了以人与他自己命运的冲突作为象征的捕鲸航程。）

7. Ishmael

（以实玛利是小说《白鲸》的叙述者。）

Ⅱ. Multiple Choice

1. A　美国十九世纪最有影响的浪漫主义小说家是霍桑。
2. C　Captain Ahab（亚哈船长）是梅尔维尔的小说 *Moby Dick*（《白鲸》）里的主人公。
3. A　纳撒尼尔·霍桑是美国文学历史上最为矛盾的作家。
4. A　《红字》（*The Scarlet Letter*）是美国 19 世纪影响最大的浪漫主义小说家和心理小说家纳撒尼尔·霍桑（Nathaniel Hawthorne）的代表作。该小说是成功运用象征手法的典范。
5. A　霍桑认为罪恶是人生来所带的标记。几乎他的每一部作品都涉及到了罪与恶。
6. B　《红字》（*The Scarlet Letter*）发表后获得巨大成功，霍桑继而创作了不少作品。其中《带有七个尖角阁的房子》（*The House of Seven Gables*）描写品钦家族的祖先（Colonel Pyncheon）谋财害命而使后代遭到报应的故事，说明财富是祸患，“一代人的罪孽要殃及子孙”；这部小说也反映了资本主义发展初期的血腥掠夺。
7. D　《黑德格医生的实验》（*Dr. Heidegger's Experiment*）是霍桑的中短篇小说。其余三项《玉石雕像》（*The Marble Faun*），《福谷传奇》（*The Blithedale Romance*），《带有七个尖角阁的房子》（*The House of Seven Gables*）都是霍桑的长篇小说。
8. B　小说《白鲸》中航程象征了对真理的探寻。

Ⅲ. Read the following quotations and answer the questions.

Passage 1

（1）Nathaniel Hawthorne

（2）In this story, “pink ribbons” appear three times. They symbolize the faith Brown holds toward God and human that religion and human are pure and upright.

（3）A symbol is a sign which suggests more than its literal meaning. In other words, a symbol is both literal and figurative. A symbol is a way of organizing the narrative and conveying thematic meanings. The best symbols are those that are believable in the lives of the characters and also fascinating as they allow readers to go beyond the literal level of the story. If the symbol is obscure or ambiguous, then the very obscurity and the ambiguity may also be part of the meaning of the story.

Passage 2

（1）This excerpt is from *The Scarlet Letter*.

（2）The author is Nathaniel Hawthorne. Much of Hawthorne's writing centers on New England, with many works featuring moral allegories with Puritan doctrines. His fiction works are considered part of the Romanticism and, more specifically, dark romanticism. His themes often center on the inherent evil and sin of humanity, and his works often have ethical messages and deep psychological complexity.

(3) When Pearl asked Mr. Dimmesdale to stand with her and her mother on the platform the next day, the minister refused. He only promised to stand together with them before the judgment-seat at the great judgment day, and thus "the daylight of this world shall not see our meeting". In fact, he did not want to announce his relationship with Hester and Pearl. So, Pearl's words "Thou wast not bold! —thou wast not true!" are ironic.

Passage 3

(1) *The Scarlet Letter*

(2) Nathaniel Hawthorne

(3) Symbolism is traditionally a sign or token of something. In the matter of literature, the definition of the literary device, symbolism is more complicated. Symbols of literature are usually metaphysical. In this novel, the scarlet letter "A" changes its meaning in many different times. This change is significant. It shows growth in the characters, and the community in which they live. The letter "A" begins as a symbol of sin. It then becomes a symbol of alone and alienation, and finally it becomes a symbol of able, angel and admirable.

Ⅳ. Short answer questions

1. The letter "A" begins as a symbol of adultery, which is worn on Hester's chest. This is the puritan way of punishing her for the crime of adultery. It then becomes a symbol of alone and alienation. Hester's social life is virtually eliminated as a result of her shameful past. And little Pearl is the only companion of her lonely life. Finally it becomes a symbol of able, angel and admirable. The villagers who condemn her now believe the scarlet letter stands for her ability to make beautiful needlework and for her unselfish assistance to the poor and sick. Hester is a strong admirable woman who goes through more emotional torture than most people go through in a lifetime. "A" may also represent Adamic, or prehistoric, an archetypal vice suggestive of "original sin".
2. For Captain Ahab, the white whale represents evil. After the loss of his leg in his encounter with the white whale, Ahab begins to hate Moby Dick and goes into lengths to kill the whale. It seems that Ahab consigned all of the evil to the white whale. For other members on the whaling ship, the white whale symbolizes the unknown, mysterious natural force of the universe. For the readers, the white whale is capable of many interpretations, for it is "paradoxically benign and malevolent, nourishing and destructive," "massive, brutal, monolithic, but at the same time protean, erotically beautiful, infinitely variable."
3. In *Moby-Dick*, Ishmael describes Ahab as mad in his narration as he intends to rebel against the forces of nature or God. However, some of the other characters in the novel whom Ishmael labels insane—notably Pip and Gabriel—might be otherwise viewed as wise, thus prompting readers to think about the possibility of making a clear distinction between sanity and insanity. Gabriel, the prophet figure aboard the *Jeroboam*, behaves irrationally and makes a number of ridiculous-sounding predictions. Gabriel's prophecies are aimed at earning fair treatment for the crew from the ship's officers and at avoiding the danger that will come from trying to hunt Moby Dick. Like Ahab, he manipulates the crew's superstitions and religious beliefs in order to gather support. But whereas Ahab's obsession is monomaniacal and selfish, Gabriel's "madness" is a response to irrational and unjust behavior on the part of those who control his ship. The ship ironically represents

the American society with fixed social status and power relationship.

4. Young Goodman Brown, essentially an allegory, which is included in Hawthorne's *Mosses from an Old Manse*, is one of his most profound tales. Through the story, Hawthorne sought to bring about the moral that, "There is evil in every human heart, which may arouse latent, perhaps, through the whole life; but circumstances may arouse it to activity."

   While using allegory to hold fast against the crushing blows of reality, the symbol serves as a weapon to attack and penetrate it. Hawthorne took his symbolism from Puritan tradition and bequeathed it to American literature in a revivified form. His view of man and history originates, to a great extent, in Puritanism. Hawthorne was burdened with a sense of guilt due to his ancestor's notorious role in Salem Witch Trials. This sensibility led to his understanding of evil being at the very core of human life, which is typical of the Calvinistic belief that human beings are basically depraved and corrupted, hence, they should obey god to atone for their sins.

V. Essay questions

1. All his life, Hawthorne seems to be haunted by his sense of sin and evil in life. Reading his tales and romances, one cannot but be overwhelmed by the "black" vision which these works reveal. The blackness of vision which comes as a natural corollary has become his trade mark. It illustrates to some extent the influence that the Calvinist doctrine of "original sin" and total depravity had upon his mind. One source of evil in Hawthorne is overweening intellect. Hawthorne's intellectual characters are usually villains, dreadful because devoid of fellow feeling.

   In *The Scarlet Letter*, the experience of Hester and Dimmesdale recalls the story of Adam and Eve because, in both cases, sin results in expulsion and suffering. But it also results in knowledge—specifically, in knowledge of what it means to be human. The real villain in *The Scarlet Letter* is Roger Chillingworth, the scholar, the embodiment of pure intellect, who commits "the Unpardonable Sin"—the violation of the human heart. He keeps preying on Dimmesdale's conscience until the poor wretch is tormented to death. The end of Chillingworth, when it comes, is also tragic enough. Dimmesdale declares God's judgment on him before he breathes his last: "Thou, too, hast deeply sinned!" And Chillingworth simply shrivels. The last time we see him, he is kneeling down beside Dimmesdale "with a blank, dull countenance, out of which the life seemed to have departed." Chillingworth's misshapen body reflects (or symbolizes) the evil in his soul, which builds as the novel progresses, similar to the way Dimmesdale's illness reveals his inner turmoil.

2. *Moby-Dick* is often referred to as "the Great American Novel" and is considered one of the treasures of world literature.

   In the novel, Melville employs stylized language, symbolism, and metaphor to explore numerous complex themes. Through the main character's journey, readers can explore the concepts of class and social status, good and evil, and the existence of gods from the perspective of Ishmael as he contemplates upon his personal beliefs and his place in the universe.

   Moby-Dick is a symbolic work, but also includes chapters on natural history. Major themes include obsession, religion, and idealism versus pragmatism, revenge, racism, sanity, hierarchical relationships, and politics. All of the members of the crew have biblical-sounding, improbable, or descriptive names, and the narrator deliberately avoids specifying the exact time of the events and some other similar details. These together suggest that the narrator is deliberately casting his tale in an epic and allegorical mode. The white whale has also been seen as a symbol for many things, including nature and those elements of life that are out of human control.

3. It is a mixture of fantasy and realism based on the South Pacific whaling industry. It might be read as an initiation story about Ishmael, the outcast, finding himself in a real world of hard work and danger and an unreal world of speculation and mystery.

   It is a fabulous dramatization of Ahab's obsessed determination to revenge himself in the pursuit of one particular whale who previously destroyed his boat and humiliated him by ripping off one of his legs. The book has so often been interpreted in so many ways, allegorically and symbolically.

   Melville is a master of allegory and symbolism. Instead of putting the battle between Ahab and the big whale into simple statements, he used symbols to indicate their confrontation. Different people on board the ship are representations of and different social, ethnic groups, facts become symbols and incidents acquire universal meanings; the Pequod is the microcosm of human society with certain power relationship and the voyage becomes a search for truth. The white whale, Moby Dick, symbolizes nature for Melville, for it is complex, unfathomable, malignant, and beautiful as well.

   For the character Ahab, however, the whale only represents evil. Moby Dick is like a wall, hiding some unknown, mysterious things behind. Moby Dick is a mystery, an ultimate mystery of the universe, and the voyage of the mind will forever remain a search, not a discovery, of the truth. The whole story turns out to be a symbolic voyage of the mind quest of the truth and knowledge of the universe, a spiritual exploration into man's deep reality and psychology.

第 6 章　惠特曼·狄金森

6.1　复习笔记

I. Walt Whitman (1819 –1892)	**I. 沃尔特·惠特曼**
1. Life	**1. 生平**
Whitman grew up in a working-class family, on Long Island, New York. He didn't have much schooling but took on a good deal of "loafing" and reading. Hungry for experience and companionable in habit, Whitman experienced plenty of jobs and obtained a direct knowledge of life and people in the new world. The life with the people and the country laid a basis as both the material and the guiding spirit for his epic, *Leaves of Grass*. When the Civil War started, he worked as a "wound dresser" in a military hospital. In 1873, paralysis condemned him to good care of by his friends in New Jersey where he continued to revise his *Leaves of Grass*.	惠特曼成长于纽约州长岛一个工人阶级家庭。他上学时间不长，四处游荡并广泛地阅读书籍。由于渴望不同的经历和喜爱社交的习性，他尝试了多种多样的工作并获得了新世界的生活和在这里生活的人们的第一手材料。惠特曼与人们往来及游览美国大好山河的经历，为他的史诗《草叶集》提供了素材和精神导向。内战开始后，他在战地医院做看护员。1873 年他患半身不遂迁至新泽西，在那儿受到朋友的照顾，修订《草叶集》直至去世。
2. Literary point of view	**2. 文学观点**
(1) Affected by the leading New Englander Emerson, Whitman claims that the greatest poet should breathe into the world the grandeur and life of the universe.	(1)受新英格兰领军人物爱默生的影响，惠特曼认为最伟大的诗人应该给世界注入宇宙的壮观和生机。
(2) Art should be based organically on nature and the poet's work grows out of nature and derives its form from within.	(2)艺术以自然为基础。诗人的作品来源于自然。
(3) Whitman embraces idealism. He relies on insight and intuition very much.	(3)惠特曼信奉理想主义。他依赖于自己的内心与直觉。
3. Themes	**3. 主题**
(1) He shows great concern for the whole diligent people and the flourishing life of cities.	(1)他关注辛勤劳动的人民和迅速发展的城市生活。
(2) He advocates the realization of the individual value. Most of the poems in *Leaves of Grass* celebrate not only the "en-masse" but also the self in word.	(2)他提倡个体价值的实现。《草叶集》中大部分的诗作不仅歌颂了全体，还有个体。
(3) Pursuit of love and happiness is endorsed constantly and affectionately in his lines. It's important to respect the individual person and his desires.	(3)他的诗行中不断深情地赞颂对爱和幸福的追求。作为个体的人和他的欲望应受尊重。
(4) Some of Whitman's poems are politically committed.	(4)惠特曼的一些诗有坚定的政治立场。诗中他向战场上丧失了

Before and during the Civil War, Whitman expressed much lamentation for the pains of the young lives in the battlefield and demonstrated a strength of will to carry on fighting fearlessly until the ultimate victory. Later, he wrote down plenty of poems to express his grief due to the loss of Lincoln, and one of the famous is "When Lilacs Last in the Dooryard Bloom'd."	年轻的生命表达哀思，并展示了坚持无畏战斗直至最后胜利的决心。之后，他写下了很多诗表达对林肯遇刺的悲痛，其中著名的一首为《当紫丁香最近在庭院开放》。
4. Writing style	**4. 写作风格**
(1) Instead of the traditional iambic pentameter, Whitman wrote "free verse", that is, poetry without a fixed beat or regular rhyme scheme.	（1）惠特曼打破了五步抑扬格的传统，并创作"自由体"诗歌，也就是没有固定韵律的诗歌。
(2) There is a strong sense of the poems being rhythmical. Parallelism and phonetic recurrence at the beginning of the lines contribute a lot to the musicality of his poems.	（2）惠特曼的诗歌有很强的节奏感，诗行前几句排比和语音重复使他的诗歌颇具音乐美感。
(3) Most of the scenes he painted with words are honest, undistorted images of various aspects of America at that time.	（3）他用语言描述的大部分画面都是反映美国社会当时各个方面的真实景象。
(4) Whitman's language is relatively simple and even rather unsubtle. Another characteristic in Whitman's language is his great usage of oral English. Whitman's vocabulary is astonishing. He would use tough, vivid, as well as rarely-used words.	（4）惠特曼语言相对简单朴实，甚至十分粗犷，另一个特点是口语化。惠特曼词汇惊人，他总能用上有力的、生动的、别人不常用的语言。
5. Whitman's influence	**5. 惠特曼的影响**
Whitman's influence over modern poetry is great in the world as well as in America. Whitman has been compared to great mountain in American literary history. For his innovations in diction and versification, his frankness about sex, his inclusion of the commonplace and the ugly and his censure of the weakness of the American democratic practice—these have led to his achievement of immortality in American literature.	惠特曼对当代诗歌的影响在美国以及世界范围内都同样深远。惠特曼被比作美国文学历史上的高山，因他在措辞和诗律方面的创新，对性这一话题的坦率，反映有平凡和丑陋的题材，以及他对美国民主弊端的指责，这些都为他在美国文学上的不朽地位奠定了基础。
6. Major works	**6. 主要作品**
Leaves of Grass	《草叶集》
"Song of Myself"	《自我之歌》
"The Poet"	《诗人》
"When Lilacs Last in the Dooryard Bloom'd"	《当紫丁香最近在庭院开放》
"O Captain, My Captain"	《哦，船长，我的船长》
"I Hear America Singing"	《我听到美国在唱歌》
"There was a Child Went Forth"	《有一个孩子向前走去》
"Out of Cradle Endlessly Rocking"	《从永久摇荡的摇篮里》
Two Riverlets	《两条小河》
Drum Traps	《桴鼓集》

7. Analysis of major works

◆*Leaves of Grass*

(1) Grass, the most common thing with the greatest energy, is not only an image of the poet himself, but also a symbol of the then rising American nation and a manifestation of his ideals about democracy and freedom.

(2) In this giant work, he pays much attention to openness, freedom, especially individualism which advocates that the rights and freedom of individual people are of most significance.

(3) He expresses warm approval of nature, democracy, labor and creation, and sings of man's dignity and equality, and of the brightest future of human beings. Most of the poems in *Leaves of Grass* sing of not only the "en-masse" but also the self.

◆"Song of Myself"

Whitman praises the perfect concept of equality and democracy and celebrates the dignity, the self-reliant spirit, and the pleasure of the common man enthusiastically. "Song of Myself" reveals a world of equality, in which there is no rank and hierarchy at all.

◆"Out of the Cradle Endlessly Rocking"

This poem can be divided into three sections. The first part discusses the ideal love and happiness, the second song depicts the pain of bereavement and love, and the third part reflects the love, death, and loneliness. The symbols in the poem include the sun and moon, day and night, land and sea, indicating the duality of nature and life.

◆"When Lilacs Last in the Dooryard Bloom'd"

It is concerned with the typical Whitmanesque love-and-death motif. It was written for President Lincoln. In the poem, when the poet looks up, he spots the western fallen star, and then when he looks around, he notices the lilac bush blossoming in the dooryard. Here the fallen star signifies death, and the lilac with a representation of life for the dead. Instead of the end, death is the beginning of life.

Ⅱ. Emily Dickinson (1830 – 1886)

1. Life

Dickinson grew up in a Calvinist family. Her father, an

7. 主要作品分析

◆《草叶集》

(1) 草叶，最为平凡却也最有生机，是诗人自己的形象，也是崛起中美国的象征和诗人关于民主自由理想的体现。

(2) 在这部巨作中，开放，自由，尤其是个体主义(主张个人的权利和自由最为重要)是诗人最为关注的。

(3) 这部作品中惠特曼也赞美了自然，民主，劳动和创新，歌颂了人的尊严和平等，憧憬了人类最美好的未来。《草叶集》中大部分诗歌赞颂了大众和自我。

◆《自我之歌》

惠特曼赞美了平等和民主的理想，赞美了人的高尚，自力更生的精神，和普通人的快乐。《自我之歌》呈现了一个没有阶层和等级的平等世界。

◆《从永久摇荡的摇篮里》

这首诗可以分为三小节。第一部分讲理想的爱和幸福，第二首歌描绘丧亲之痛和爱，第三部分体现死亡，孤独与爱。诗中的象征包括太阳和月亮，白天和夜晚，陆地和海洋，它们体现了自然和生命的双重性。

◆《当紫丁香最近在庭院开放》

这首诗体现了典型的惠特曼作品中的爱与死的主题。诗人为纪念林肯总统而作。在这首诗中，当诗人仰望天空，他看到西天星星陨落；当他环望四周，他发现了紫丁香花在庭院的开放。这里陨落的星星是死亡的象征，丁香花丛是死者生命的象征。死亡不是终点，而是新生的开始。

Ⅱ. 艾米莉·狄金森

1. 生平

狄金森生于一个信奉加尔文教

old Puritan, with a heart "pure and terrible", had a great effect on his daughter. She was timid, sensitive, but rebellious from time to time. Emily had become a recluse since she was twenty-year-old. She wanted to live simply as a completely independent person.	的家庭。她的父亲，有着"纯洁而可怕的心"的一位虔诚清教徒，对女儿产生了很大的影响。她害羞，思想敏感，有时具有反叛精神。在她二十多岁时她成为一名隐士。她希望完全独立，过简单的生活。
2. Themes	**2. 主题**
(1) Inspired by her own life experiences, joys or sorrows, she writes about doubt and belief about religious subjects, suffering and frustration due to love, success and failure.	(1) 基于她个人的经历和喜悲，她的诗歌主题是关于宗教主题的疑惑和信仰，爱情中的痛苦和挫折，成功与失败。
(2) Dickinson's poetry attaches great attention to death and immortality. In Dickinson's perspective, death brings about immortality.	(2) 狄金森的大部分诗歌是关于死亡与永生的。对狄金森来说，死亡导向永生。
(3) Nature is considered as both gaily benevolent and cruel.	(3)狄金森视自然为仁慈并冷酷残忍的。
(4) Ethically Dickinson believes that beauty, truth and goodness are not separated from each other.	(4) 在伦理的层面上，狄金森认为真善美是合而为一的。
(5) She gives special importance to free-will and responsibility belonging to human.	(5) 她强调自由意志和人类责任。
3. Writing styles	**3. 写作风格**
(1) Her poetry is filled with telling images. In the best of her poems, every word constitutes a picture. As a result, she is considered as the precursor of Imagism poetry.	(1) 她的诗歌描绘有各种意象。在她创作的最好的诗歌中，每一个词都是一幅画。所以她被视作意象派诗歌的先驱。
(2) Her poetic idiom is well-known for its conciseness, directness and great usage of the plainest words.	(2) 她诗歌的风格简明，直接，善用最平易的词。
(3) Dickinson's poems are usually short, and the first line of Dickinson's poems tends to be the title at the same time.	(3) 狄金森的诗歌通常篇幅较短，第一句往往是诗歌的题目。
(4) The capital letters in her poems are used for prominence.	(4) 诗歌中要强调的词均大写。
4. Comparison: Whitman VS. Dickinson	**4. 比较：惠特曼 VS. 狄金森**
Similarities:	**相同点：**
(1) On the level of theme, they both sing the praise of, an emergent America, its expansion, its individualism and its Americanness, whose poetry constitutes "American Renaissance" from different perspectives.	(1) 主题选择上，他们都用不同的方式歌颂了一个新兴的美国，辽阔，个人主义和自身特色，他们的诗歌是"美国文艺复兴"的组成部分。
(2) On the level of writing technics, they both added to the literary independence of the new nation by breaking free of the tradition of the iambic pentameter and displaying freedom in form unprecedented in history: they were pioneers in American poetry.	(2) 写作技巧上，他们打破了传统诗歌创作的五步抑扬格，给诗歌创作形式上以很大的自由，在新兴的国家独立地创作，这是史无前例的。他们是美国诗歌的先驱。

Differences: (1) Whitman seems to keep his eye on society on a large scale; Dickinson explores the inner life from the individual perspective. (2) Whereas Whitman is "national" in his interpretation, Dickinson is "regional". (3) Dickinson prefers the "catalogue technique" (direct, simple style) which Whitman doesn't approve.	不同点: (1)惠特曼更细致地关注社会生活，而狄金森更倾向于探索人的内心世界。 (2)惠特曼的视野放眼"全国"，而狄金森关注"地方"。 (3)狄金森创作风格直接简洁，而惠特曼并非如此。
5. Influence Dickinson's poetry is filled with telling images. Her poetic idiom is well-known for its laconic brevity, directness and great usage of the plainest words. All these features of her poetry were to become well-liked by Stephen Crane with the Imagists such as Ezra Pound and Amy Lowell in the twentieth century. She was considered as the precursor of the Imagist movement.	**5. 影响** 狄金森的诗歌意象丰富，诗歌风格简洁，直接，用词平易。这些特点很受斯蒂芬·克兰和20世纪意象派诗人艾兹拉·庞德和艾米·洛威尔的欢迎。她被视作意象派诗歌的先驱。
6. Major works "The Soul selects her own Society" "My life closed twice before its close" "Because I could not stop for Death" "I heard a fly buzz when I died" "Mine—by the Right of the White Election" "Wild Nights—Wild Nights" "Death is a Dialogue between" "I died for Beauty—but was scarce"	**6. 主要作品** 《心灵选择了自己的友伴》 《我的生命在结束之前已结束了两次》 《因为我不能停步等待死神》 《我死时听到了苍蝇的嗡嗡声》 《我的——根据白色选举的权利》 《狂风夜——狂风夜!》 《死是一场对话》 《我为美而死》

6.2 考研真题与典型题详解

I. Fill in the blanks.

1. Author __________ Title __________(南京大学2008研)

   Not one of all the purple host
   Who took the flag today
   Can tell the definition,
   So clearly, of victory.

2. *Leaves of Grass*, either in content or form, is an epoch-making work in American literature; its democratic content marked the shift from __________ to __________, and its __________ form broke from old poetic conventions to open a new road for American poetry.

3. In __________, Whitman's own early experience may well be identified with the childhood of a young growing America.

4. The poetic style Walt Whitman devised is now called __________, that is poetry without a fixed beat or regular rhyme scheme.

5. In his cluster of poems called *Leaves of Grass*, __________ gave America its first genuine epic poem.

Ⅱ. Multiple Choice

1. Which ONE of the following is the author of the poem *Song of Myself*?（四川大学 2008 研）

A. Walt Whitman　B. Stephen Crane

C. Edgar Allan Poe　D. Henry Wadsworth Longfellow

2. "By day her meals untouch'd, then at night fitfully sleeping, often waking" is taken from "I Hear America Singing". The female described here is the __________ of the dead person.（首师大 2009 研）

A. mother　B. wife　C. sister　D. daughter

3. "I celebrate myself, and sing myself, /And what I assume you shall assume, /For every atom belonging to me as good belongs to you."

In the above quoted verse lines taken from Walt Whitman's poem "Song of Myself", what does the central image "myself" refer to?（四川大学 2009 研）

A. Merely the poet himself.　B. The common people of America.

C. Masculine sublime ego.　D. American puritans.

4. Which ONE of the following is an influential poet whose poems often express a thematic concern about the issue of death and eternity?（四川大学 2009 研）

A. Walt Whitman　B. Ralph Waldo Emerson

C. Henry Wadsworth Longfellow　D. Emily Dickinson

5. The following poems were all composed by Emily Dickinson EXCEPT __________.（四川大学 2007 研）

A. "Because I Could Not Stop for Death"　B. "A Psalm of Life"

C. "I Died for Beauty—but Was Scarce"　D. "I Heard a Fly Buzz—When I Died"

6. Which of the following features cannot characterize poems by Walt Whitman?

A. Lyrical and well-structured.　B. Free-flowing.

C. Simple and rather crude.　D. Conversational and casual.

7. In Walt Whitman's "There was a Child Went Forth." the child refers to __________.

A. the poet himself as a child　B. any American child

C. the young America　D. one of the poet's neighbor

8. American literature produced only one female poet during the 19th century. She was __________.

A. Anne Bradstreet　B. Jane Austen　C. Emily Dickenson　D. Harriet Beecher

9. The main theme of Emily Dickinson is the following except __________.

A. religion　B. love and marriage

C. life and death　D. war and peace

10. Emily Dickinson's poetic idiom is noted for the following except __________.

A. brevity　B. directness　C. plainest words　D. obscure

Ⅲ. Explain the following term.

1. free verse（首师大 2009 研）

Ⅳ. Read the following quotations and answer the questions.

Passage 1（北航 2008 研）

I Heard a Fly Buzz—when I died—

The Stillness in the Room
Was like the Stillness in the Air—
Between the Heaves of Storm—
The Eyes around—had wrung them dry—
And Breaths were gathering firm
For that last Onset—when the King
Be witnessed—in the Room—
I willed my Keepsakes—Signed away
What portion of me be
Assignable—and then it was
There interposed a Fly—
With Blue—uncertain stumbling Buzz—
Between the light—and me—
And then the Windows failed—and then
I could not see to see—

Questions:

(1) Identify the author of the passage.

(2) What are the effect and the meaning of "I heard a Fly buzz—when I died—"?

(3) What is the meaning of the last two lines?

Passage 2

"I celebrate myself, and sing myself.
And what I assume you shall assume,
For every atom belonging to me as good belongs to you."

Questions:

(1) Who wrote these lines? What is the poet celebrating?

(2) Whom does "you" refer to?

(3) What are the two principle beliefs that the poet set forth on this poem?

Passage 3

Because I could not stop for Death—
He kindly stopped for me—
The Carriage held but just Ourselves—
And Immortality.

Questions:

(1) Who is the writer of these lines?

(2) In which category would you place this poem?

(3) Emily Dickinson is noted for her use of ____________ to achieve special effects.

V. Short answer question

1. Why *Leaves of Grass* is considered a milestone in American literature?

Ⅵ. Essay question

1. Discuss the themes and artistic features of Emily Dickinson's poems. （山东大学 2016 研）

参考答案及解析

I. Fill in the blanks.

1. Emily Dickinson; *Success is Counted Sweetest*

(题目节选自狄金森的 *Success is Counted the Sweetest*《成功最甜美》。艾米莉·狄金森，美国最富传奇性的抒情诗人。生前只发表了 7 首诗，诗作几乎全部在她死后才发表。她被视为 20 世纪现代主义诗歌的先驱之一，和美国文学之父欧文、诗人惠特曼比肩。)

2. Romanticism; Realism; free verse

(《草叶集》无论是从内容上还是形式上都是美国文学划时代的作品，它有关民主的内容标志着浪漫主义到现实主义的转变，它采用自由体，从而打破了旧时诗歌的传统，为美国诗歌独辟蹊径。)

3. *Song of Myself*

(在惠特曼的《自我之歌》中他将自己早期的经历同一个正在成长中的美国等同起来。)

4. free verse

(沃尔特·惠特曼(Walt Whitman, 1810－1892)是美国著名诗人、人文主义者，他创造性地运用了诗歌的自由体(Free Verse)，其代表作品是诗集《草叶集》(*Leaves of Grass*)。自由诗是诗体的一种，其结构自由，段数、行数、字数没有一定规格；语言有自然节奏而不用韵。)

5. Walt Whitman

(《草叶集》(*Leaves of Grass*)是十九世纪美国作家沃尔特·惠特曼(Walt Whitman)浪漫主义诗集。《草叶集》是惠特曼一生创作的总汇，也是美国诗歌史上一座灿烂的里程碑。作品包含了丰富而深刻的思想内容，充分反映了十九世纪中期美国的时代精神。)

Ⅱ. Multiple Choice

1. A　Walt Whitman(沃尔特·惠特曼)，美国著名诗人，*Song of Myself*(《自我之歌》)代表其创作的最高峰，后来收录在他的 *Leaves of Grass*(《草叶集》)中。
2. A　这首诗是惠特曼“Come Up From The Fields, Father”里的几句，描写的是母亲接到儿子的死讯以后痛苦的心情。节译：白天她茶饭不思，晚上她无法安睡。
3. B　惠特曼在《自我之歌》里歌颂的是伟大的美国劳动人民。
4. D　艾米丽·狄金森的诗歌表达了一种对于死亡和永恒的关注，如“因为我不能停下来等待死亡”“我死前听见一只苍蝇在嗡嗡”等。
5. B　《人生礼赞》的作者是美国诗人 Henry Wadsworth Longfellow(朗费罗)，其余选项都是狄金森的诗作。
6. A　沃尔特·惠特曼创造性地运用了诗歌的自由体(Free Verse)自由诗是诗体的一种，其结构自由，段数、行数、字数没有一定规格；语言有自然节奏而不用韵。
7. C　惠特曼的诗歌《有一个孩子向前走去》中孩子是指成长中的美国。
8. C　Emily Dickenson 是 19 世纪美国浪漫主义时期的唯一的女诗人，Anne Bradstreet 是 17 世纪的女诗人，Jane Austen 是英国 18 世纪末的小说家，Harriet Beecher 是美国 19 世纪的小说家。
9. D　艾米丽·狄金森诗歌的主题不涉及战争与和平。
10. D　艾米丽·狄金森的用词简洁、直率、平易，而非晦涩。

Ⅲ. Explain the following term.

1. Free verse is a term describing various styles of poetry that are written without using a strict rhyme scheme, but still recognizable as poetry by virtue of complex patterns of one sort or another that readers will perceive to be part of a coherent whole. Walt Whitman is a representative who employed free verse successfully.

Ⅳ. Read the following quotations and answer the questions.

Passage 1

(1) The author is Emily Dickenson.

(2) In this poem, the speaker is waiting for her last moment. The room is still, and the eyes of her relatives have been dry. All these together create a solemn and woeful atmosphere. The speaker is going to see the "King", but at this time, she hears a fly buzz. Fly is generally regarded as a disgusting creature, and sometimes it gathers around the corpse. Its appearance disconcerts us and makes the "immortality" doubtful.

(3) The fly's wings cut the speaker off from the light, and then the speaker closes her eyes and dies. Here, the light that she sees is from the Heaven. The speaker imagines that she is on the way to the Heaven. Just at this moment, the fly appears, between the speaker and the heaven. Thus, her hope of immortality becomes doubtful. The speaker is not sure whether she can really go to the heaven with "the King".

Passage 2

(1) These lines are taken from Walt Whitman's *Songs of Myself*. The poet is celebrating individualism and nationalism in this poem. Here "I" does not necessarily mean the poet or a particular person, because the poet mingles the first person with the second person by the word "assume".

(2) Here "you" refers to the democratic "en-masse" of America.

(3) The two beliefs are the theory of universality and the belief in the singularity and equality.

Passage 3

(1) Emily Dickinson

(2) dramatic

(3) slant rhyme

V. Short answer question

1. Whitman's *Leaves of Grass* has always been considered a monumental work because of its uniquely poetic embodiment of American democratic ideal.

   In this work, the abundance of themes voices freshness. Whitman shows concern for the whole hardworking people and the burgeoning life of the cities. The realization of the individual value also found a tough position in Whitman's poems in a particular way. In celebrating the self, Whitman gives emphasis to the physical dimension of the self and openly celebrates sexuality. And some of Whitman's poems are politically committed.

   Stylistically, Whitman experiments with a mixture of the colloquial diction and prose rhythm of journalism. The direct address is another salient feature of his poetry. He constructs a democratic "I", a voice that sets out to celebrate itself and the rapture of its sense experiencing the world. In addition, Whitman initiated the form of free verse in America that endows his poems with a flow of musicality and a sense of rhythm.

VI. Essay question

1. (1) themes:

①Love, death, pain and nature are subjects Dickinson dwells on and Dickinson's poems are usually based on her own experiences, her sorrows and joys. Among these themes, death is the most important one.

②Emily Dickinson was a pessimistic poet, Dickinson had a tragic message. Dickinson seems to have accepted death as an inevitable conclusion of life. Her greatest lyrics are on the theme of death, personified as a monarch, a lord, or a kind but irresistible lover, yet her moods varied widely from melancholy to exuberance, grief to joy, leaden despair to spiritual intoxication. She sensed the inherent beauty and the frightening coldness of the world. She perceived beauty in the wholeness and harmonious relationships of nature, and her works reflected a spiritual unrest and an awareness of the human predicament that defied all easy categories.

③She wrote of God, man, and nature with a knowledge that seemed impossible for a person so limitedly experienced. She knew love and death as few would have known them.

(2) artistic features:

①Her poem is short, condensed and often based on a single image or symbol, it is remarkable for its variety, subtlety, and richness. Dickinson's poetry is unique and unconventional in its own way. Her poems have no titles, hence are always quoted by their first lines.

②Influence of Christian tradition: She used the Biblical language and allusions and strikingly illuminated hidden recesses in the human soul. She was religiously oriented. She wrote poems that could be sung, as a matter of fact, just like a Christian hymn.

③Use of the persona "I." She would pretend to be a small girl and write cute little poems with which she examined personal emotion.

④Use of paradox and irony, unorthodox syntax and punctuation. For example, she used the subjunctive where the indicative should be used. She often did not inflect the third person singular form of the verb. She just left it uninflected. Her capitalization and dashes were often used willfully.

⑤Counter-poetic style. Her counter-poetic style is characterized by lexical surprises, frequent use of oxymoron and synaesthesia, which creates a world of resonant possibility.

⑥Innovation in rhyme. She was not restricted by full rhyme. "Moon, soon, coon, swoon" are full rhymes with the same vowel and the same consonant. But she used "consonance" which means similarity of final consonants, but not vowels such as "reach—touch." And the other kind of rhyme she used is assonance. For assonance, the final vowel sounds correspond, but the consonants are different. Consonance and assonance break the rules of poetry.

⑦On the whole, her poetry is irregular in rhyme and rhythm. Dickinson's style is characteristic of frequent use of dashes, sporadic capitalization of nouns, convoluted and ungrammatical phrasing, off-rhymes, broken meters, bold and unconventional and often startling metaphors, and aphoristic wit.

第7章 埃德加·爱伦·坡

7.1 复习笔记

I. Edgar Allan Poe

1. Life

Poe's childhood was a miserable one. His parents passed away when he was young, and he was taken care of by a wealthy merchant of Virginia, John Allan. But Poe enjoyed nothing but an unhappy relationship with the Allans. At 17 Poe entered the University of Virginia but did not finish. He went to West Point as a cadet but was expelled from the school for misconduct. Throughout his short life, Poe spent much time writing and editing. He was poor all his life. At 27 he married his thirteen-year-old cousin, whose death in 1847 was a great grief to him. In October, 1849, he died mysteriously. For a long time after his death Poe remained probably the most controversial and most misunderstood literary figure in the history of American literature. But today Poe is recognized as a great novelist, a first-rate poet, and a critic of great insight. His works are widely read around the world and win appreciation and understanding.

2. View of literary criticism

Poe's theories are excellent in their clarity and are primely elucidated in "The Philosophy of Composition" and "The Poetic Principle." George Bernard Shaw regarded him as "the greatest journalistic critic of his time".

(1) Theories for short story

①The length of the short story should be brief and concise to ensure the reader's impression of the story as a whole.

②The first sentence ought to help to bring out the "single effect" of the story. Do not use words which do not fit the "pre-established" design of the work (compression).

③The novel should reveal some logical inspiration, and should end with the last sentence, which can leave a sense of finality with the reader.

I. 埃德加·艾伦·坡

1. 生平

坡有着悲惨的童年。他年幼时父母双亡，他被弗吉尼亚富商约翰·爱伦收养，但他与养父家之间的关系并不好。17岁时坡进入弗吉尼亚大学学习，但是没能完成学业。后来去了西点军校，却又因为行为不端而被校方开除。他短暂的一生中大部分时间都在从事写作和编辑工作。他终身贫困潦倒。27岁时，他和13岁的表妹结婚，1847年妻子的离世使他悲痛万分。1849年10月，他离奇地去世。坡死后相当长的时间里仍是美国文学史上最具争议性、被误解最深的文学家。而现在坡被认为是一位伟大的小说家、一流的诗人和具有敏锐洞察力的批评家。他的作品在世界范围内被广泛阅读，并获得了赞赏和理解。

2. 文学批评观

坡的文学理论明白晓畅，在《创作哲学》和《诗学原理》中得到了最好的阐述。萧伯纳认为他是"那个时代最伟大的新闻批评家"。

(1) 短篇小说理论

①短篇小说的篇幅应简洁，这样可以确保读者对故事的整体印象。

②第一句话应当帮助引出故事的"单一效果"。不使用不符合"预先制定"情节的词(紧凑)。

③小说应当具备一些符合逻辑的启发，最后一句应给人一种"完结感"。

(2) Theories for poetry ①Poems should be short and concise, so that readers can read them all at once. ②The aim of poem writing is to express beauty; the most beautiful thing described by a poem is the death of a beautiful woman; the best tone of a poem is melancholy. ③Poe dislikes poems which are designed to teach people a moral lesson. ④Poe emphasized the form of poem, especially the beautiful and neat rhyme. He declared that "music is the perfection of the soul, or idea, of poetry" and defined poetry as "the rhythmic creation of beauty". **3. Theme and style** Poe is a romantic poet, preoccupied with the theme of the death of one's beloved lover, who is a combination of intelligence and beauty. In versification, he opposes the didactic and calls for "pure" poetry. He emphasizes the musicality of poetry and insists on an even metrical flow in poetry. He also writes short stories about horror (Gothic novels), murder, and insanity, excavating the human mind. Some of his stories fall in the genre of the detective. Poe's style is traditional and very rational, too ordinary to reflect the peculiarity of his theme. Somehow he fails to incorporate the newness of his idea into his style, so it is difficult to make his central theme understood. He is not easy to read. Poe's choice of words and his syntax is the reason why his works are difficult to understand. **4. Reputation and Influence** Poe became famous first in France through Charles Baudelaire's criticism and translation and influenced other French poets and critics such as Stephane Mallarme and Paul A. Valery. Though Poe was not welcomed in his own country, he enjoyed respect in Europe. Swinburne, Bernard Shaw, D. H. Lawrence, and W. H. Auden spoke highly of him, writers such as R. M. Rilke and Dostoevsky were indebted to him. Poe's relationship to Chinese literature cannot be ignored. Recent studies show the fact that modern Chinese masters like Lu Xun and Guo Mo-ruo all read and made comment on his works.	**(2)诗歌理论** ①诗歌应该简短，使读者可以一口气读完。 ②诗歌创作的目的是表现美；最富诗意的美莫过于美丽女子的死亡；诗的最佳基调应是忧郁。 ③坡反感说教性的诗歌。 ④坡强调诗歌的形式，尤其强调韵律的美感。他宣称“音乐是诗歌灵魂或思想的完美体现”，认为诗是“美的节奏性创造”。 **3. 主题及写作风格** 坡是浪漫主义诗人，专注于深爱的情人之死这样的主题，通常她们集智慧与美丽于一身。在诗歌创作上，他反对说教，呼吁“纯粹”的诗歌。他强调诗歌的音乐性并坚持诗歌中匀称的韵律。他也写短篇恐怖小说（即哥特式小说），书写谋杀及精神错乱，探索人的心灵。他的一些小说属于侦探小说类型。 坡的写作风格很传统，很重理性，让人觉得太过平常而不易发掘他写作主题的特性。他不能将他想法的新意揉进他的风格，从而他难以使他作品的主题思想被人看透。他的作品不好理解，作品的选词和句法是他散文难以理解的原因。 **4. 名誉与影响** 由于波德莱尔的评论和翻译，坡首先在法国成名，并影响了其他法国诗人和评论家，如斯蒂芬·马拉美和保罗·瓦莱里。虽然坡在自己的国家不受欢迎，但他在欧洲受到尊敬。斯温伯恩、萧伯纳、D·H·劳伦斯和W·H·奥登对他评价很高，里尔克和陀思妥耶夫斯基等作家都受到了他的影响。爱伦坡与中国文学的关系也不容忽视。最近的研究表明，鲁迅、郭沫若等中国现代文学大家都曾阅读并评论过他的作品。

His influence on modern literature is worldwide. His aesthetic views, superb writing skills and his attack on the didactic function of literature, and the call for "the rhythmical creation of beauty" have made impact on French symbolists and the devotees of "art for art's sake". Poe is the father of psychoanalytic criticism and the father of detective fiction.

坡对现代文学的影响是世界性的。他的美学观点和精湛的写作技艺，对文学说教功能的抨击，以及他倡导的"诗是美的节奏性创作"对法国象征主义者和"为艺术而艺术"的信徒产生影响。坡是精神分析批评之父和侦探小说之父。

5. Major works

The Narrative of Arthur Gordon Pym
Tales of the Grotesque and the Arabesque
"MS. Found in a Bottle"
"The Murders in the Rue Morgue"
"The Fall of the House of Usher"
"The Masque of the Red Death"
"The Cask of Amontillado"
"The Tell-Tale Heart"
"Ligeia"
"The Raven"
"Sonnet—To Science"
"Israfel"
"Annabel Lee"
"To Helen"
"The Philosophy of Composition"
"The Poetic Principle"

5. 主要作品

《阿瑟·戈登·皮姆的故事》
《奇异怪诞故事集》
《瓶子里发现的手稿》
《毛格街杀人案》
《厄舍古屋的倒塌》
《红色死亡的化妆舞会》
《一桶酒的故事》
《泄密的心》
《丽姬娅》
《乌鸦》
《十四行诗——致科学》
《伊斯拉菲尔》
《安娜贝尔李》
《致海伦》
《创作哲学》
《诗歌原理》

6. Analysis of major works

◆"To Helen"

"To Helen" is one of Poe's most famous lyric poems. It was inspired by the beauty of a classmate's mother when Poe was at school in Richmond, Virginia. The poem is famous for a number of things, for example, its rhythm, varied line lengths, the metaphor of a travel on the sea, and the frequently quoted lines, "To the Glory that was Greece/And the grandeur that was Rome."

◆"The Raven"

"The Raven" embodies Poe's theory of poetry creation. It has about 100 lines (108 in fact), perfectly readable at one sitting. A sense of melancholy over the death of a beloved beautiful young woman pervades the poem: a young man mourning the passing of Lenore. The bird that appears at the beginning of the poem repeats a word, which turns the man's grief into madness.

6. 主要作品分析

◆《致海伦》

《致海伦》是坡最著名的抒情诗之一。这首诗的灵感来源于坡在弗吉尼亚州里士满上学时一位同学母亲的美貌。该诗以其韵律、多变的句子长度、海上旅行这一比喻及经常被引用的诗行"光荣属于希腊，伟大属于罗马"而著称。

◆《乌鸦》

《乌鸦》体现了坡的诗歌创作理论。这首诗大概有一百行(实际上是108行)，读者可以一气呵成，读完全诗。整首诗弥漫着因心爱的年轻美人逝去而忧郁的气氛。诗歌描写了一位年轻人哀悼逝去的丽诺，诗歌开篇出现的鸟儿反复重复一个词，在此影响下，他的悲伤继而转化为疯狂。

On the verge of a mental collapse, the young man outpours his sorrow to the bird when he is half asleep and half awake. The phantom of the bird is a poetic imagination, enhancing the effect of the tragedy of the bereavement. The poem is heavily tinted in a dreamy, hallucinatory color and the narrator is in a semi-conscious state. This particular feature is prominent in Poe's poems, which is reflected in poems such as "Annabel Lee", "The Sleeper" and "A Dream Within a Dream".	这位年轻人的精神濒临崩溃的边缘，在半梦半醒之间，面对鸟儿倾吐自己的悲伤。鸟儿的幻影是一种诗意的想象，增强了失去爱人的悲剧性。这首诗歌中梦幻的色调较重，叙述者处于一种半昏迷的状态。这一特点在爱伦坡的诗歌中尤为突出，在《安娜贝尔·李》《沉睡者》和《梦中梦》等诗中也有体现。
◆"Sonnet—To Science"	◆《十四行诗——致科学》
In the poem, science, an abstraction, is personified and treated as a villain by the speaker. The animalized science has relieved the world of a lot of its myth and offer room for poetic imagination: The romance of Diana, Hamadryad, Naiad, and the Elfin is broken, so is the poet's "summer dream beneath the tamarind tree." The poet's aspirations are baffled. The tension between science on the one hand and art and imagination on the other endows the poem with a unique power and significance. The poem indicates that Poe was in essence a Renaissance man. He derived in part from Plato the notion that the universe was endowed with myth, and tried to restore it to the primordial unity which the cosmos once possessed.	在这首诗中，科学这一抽象概念被拟人化，并被说话者视为恶棍。被动物化的科学将神话的束缚从世界身上解除，也为诗意的想象提供了空间：戴安娜、哈玛德里亚德、奈阿德和精灵的浪漫故事被打破了，诗人"罗望子树下的夏日梦"也被打破了。诗人的抱负遇到了阻碍。科学与艺术和想象之间的张力赋予了诗歌独特的力量和意义。这首诗说明了坡本质上是一位博学之人。他部分地从柏拉图那里得到了宇宙被赋予神话的观念，并试图将其恢复到宇宙曾经拥有的原始统一性。

7.2 考研真题与典型题详解

I. Fill in the blanks.

1. In consideration of the beauty of poems, __________ concludes that "the death of a beautiful woman is unquestionably the most poetical topic in the world."（天津外国语学院 2007 研）
2. __________ is regarded as the father of psychoanalytic criticism and the detective story.（首师大 2008 研）
3. __________ is generally thought of as the true beginner of the short stories because he was the first writer who formulated poetics of the short stories.
4. __________ is usually acknowledged as the originator of detective stories. He is also credited with developing many of the standard features of detective fiction. His detective M August Dupin of *The Murders in the Rue Morgue* and *The Purloined letter* is the forerunner of a long line of fictional detectives who are eccentric and brilliant.
5. __________'s poems have the musical quality and romantic beauty. *The Raven* is his best-known poem.

Ⅱ. Multiple Choice

1. Mark the novelist whose major works are characterized by the elements of the "grotesque"? (四川大学 2008 研)

   A. Philip Freneau　　B. Edgar Allan Poe

   C. Washington Irving　　D. Emily Dickson

2. Edgar Allan Poe's first collection of short stories is ________.

   A. *Tales of a Traveller*　　B. *Leatherstocking Tales*

   C. *Canterbury Tales*　　D. *Tales of the Grotesque and Arabesque*

Ⅲ. Read the following quotations and answer the questions.

Passage 1 (人大 2007 研)

"Prophet!" said I, "thing of evil! —prophet still, if bird or devil! —
Whether tempter sent, or whether tempest tossed thee here ashore,
Desolate yet all undaunted, on this desert land enchanted—
On this home by horror haunted—tell me truly, I implore—
Is there—is there balm in Gilead? —tell me—tell me, I implore!"

Questions:

(1) Give the title of the work and the full name of the author.

(2) Explain the implications of the underlined parts.

Passage 2 (北航 2007 研)

Although, as boys, we had been even intimate associates, yet I really knew little of my friend. His reserve had been always excessive and habitual. I was aware, however, that this very ancient family had been noted, time out of mind, for a peculiar sensibility of temperament, displaying itself through long ages, in many works of exalted art, and manifested, of late, in repeated deeds of munificent yet unobtrusive charity, as well as in a passionate devotion to the intricacies, perhaps even more than to the orthodox and easily recognizable beauties, of musical science. I had learned, too, the very remarkable fact, that the stem of the Usher race, all time-honored as it was, had put forth, at no period, any enduring branch; in other words, that the entire family lay in the direct line of descent, and had always, with very trifling and very temporary variation, so lain. It was this deficiency, I considered, while running over in thought the perfect keeping of the character of the premises with the accredited character of the people, and while speculating upon the possible influence which the one, in the long lapse of centuries, might have exercised upon the other—it was this deficiency, perhaps, of collateral issue, and the consequent undeviating transmission, from sire to son, of the patrimony with the name, which had, at length, so identified the two as to merge the original title of the estate in the quaint and equivocal appellation of the "House of Usher"—an appellation which seemed to include, in the minds of the peasantry who used it, both the family and the family mansion.

Questions:

(1) Which fiction is this excerpt from?

(2) Who is the author? What are the artistic features of the author?

(3) What literary technique is the fiction famous for, as embodied in this excerpt?

Ⅳ. Short answer question

1. How does Edgar Allan Poe anticipate the 20th-century literature?（国际关系学院 2007 研）

V. Essay question

1. What are the artistic achievements of Edgar Allan Poe?

参考答案及解析

I. Fill in the blanks.

1. Edgar Allan Poe

（爱伦·坡认为，美的效应在于使灵魂激动而变得高尚；无论哪种美，其最高形式必然使敏感的灵魂悲泣。因此，诗的基调应该是"忧郁"。人最感到忧郁的事莫过于死，而最富于诗意的死莫过于心爱的年轻女子离世。）

2. Edgar Allan Poe

（爱伦·坡被认为是精神分析批评之父和侦探小说的鼻祖。）

3. Edgar Allan Poe

（爱伦·坡被视作短篇小说的真正始祖因为他是第一个在小说中赋予了诗意的作家。）

4. Edgar Allan Poe

（爱伦·坡被视作侦探小说的鼻祖。）

5. Edgar Allan Poe

（爱伦·坡的诗歌富有音乐感和浪漫主义色彩，《乌鸦》是最知名的一首。）

Ⅱ. Multiple Choice

1. B　Edgar Allan Poe（爱伦·坡），美国著名诗人、短篇小说家、文学评论家。他的短篇小说着意描写人的内心世界，对表现人的思想病态尤其感兴趣。其后期的短篇小说，经常充满一种恐怖气氛，情节阴森古怪，令人毛骨悚然。

2. D　埃德加·爱伦·坡（Edgar Allan Poe）（1809 ~ 1849）十九世纪美国诗人、小说家和文学评论家，在世时长期担任报刊编辑工作。《怪异故事集》（*Tales of the Grotesque and Arabesque*）是爱伦·坡的第一部短篇小说集。

Ⅲ. Read the following quotations and answer the questions.

Passage 1

（1）*The Raven* by Edgar Allan Poe

（2）Prophet：The narrator here calls the raven as a prophet, who can give him some clues to his puzzle of his beloved one.

implore：This word means that the narrator anxiously asks the raven to tell him whether there are ways to cure his pain.

balm in Gilead：This sentence is quoted from the Bible, which means that whether there are some medicines to ease the narrator's pain.

Passage 2

（1）This excerpt is from "The Fall of the House of Usher."

（2）The author is Edgar Allan Poe. As a remarkable poet and critic, Poe emphasizes rhythm, considers true poetry as "the rhythmical creation of beauty," and advocates that "music is the perfection of the soul, or idea, of poetry." Poe is a short-story writer of the imagination. In his psychological fiction, he puts the subconscious mental state under investigation and explores beneath the surface of normal existence. He was the first author in American literature to make the neurotic the heroic figure, the protagonist, in his stories. He is the father of many things including psychoanalytic criticism and the detective novel.

(3) *The Fall of the House of Usher* possesses the essential features of the Gothic novel. It is a literary genre that combines elements of both horror and romance. The outstanding features of Gothic fiction include terror (both psychological and physical), mystery, the supernatural, ghosts, haunted houses and Gothic architectures, castles, darkness, death, decay, doubles, madness, secrets, and hereditary curses.

Ⅳ. Short answer question

1. Allan Poe anticipates the 20th century literature and his influence is world-wide in modern literature. He was one of the earliest American practitioners of the short story and is considered the father of psychoanalytic criticism and the detective novel. Poe is further credited with contributing to the emerging genre of science fiction. His aesthetic views and superb writing skills attack on the didactic function of literature, and his call for "the rhythmical creation of beauty" have an impact on French symbolists and the advocates of "art for art's sake."

Ⅴ. Essay question

1. Edgar Allan Poe has been recognized as a great writer of fiction, a first-rate poet, and a critic with deep insight. Poe is the father of many things, one of which is psychoanalytic criticism, the other being the detective novel.

   Poe was good at generalizing. He tried to cash in on his literary practice to rationalize about literary creation. His poetic theories are clear, which are best reflected in his "The Philosophy of Composition" and "The Poetic Principle." He believes that the poem should be short and its aims are to produce a sense of beauty and melancholy. Moreover, he insists on a metrical flow in versification.

   His theories for the short story are equally remarkable. In his opinion, the short story should be short and reveal some logical truth. Poe is a short-story writer of the imagination. In terms of the theme, Poe anticipates the twentieth-century literature in his treatment of the division of the self. He puts the subconscious mental state under investigation and explores beneath the surface of normal existence.

第8章　现实主义时期·豪威尔·詹姆斯

8.1　复习笔记

Ⅰ. Realism: Social Background	**Ⅰ. 现实主义：社会背景**
(1) The Civil War had significant influence on American literature. The war marked the win of the factory over the farm, which made America head towards capitalism. The postbellum period is characterized by the question of the assumptions of Transcendentalism such as natural goodness, the optimistic view of nature and man, and benevolent God.	(1)南北战争对美国文学产生了重大影响。这场战争标志着工厂对农场的胜利，使美国走向资本主义。战后时期的特点是对诸如自然善良，对自然和人的乐观看法，以及仁慈上帝等超验验主义假设的质疑。
(2) Increasing industrialization and mechanization of the country, now in foil swing after the war, soon produced extremes of wealth and poverty. Self-reliance spirit was replaced by the ambition and lust for money and power. Besides, the American frontier was closing. Suffering and unhappiness lay behind the superficial prosperity.	(2)国家的工业化和机械化程度不断提高，在战后处于摇摆状态，很快就产生了贫富两极分化。自力更生的精神被对金钱和权力的野心和欲望所取代。此外，美国的边境正在关闭。在表面的繁荣背后隐藏着痛苦和不幸。
(3) With the waning of New England Renaissance, writers and celebrities of the older generation such as Emerson, Longfellow and Melville began to wane in American literary scene. Boston and New England ceased to be the cultural center of the country. Younger writers such as William Dean Howells, Henry James, Mark Twain, Bret Harte, Edward Eggleston and Loiusa May Alcott began to appear and made their voices heard.	(3)随着新英格兰文艺复兴运动的衰落，爱默生、朗费罗、梅尔维尔等老一辈作家和名人在美国文坛的地位开始式微。波士顿和新英格兰不再是这个国家的文化中心。年轻的作家如威廉·迪恩·豪威尔斯、亨利·詹姆斯、马克·吐温、布雷特·哈特、爱德华·埃格尔斯顿和路易莎·梅·奥尔科特开始出现，并发出了自己的声音。
Ⅱ. Realism: Theme and Style	**Ⅱ. 现实主义：主题和风格**
Realism as a literary movement aiming to reflect reality itself reacts against romanticism and sentimentalism, paving the way to modernism.	现实主义是对浪漫主义和感伤主义的一种反抗，并为现代主义做了铺垫。
During this period a new generation of writers, dissatisfied with the Romantic ideas in the older generation, came up with a new inspiration. This new attitude was characterized by a great interest in the realities of life. It aimed at the interpretation of the realities of any aspect of life, free from subjective prejudice, idealism, or romantic color. Instead of thinking	在这一时期，新一代的作家对浪漫主义观点颇为不满，于是提出了新的思想。新的理念对现实生活产生极大的关注，目的在于真实地反映现实生活的各个方面，摒弃主观的偏见，理想主义或是浪漫主义

about the mysteries of life and death and heroic individualism, people's attention was now directed to the interesting features of everyday existence, to what was brutal or sordid, and to the open portrayal of class struggle.

So writers began to focus on the world of experience, of the commonplace, the familiar and the low. They described the integrity of human characters reacting under various circumstances and picture the pioneers of the Far West, the new immigrants and the struggles of the working classes.

Mark Twain, Howells and Henry James are three leading figures of the American Realism. Realism became a major trend in the 1870's and 1880's.

Ⅲ. William Dean Howells

1. Life

Although he came from a small and humble town (Martins Ferry) in Ohio, he made a remarkably successful life by his magnificent letters. He had little formal education but read widely. He was the first president of the American Academy of Arts and Letters, once the editor-in-chief of the country's most influential journal, *The Atlantic Monthly*. As a prolific writer, he produced volumes of drama, poetry, and novels as well as criticism, travelogues, and autobiography.

2. Literary point of view

(1) He defines realism as "fidelity to experience and probability of motive". Realism should mirror commonness rather than uniqueness.

(2) Howell's fictions are devoted to displaying human in his natural and honest stupidity.

(3) The core principle of realism is to grasp characters' "motives" and inward conflicts rather than simply to reflect the appearance strictly.

(4) The American spirit was best expressed through realism's sympathetic analysis of the "common feelings of commonplace people".

(5) Howells thinks that literary criticism should not contain subjective and unreasonable judgements but should analyze a book objectively and reasonably as doing scientific description, interpretation, and classification.

色彩。人们不再考虑生与死的神秘和个人英雄主义，而是直接关注日常生活的特点，写生活的残忍和卑贱，坦率地描述阶级斗争。

作家开始聚焦于经验世界，书写平常、熟悉、低贱的事物。他们描述各种各样环境下人性格当中的正直，并描写在遥远西部的拓荒者，新移民和工人阶级的斗争。

马克吐温，豪威尔斯，和亨利·詹姆斯是美国现实主义的代表作家。现实主义成为了美国 19 世纪七八十年代的主流。

Ⅲ. 威廉姆·迪恩·豪威尔斯

1. 生平

尽管豪威尔斯出生在俄亥俄州一个小城镇，在一个卑微的环境中成长，但是他凭借精湛的文字艺术最终功成名就。他没有受过多少正规的教育，但阅读涉猎广泛。他曾是美国艺术文学院的院长，并曾担任过国内最有影响力的期刊——《大西洋月刊》的主编。他是一位多产的作家。他写了大量的戏剧、诗歌和小说，另外还有评论文、旅行见闻及自传。

2. 文学批评观

(1) 他指出，"现实主义忠实于生活，反映动机的可能性"，寻求表现一般性和习惯性，而不是特殊性或独特的高尚或卑微现象。

(2) 他表现的主体是自然、不矫揉造作而愚笨无聊的人。

(3) 现实主义的中心原则是把握人物的"动机"及其心理矛盾，而不是简单而僵硬地反应事物的表面。

(4) 现实主义饱含同情地分析了"普通人的日常情感"，由此，美国精神得到了最好的诠释。

(5) 关于文学批评，豪威尔主张文学批评家不应随意地主观地去评价作品，应该客观地去做准确精炼的描述，阐释和分类。

3. Major works

The Rise of Silas Lapham

A Modern Instance

A Hazard of New Fortunes

Criticism and Fiction

4. Analysis of major work

◆*The Rise of Silas Lapham*

Howell's novelist qualities are illustrated thoroughly by this novel. It tells the story of a Boston new upstart in the mid-19th century. It sets a classic example for American realism. This novel is loyal to the realistic principle of mirroring commonness rather than uniqueness.

In this novel the author emphasizes ethics, the need for sympathy and moral integrity, and the need for a harmonious interaction between different social classes. The author criticizes the rise of materialism in American life.

3. 主要作品

《塞拉斯·拉帕姆的发迹》

《一个现代的例证》

《时来运转》

《批评与小说》

4. 主要作品分析

◆《塞拉斯·拉帕姆的发迹》

该小说充分体现了豪威尔斯这位小说家的素养。它讲述了19世纪中期波士顿一个暴发户的故事。它是美国现实主义文学的典范。这里没有英雄主义，没有戏剧化或非同寻常的情节。豪威尔斯专注于描写渺小、琐碎及平常的事务。

在这部小说中作者强调道德，强调同情心、道德高尚以及不同社会阶层互相适应、和谐相处的必要性。作者批判了美国生活中物质主义的兴起。

Ⅳ. Henry James (1843 –1916)

Henry James is considered the founder of psychological realism. He was the first of the modern psychological analysts in the novel and anticipated the modern stream-of-consciousness technique of modern literature. He was the first American writer to conceive his artistic work in international themes.

1. Life

Henry James came from a rich New England cultured family. His brother, William James, was a renowned philosopher and psychologist. To some extent, his family background decides his theme: he wrote about the wealthy, deep-rooted leisure class. The European culture influenced him since he was a baby. The French culture may stamp on him most as he called Balzac his "greatest master". In 1876, he settled down in London and almost spent the rest of his life there.

2. James' literary point of view

(1) As a realist, he holds that life is bound with art and representing life is the goal of a novel. He advocates novel-writing must get rid of numerous limitations and welcome vulgar and mediocre items.

Ⅳ. 亨利·詹姆斯

亨利·詹姆斯是心理现实主义的先驱。他是小说领域最早的现代心理分析学家，开创了现代文学中的现代意识流手法。他是美国第一个致力于国际题材的作家。

1. 生平

亨利·詹姆斯生于新英格兰一个家境富裕的书香门第。他的哥哥威廉·詹姆斯是著名的哲学家和心理学家。在一定程度上，他的家庭背景决定了他写作的主题：他的作品主要是叙述富有悠闲的上流社会的生活。他早年深受欧洲文化的影响。也许法国文化对他影响最深，正如他称巴尔扎克是他的"最出色的老师"。1876年他定居伦敦，几乎在那里度过余生。

2. 詹姆斯的文学批评观

(1) 作为一个现实主义作家，他认为艺术与生活息息相关，小说的目的就是表现生活。他主张给予小说写作极大的自由，作品应欢迎粗俗和平庸的事物。

(2) James's psychological analysis of his topic characterizes his realism. His characters' inner awareness and inner conflicts against reality are the focus in his works rather than the details of their surroundings.

(3) The aesthetics of his novels centers on "point of view". James endeavors to refrain from the artificial omniscience and attempts to make his characters reveal themselves.

3. Theme

James established himself as a legendary writer with "the international theme": the meeting of America and Europe, American innocence in contact and contrast with European decadence, and its moral and psychological complications. The meeting symbolizes America's growth from innocence to maturity.

4. Style

It is hard to understand James. He is often highly refined and insightful. His large vocabulary enables his word selection to be exact and appropriate for his literary imagination. Therefore Henry James is not only one of the most important realists of the period before the First World War, but also the most expert stylist of his time.

5. Major works

The American
Daisy Miller
The Portrait of a Lady
The Bostonians
The Princess Casamassima
The Turn of the Screw
What Maisie Knew
The Ambassadors
The Wings of the Dove
The Golden Bowl
The Art of Fiction

6. Analysis of major works

◆*The Portrait of a Lady*

An optimistic and innocent Jamesian American girl, Isabel Archer, arrives in Europe to live a free and noble life, only to be the victim of two vulgar and corrupt expatriates, Madame Merle and Gilbert Osmond. Her ignorance of evil around her and her wealth destroy her dreams and hope.

（2）詹姆斯作品的题材有明显的心理分析的特点，他不仅仅细致地描述外部环境，更多的是强调人物的内心活动。

（3）詹姆斯关心叙事视角，这是他小说美学的关键。他避免用全知视角而尝试让角色表现他们自己。

3. 主题

詹姆斯的名声主要建立在他小说的"国际主题"上，即美国和欧洲的相遇。美国的天真和欧洲的堕落、道德和心理上的复杂性相接触且相对照。对美国人而言，这是一个从积累经验、增长知识到走向成熟的过程。

4. 写作风格

詹姆斯的作品不易理解。他语言优美，眼光独到。他词汇量丰富，选词准确，力求寻找能够表达他所想的最佳表达方式。因此詹姆斯不仅是一战前这段时期最重要的现实主义作家之一，也是那个时代最老练的文体家。

5. 主要作品

《美国人》
《黛西·米勒》
《贵妇人的画像》
《波士顿人》
《卡萨玛西玛公主》
《拧螺丝》
《梅西见闻》
《专使》
《鸽翼》
《金碗》
《小说的艺术》

6. 主要作品分析

◆《贵妇人的画像》

典型的詹姆斯式的美国姑娘伊莎贝尔·阿切尔来到欧洲，满怀希望过一种自由和高贵的生活，却不幸沦为两个粗野且不择手段的美国侨民——默尔太太和吉尔伯特·奥斯蒙德的受害者。伊莎贝拉的美梦和期望破碎了：她对周围邪恶的无知和她的财富摧毁了她的梦想和希望。

◆ *The Ambassadors* James considered *The Ambassadors* as his "most perfect" artistic work, which parodies American and European manners. Although Strether, a middle-aged commonplace American, is expected to bring back his wealthy fiancée's son Chad, who is crazy about the European culture, to inherit the Newsome family business in New England, he is turned to believe that Paris should be home to Chad and himself. James stresses mutual understanding and sympathy between European traditionalism and American individualism, and the harmonious combination of the best of both.	◆《专使》 《专使》是詹姆斯自认为最完美的著作。它是一部关于美国和欧洲习俗的喜剧。它讲述了平庸的中年美国男子斯特雷瑟赴巴黎接一位迷恋欧洲的年轻人回新英格兰继承家业，但是最终却相信巴黎才是这个年轻人和他自己应该生活的地方。詹姆斯强调欧洲传统主义和美国个人主义之间的相互理解和同情，以及两者的和谐结合。

8.2 考研真题与典型题详解

I. Fill in the blanks.

1. The American novelist __________ probed deeply at the individual psychology of his characters, writing in a rich and intricate style that supported his intense scrutiny of complex human experience.（人大 2006 研）
2. *Daisy Miller* was written by __________.（大连外国语学院 2007 研）
3. The name of the heroine in *The Portrait of a Lady* is __________.（人大 2006 研）
4. The Age of Realism is also what Mark Twain referred to as "__________".
5. By 1875, American writers were moving toward __________ in literature. We can see this in the true-to-life descriptions of Bret Harte, William Dean Howells, Hamlin Garland.
6. The most straightforward definition of realism is probably the one given by the American realist __________: that is, "nothing more and nothing less than the truthful treatment of material."
7. Howells' __________ is a fine specimen of American realistic writing.

Ⅱ. Multiple Choice

1. __________ divides the 19th century into the age of romanticism and realism in American literature.（北二外 2009 研）

   A. The Spanish-American war　　B. The Civil War
   C. WWI　　D. WWII

2. Realism in American literature stretches from __________ to the end of 19th. C.（北二外 2007 研）

   A. early 17th. C　　B. early 18th. C
   C. American Civil War　　D. Spanish-American War

3. William Dean Howells explores the life of __________ Americans.（北二外 2009 研）

   A. lower-class　　B. upper-class　　C. working-class　　D. middle-class

4. Which of the following works by Henry James does not deal with "the international theme"? __________（天津外国语学院 2009 研）

   A. *Daisy Miller*　　B. *The Turn of the Screw*

C. *The Portrait of a Lady*　　D. *The Ambassadors*

5. Which of the following novels is not written by Henry James? (天津外国语学院 2007 研)

A. *Daisy Miller*　　B. *The Golden Bowl*

C. *What Maisie Knew*　　D. *The Rise of Silas Lapham*

6. Which ONE of the following concepts is related to the understanding of literary realism? (四川大学 2010 研)

A. spontaneous outflow of feelings

B. faith in individualism, independence of mind and self-reliance

C. representation of characters, human nature and social actualities in a non-idealized way

D. survival of the fittest

7. With William Dean Howells, James, and Mark Twain active on the scene, ________ became the major trend in the seventies and eighties of the nineteenth century.

A. sentimentalism　　B. romanticism　　C. realism　　D. naturalism

8. Where Mark Twain and William Dean Howells satirized European manners at times, ________ was an admirer.

A. O. Henry　　B. Henry James　　C. Walt Whitman　　D. Jack London

9. Choose the novel which is not written by Henry James.

A. *The Ambassadors*　　B. *The Wings of the Dove*

C. *The Bostonians*　　D. *The Mysterious Stranger*

10. The main theme of ________ *The Art of Fiction* reveals his literary credo that representation of life should be the main object of the novel.

A. Henry James'　　B. William Dean Howells'

C. Mark Twain's　　D. O. Henry's

Ⅲ. Explain the following terms.

1. The Age of Realism in American Literature (四川大学 2010 研)
2. Realism (合肥工业大学 2023 研)
3. Psychological realism

Ⅳ. Read the following quotations and answer the questions.

Passage 1 (人大 2006 研)

Isabel always felt an impulse to pull out the pins; not that she imagined they inflicted any damage on the tough old parchment, but because it seemed to her aunt might make better use of her sharpness. She was very critical herself—it was incidental to her sex, and her nationality; but she was very sentimental as well, and there was something in Mrs. Touchett's dryness that set her own moral fountains flowing.

Questions:

(1) Give the title of the work and the full name of the author.

(2) Explain the implications of the underlined parts of the passage.

Passage 2

Isabel always felt an impulse to pull out the pins; not that she imagined they inflicted any damage on the tough old parchment, but because it seemed to her her aunt might make better use of her sharpness. She was very critical herself—it was incidental to her sex, and her nationality but she was very sentimental as well, and there was something in Mrs. Touchett's dryness that set her own moral fountains flowing.

"Now what's your point of view?" she asked of her aunt. "When you criticize everything here you should have a point of view. Yours doesn't seem to be American you thought everything over there so disagreeable. When I have mine; it's thoroughly American!"

"My dear young lady", said Mrs. Touchett, "there are as many points of view in the world as there are people of sense to take them. You may say that doesn't make them very numerous. American? Never in the world; that's shockingly narrow. My point of view, thank God, is personal!"

Isabel thought this a better answer than she admitted; it was a tolerable description of her own manner of judging, but it would not have sounded well for her to say so.

Questions:

(1) This passage is taken from a well-known novel. What is the name of the novel?

(2) Who is the author of this novel?

(3) Make a brief comment on the heroine Isabel Archer.

(4) What is Jamesian theme?

Passage 3

Under certain circumstances there are few hours in life more agreeable than the hour dedicated to the ceremony known as afternoon tea. There are circumstances in which, whether you partake of the tea or not—some people of course never do—the situation is in itself delightful. Those that I have in mind in beginning to unfold this simple history offered an admirable setting to an innocent pastime. The implements of the little feast had been disposed upon the lawn of an old English country-house, in what I should call the perfect middle of a splendid summer afternoon. Part of the afternoon had waned, but much of it was left, and what was left was of the finest and rarest quality. Real dusk would not arrive for many hours; but the flood of summer light had begun to ebb, the air had grown mellow, the shadows were long upon the smooth, dense turf. They lengthened slowly, however, and the scene expressed that sense of leisure still to come which is perhaps the chief source of one's enjoyment of such a scene at such an hour. From five o'clock to eight is on certain occasions a little eternity; but on such an occasion as this the interval could be only an eternity of pleasure.

Questions:

(1) From which novel is this paragraph taken from?

(2) Who is the author of this novel?

(3) What is conveyed in this opening paragraph about English convention?

V. Short answer questions

1. How does Henry James describe the Americans in his novels? (国际关系学院 2007 研)
2. Who are the three dominant figures of the American Realistic Period and what are their literary differences?

VI. Essay questions

1. What literary movements dominated the periods immediately before and after the American Civil War? What factors mainly caused the shift? Please name two representative authors respectively.

（西安交大 2008 研）

2. What led to the rise of American Realism?（北航 2007 研）
3. According to Henry James's viewpoint, what is the conflict between the American personalities and European personalities?
4. What is the most famous theme in Henry James' fiction? What is his favorite approach in characterization, which makes him different from Mark Twain and W. D. Howells as realists? Please take *The Portrait of a Lady* as an example to give sound ground for your points.

参考答案及解析

I. Fill in the blanks.

1. Henry James

（美国小说家亨利·詹姆斯的作品善于挖掘人物心理。）

2. Henry James

（《黛西·米勒》是美国作家 Henry James 的国际主题小说。）

3. Isabel Archer

（《一位贵妇的画像》(*The Portrait of a Lady*)是亨利·詹姆斯的早期代表作，也是他的杰作之一。该小说的女主人公是伊莎贝尔·阿切尔。）

4. The Gilded Age

（现实主义时期被马克·吐温看作"镀金时代"。）

5. realism

（到 1875 年后美国文学过渡到了现实主义时期，我们可以在布勒特·哈特，威廉姆·迪恩·豪威尔斯和哈姆林·加兰的作品中找到对生活逼真的描述。）

6. William Dean Howell

（现实主义最明确的定义是威廉姆·迪恩·豪威尔斯提出来的，"对材料的处理很真实，恰到好处。"）

7. *The Rise of Silas Lapham*

（豪威尔的《塞拉斯·拉帕姆的发迹》是美国现实主义的优秀作品。）

Ⅱ. Multiple Choice

1. B　内战是美国浪漫主义文学和现实主义文学的分水岭。
2. C　美国的现实主义阶段是从南北战争到 19 世纪。
3. D　豪威尔斯擅长描写上升中的美国中产阶级，其代表作是《塞拉斯·拉帕姆的发迹》。
4. B　*The Turn of the Screw*(《螺丝在拧紧》)是亨利·詹姆斯的一部哥特式心理小说，描写的是一位年轻女教师应聘到乡下一家富户照看两个失去双亲的孩子，在其家中见到死去的前任女教师及这家男仆的幽影，气氛越来越紧张，最后一个孩子死去，另一个精神错乱。其余三个选项都是詹姆斯关于"国际题材"的作品。
5. D　*The Rise of Silas Lapham*(《塞拉斯·拉帕姆的发迹》是 William Dean Howell(豪威尔斯)的作品，其余都是亨利·詹姆斯的作品。
6. C　现实主义的核心观念为客观再现当代社会现实，展现人物性格、人类本质和社会现实。选项 A 是浪漫主义的核心观念，选项 B 是个人主义的观念，选项 D 是达尔文的"适者生存"观念。

7. C 19世纪七、八十年代现实主义成为美国文学的主流。威廉·豪威尔斯、亨利·詹姆斯和马克·吐温是这一时期的代表作家，他们在理论和实践上都对美国现实主义文学的发展做出了重大贡献。

8. B 马克·吐温、亨利·詹姆斯和威廉·豪威尔斯并驾齐驱，被誉为是19世纪美国现实主义文学的三大倡导者。欧洲风情受到亨利·詹姆斯的赞美，却不时成为马克·吐温和威廉·豪威尔斯讽刺的对象。

9. D 《神秘的陌生人》(*The Mysterious Stranger*)是马克·吐温的作品，其余三项《大使》(*The Ambassadors*)，《鸽翼》(*The Wings of the Dove*)，《波士顿人》(*The Bostonians*)都是亨利·詹姆斯的作品。

10. A 除小说以外，亨利·詹姆斯(Henry James)对文学贡献的另一部分是他的文学批评。在《小说的艺术》(*The Art of Fiction*)中詹姆斯明确指出，小说的目的是反映现实生活。

Ⅲ. Explain the following terms.

1. In American literature, the Civil War brought the Romantic Period to an end. The Age of Realism came into existence. It came as a reaction against the lie of romanticism and sentimentalism. Realism turned from an emphasis on the strange toward a faithful rendering of the ordinary, a slice of life as it is really lived. It expresses the concern for commonplace and the low, and it offers an objective rather than an idealistic view of human nature and human experience.
2. Realism: It's a mode of writing that gives the impression of recording or reflecting faithfully an actual way of life. Realism in literature attempts to describe life without idealization or romantic subjectivity. The representatives of American Realism are Henry James, William Dean Howells and Mark Twain.
3. Psychological realism: It is the realistic writing that probes deeply into the complexities of characters'thoughts and motivation. Henry James' novel *The Ambassadors* is considered to be a masterpiece of psychological realism.

Ⅳ. Read the following quotations and answer the questions.

Passage 1

(1) *The Portrait of a Lady*, Henry James

(2) parchment: This word implies the old European culture with a long history.
incidental to her sex, and her nationally: This phrase implies it's her aunt's nature to be sharp because sharpness is the nature of a woman and an English person.

Passage 2

(1) *The Portrait of a Lady*

(2) Henry James

(3) An optimistic and innocent Jamesian American girl, Isabel Archer, arrives in Europe to live a free and noble life, only to be the victim of two vulgar and corrupt expatriates, Madame Merle and Gilbert Osmond. Her ignorance of evil around her and her wealth destroy her dreams and hope.

(4) Jamesian theme refers to Henry James's handling of his major fictional theme, "the international theme": the meeting of America and Europe, American innocence in contact and contrast with

European decadence and its moral and psychological complications.

Passage 3

(1) *The Portrait of a Lady*

(2) Henry James

(3) In English society, it seems that everything goes according to convention. Afternoon tea is almost a routine ritual in English society and English men's seriousness about this process is a reflection of their conservative character.

V. Short answer questions

1. The novels of Henry James largely dealt with "the international theme": the meeting of America and Europe. James enjoyed juxtaposing American moral innocence with the somber decadence of Europe. In his novels, the Americans are usually innocent, fresh, full of energy and curiosity, open and assertive. When confronting European sophistication, some of them triumph over it and some others are overwhelmed.

2. The three dominant figures of the period were William Dean Howells, Mark Twain, and Henry James. Though the three prominent writers all worked for realism, they had different understandings of "truth". While Mark Twain and Howells seem to have paid more attention to the "life" of the Americans, Henry James has apparently laid a greater emphasis on the "inner world" of man. He is a realist of the inner life. Though Twain and Howells both share the same concern in presenting the truth of the American society, they have each of them different emphasis. Howells focuses his discussion on the rising middle class and the way they live, while Twain deals with his own region and people of the lower class of society at the forefront of his stories. James writes mostly of the upper reaches of American society.

VI. Essay questions

1. Transcendentalism dominated the periods immediately before the American Civil War and realism dominated after the American Civil War.

    Literary theme and technique are influenced by and switch in accord with political and social events. The sweeping factory, which beat the farm boosted the American capitalism. The Civil War from 1861 to 1865 not only changed the American social structure but also altered the nature of American morality.

    Since the end of the Civil War, the national economy is dominated by commerce. In the east, urbanization rate reached 50% till 1880, and meanwhile the trend toward towns and cities was obvious. Although the tremendous and rapid industrialization and mechanization produced abundant wealth, the gap between wealth and poverty was enlarged to extreme degrees.

    What makes the gap worse was the disappearing frontier. The ideals of the New World are less attractive to people. For example, people began to doubt whether pursuing an American dream was worthwhile or whether the charm of the New World is true. Suffering and unhappiness began to surface in the prosperous phenomenon. Feelings of disenchantment and frustration swept the country from coast to coast. The "Golden Age" was indeed a "Gilded" one as nicknamed by Mark Twain.

    The literary movement, realism, developed as an opposite posture against romanticism and sentimentalism. It was concerned with and was devoted to displaying reality itself no matter whether it was beautiful or not. It tried to represent commonness rather than uniqueness. William Dean Howells, Henry James, and Mark Twain pushed realism into the central literary movement through the 1870s and the 1880s.

2. Literary theme and technique are influenced by and switch in accord with political and social events. The sweeping factory, which beat the farm boosted the American capitalism. The Civil War from 1861 to 1865 not only changed the American social structure but also altered the nature of American morality.

   Since the end of the Civil War, the national economy is dominated by commerce. In the east, urbanization rate reached 50% till 1880, and meanwhile the trend toward towns and cities was obvious. Although the tremendous and rapid industrialization and mechanization produced abundant wealth, the gap between wealth and poverty was enlarged to extreme degrees.

   What makes the gap worse was the disappearing frontier. The ideals of the New World are less attractive to people. For example, people began to doubt whether pursuing an American dream was worthwhile or whether the charm of the New World is true. Suffering and unhappiness began to surface in the prosperous phenomenon. Feelings of disenchantment and frustration swept the country from coast to coast. The "Golden Age" was indeed a "Gilded" one as nicknamed by Mark Twain.

   The literary movement, realism, developed as an opposite posture against romanticism and sentimentalism. It was concerned with and was devoted to displaying reality itself no matter whether it was beautiful or not. It tried to represent commonness rather than uniqueness. William Dean Howells, Henry James, and Mark Twain pushed realism into the central literary movement through the 1870s and the 1880s.

3. H James established himself as a legendary writer with "the international theme": the meeting of America and Europe, American innocence in contact and contrast with European decadence, and its moral and psychological complications. American heroes and heroines tackling European sophistication are always the focus among Henry James' novels. His novels represent these characters' ruin or success.

   He saw that Americans often regarded Europeans as over-refined, degenerate, and artificial, and that many Europeans considered Americans naive, vulgar, and ignorant. The misunderstanding caused personality conflicts. The national differences provided an opportunity for contrasts of characters. The typical American in a James novel is fresh, enthusiastic, not perhaps as cultured as he might be, but eager to learn, and basically "good" in spite of his disregard of the outworn conventions and social graces of Europe. The European, on the other hand, is highly cultivated, urban, sometimes boring, but always correct. He was, however, sometimes unprincipled. In James, the Americans often appeared to stand for morality, the Europeans for manners. This is true even the case of characters like Daisy Miller.

4. His main theme is the innocence of the New World (America) in conflict with the corruption and wisdom of the Old (Britain).

   His favorite approach in characterization is psychological approach, and unlike W. D. Howells and other realists, his realism is called psychological realism.

The Portrait of a Lady explores the conflict between the individual independence and the British society's convention. Isabel Archer is a young American woman who must choose between her independent spirit and the demands of social convention. After professing and longing to be an independent woman, autonomous and answerable only to herself, Isabel falls in love with and marries the sinister Gilbert Osmond, who wants her only for her money and who treats her as an object, almost as part of his art Collection. Isabel must then decide whether to honor her marriage vows and preserve social propriety or to leave her miserable marriage and escape to a happier, more independent life, possibly with her American suitor Caspar Goodwood.

The most important part of the book is where she realizes her mistake. She sits all alone, late at night, in her "house of darkness". James shows her inner consciousness in this quiet moment. There is a great drama in his description of her "motionlessly seeing" the mistake she has made. The drama is not created by her actions but by the thoughts in her mind.

James is one of America's great psychological realists, and he uses all his creative powers to ensure that Isabel's conflict is the natural product of a believable mind, and not merely an abstract philosophical consideration.

第9章　地方色彩小说·马克·吐温

9.1　复习笔记

I. Local Colorism	Ⅰ. 地方色彩主义
Local colorism as a trend became dominant in American literature in the late 1860s and early 1870s. As a variation of American literary realism, it shows the cohesion of historical and aesthetic energy.	19世纪60年代末70年代初，地方色彩主义成为美国文学的主流。作为美国现实主义文学的一个分支，它体现了历史与艺术的结合。
The development of local colorism was influenced by the social and cultural climate of the country. Socially, the country was expanding westward, and the psychological need of seeking for cultural identity motivated people to show their local features. Culturally, the frontier humorists prospered "talk tales" and provided conditions for the development of local colorism.	地方色彩主义的发展受到当时社会文化环境的影响。从社会层面来说，国家向西扩张，寻求文化认同的心理需求促使人们展现地方特色。文化上，边疆幽默作家发展了话本故事，为地方色彩主义的发展提供了条件。
Local colorists concentrated on the elements which characterize the local culture, such as speech, customs, and more peculiar to one particular place. They emphasize the physical settings and those distinctive qualities of landscape which condition human thought and behavior. Major local colorists are Bret Harte, Hanlin Garland, Harriet Beecher Stowe, Kate Chopin and Mark Twain.	地方色彩主义作家关注的是当地文化的特征要素，如语言、习俗，以及某个特定的地方的独特之处。他们强调自然环境和那些影响人类思想和行为的独特的景观特点。主要的地方色彩主义作家包括布莱特·哈特、汉林·加兰德、哈里耶特·比彻·斯托、凯特·肖邦及马克·吐温等。
II. Mark Twain (1835 – 1910)	**Ⅱ. 马克·吐温**
1. Life	**1. 生平**
Mark Twain, whose real name is Samuel Longhorn Clemens, is a great master of American literature. He grew up in the river town of Hannibal, Missouri. After his father died, he left school and began to seek his own fortune. He once worked as a printer's apprentice, a tramp printer, a silver miner, a steamboat pilot and a frontier journalist. Twain's writing took the form of humorous journalism of the time, and it enabled him to master the technique of narration. The short story *The Celebrated Jumping Frog of Calaveras County* brought him international attention. Two of the best books during his period are *The Adventure of Tom Sawyer* and *The Adventures of*	马克·吐温，原名萨缪尔·朗赫恩·克莱门斯，是一位美国文学巨匠。他在密苏里州的河畔小镇汉尼拔长大。他父亲去世后，他离开了学校，开始自谋出路。他当过印刷所学徒、排字工、银矿矿工、舵手还有记者。马克·吐温的写作采用了当时的幽默新闻的形式，体现出叙述的技巧。短篇小说《卡拉维拉斯县著名的跳蛙》使他获得了国际关注。在他的时代，最好的两本书是《汤姆·索亚历险记》和《哈克贝利·费恩历险记》。前者被认为

Huckleberry Finn. The former was regarded as a classic book written for boys, while the latter is Twain's most representative work. His early works show his optimistic attitude towards life. But later in his work, he changed writing styles and turned into a despairing and cynical determinist. His tragic experience led to this change, but more importantly, he saw the dark side of social life.

是写给男孩们的经典著作，而后者是马克·吐温的代表作。他的早期作品表现了他乐观的人生态度。但后来在他的作品中，他改变了写作风格，变成了一个绝望和讽刺的宿命论者。他的悲惨经历造成了这一改变，但更重要的是，他看到了社会生活的阴暗面。

2. Comparisons among Howells, Henry James and Mark Twain

Although Howells, James and Mark Twain all worked for realism, there were obvious differences between them.

(1) In terms of the theme, James focused on the upper class of American society. Howells paid more attention to the daily life of the middle class, while Mark Twain concentrated on the life of the lower class.

(2) Technically, Howells wrote in a gentle way, and James worked on a kind of imaginative or psychological realism. Mark Twain made remarkable contributions to the development of American literature in terms of realistic novel theory and novel language style.

2. 豪威尔斯、亨利·詹姆斯和马克·吐温的比较

尽管豪威尔斯、亨利·詹姆斯和马克·吐温都是美国现实主义作家，但是三者之间具有明显的不同。

(1)就主题而论，亨利·詹姆斯主要写美国的上层社会，豪威尔斯侧重写社会中层，而马克·吐温则写社会下层人民的生活。

(2)从技巧上讲，豪威尔斯运用的是温文尔雅的现实主义风格，亨利·詹姆斯致力于一种"想象"处理或者心理现实主义。而马克·吐温在现实主义小说理论和小说语言风格方面，为美国文学的发展做出了卓越贡献。

3. Comments on Mark Twain

(1) Mark Twain was a famous American literary giant. He was a humorist and acclaimed as "the true father of our national literature" by Mencken.

(2) Mark Twain portrayed familiar places for American people to reflect local social life. His works are based on his abundant knowledge about people and events.

(3) Mark Twain's extensive use of the colloquial speech has made it a highly regarded form of American literature. His style of language influenced many later writers like Sherwood Anderson, Hemingway, etc.

(4) Mark Twain was also a social critic. He loved life and people, advocated freedom and justice, and respected fraternity and mutual assistance among people. He hated hegemonism and despised injustice and cruelty.

3. 对马克·吐温的评价

(1)马克·吐温是美国一位著名的文学巨匠。他是一位幽默大师，被门肯评价为"我们真正的民族文学之父"。

(2)马克·吐温的小说用了人们熟悉的地方来描述美国的社会生活。他的作品是基于他对人和事的丰富了解。

(3)马克·吐温对口语的大量运用使其成为美国文学中备受推崇的一种文学形式。他的语言风格还影响了舍伍德·安德森和海明威等很多后世作家。

(4)马克·吐温同时也是一位社会批评家。他热爱生活和人民，主张自由和正义，推崇人与人之间的友爱互助。他厌恶霸权主义，蔑视不公和残暴。

(5) Mark Twain was a friend of the Chinese. He cared about the Chinese people who were oppressed in the United States and the Chinese people who were humiliated by the great powers.

4. Major works

Innocents Abroad
Roughing it
The Gilded Age
The Adventures of Tom Sawyer
The Prince and the Pauper
Life on the Mississippi
The Adventures of Huckleberry Finn
A Connecticut Yankee in King Arthur's Court
The Man That Corrupted Hadleyburg
The Mysterious Stranger
Autobiography

5. Analysis of major works

◆*The Adventures of Huckleberry Finn*

(1) It is a sequel to *The Adventures of Tom Sawyer*, but much deeper and more mature in theme and technique. It is generally considered to be one of the most excellent works of western literature and western civilization. Hemingway described it as the book from which "all modern American literature comes".

(2) It tells a story of a teenager Huck who finds himself floating on a raft down the Mississippi River with an escaping slave, Jim. In their adventurous journey, Huck and Jim encounter danger and finally Huck abandons his discrimination against the black people, realizing that Jim is his close friend.

(3) This novel is a portrayal of real life. It discusses some social and cultural issues from the perspective of a child, showing the collision between wilderness and civilization. It is a classic local colorism novel. By describing the experience of Huck's adventure, the novel tells us a universal value that humanity will prevail.

(4) Another notable feature of the novel is its language. Mark Twain used the informal language of uneducated Americans, making oral style a highly respected literary form in the history of American literature.

(5)马克·吐温是中国人民的朋友。他关心在美国饱受压迫的华侨，关心备受列强凌辱的中华民族。

4. 主要作品

《傻子出国记》
《艰难时代》
《镀金时代》
《汤姆·索亚历险记》
《王子与贫儿》
《密西西比河上的生活》
《哈克贝利·费恩历险记》
《亚瑟王宫廷中的美国佬》
《败坏哈德莱堡的人》
《神秘的陌生人》
《自传》

5. 主要作品分析

◆《哈克贝利·费恩历险记》

(1) 这部小说是《汤姆·索亚历险记》的续篇，但是其主题更深刻，写作技巧更成熟。它通常被认为是西方文学和西方文明最伟大的著作之一。海明威曾评价其为“现代美国文学之源”。

(2) 它讲述了一个少年哈克发现自己和一个逃跑的奴隶吉姆一起在密西西比河上漂流的故事。在冒险的旅程中，哈克和吉姆遇到了危险，最终哈克放弃了对黑人的歧视，意识到吉姆是他的好朋友。

(3)这部小说是对现实生活的真实写照。它从一个孩童的角度讨论了一些社会文化问题，展现了野蛮与文明的碰撞。这是一部经典的地方色彩小说，通过描述哈克的冒险经历，小说告诉我们一个普遍的价值观，即人性将战胜一切。

(4)小说的另一个特点就是其语言。马克·吐温使用未受过教育的美国人的非正式语言，使口语体成为美国文学史上一种备受推崇的文学形式。

9.2 考研真题与典型题详解

I. Fill in the blanks.

1. Mark Twain, pseudonym of Samuel Langhorne ________, started off as a ________ colorist. His novel ________ is the one book from which, as Hemingway noted, "all ________ American literature comes". (国际关系学院 2010 研)
2. Harriet Beecher Stowe's masterpiece is ________.
3. One of Samuel Langhorne Clemens' best books ________ is built around his experiences as a steamboat pilot.
4. The result of Mark Twain's European trip was a series of newspaper articles, later published as a book called ________.
5. William Sidney Porter, whose pen name was ________, was the author of *The Cop and the Anthem.*
6. Many of O. Henry's stories tell about the life of poor people in ________.

II. Multiple Choice

1. West Humor is best represented in ________'s short story writing. (北二外 2007 研)

   A. O Henry　　B. Flannery O'Connor

   C. Henry James　　D. Mark Twain

2. ________'s stories still had many unrealistic qualities: "tall tales" and unlikely coincidences. He is never a pure realist.

   A. Henry James　　B. Mark Twain

   C. Nathaniel Hawthorne　　D. Henry David Thoreau

3. Mark Twain wrote most of his literary works with a ________ language.

   A. grand　　B. pompous　　C. simple　　D. vernacular

4. Mark Twain was a great social critic and a friend of the Chinese. His *Disgraceful Persecution of a Boy* is a scathing piece of criticism directed against the persecution of the ________ immigrants in California.

   A. Quakers　　B. Chinese　　C. French　　D. Japanese

Ⅲ. Explain the following term.

1. Local Colorism (山东大学 2016 研; 北二外 2008 研; 四川大学 2009 研)

Ⅳ. Read the following quotations and answer the questions.

Passage 1

I took the sack of corn meal and took it to where the canoe was hid, and shoved the vines and branches apart and put it in; then I done the same with the side of bacon; then the whisky-jug. I took all the coffee and sugar there was, and all the ammunition; I took the wadding; I took the bucket and gourd; took a dipper and a tin cup, and my old saw and two blankets, and the skillet and the coffee-pot. I took fish-lines and matches and other things—everything that was worth a cent. I cleaned out the place. I wanted an ax, but there wasn't any, only the one out at the woodpile, and I knew why I was going to leave that. I fetched out the gun, and now I was done.

Questions:

(1) Which novel is this passage taken from?

(2) Analyze the language style of this passage.

V. Short answer questions

1. Why is Mark Twain considered a social critic?(国际关系学院 2007 研)
2. In *The Adventures of Huckleberry Finn*, Huck Finn is a thirteen-year-old boy. Why does Mark Twain use a child as the center of consciousness in this book?
3. What is special about Mark Twain's realism?
4. How do you understand Mark Twain's use of Local Color in his writing?

VI. Essay questions

1. Charles Dickens and Mark Twain are both well-known literary realists. Name one of the masterpieces by each of them and make a brief comparison and/or contrast so as to tell the similarities and/or differences between British and American realism.(武汉大学 2007 研)
2. What's the difference between Henry James's realism and Mark Twain's realism?

参考答案及解析

I. Fill in the blanks.

1. Clemens; local; *The Adventures of Huckleberry Finn*; modern

(马克·吐温(Mark Twain),原名萨缪尔·兰亨·克莱门(Samuel Langhorne Clemens)是美国的作家,19 世纪后期美国现实主义文学的杰出代表。开始时他是个乡土作家,《哈克贝利·芬恩历险记》被海明威称为"现代美国文学之源"。)

2. *Uncle Tom's Cabin*

(比彻·斯托夫人(Harriet Beecher Stowe 1811 – 1896)的名作长篇小说《汤姆叔叔的小屋》(*Uncle Tom's Cabin*)是 19 世纪最畅销的小说(以及第二畅销的书,仅次于最畅销的书《圣经》)并被认为是刺激 1850 年代废奴主义兴起的一大原因。)

3. *Life on the Mississippi*

(马克·吐温凭着年轻时驾驶河船的经验,写成了脍炙人口的自传《密西西比河上的生活》(*Life on the Mississippi*)。以密西西比河及沿岸的城镇为舞台背景,生动地写下作者的生活体验、童年岁月以及他所热爱的乡土。)

4. *Innocents Abroad*

(马克·吐温游历欧洲时写了一系列文章,讽刺而幽默地记录他的所见所闻,这些文章后来整理出版成书,名为《傻子旅行》(*Innocents Abroad*)。)

5. O. Henry

(欧·亨利(O. Henry),原名为威廉·西德尼·波特(William Sydney Porter),他是美国著名批判现实主义作家,世界三大短篇小说大师之一。《警察与赞美诗》是其著名的短篇小说。)

6. New York

(欧·亨利(O. Henry)善于描写美国社会尤其是纽约(New York)百姓的生活。他的作品构思新颖,语言诙谐,结局总使人"感到在情理之中,又在意料之外";又因描写了众多的人物,富于生活情趣,被誉为"美国生活的幽默百科全书"。)

II. Multiple Choice

1. D　美国西部幽默的代表人物是马克·吐温。
2. B　马克·吐温的小说中有很多不现实的特质，荒诞不经的故事和不大可能发生的巧合。
3. D　马克·吐温大多数的作品都是用口语化的语言写的。
4. B　美国作家马克·吐温是伟大的社会批评家、中国人民的朋友。对于迫害加利福尼亚州华人的行为，马克·吐温在 *Disgraceful Persecution of a Boy* 中给予了辛辣的抨击。

III. Explain the following term.

1. Local Colorism: Local Colorism is an unique variation of American literature realism. Generally, the works by localism are concerned with the life of a small region or province. This kind of fiction depicts the characters from a specific settings or an era, which are marked by its customs, dialects, landscape, or other peculiarities that have escaped standardizing cultural influence. Task of local colorism is to write or present local characters of their regions in truthful depiction distinguished from others. Mark Twain's *The Adventures of Huckleberry Finn* is the most representative one.

Ⅳ. Read the following quotations and answer the questions.

Passage 1

(1) *The Adventures of Huckleberry Finn*

(2) In addition to several words, most of the words are simple colloquial words. These words are short, concrete and easy to understand.

Most of the sentence structures are simple or compound sentences, with connective words such as "and" and "then" being used.

In the article, repeated verbs are widely used, and the concrete picture is presented through the description of specific characters and actions.

One other specific peculiarity is that the style of the book does approximate the actual speech habit of an uneducated American boy at that time.

V. Short answer questions

1. Mark Twain is a satirist for he criticized many aspects of the American society. He dealt largely with the lower strata of society and preferred to represent social life through portraits of local places which he knew best. Mark Twain is also a strong supporter of anti-imperialism, abolition, emancipation, anti-racism and women's rights.
2. In using a child protagonist, Twain is able to imply a comparison between the powerlessness and vulnerability of a child and those of a black man in pre-Civil War America.

   Huck and Jim frequently find themselves in the same predicaments: each is abused, each faces the threat of losing his freedom, and each is constantly at the mercy of adult white men. As we see in Huck's moral dilemmas, however, Jim is also vulnerable to Huck, who, although he occupies the lowest rung of the white social ladder, is white nonetheless.

   Twain also uses his child protagonist to dramatize the conflict between socialized or received morality on the one hand and a different kind of morality based on intuition and experience on the other. As a boy, Huck is a character who can develop morally, whose mind is still open and being formed, who does not take his principles and values for granted.

By tracing the education and experiences of a boy, Twain shows that conclusions about right and wrong that are based on logic and experience often stand at odds with the society's rules and morals, which are often hypocritical rather than logical.

3. Mark Twain's contribution to the development of realism and to American literature as a whole was partly through his theories of Local Colorism in American fiction, and partly through his colloquial style.

   Mark Twain drew heavily from his own rich fund of knowledge of people and places. He confined himself to the life with which he was familiar. By quoting from his own experience, Mark Twain managed to transform art into the freedom and humor, in short, the finest elements of Western culture.

   Another feature of Mark Twain's realism is its language. He reproduced actual daily speech with a degree of accuracy and made colloquial speech an accepted, respectable literary medium in the literary history of America.

4. Mark Twain's narratives are distinguished for his use of local color. This may be defined as the careful attention to details of the physical scene and to those mannerisms in speech, dress, or behavior peculiar to a geographical locality.

   Twain emphatically insisted that the job of the native novelists was not to generalize the nation but to depict each of the country's regions and peoples accurately. Only in this way, the peculiarity of American experience, the polyglot tongues of its people, and the vastness of the continent could be captured.

   After the civil war a number of American writers exploited the possibilities of local color in various parts of America.

VI. Essay questions

1. In the nineteenth century, many progressive writers wrote excellent works to unveil the dark society. Charles Dickens (1812 ~ 1870) and Mark Twain (1835 ~ 1910) were the most outstanding representatives of them. *Oliver Twist* is the masterpiece of Charles Dickens and Mark Twain's masterpiece is *The Adventures of Huckleberry Finn*. The two books share the theme of a corrupt adult society, and the irony in both works is often centered on racism and religion. Both novels are adventures of children.

   Oliver Twist is based on real life materials such as the New Poor Law of 1834 and the current trial of a notorious fence and thief-trainer. By following the most unfortunate experience of a poor orphan boy, Oliver, the author means to give a vivid picture of the underworld with all kinds of thieves, prostitutes and murderers as well as the horrible cruelty of the workhouse system of the time. Oliver is the first of that brilliant group of child characters who are the very images of innocence, love and honesty. The novel leads to a happy ending. Dickens lives and writes in the Victorian age when English society began to feel the impact of change but still managed to keep the old values intact. Industrialization and capitalism had begun to bring wretchedness into the country, but life had not become totally impossible. So, English realist writers like Dickens were basically optimistic. They were aware of modern ills which they lost no time to castigate, but still wrote with the notion that the world was basically good and could become better.

The Adventures of Huckleberry Finn tells a story about the United States before the Civil War, around 1850, when the great Mississippi Valley was still being settled. Here lies an America, with its great national faults, full of violence and even cruelty, yet still retaining the virtues of "some simplicity, some innocence, some peace." Here is a "hymn" to that ante bellum America, the moral values of which vanished with the war. The machine and the worship of money were on their way in, but the river-god, with its "sunlight, space, uncrowded time, stillness, and danger," has not been forgotten. Similar to English realists, American realist novelists took the side of the defenseless or oppressed, and fought corruption, privilege and abuse of the society, but the Civil War and the American Dream played important roles in their writing.

2. Although Henry James and Mark Twain were both American realistic writers, there were obvious differences between them. In terms of the theme, James focused on the upper class of American society, while Twain concentrated on the life of the underclass. Technically, James worked on a kind of imaginative or psychological realism, but Mark Twain made remarkable contributions to the development of American literature in terms of realistic novel theory and novel language style.

   Henry James believed that the only reason for the existence of a novel is that it does attempt to represent life. Such realism is therefore merely the obligation that the artist assumes to represent life as he sees it, which may not be the same life as it "really" is. James shifted the ground of realistic art from the outer to the inner world.

   Mark Twain preferred to represent social life through portraits of local places that he knew best. He drew heavily from his own rich fund of knowledge of people and places. He confined himself to the life with which he was familiar. By quoting from his own experience, Mark Twain managed to transform art into the freedom and humor, in short, the finest elements of western culture.

第 10 章 美国自然主义·克兰·诺里斯·德莱赛·罗宾逊

10.1 复习笔记

I. American Naturalism	I. 美国自然主义
1. Historical Background	**1. 历史背景**
(1) In the decades after the Civil War, "Modern America" has risen. The promotion of industrialization caused polarization between the rich and the poor. The number of slums increased drastically, and the urban poor people were homeless, suffering from torture and violence.	(1)内战以后，现代美国开始崛起。工业化的推广造成贫富两极分化。贫民窟的数量急剧增加，城市的贫民生活没有着落、饱受折磨和暴力的侵袭。
(2) The westward expansion continued, and the frontier extended to the Pacific coast. People were ruthlessly manipulated by various forces, including railways. The high freight rates of railway goods forced farmers to go bankrupt.	(2)西进扩张继续推进，边疆推至太平洋沿岸。人们被各种力量无情地操纵着，例如高昂的铁路货物运费逼得农民破产。
(3) People who lived in a cold, indifferent, and godless world no longer had free will. People began to be pessimistic. Darwinian evolutionary thoughts such as "survival of the fittest" or "human beasts" became popular terms and moral standards in this morally degraded world.	(3)生活在冷酷、淡漠、没有上帝的世界里的人们早已没有自由意志可言。人们开始悲观，"适者生存"或"人类畜类"这一类的达尔文进化思想在这个道德沦丧的世界成为流行用语、道德标准。
2. Features of Naturalist writings	**2. 自然主义作品的特点**
(1) American naturalism is a new and harsher realism. Naturalism is derived from realism, but it is a step forward than realism in describing social reality.	(1) 美国自然主义是一种新的更为严苛的现实主义。自然主义源于现实主义，但在描述社会现实方面比现实主义更向前一步。
(2) American naturalist writers no longer portray social reality gently. They describe the weakness and helplessness of human beings in the cruel world, as well as their lack of dignity in the face of crushing forces such as the environment and genetic factors.	(2)美国自然主义作家不再温和地描绘社会现实，他们描写在冷酷的世上人类无助及微不足道，以及其在面临环境、遗传因素等粉碎性力量面前缺乏尊严。
(3) The works of naturalism reveal a miserable world. People live in a cold, harsh, and indifferent environment to fight hopelessly against overwhelming forces. The power that human beings cannot manipulate determines people's life. The style of the work is gloomy, and the overall tone is hopeless or even desperate.	(3)自然主义的作品揭示了一个悲惨的世界，在这样的世界里人类在冷酷、恶劣又无动于衷的环境下与压倒一切的力量做无望的斗争，他们的人生由自身无法决定的力量操控。作品中整个画面阴郁而黑暗，总体基调是无望甚至是绝望。

3. Major American Naturalists

Stephen Crane

Frank Norris

Theodore Dreiser

Edwin Arlington Robinson

Jack London

Upton Sinclair

II. Stephen Crane (1871 –1900)

1. Life

Stephen Crane was born into a Methodist family in New Jersey. He had been in a military preparatory school for less than a year. Then he moved to New York and became a freelance writer. His first-hand knowledge of the New York slums provided the writing material for his work *Maggie: A Girl of the Streets*. *The Red Badge of Courage* published in 1895 and his first collection of poems *The Black Riders*. He reported the Spanish-American War as a war correspondent in Cuba. He left the United States and settled in the United Kingdom for his marriage. He became good friends with Conrad and James there.

2. Literary contributions

(1) Crane was a pioneer of American naturalism. His writings provided "a sudden direction and a fresh impulse" for the entire aesthetic movement in the 1890s.

(2) Crane was also a pioneer of modern poetry. His early poems were concise and catchy without rhyme. His poetry broke the orthodoxy with impressive imagination, which had a huge impact on modern poetry.

3. Major works

Maggie: A Girl of the Streets

The Black Riders

The Red Badge of Courage

"The Open Boat"

"The Blue Hotel"

"An Experiment in Misery"

4. Analysis of major work

◆*Maggie: A Girl of the Streets*

The story takes place in the slums of New York. Maggie's

3. 美国自然主义主要作家

斯蒂芬·克兰

弗兰克·诺里斯

西奥多·德莱赛

埃德温·阿灵顿·罗宾森

杰克·伦敦

厄普顿·辛克莱尔

II. 史蒂芬·克兰(1871 –1900)

1. 生平

史蒂芬·克兰出生在新泽西的一个卫理公会教派的家庭。他曾在一所军事预备学校待了不到一年。然后他移居到了纽约，成为了一名自由撰稿人。他对纽约贫民窟的第一手了解为他的《街头女郎玛吉》提供了写作素材。1895 年出版的《红色英勇勋章》和他的第一部诗集《黑衣骑士》使他成为著名的作家。他曾在古巴做战地记者报道美西战争。由于其婚姻关系，他离开美国定居英国，并与康拉德和詹姆斯成为好朋友。

2. 文学贡献

(1) 克兰是美国自然主义的先驱。他的作品为 19 世纪 90 年代整个美学运动提供了“一个突然的方向和新鲜的动力。”

(2) 他也是现代诗歌的先驱。他早期的诗歌语言简练，朗朗上口，没有韵脚，打破正统地简洁，想象力令人印象深刻，这些都对现代诗歌产生了巨大的影响。

3. 主要作品

《街头女郎玛吉》

《黑衣骑士》

《红色英勇勋章》

《海上扁舟》

《蓝色宾馆》

《悲苦中的实验》

4. 主要作品分析

◆《街头女郎玛吉》

故事发生在纽约的贫民窟。玛

parents are both alcoholics. They are very rude to the children, and Maggie can't feel any warmth at home. She grows into a beautiful girl and becomes a female worker in a shirt factory. Her brother's friend Peter tempted her with money and clothing. Soon Peter abandons Maggie and finds a new partner. Maggie loses her job at the shirt factory. Her mother, who had a strong religious mindset, refuses to allow her to go home. She has to work as a prostitute on the streets for several months before ultimately committing suicide in despair. As Crane says, environment is a "tremendous" thing for an insignificant human being to battle against.

吉的酒鬼父母粗暴对待孩子们，玛吉在家里感受不到一点温暖。后来她长成了一位美丽的少女，在衬衫厂里找到了工作。她哥哥的朋友彼特，以金钱和衣装诱惑她在一起，不久后又抛弃了玛吉，另寻新欢。玛吉失掉了衬衫厂的工作。而她的母亲受宗教思想影响，不准她回家，她只得流落街头，做了几个月的妓女，最后在失望中投河自尽。正如作者所说，对于一个微不足道的人而言，环境会给人带来巨大的压力。

◆ *The Red Badge of Courage*

(1) The story is set in the American Civil War. The basic theme is human life in a cold, manipulating world. In this work, Crane explores the primeval emotions of man and tries to tell the basic facts of human life.

(2) Crane's exposure of the war shows the feature of modernism. In this novel, war is nothing more than a slaughterhouse. There is no heroism on the battlefield. There is only fear of death, timidity, and the human instinct to run away from dangerous situations. Crane's non-romantic and non-heroic treatment of the war started the modernist tradition of telling the truth about the basic human condition by all means and describing the war according to real human experience.

◆《红色英勇勋章》

（1）故事以美国内战为背景。基本主题是在冰冷且操纵一切的世界中的人类。在这部作品里，克兰探究了人的原始情感并试图讲述人类生活的基本事实。

（2）克兰对战争的揭露具有现代派独有的特点。在这部小说中战争只不过是个屠宰场。战场上没有英勇或英雄主义，有的只是对死亡的恐惧、胆怯，以及人想要逃离险境的本能。克兰这种对战争非浪漫主义和英雄主义的处理，开创了现代派的传统，即不计一切代价讲述人类基本生存状况的真相，将战争描写成人真实的经历。

III. Frank Norris (1870 – 1902)

1. Life

Frank Norris was born in Chicago and his family moved to San Francisco in 1884. During the year at Harvard, he wrote *McTeague*. He had planned to write a trilogy on the production, sale and consumption of wheat. His first work, *The Octopus*, was his best work, the second, *The Pit*, and the third, *The Wolf*, was unfinished. Frank Norris was a literary critic as well. His essays were collected in *The Responsibility of the Novelist*. He died of meningitis in 1902. Norris had a great influence on the writers of the 1920s and 1930s including William Faulkner and John Steinbeck.

III. 弗兰克·诺里斯

1. 生平

弗兰克·诺里斯生于芝加哥，1884年举家搬到了旧金山。在哈佛逗留的那一年他写了《麦克提格》。他生前计划写关于小麦生产、销售和消费的三部曲。第一部《章鱼》是他的最佳作品，第二部是《粮食交易所》，第三部《狼》未完成。诺里斯也是一位文学批评家。他的文学评论文章收集在他的《小说家的责任》一书内。他于1902年死于脑膜炎。诺里斯对威廉·福克纳和约翰·斯坦贝克等20世纪二三十年代的作家产生了巨大的影响。

2. Writing style Mr Norris's works are sometimes loose and thrilling, but the language is simple and catchy, like poetry. His innovative images are also one of the precious treasures of literature in that period.	**2. 写作风格** 诺里斯的作品有时结构松散，情节过于惊险，但是语言简洁，朗朗上口，宛如诗歌。他那清新的意象也是这一时期文学的宝贵财富之一。
3. Major works *Mcteague* *The Octopus* *The Pit* *The Responsibility of the Novelist*	**3. 主要作品** 《麦克提格》 《章鱼》 《粮食交易所》 《小说家的责任》
4. Analysis of major work ◆*McTeague* (1) It is "the first full-bodied naturalist American novel" and "a consciously naturalistic manifesto." It is a classic about the inevitable impact of environment and genetics on human life. (2) McTeague is a typical "human beast". His behavior is primitive and ancestral with wild desires. His tragedy is reflected in his inability to get rid of the wild power which is destined to destroy him. (3) This novel added vitality to the naturalism that just begun to rise in the United States.	**4. 主要作品分析** ◆《麦克提格》 (1)《麦克提格》被誉为"第一部全面的美国自然主义小说"及"美国自然主义的宣言"。它是关于环境及遗传对人类生活产生不可避免影响的经典之作。 (2) 主人公麦克提格是"人形兽类"的典型，他的行为原始且具有返祖性，他还有着野性的欲望。他的悲剧性在于无法摆脱注定要毁灭他的野性力量。 (3) 这部小说给刚刚开始影响美国的自然主义增添了力量。
Ⅳ. Theodore Dreiser (1871 –1945) Dreiser was the most accomplished American literary naturalist.	**Ⅳ. 西奥多·德莱赛** 德莱赛是美国最伟大的自然主义作家。
1. Life Dreiser was born in Indiana as the ninth child. His parents were German immigrants, and the family was extremely poor. His first novel, *Sister Carrie*, was rejected because it ruthlessly revealed the essence of American life. *Sister Carrie* was published in 1900, and his other works were also published later. Dreiser's thoughts are left-sided. He visited Russia once and came back with great sympathy for socialism. With his *Dreiser Looks at Russia* and *Tragic America*, he conveyed his new belief. He then joined the American Communist Party.	**1. 生平** 德莱赛出生在印第安纳州，是家中第九个孩子，父母是德国移民，童年极度贫困。其第一部小说《嘉莉妹妹》因其无情地揭示美国生活的本质而被拒绝出版。1900年《嘉莉妹妹》出版，其他作品也相继出版。德莱赛思想偏左，他访问过俄国并对社会主义产生了极大的同情，并写下《德莱塞访苏印象记》和《悲惨的美国》表达其新信仰。他在去世前加入了共产党。
2. Dreiser's points of view (1) Dreiser believes in social Darwinism. He believes that man is just an animal driven by greed for survival. Only	**2. 德莱赛的观点** (1)德莱赛信奉社会达尔文主义。他认为人只是为了生存而被贪

the fittest can survive in the struggle for survival. Life is fixed, and people have no right to express their wishes.	婪驱使的动物，在生存斗争中只有适者才能生存。人生既定，人无权表达自己的意愿。
(2) He severely criticized his country because he believed that the moral model of American society distorted human nature.	(2)他严厉批判他的国家，因为在他的眼里美国的社会道德模式歪曲了人的本性。
3. Major works	**3. 主要作品**
Sister Carrie	《嘉莉妹妹》
Jennie Gerhardt	《珍妮姑娘》
The Financier	《金融家》
The Titan	《巨头》
The Stoic	《斯多噶》
The Genius	《天才》
An American Tragedy	《悲惨的美国》
Dreiser Looks at Russia	《德莱塞访苏印象记》
Tragic America	《美国悲剧》
The Bulwark	《堡垒》
4. Analysis of major work	**4. 主要作品分析**
◆*Sister Carrie*	◆《嘉莉妹妹》
(1) *Sister Carrie* is a story about a country girl who went to Chicago to seek a better life and realize the American dream.	(1)《嘉莉妹妹》是一个乡村女孩到芝加哥寻求更好生活和实现“美国梦”的故事。
(2) *Sister Carrie* embodies Dreiser's naturalistic idea that human inheritance, instinct, and coincidence will control and restrict people.	(2)《嘉莉妹妹》体现了德莱赛的自然主义的观点，即人总是被遗传、本能和机缘巧合操控及限制。
(3) In a cruel and indifferent world, the lonely and helpless Sister Carrie is mechanically driven by desire and blindly seizes opportunities to survive better. She can only be manipulated by forces that she cannot understand and control.	(3) 在残酷冷漠的世界，孤独无助的嘉莉妹妹机械地被欲望驱使，盲目的抓住机会以便能更好地生存。她只能受自己不能理解和控制的力量所摆布。
(4) As the most noteworthy symbol in the novel, the rocking chair represents the uncertainty of life.	(4) 小说中最明显的象征是那把摇椅，它代表了人生的不确定性。
V. Other authors of the period	**V. 同时期其他作家**
1. Edwin Arlington Robinson (1860 – 1935)	**1. 埃德温·阿灵顿·罗宾逊**
Robinson was the most accomplished poet in America in the 1920s.	罗宾逊被认为是20世纪20年代美国最伟大的诗人。
◆Major works	**◆主要作品**
“The Man Against the Sky”	《天边人影》
“Richard Cory”	《理查德·科里》
“Miniver Cheevy”	《米尼弗·契维》
“Flammonde”	《弗拉蒙德》

2. Jack London (1876 –1916) Jack London was very popular in the early 20th century. He moved from the lower class to the upper class through hard work. After he became a millionaire, he found that life in mainstream society was empty and dull. So he was frustrated and committed suicide.	**(2) 杰克·伦敦** 杰克·伦敦是20世纪初美国著名的作家。他来自社会的底层，努力的工作并跻身于社会的上流阶层。但是当他成为百万富翁后，他发现主流社会的生活是空虚、索然无味的。他在绝望中自杀。
◆Major works *The Call of the Wild* *White Fang* *The Sea Wolf* *Martin Eden*	**◆主要作品** 《野性的呼唤》 《白獠牙》 《海狼》 《马丁·伊登》
3. O. Henry (1862 –1910) O. Henry is the pen name of William Sidney Porter. He has many popular works as a famous short story writer in the world.	**(3) 欧·亨利** 欧·亨利是威廉·西德尼·波特的笔名。他十分多产，是世界著名的短篇小说家。
◆Major works "The Gift of the Magi" "The Cop and the Anthem" "The Last Leaf"	**◆主要作品** 《麦琪的礼物》 《警察与赞美诗》 《最后一片叶子》

10.2 考研真题与典型题详解

I. Fill in the blanks.

1. Dreiser's novel __________, a commercial and critical failure when first published in 1900, was reissued in 1907 and won high praise for its grim, naturalistic portrayal of American society. (人大2006研)
2. Naturalism stresses the determinism of __________ and __________.（国际关系学院2009研）
3. __________ is the novel into which Jack London put most of himself. (人大2006研)
4. The impact of Darwin's evolutionary theory on the American thought and the influence of the nineteenth century French literature on the American men of letters gave rise to another school of realism: American __________.
5. In 1859, Darwin published __________, which exerted great influence on American Naturalism.
6. __________ is the pioneer who wrote in the naturalistic tradition.
7. War in Crane's novel __________ is a plain slaughterhouse. There is nothing like valor or heroism on the battlefield, and if there is anything, it is the fear of death, cowardice, the natural instinct of man to run from danger.
8. __________ had an evident influence on naturalism. It seemed to stress the animality of man, to suggest that he was dominated by the irresistible forces of evolution.

9. The identification of potency with money is at the heart of Theodore Dreiser's masterpiece ________.

10. The protagonist of Theodore Dreiser's *Trilogy of Desire* is ________.

11. ________ is the pioneer who wrote in the naturalistic tradition.

12. Stephen Crane's novel ________ relates the story of a good woman's down fall and destruction in a slum environment.

13. Benjamin Frank Norris's novel ________ has been called "the first full-bodied naturalistic American novel" and "a consciously naturalistic manifesto".

14. O. Henry's ________ is a very moving story of a young couple who sell their best possessions in order to get money for a Christmas present for each other.

15. In ________, a novel about American Civil War, the protagonist keeps asking himself the question, "Will I run from a battle?" and at last he does run away from the battle field. (天津外国语学院 2009 研)

16. In *The Octopus* written by ________, wheat farmers struggle to grow crops and send them to market for a profit, while being beleaguered by the inflated prices of the giant railroad conglomeration. (大连外国语学院 2008 研)

17. As a literary movement, ________ came in the latter half of the 19th century as a reaction against the "lie" of romanticism and sentimentalism. (天津外国语学院 2007 研)

II. Multiple Choice

1. Which of the following books deals with American Civil War? (天津外国语学院 2008 研)

A. *The Red Badge of Courage* B. *For Whom the Bell Tolls*

C. *Slaughterhouse-Five* D. *Catch 22*

2. ________ does not belong to Theodore Dreiser's *Trilogy of Desire*. (首师大 2009 研)

A. *The Financier* B. *The Titan*

C. *The Stoic* D. *An American Tragedy*

3. All the following concepts can be found in American naturalistic fiction EXCEPT ________. (四川大学 2008 研)

A. determinism

B. survival of the fittest

C. effects of hereditary and environmental forces

D. search for identity

4. "The Lure of the Spirit: The Flesh in Pursuit" is the title of one chapter in Dreiser's novel ________.

A. *An American Tragedy* B. *Sister Carrie*

C. *Dreiser Looks at Russia* D. *Jannie Gerhardt*

5. "________" was a term created by the French novelist, Emile Zola.

A. realism B. transcendentalism

C. naturalism D. veritism

6. Jack London was at his height of his powers when he wrote ________, which is deeply influenced by Darwinism.

A. *The Sea Wolf*　　B. *To Build a Fire*

C. *The Call of the Wild*　　D. *Martin Eton*

Ⅲ. Explain the following term.

1. American Naturalism(北二外 2007 研；南开大学 2008 研)

Ⅳ. Read the following quotations and answer the questions.

Passage 1（西安交大 2008 研）

When Carolin Meeber boarded the afternoon train for Chicago, her total outfit consisted of a small truck, a cheap imitation alligator-skin satchel, a small lunch in a paper box, and a yellow leather snap purse, containing her ticket, a scrap of paper with her sister's address in Van Buren Street, and four dollars in money. It was in August, 1889. She was eighteen years of age, bright, timid, and full of the illusions of ignorance and youth... When a girl leaves her home at eighteen, she does one of two things. Either she falls into saving hands and becomes better, or she rapidly assumes the cosmopolitan standard of virtue and becomes worse. Of an intermediate balance, under the circumstances, there is no possibility. The city has its cunning wiles, no less than the infinitely smaller and more human tempter. There are large forces which allure with all the soulfulness of expression possible in the most cultured human. The gleam of a thousand lights is often as effective as the persuasive light in a wooing and fascinating eye. Half the undoing of the unsophisticated and natural mind is accomplished by forces wholly superhuman. A blare of sound, a roar of life, a vast array of human hives appeal to the astonished senses in equivocal terms. Without a counselor at hand to whisper cautious interpretations, what falsehoods may not these things breathe into the unguarded ear! Unrecognized for what they are, their beauty, like music, too often relaxes, then weakens, then perverts the simpler human perceptions.

Questions:

(1) What novel is the above passage taken from? Who is the author?

(2) How many types of tempters exist? What are they?

(3) Please identify all the instances of "large forces". What can these large forces do?

(4) What is suggested as a solution to an eighteen-year-old girl's falling into folly?

(5) What realistic features are revealed in the passage? Please expound your argument in detail.

(6) What naturalistic ideas are revealed in the passage? Please explain your argument in detail.

Passage 2（国际关系学院 2007 研）

When a girl leaves her home at eighteen, she does one of two things. Either she falls into saving hands and becomes better, or she rapidly assumes the cosmopolitan standard of virtue and becomes worse. Of an intermediate balance, under the circumstances, there is no possibility. The city has its cunning wiles, no less than the infinitely smaller and more human tempter. There are large forces which allure with all the soulfulness of expression possible in the most cultured human. The gleam of a thousand lights is often as effective as the persuasive light in a wooing and fascinating eye. Half the undoing of the unsophisticated and natural mind is accomplished by forces wholly superhuman. A blare of sound, a roar of life, a vast array of human hives, appeal to the astonished senses in equivocal terms. Without a counselor hand to whisper cautious interpretations, what falsehoods may not these things breathe into the unguarded ear? Unrecognized for what they are, their beauty, like music, too often relaxes, then weakens, the perverts the simpler human perceptions.

Questions:

(1) Who is the author of the novel from which this paragraph is taken? What is the title of the novel?

(2) With which literary school is the author usually identified?

(3) How does the paragraph express the main points of that school?

(4) What do you think about the author's way of writing as reflected in the paragraph?

V. Short answer question

1. What are the characteristics of O. Henry's writing?

Ⅵ. Essay questions

1. In what ways does *Sister Carrie* or some other major works by Theodore Dreiser reveal his perception of the "American Dream"? What do you know and think of the controversy about Dreiser as a man and as a writer?（人大 2007 研）
2. Please briefly comment on Theodore Dreiser's novel *Sister Carrie*.（四川大学 2007 研）
3. Discuss Jack London's writing style and theme.
4. Discuss Theodore Dreiser's style.
5. Discuss the reflection of realistic and naturalistic tendencies on the American 19th-century novels.

参考答案及解析

I. Fill in the blanks.

1. *Sister Carrie*

（德莱赛的《嘉莉妹妹》在 1900 年首次出版时在商业上和文学批评界是失败的，在 1907 年重新被发现，因其对美国社会的自然描写赢得了很高的评价。）

2. heredity; social environment

（自然主义强调遗传和社会环境决定论。）

3. *Martin Eden*

（杰克·伦敦名作《马丁·伊登》(*Martin Eden*)是一部带有自传色彩的长篇小说。）

4. naturalism

（达尔文的进化论对美国思想和 19 世纪法国文学产生深远影响，从而产生了美国自然主义这一新的学派。）

5. *Origin of the Species*

（1859 年达尔文发表的《物种起源》对美国自然主义产生了很大的影响。）

6. Stephen Crane

（史蒂芬·克兰是美国文学自然主义传统的先锋人物。）

7. *The Red Badge of Courage*

（克兰的小说《红色英勇勋章》中战争是就一个屠场，战争中并没有展示战士的勇猛和英雄主义，只是对死亡的恐惧，懦弱和人性中逃离危险的自然本能。）

8. Darwinism

（达尔文主义(Darwinism)对自然主义(Naturalism)影响深远。达尔文主义强调人的"动物本性"，认为人是由遗传和不可抗拒的外部力量共同支配的。）

9. *An American Tragedy*

(德莱塞代表作长篇小说《美国的悲剧》(*An American Tragedy*)(1925)通过一个穷教士儿子克莱特·格里菲斯为追逐金钱财势堕落为蓄意杀人犯的故事，揭示了利己主义恶性膨胀的严重后果，同时更揭露了金钱至上的美国生活方式对人的普遍的罪恶性腐蚀毒害作用。)

10. Frank Cowperwood

(西奥多·德莱塞的《欲望三部曲》(*Trilogy of Desire*) 包括《金融家》(*The Financier*)，《巨人》(*The Titan*)，《斯多葛》(*The Stoic*)。《欲望三部曲》的主人公是法兰克·柯帕乌(Frank Cowperwood)。)

11. *Stephen Crane*

(斯蒂芬·克兰(Stephen Crane，1871~1900)，是美国著名作家，他是美国自然主义文学的先驱者，其代表作有《街头女郎玛吉》(*Maggie*：*A Girl of the Streets*)和《红色英勇勋章》(*The Red Badge of Courage*)。)

12. *Maggi*：*A Girl of the Streets*

(美国自然主义作家斯蒂芬·克兰第一部小说《街头女郎玛吉》(*Maggie*：*A Girl of the Streets*)是美国文学史上重要的自然主义作品。他通过小说的主人公玛吉的成长历程来探索主体的社会化过程，最终寻找促使玛吉走向毁灭的"现实"。本文旨在从社会心理学的角度探讨该部作品，进而挖掘其小说的社会心理表征。)

13. *McTeague*

(美国自然主义作家弗兰克·诺里斯(Frank Norris 1870－1902)的小说《麦克提格》(*McTeague*) 是美国文学史上第一部真正意义上的自然主义作品，被称为美国自然主义流派小说的宣言。)

14. *The Gift of the Magi*

(《麦琪的礼物》(*The Gift of the Magi*)是美国著名文学家欧·亨利的一篇短篇小说，它描写了一个感人的故事：在圣诞节前一天，一对小夫妻互赠礼物，结果阴差阳错，两人珍贵的礼物都变成了无用的东西，而他们却得到了比任何实物都宝贵的东西——爱。)

15. *The Red Badge of Courage*

(《红色英勇勋章》是以美国内战为背景，讲的是名叫亨利的青年怀着对战争的美妙幻想，不顾母亲的反对，参加了北方军。虽然战争很刺激，但是面对死亡的威胁，他动摇了。他一直问自己："我会从战场上逃跑吗?"后来，他还是从阵地上逃跑了。后来，他为此十分内疚，重上战场，获得显赫战功，但是无论他逃跑时的怯弱还是冲锋时的英勇都不过是一种歇斯底里的表现。)

16. Frank Norris

(弗兰克·诺里斯，美国小说家，《章鱼》是其代表作。)

17. Realism

(作为一场文学运动，现实主义作为对浪漫主义和感伤主义的"谎言"的对抗出现在19世纪后半期。)

II. Multiple Choice

1. A 《红色英勇勋章》是美国作家 Stephen Crane 的小说，描绘了美国内战的残酷。《丧钟为谁而鸣》是美国作家 Ernest Miller Hemingway 以西班牙内战为背景的小说。《第五屠宰场》是美国小说家 Kurt Vonnegut 关于第二次世界大战的反战科幻小说。《第二十二条军规》是美国作家 Joseph Heller 以第二次世界大战为背景的小说。

2. D　德莱塞的欲望三部曲包括《金融家》《巨人》和《斯多葛》。
3. D　自然主义小说家们推崇生物决定论和适者生存，认为生理遗传和社会环境都是人类社会发展的决定性因素。
4. B　《嘉莉妹妹》(*Sister Carrie*)是德莱塞创作的第一部小说。该小说体现了作者的自然主义观点。德莱塞认为人是由遗传、本能和机遇控制与操纵的。其中"灵的诱惑：肉的追求"("The Lure of the Spirit: The Flesh in Pursuit")是《嘉莉妹妹》20 章和 21 章的标题。
5. C　自然主义是由法国小说家左拉提出的。这一术语对美国自然主义产生了深远影响。
6. C　《野性的呼唤》是杰克伦敦在其鼎盛时期写的一部深受达尔文主义影响的小说。

Ⅲ. Explain the following term.

1. American Naturalism appeared in the late 19th to early 20th century. The movement was inspired by the principles and methods of natural science, especially Darwinism, Naturalism is derived from realism, but it is a step forward than realism in describing social reality. The works of naturalism reveal a miserable world. People live in a cold, harsh, and indifferent environment to fight hopelessly against overwhelming forces. The power that human beings cannot manipulate determines people's life. The style of the work is gloomy, and the overall tone is hopeless or even desperate. Typical American Naturalism is represented by Stephen Crane's *The Red Badge of Courage*, Frank Norris's *McTeague* and Theodore Dreiser's *Sister Carrie*.

Ⅳ. Read the following quotations and answer the questions.

Passage 1

(1) The above passage is taken from Theodore Dreiser's *Sister Carrie*.

(2) There are two types of tempters. One is the luxury life in the city; another is the tempter from human.

(3) "Large forces" include the gleam of a thousand lights, the persuasive light in a wooing and fascinating eye, a blare of sound, a roar of life and a vast array of human hives. The forces will relax, then waken, then pervert the simpler human perceptions.

(4) A counselor who can recognize the tempters tells them all the time and teaches them to recognize the tempters.

(5) Firstly, realism emphasizes a faithful rendering of the ordinary, the slice of life as it really lives. In this paragraph, the life of Carrie, a girl from countryside to Chicago to realize her American Dream, is described in detail. What she is bringing, even very tidy items, are listed faithfully. Secondly, realism is objective rather than idealized with close observation of life. In the first description of Carrie, the author doesn't make a judge of her, but tells her situation in an objective way by words like board, consist, outfit. Thirdly, realism is concerned with social problems, revealing the frustrations of characters in an environment of depravity. In the second half of this paragraph, the author uses many sentences to depict the tempters of city and the depravity.

(6) American naturalist writers no longer portray social reality gently. They describe the weakness and helplessness of human beings in the cruel world, as well as their lack of dignity in the face

of crushing forces such as the environment and genetic factors. The works of naturalism reveal a miserable world. People live in a cold, harsh, and indifferent environment to fight hopelessly against overwhelming forces. The power that human beings cannot manipulate determines people's life. The style of the work is gloomy, and the overall tone is hopeless or even desperate. In this paragraph, there are only two ways for a young girl in such condition—if she has others' help, she will be better; if she assumes the social standard, she will be worse. She can't make a change by her struggle for there are so many strong forces. Man is negative to act. What's more, the cruel realities of capitalism are revealed, which is one respect of naturalism.

Passage 2

(1) The author is Theodore Dreiser. The title of the novel is *Sister Carrie*.

(2) Theodore Dreiser belongs to American Naturalism. American Naturalism reported truthfully and objectively, with a passion for scientific accuracy and an overwhelming accumulation of factual detail. They painted life as it was lived in the slums, and were accused of telling just the hideous side of it and making "a god of the dull commonplace."

(3) American naturalist writers no longer portray social reality gently. They describe the weakness and helplessness of human beings in the cruel world, as well as their lack of dignity in the face of crushing forces such as the environment and genetic factors. The works of naturalism reveal a miserable world. People live in a cold, harsh, and indifferent environment to fight hopelessly against overwhelming forces. The power that human beings cannot manipulate determines people's life. In this paragraph, there are only two ways for a young girl in such condition—if she has others' help, she will be better; If she assumes the social standard, she will be worse. She can't make a change by her struggle for there are so many strong forces. Man is negative to act.

(4) ①As a naturalist, Theodore Dreiser attempted to achieve extreme objectivity and frankness. For example, in this paragraph, "When a girl leaves her home at eighteen, she does one of two things... Of an intermediate balance, under the circumstances, there is no possibility." This sentence is very objective in tone. This is also an evidence to show that he also mixed philosophical speculations with scenes of the harsh society in this novel. ②Dreiser is good at using the journalistic repetitive methods to leave a deep impression on readers. He showed his interest in painting through the text and pictures, the sharp contrast, the authenticity of colors and the dynamic sense of outline. For instance, "The city has its cunning wiles, no less than the infinitely smaller and more human tempter. There are large forces which allure with all the soulfulness of expression possible in the most cultured human. The gleam of a thousand lights is often as effective as the persuasive light in a wooing and fascinating eye."

V. Short answer question

1. His stories are usually short. The plots are exceedingly clever and interesting, humor abounds with the surprising ending. A story usually has two endings, the first is an unexpected ending, and the other is a completely different ending and contains a better surprise. Many of his stories contain a lot of spoken and local expressions, which makes them difficult to understand by outsiders. This form of language is used to show partial color, so that the story matches the characters

and scenes described. O. Henry's style, whether spoken or written, is always pure and clear.

VI. Essay questions

1. Each of Dreiser's characters in *Sister Carrie* search for their own "American Dreams"— the ones offered by a growing and prosperous democratic country. Carrie, a poor country girl, arrives in Chicago, filled with the expectations of acquiring the better things in life. She imagines the elegant clothes she will wear, the exciting places to which she will go, and the fashionable people with whom she will associate, thinking that everyone who lives beyond the boundaries of her Midwestern state has achieved that higher status. Drouet seeks his own version of the American Dream. He has achieved a certain station in life and wears the clothes to prove it. He frequents the important establishments in town and has befriended many of the right people. Yet, he pursues the other appointments that represent his dream, such as a beautiful woman to adorn his arm and his own home. Hurstwood has the woman, the established home and family, and a good position. He, though, wants more. He knows that his employers leave him out of important decision making, and he knows his friends like him for his position. He seeks love, appreciation, and more prestige. However, at the end of the story, each of them ends up disillusioned.

   Dreiser was controversial throughout his life. He was accused of immoral behavior, improper thinking as a political activist. People criticized him for his heavy style and weak narrative consciousness. As a man who grew up in a harsh environment and a low class, Dreiser had an American dream. He wanted to be rich and respected. But he also saw the cruel reality of American society and the tragedy of chasing the American dream. As a writer, he has the responsibility to reveal reality and awaken people. Among all contemporary writers, he is the bravest man willing to show the true face of society. Over time, Dreiser was recognized as a foresight critic of American values and an influential novelist.
2. *Sister Carrie* is a story about a country girl who went to Chicago to seek a better life and realize the American dream. *Sister Carrie* embodies Dreiser's naturalistic idea that human inheritance, instinct, and coincidence will control and restrict people. Dreiser described the three different worlds in which Sister Carrie lived in detailed records. These scenes present a rough and barbaric panorama of social life in the early 20th century. The details of the novel reflect surprising completeness and precision. In a cruel and indifferent world, the lonely and helpless Sister Carrie is mechanically driven by desire and blindly seizes opportunities to survive better. She can only be manipulated by forces that she cannot understand and control.
3. Jack London was very popular in the early 20th century. His writing style is full of vitality and color. Instead of words, he tells his story through actions and rarely stops to communicate with the readers. His early magazine experience is very helpful to him. Every sentence in his prose can arouse readers' interest. His shortcomings are that his character is usually very rigid and his dialogue is stereotyped. London's themes focus on primitive violence, biological evolution, class warfare, and mechanism determinism. He believes that human beings are victims of forces beyond people's control. Human beings have been manipulated by the animal instincts of lower animals. Survival is a non-stop war. The strong and the weak are often engaged in cruel struggles.
4. Theodore Dreiser's style has always attracted attention. So far, people have realized that Dreiser's

novels have obvious shortcomings and advantages. His writing is sometimes formless and clumsy, and the characters in the story are relatively simple. But Dreiser's stories are always fascinating and interesting with the clear plot and dynamic characters. Dreiser is good at using the journalistic repetitive methods to leave a deep impression on readers. He showed his interest in painting through the text and pictures, the sharp contrast, the authenticity of colors and the dynamic sense of outline. This is the key for Dreiser to become one of the most important American novelists.

5. Since William Dean Howells first proposed realism in American literature, many realist works with personal characteristics have emerged in the United States. American realists uphold the principle of being honest with life and focus on the faithful reflection of human society.

   The Rise of Silas Lapham, Howell's best-known novel, is the study of a self-made businessman who is ultimately ruined financially by his determination not to compromise his integrity; Mark Twain successfully used local color and historical settings to illustrate and shed light on the contemporary society. The employment of the local dialects and the colloquial language gives impetus to his works. Henry James, however, explored the literary possibility of the inner life in the characters.

   As to the naturalist writers, Stephen Crane's *The Red Badge of Courage*, Frank Norris's best-known works *McTeague* and *The Octopus* reflect the concern with social and economical forces and their effect on human lives. And Dreiser's naturalist idea found expression in almost every book he wrote.

第 11 章　20 世纪 20 年代 · 意象派 · 庞德

11.1　复习笔记

I. Overview of the 1920s

1. Background

(1) The 1920s was in between two important historical events: WWI and the Great Depression.

(2) In the post-war years, the country's development became increasingly urbanized, and a new industrial economy began to develop. Production and consumption at large scale, and entertainment became essential parts of economic and cultural life, and quickly turning into the dominant culture and customs of the nation.

(3) After the war, the heroism, patriotism, and enthusiasm for democracy that a generation had believed in, the romantic feelings for war, proved to be false and meaningless.

(4) At the social level, the entire American society is in a state of low tolerance. All radical forms and all claims of social and religious rights are considered intolerable.

(5) Darwin's theory of evolution made people lose their faith, and this crisis of faith was severely intensified in the 20th century. Without faith, life was fragmented and chaotic. People found themselves living in a spiritual wasteland.

2. New expressions in the field of art and literature

Impressionism
Dadaism
Expressionism
Symbolism
Surrealism

II. The coming of the image

The Imagist poem was a movement initiated by some English and American poets in the early 20th century to seek new ways of writing poetry. This movement went through three stages.

I. 20 世纪 20 年代概况

1. 背景

(1) 20 世纪 20 年代被夹在第一次世界大战和经济危机两大重大历史事件之间。

(2) 战后这些年国家发展日趋城市化，一种新的工业经济开始发展。大规模生产、大规模消费和娱乐成为经济文化生活的要素，并迅速成为国家文化和习俗的主导。

(3) 战后，一代人曾信仰的英雄主义、爱国主义及对民主的热情这些对战争的浪漫情怀被证明是虚假毫无意义的。

(4) 在社会层面上，整个美国社会处于一种高度的不容异说的状态。所有的激进形式和所有对社会和宗教权利的主张都被认为是无可容忍的。

(5) 达尔文进化论使人们丧失了信仰，这种信仰危机在 20 世纪严重加剧。失去信仰，生活支离破碎、混乱不堪。人们发现自己生活在精神的荒原之中。

2. 文学艺术领域的新表达形式

印象主义
达达主义
表现主义
象征主义
超现实主义

II. 意象主义的兴起

意象派诗歌运动是 20 世纪初由一些英美诗人发起的寻求诗歌新的写作方式的运动。这个运动经历了三个发展阶段。

1. Phase Ⅰ (1908 –1909) The British poet T. E. Hulme founded a Poets' Club in 1908, where poets met and discussed poetry in Soho, London every Wednesday. Hulme favored absolutely accurate expression and no verbiage.	**1. 第一阶段** 英国诗人 T. E. 休姆于 1908 年创立了一个"诗人俱乐部"，每周三在伦敦索豪区一处会餐和讨论诗歌问题。休姆强调绝对准确表达和不讲空话。
2. Phase Ⅱ (1912 –1914) Ezra Pound was the leading figure of this phase. He and Flint created the Poetic Principle's as follows: (1) Direct description of the "thing", either subjective or objective thing; (2) To avoid words that does not contribute to the presentation; (3) In terms of rhythm, to compose in accordance with the musical phrase, instead of a metronome.	**2. 第二阶段** 埃兹拉·庞德是这一阶段的领军人物。庞德和弗林特制定的诗歌原则为： (1) 直接主观或客观地描绘"事物"； (2) 不使用任何与表达该事物无关的词语； (3) 至于诗歌的韵律，应按音乐的小节而不是按节拍器来组织。
3. Phase Ⅲ (1914 –1917) After Pound, Amy Lowell took the movement into the "Amygism" period. Disagreements emerged among the Imagist poets and the Imagist movement gradually lost its momentum.	**3. 第三阶段** 艾米·洛威尔代替庞德把运动推向"艾米主义"时期。意象派诗人之间出现分歧，意象派诗歌运动逐渐失去发展动力。
4. Conception of image T. E. Hulme: The image must enable one "to dwell and linger upon a point of excitement, to achieve the impossible and convert a point into a line". Ezra Pound: An image is "that which presents an intellectual and emotional complex in an instant of time". Richard Aldington: Accurate choice of words can make the image produced by the reader consistent with the image when the author is writing.	**4. 意象的概念** T. E. 休姆：意象必须能使人留恋某个令人兴奋的时刻，使不可能变为现实，能使一个点变成一条线。 埃兹拉·庞德：意象描绘瞬间出现在脑际的复杂的思想与情感。 理查德·奥尔丁顿：精准的选词能让读者眼前产生的意象与作者写作时的意象一致。
5. American Imagists Ezra Pound Amy Lowell William Carlos Williams Wallace Stevens T. S. Eliot Carl Sandburg	**5. 美国意象派诗人** 埃兹拉·庞德 艾米·洛厄尔 威廉·卡洛斯·威廉斯 华莱士·史蒂文森 T. S. 艾略特 卡尔·桑德堡
Ⅲ. Ezra Pound (1885 –1972) Ezra Pound is known as the father of modern American poetry and the most influential leader of the Imagist Movement.	**Ⅲ. 埃兹拉·庞德** 埃兹拉·庞德被称为"美国现代诗歌之父"，他也是意象派诗歌运动最具影响力的领军人物。

1. Life Pound was born in Hailey, Idaho in 1885 and grew up in Pennsylvania. He majored in Roman language at Hamilton College and the University of Pennsylvania. Pond arrived in Europe in 1908 and published his first collection of poetry, *A Lume Spento* in Venice. After arriving in London, he met T. E. Hulme and participated in his Poets' Club, and later launched Imagism with H. D. and Richard Aldington. In 1914 he parted ways with Amy Lowell and turned to Vorticism; the aesthetics of both movements left an indelible mark on his works. Pound is also the most controversial figure in the history of American literature. After the outbreak of WWII, he began to deliver some pro-Fascist speeches against Britain and America. He was arrested and charged with treason after the War. He was detained in an American prison near Pisa, and was later then declared insane and interned at St. Elizabeths Hospital. In 1958, with the efforts of celebrities such as T. S. Eliot, Frost and Hemingway, Pound was released in 1958 and returned to Italy, where he worked until his death in 1972.	**1. 生平** 庞德1885年出生于美国爱达荷州的海利镇，在宾夕法尼亚长大。他在汉密尔顿大学和宾夕法尼亚大学学习，主修罗马语。1908年庞德到达欧洲并在威尼斯出版了他的第一部诗集《灯光熄灭之时》。到达伦敦后他结识了休姆并参加了“诗人俱乐部”，后来与H. D. 和理查德·奥尔丁顿发起意象新诗运动。1914年他与艾米·洛厄尔分道扬镳，转向“漩涡主义”，这两个运动的美学思想在他的作品中留下了不可磨灭的印记。庞德也是美国文学史上一位饱受争议的作家。二战爆发后，他发表了一些亲法西斯反对英美的演说。战后，他以叛国罪被捕。他被关押在比萨附近的一所美国监狱，后来被宣布精神失常，被拘禁圣伊丽莎白医院。经过T. S. 艾略特、弗罗斯特和海明威等名人的努力，1958年庞德获释回到意大利，在那里工作直到1972年去世。
2. Features of literature (1) What Pound saw in the West in the early years of the 20th century was a chaotic, broken, and barbaric world. He believes that he has an obligation to protect the crumbling civilization. He tries to discover the standards of the past culture and resurrect the lost principles of order. (2) We can find easily in his poetry the traits of Greek, Provencal, Latin, Anglo-Saxon poetic traditions. (3) Pound was also deeply influenced by Chinese culture, especially Confucius. The pictographic features and colorful images in Chinese poetry also have a profound impact on Pound's poetry.	**2. 文学特点** (1) 庞德看到20世纪初的西方是一个混乱、破碎、野蛮的世界。他认为有义务保护摇摇欲坠的文明，他试着发掘过去文化的标准、复活失去的秩序。 (2) 在他的诗作中不难发现古希腊、意大利、古英语以及普罗旺斯诗歌传统的痕迹。 (3) 庞德也深受中国文化的影响，特别是孔子的影响。中国诗歌中语言象形表意的特点以及多姿多彩的意象也对庞德的诗歌创作产生了深刻的影响。
3. Major works *A Lume Spento* *Personae* *The Spirit of Romance* *Cathay*	**3. 主要作品** 《灯火熄灭之时》 《人物》 《罗曼斯精神》 《华夏》

Homage to Sextus Propertivs
Hugh Selwyn Mauberley
Cantos
"In a Station of the Metro"

《向塞克斯特斯普罗波蒂斯致敬》
《休·赛尔温·毛伯利》
《诗章》
《在地铁车站》

4. Analysis of major works

◆"In a Station of the Metro"

One of the most representative and classical pieces of work of Pound. Pound was once in a subway station in Paris and was struck by the faces of some pretty women and children hustling out of the damp and somber station. This scene left an extremely deep impression on him, so he decided to describe this picture in poetic language. That was where this poem came from. "The object" is those faces in that dim station. The impression is represented vividly by the simple image of flower petals on a wet, black bough, which serves as the most concise, direct, and accurate representation of the "faces in the crowd".

◆*The Cantos*

(1) *The Cantos* is called Pound's "intellectual diary since 1915". There are in total 117 poems included in this collection. It is a social history, integrating heterogeneous cultures and languages. The world in *The Cantos* is depressive and somber. The poet attempts to give order and meaning to the chaotic and meaningless world through art.

(2) An important theme of The cantos is usury which, in Pound's eyes, is like a beast with a hundred legs that destroys light, life, and love.

(3) Pound found strength and wisdom in Chinese history and Confucianism, which is in contrast to the gloom and chaos of the West. The ideals of harmony and order could be found shining in many chapters of *The cantos*.

◆*Hugh Selwyn Mauberley*

Hugh Selwyn Mauberley is probably the best poem written by Pound, consisting of two parts and 400 lines. It charts Pound's evolution as a poet from paying homage to Propertius in "Homage to Sextus Propertius" to realizing that aestheticism

4. 主要作品分析

◆《在地铁车站》

这是意象派诗歌的一首经典佳作。庞德有次在巴黎地铁站被眼前的景象所打动。在人群中，他看到几个漂亮的女人和孩子的面孔。他们正匆匆忙忙地走出潮湿幽暗的地铁站。这场景给他留下了极其深刻的印象，于是他决定以诗歌的语言来展现这幅画面。最后写成了这首诗。诗中描写的对象是潮湿幽暗环境中的面孔。诗人用一枝湿漉漉的黑色粗枝上的花瓣这一简单的主导意象来形象地表达出这种印象。花瓣简洁、直接、确切地代表了"人群中的面孔"。

◆《诗章》

(1)《诗章》被称为庞德"1915年后的思想日记"，共117首。它是社会历史，是多种语言文化的混合凝练。诗人企图通过艺术赋予杂乱无章、毫无意义的世界以秩序和意义。《诗章》描写了一个沉闷阴郁的世界。

(2)《诗章》的一个重要主题就是高利贷的思考。在庞德的眼中，高利贷就像多脚猛兽摧毁了光明、生活和爱。

(3)庞德在中国历史和儒家思想中找到了力量和智慧的源泉，这与西方的阴郁与混乱是相对的。许多章节闪耀着和谐与秩序理想的光芒。

◆《休·塞尔温·莫伯利》

《休·塞尔温·莫伯利》是庞德写过的最优秀的诗之一，共有两个部分，共400行。从他向《方浩姆斯》中的普罗彼提乌斯致敬到最终意识到审美主义在现代世界中行

is not viable in the modern world. The poem incorporates many autobiographical elements.

(1) The first part expresses the poet's discontent with the commercialization and degradation of art, along with frustration and failure in a conservative and philistine world.

(2) The second part introduces Mauberley, a literary figure with multiple layers of significance. Mauberley serves as a foil to the narrator-poet but differs significantly in character.

The poem showcases a mature poet-narrator looking back and inward, celebrating his successful "escape," reaffirming his faith in beauty, and foreshadowing a new beginning in his endeavor.

5. Pound's War Crime

(1) After the First World War, Pound's focus has been turned from poetry to economics.

(2) After the Second World War, he was arrested for treason, and later declared insane and sent to St. Elizabeth's Hospital in Washington, D. C. While at the hospital, he completed several literary works, including the *Rock Drill Cantos*, and a translation of the Chinese classic, *The Classic Anthology Defined by Confucius*.

6. Pound's Connection with Chinese Culture

Pound became the literary executor of American Orientalist Ernest Fenollosa, leading to his deep exploration of Chinese culture, resulting in the publication of *Cathay*, a volume of Chinese translations. Pound's admiration for Chinese civilization, particularly Confucianism, influenced his career, as he believed it could enlighten and civilize the Western world. He saw in Chinese characters an ideal medium for poetry.

7. Pound's Reputation

(1) Pound is one of the poetic giants of English and American Modern poetry. He had a huge impact on the modernist writers in Britain and America after WWⅡ.

(2) Pound's early poems are fresh and lyrical, but his Chinese translations are inconsistent, regarded as a significant failure.

(3) He is known for his autobiographical and personal style, as well as for his open, spontaneous and sometimes grammatical expressions. He became a representative figure of postwar poets.

不通，这首诗记录了庞德作为诗人的成长历程。许多诗中元素显然是自传性质的。

(1)第一部分表达了诗人对艺术商业化和堕落的不满，以及对保守庸俗世界的挫折感和失败感。

(2) 第二部分介绍了文学人物莫伯莱，他在不同层面上有着多重意义。莫伯莱可以视为与诗人相对照的形象，但两者在性格上有很大的区别。

诗人在诗中回顾和反省自己的过去，庆祝了他"逃离"的成功，重新确认了他对美的信仰，并预示了他新的开始。

5. 庞德的战争罪行

(1)第一次世界大战后，庞德的研究重点从诗歌转向经济学。

(2)第二次世界大战后，他因叛国罪被捕，后被宣布精神失常，送往华盛顿特区的圣伊丽莎白医院。在医院期间，他完成了多部文学作品，包括《钻岩诗篇》和翻译中国古典著作《孔子释经》。

6. 庞德与中华文化的连结

庞德成为美国东方学家欧内斯特·费诺洛萨的文学执行人后，开始深入学习中文和中国古代文化，并以《中国诗选》完成了中文翻译。他对中国文化的崇敬影响了他的创作，尤其是儒家思想，认为儒家可以启蒙和"文明化"野蛮的西方社会。他认为汉字是理想的诗歌表现媒介。

7. 庞德的历史声誉

(1)庞德是英美现代派诗歌的一位巨匠，对二战后英美的现代作家产生颇多影响。

(2)庞德早期的诗歌新颖而抒情，但其汉译作品质参差不齐，被认为是巨大的失败。

(3)他因其自传体和个人化的风格，以及开放、自发和有时不按语法规则的表达。他成为战后诗人的代表人物。

(4) With time, people have begun to forget his wartime misbehavior and recognize his achievements as a poet, understanding his role in shaping modern poetry in the West. He will be remembered as such.	(4)随着时间的推移，人们开始忘记他在战时的不当行为，并认识到他作为诗人的成就，理解他在塑造西方现代诗歌中所扮演的角色，他将因此被铭记。

11.2 考研真题与典型题详解

I. Fill in the blanks.

1. "In a Station of the Metro" by Ezra Pound goes like this: The apparition of these faces in the crowd; ________. (首师大 2008 研)
2. ________, by Ezra Pound, employs the complex association of scholarly lore, anthropology, modern history and personages, private history and Witticism, and obscure literary interpolations in various languages. (人大 2006 研)
3. Author ________ Title ________(南京大学 2007 研)
   The apparition of these faces in the crowd;
   Petals on a wet, black bough.
4. Ezra Pound's lifelong endeavor had been devoted to the writing of ________, which contains ________ poems. (国际关系学院 2007 研)
5. Pound was the leader of a new movement in poetry which he called the "________" movement.

II. Multiple Choice

1. Imagist poems are mainly composed in the form of ________. (北二外 2008 研)
   A. blank verse B. free verse C. sonnet D. Quatrain
2. The Imagist writers followed three principles. They respectively are direct treatment, economy of expression and ________.
   A. local color B. irony C. clear rhythm D. blank verse
3. ________ showed great interest in Chinese literature and translated the poetry of Li Po (Li Bai) into English, and was influenced by Confucian ideas.
   A. Ezra Pound B. Robert Frost C. T. S. Eliot D. E. E. Cummings
4. ________ championed the imagist movement from 1912 to 1914, setting down the imagist principles. Then Amy Lowell led the movement into the period of "Amygism," as Pound called it, from 1914 to 1917.
   A. T. S. Eliot B. H. D. C. Ezra Pound D. Carl Sandburg

III. Explain the following terms.

1. Imagism (北外 2009 研; 南开大学 2009 研; 北京邮电大学 2010 研)
2. Avant-Garde (上海交大 2007 研)

IV. Read the following quotation and answer the questions.

Passage 1 (北航 2009 研)

The apparition of these faces in the crowd;

Petals on a wet, black bough.

Questions:

(1) What is the title of this short poem?

(2) Who is the author?

(3) What two images are juxtaposed or placed next to each other in this poem?

V. Short answer questions

1. Why the decade of the 1920s can be termed the second renaissance in the history of American literature? (厦门大学 2007 研)
2. Comment on the artistic features of the poem "In a Station of the Metro" by Ezra Pound. (南京大学 2008 研)

参考答案及解析

I. Fill in the blanks.

1. Petals on a wet, black bough.
   (这是意象派诗人庞德的名作，意为：人群中这些面孔幽灵一般显现，湿漉漉的黑色枝条上许多花瓣。)
2. *The Cantos*
   (庞德的《诗章》包罗万象，是庞德的代表作。)
3. Author: Ezra Pound　Title: "In a Station of the Metro"
   (题目节选自庞德的《在一个地铁车站》，该诗是以一个意象作为叙述语言的典型范例。)
4. *The Cantos*; 117
   (庞德把毕生精力都投入到写作《诗章》当中，《诗章》共包括 117 首诗。)
5. Imagist
   (庞德是意象主义运动的领军人物。)

II. Multiple Choice

1. B　意象派诗人主张诗歌创作在韵律上突破英诗传统格律五音步抑扬格的限制，追求一种更加灵活的自由体。

2. C　意象主义在其宣言中提出了三大原则，分别是：(1) 直接主观或客观地描绘"事物"；(2) 不使用任何与表达该事物无关的词语；(3) 至于诗歌的韵律，应按音乐的小节而不是按节拍器来组织。

3. A　庞德对中国文学很感兴趣，他将李白的诗歌翻译成英文，并且深受儒家思想的影响。

4. C　庞德是意象主义第二阶段的领导者，而艾米·洛威尔是第三个阶段的领导者。

III. Explain the following terms.

1. Imagism is a literary movement that took shape in Britain and U. S. in about 1910. It is a reaction to traditional English poetry and aims to express the sense of fragmentation and dislocation. The imagists, with Ezra Pound as the leading figure, believe that the best means to express momentary impressions is to use one dominant image. Three poetic principles of Imaginism are as follows: i) direct treatment of subject matter; ii) economy of expression; iii) in terms of rhythm, to compose in the sequence of the musical phrase, instead of a metronome. Ezra Pound's "In a Station

of the Metro" is a well-known imagist poem.

2. Avant-garde, a French word referring to the vanguard of an army or political movement. Its definition was extended since the late 19th century to those artists and writers who are dedicated to making art as an experiment and revolt against tradition. Ezra Pound's view that 'Artists are the antennae of the race, is a distinctly modern one, implying a duty to stand ahead of one's time by constantly innovating in terms of forms and subjects.

Ⅳ. Read the following quotation and answer the questions.

Passage 1

(1) *In a Station of the Metro*

(2) Ezra Pound

(3) The writer uses the image of "petals" on another image, that is, "wet, black bough". The poem is considered one of the most significant poems of the Imagist. It is written in a Japanese haiku style. There are only fourteen words in this poem, manifesting that Imagism focuses on the concision of language, the precision of imagery and that it experiments with non-traditional verse forms. Pound contrasts the actual, mundane image that he saw with a metaphor from nature and thus incorporates this "apparition" with visual beauty. The word "apparition" is regarded as crucial since it creates an uncanny and supernatural sense of imprecision which is then enhanced by the metaphor of the second line. The poem reflects the moment of revelation and intense emotion Pound felt at the Metro in Paris. Due to its treating subject's appearance by way of the poem's own vision, it is regarded as a typical Imagist text.

V. Short answer questions

1. The 1920s was in between the two most significant historic events, WWI and the Great Depression. There were at least two important reasons that made the decade different from the other periods: WWI, and the sense of life being dislocated and fragmented which was more strongly felt in the first years of the twentieth century. The 1920s was a peculiar period, in which the economic boom after the war and the sense of spiritual disorder were mixed. The greatness of the literature in this period is that it tried to capture that mood and record that for future generations. Just as Emerson and his contemporaries showcase the spirit of their age in their works, T. S. Eliot and Hemingway, and other writers also constituted a lot in terms of recording the spirit of their times.

2. ①It is identified as one of the most significant poems of the Imagist. There are only fourteen words in this poem, manifesting that Imagism focuses on the concision of language, the precision of imagery and that it experiments with non-traditional verse forms. ②It is written in a Japanese haiku style. ③It is a work produced at the early stage of Modernist poetry. It attempts to "break from the pentameter", incorporates the use of visual spacing as a poetic instrument, and contains not a single verb. ④Eight words were arranged in the first line and six in the second, mirroring the octet-sestet, mirroring octet-sestet of the Italian sonnet form .

第12章 艾略特·史蒂文斯·威廉斯

12.1 复习笔记

I. T. S. Eliot (1888 – 1965) T. S. Eliot is a great modern American poet, playwright and literary critic.	**I. T. S. 艾略特** T. S. 艾略特是一位伟大的美国现代诗人，剧作家和文学评论家。
1. Life Elliot was born in St. Louis, Missouri, where his grandfather organized University of Washington. Both of his parents were cultured and educated, so Eliot received a good education from an early age, especially in classical literature. In 1906 Eliot entered Harvard University, where he studied under Santayana, Barrett Wendell and Irving Babbitt, and was deeply influenced by their neo-humanist ideas. After receiving his master's degree from Harvard, Eliot went on to study in Paris and Oxford. He settled in England in 1915, where he worked as a teacher and bank clerk, and wrote book reviews for publishers. He became a British citizen in 1927 and was awarded the Nobel Prize for Literature in 1948 for his work on *The Four Quarters*.	**1. 生平** 艾略特出生在密苏里州的圣路易斯，他的祖父在那儿筹办了华盛顿大学。他的父母都是有文化教养的人，因此艾略特自幼就受到良好的教育，特别是在古典文学方面。1906年艾略特进入哈佛大学学习，师从桑特亚那、巴雷特·温德尔和欧文·巴比特，并深受他们新人文主义思想的影响。艾略特在哈佛获得硕士后，又在巴黎和牛津学习过。1915年他定居英国，先后做过教师和银行职员，并为出版商撰写书评。他1927年成为英国公民。1948年因创作《四个四重奏》而获诺贝尔文学奖。
2. As a poet (1) Eliot's poetry mainly reveals the barrenness and uselessness of Western culture, expresses people's frustration and despair, and pursues the reconstruction of the spiritual world. (2) In his poetry, Eliot was adept at using symbolism, juxtaposition and complex literary allusions. (3) Eliot's poetry has no fixed poetic style or rhyme. But people are able to find rules in irregularities and taste rhymes in irregular rhythms.	**2. 诗歌艺术方面** (1)艾略特的诗歌主要揭示西方文化的贫瘠与无用，表达人们的沮丧与绝望，追寻精神世界的重建。 (2)在其诗歌创作中，艾略特善于运用象征主义、并列和复杂的文学典故。 (3)艾略特的诗歌没有固定的诗体或诗韵，但是人们能够在不规则中找到规则，在不固定的韵律中品出韵律。
3. As a critic (1) The basic themes of Eliot's literary criticism are the relationship between tradition and individual talent, and the relationship between the past, present and future, etc.	**3. 文学批评方面** (1)艾略特文艺评论的基本主题是传统与个人才能间的关系，以及过去、现在和未来之间的关系等。

(2) Eliot's most famous theory is the "impersonal theory" or the theory of impersonality and objectivity. He also proposed that the focus of literary criticism should be the poem itself rather than the poet, and that the literary work itself is a separate entity. These ideas drove the emergence of the New Criticism.

(3) Eliot also contributed greatly to the re-evaluation and popularization of "Metaphysical Poets" of the 17th century and French symbolism in the late 19th century.

4. Major works

The Love Song of J. Alfred Prufrock
"Gerontion"
The Waste Land
"Hollow Man"
Ash Wednesday
Four Quartets
Murder in the Cathedral
Cocktail Party
The Confidential Clerk
"Tradition and the Individual Talent"

5. Analysis of major works

◆ *The Love Song of J. Alfred Prufrock*

(1) This poem is about a timid and timid middle-aged man who wants to propose to a young woman and is apprehensive all the way.

(2) The poem uses an inner monologue like Browning's poetry, and the themes of the poem are frustration and emotional conflict.

(3) Prufrock is a depressed, unhappy and tragic figure of a 20th century Western intellectual, who is divided by passion and cowardice, desire and incompetence.

(4) The title of the poem is very ironic. In fact, the "love song" is a song without love.

◆ *The Waste Land*

(1) *The Waste Land* is a landmark epic. It depicts the spiritual crisis in post-war Europe and reads like a manifesto for the "lost generation". It also established Eliot's position in the literary world.

(2)艾略特最著名的理论是"非个人化理论"或非个人化和客观性理论。他还提出文学评论的焦点应该是诗歌本身而不是诗人，文学作品本身是独立的实体。这些观点推动了新批评的产生。

(3)艾略特也为重新评价、普及17世纪的"玄学派诗人"和19世纪晚期的法国象征主义做出了巨大的贡献。

4. 主要作品

《普鲁弗洛克的情歌》
《小老头》
《荒原》
《空心人》
《圣灰节》
《四个四重奏》
《大教堂的凶杀案》
《鸡尾酒会》
《机要秘书》
《传统与个人才能》

5. 主要作品分析

◆《普鲁弗洛克的情歌》

(1)这首诗歌讲述的是一个胆小怯懦的中年男人欲向一位年轻女人求婚而又一路忐忑忧虑。

(2)这首诗采用了像勃朗宁诗歌一样的内心独白。诗的主题是沮丧和情感冲突。

(3)普鲁弗洛克是一位抑郁不乐、颇具悲剧性的20世纪西方知识分子的形象，是一个被激情与怯懦、欲望与无能分割的现代知识分子。

(4)该诗的题目极具讽刺意味。事实上"情歌"竟是"没有情感之歌"。

◆《荒原》

(1)《荒原》是具有划时代意义的史诗。描绘了战后欧洲的精神危机，读起来像是"迷惘的一代"的宣言书。它也奠定了艾略特的在英美文坛的地位。

(2) The poem's inscription is quoted from the first-century Roman satirist Petronius' *Satyricon*. The title of the poem is based on the Fisher King Legend.	(2)该诗的题记引自一世纪古罗马讽刺家佩特罗尼斯的《风流韵事记》。诗的题目引自"渔王"传说。
(3) An important feature of the poem is that the failure of sexuality implies spiritual emptiness.	(3)该诗的一个重要特点就是性爱的失败意味着精神的虚空。
(4) The poem is a bold innovation in rhyme and style. It not only presents the full picture of the chaos of the modern Western material world and the desolation of the spiritual world, but also reflects the general mood of frustration and despair of the entire post-war generation.	(4)该诗在韵律和文体上进行了大胆的创新。它不仅展现了现代西方物质世界混乱、精神世界荒凉的全貌，也反映了整个战后一代普遍的沮丧与绝望情绪。
(5) The poem is divided into five separate sections: "The Burial of the Dead," "A Game of Chess," "The Fire Sermon," "Death by Water," and "What the Thunder Said". Through the absence of intervals, connectives and dissonance, the poet wants the reader to see and feel the fragmentation of life.	(5)该诗共分为五个独立的部分:《死者葬礼》《对弈》《火诫》《水里的死亡》《雷霆的话》。通过间隔、连接词的缺省及不和谐的缺省，诗人想要读者看到和感受生活的支离破碎。
6. Reputation	**6. 作品认知**
Four Quartets is Eliot's significant work from the later phase of his career, considered one of the best long poems of the 20th century. It consists of four parts: "Burnt Norton," "East Coker," "The Dry Salvages," and "Little Gidding." In contrast to his earlier representative work *The Waste Land*, which reflects High Modernism, "Four Quartets" shows aspects of Postmodernism in its speech, mood, and tone.	《四个四重奏》是艾略特晚期的代表作，被誉为20世纪最杰出的长诗之一。包含四个部分:"烧伤的诺顿""伊斯特科克""干燥的救赎"和"小吉丁"。与他早期代表作《荒原》不同，《四个四重奏》在言语、情绪和语调上呈现出后现代主义风格。
The poemof Eliot incorporates elements of personal memories and meditation, making it more accessible to readers.	艾略特的诗中融入了个人回忆和冥思的元素，更易于阅读。
II. Wallace Stevens (1879 –1955)	**Ⅱ. 华莱士·史蒂文斯**
1. Life	**1. 生平**
Wallace Stevens was an unusual poet in modern American literary history. He began his literary work relatively late, publishing his first collection of poetry at the age of 44. He was both a successful businessman and a famous poet. He won the Pulitzer Prize and the National Book Award in the year of his death.	华莱士·史蒂文斯是美国文学史上一位与众不同的诗人。他开始文学创作比较晚，44岁时才出版了第一部诗集。他既是一位成功的商人，也是一位著名的诗人。他在去世的那一年获得了普利策奖和国家图书奖。
2. Stevens' Aesthetics	**2. 美学观点**
(1) Wallace Stevens insisted that poets lived in two worlds, the real and the imaginary, and strived to build a bridge between them. He believed that poets should find beauty, joy and meaning in the filthy reality.	(1)华莱士·史蒂文斯坚持认为诗人生活在现实和想象两个世界，并努力搭建它们之间的桥梁。他认为诗人应从污秽的现实中发现美、快乐和意义。

(2) Stevens believed that a poem could have multiple interpretations, and he was against providing explicit meanings for his poems. He cherished the ambiguity and uncertainty that arise from imagination and emotion, as these qualities add depth to the poetic experience. (3) Stevens viewed poetry as a modern form of revelation. It reveals the heroism of modern man, who, despite acknowledging the existential void, brings order and meaning to a chaotic and seemingly meaningless world. The poet operated in both the real and imagined spheres, anchoring poetry in the present reality. (4) For Stevens, poetry creates an aesthetic order that also transforms stressful, ominous and destructive environments into explainable, submissive ones. Stevens brought imagination and art to the pinnacle of success in American literary history.	(2)史蒂文斯认为诗歌可以有多种解释，他不赞成为他的诗歌提供明确的意义。他珍视想象力和情感所带来的模棱两可和不确定性，因为这些特质赋予了诗歌体验更深层次的内涵。 (3)史蒂文斯认为诗歌是一种现代的启示形式。它揭示了现代人的英勇精神，尽管承认了存在的虚无，但能够将秩序和意义带入混乱和看似毫无意义的世界。诗人活跃于现实和想象的两个领域，将诗歌牢牢地锚定在现实世界中。 (4)对史蒂文斯来说，诗歌创造了一种美学秩序，也把充满压力，带有恶兆和毁灭性的环境转变为可解释的、顺从的环境。史蒂文斯使想象和艺术在美国文学史上的成功达到顶峰。
3. The Basic Features of Stevens (1) Stevens sought the artistic beauty of poetry, and he often used musical and pictorial techniques to add to the artistic appeal of his poetry. (2) Stevens's poetry exudes a spirit of optimism rarely found in modern Western poetry. (3) Stevens, like Keats, is a poet of the senses. He likes to depict the world that can be felt by the senses, hoping to relieve the dull and dreary feeling of daily life by discovering the pleasure of the senses. Among the senses, sight is highly valued by Stevens, and his visual imagery frequently revolves around the theme of vision. (4) Colors hold significant meaning in Stevens' poems. (5) Later in his poetic career, Stevens' style became contemplative, even puzzling, and more difficult to appreciate.	**3. 诗歌特点** (1)史蒂文斯追求诗歌的艺术美，他经常运用音乐和绘画技术来增加诗歌的艺术魅力。 (2)史蒂文斯的诗歌流露着现代西方诗歌少有的乐观精神。 (3)史蒂文斯和济慈一样是一位感官诗人。他喜欢描绘感官可以感受到的世界，希望通过发掘感官的快乐来缓解每日生活的枯燥沉闷感。在感官中，史蒂文斯特别珍视视觉，他的视觉意象常围绕视觉主题展开。 (4)色彩在史蒂文斯的诗歌中具有重要的意义。 (5)在他的诗歌创作后期，史蒂文斯的诗风变得富于沉思甚至是令人费解并且更加难以欣赏。
4. Major works *Harmonium* *Ideals of Order* *The Man with the Blue Guitar* *Parts of a World* *Transport to Summer*	**4. 主要作品** 《风琴》 《关于秩序的思想》 《携蓝色吉他的人》 《世界的某些部分》 《转入夏季》

The Auroras of Autumn *The Necessary Angel* *Collected Poems* *Opus Posthumous*	《秋天的晨曦》 《必不可少的天使》 《诗集》 《遗作集》
5. Analysis of major poems	**5. 主要诗歌分析**
◆"Anecdote of the Jar"	◆《坛子的故事》
(1) In a way, the poem is rather odd and not easy to explain. Wallace Stevens was rather opposed to telling people what his poems mean. Therefore, we can only get the meaning of this poem by placing them in the larger context of his aesthetic tenets and related themes.	(1)在某种程度上，这首诗比较怪异，不易解释。华莱士·史蒂文斯相当反对告诉人们他的诗的意思。因此，我们只能把诗歌置于他的美学信条和相关主题的大环境中，以此来得到其诗歌的意思。
(2) The "Jar" in the poem may be a symbol of the art world and, by extension, of the imagination, as the poem seems to be discussing the relationship between art and nature. Art and imagination give form and meaning to nature and the real world. A society without art is a society without order. Man creates order according to his own perceptions, and half of the world he lives in is of his own making.	(2)诗中的"Jar"可能是艺术世界的象征，推而广之是想象的象征。这首诗歌似是讨论艺术和自然之间的关系。艺术和想象力赋予自然和现实世界以形式和意义。没有艺术的社会是没有秩序的社会，人按自己的认知创造秩序，人所生活的世界有一半是他自己创造的。
◆"The Idea of Order at Key West"	◆《在基韦斯特岛边关于秩序的想法》
This poem depicts a girl who confronts the chaotic world of nature. While walking, she sings, and through her singing, the world seems to transcend its chaos and becomes orderly.	这首诗歌描述了一个女孩面对混乱的自然世界，她边行走边唱歌。在她唱歌的时候，世界似乎停止了混乱，变得有序起来。
Stevens maintains a balance between art and real-life in his creative work. He is well aware that the world of reality sets the boundaries for art, and imagination can only construct based on the natural world.	史蒂文斯在他的创作中保持了艺术与现实生活之间的平衡。他深知现实世界决定了艺术的限度，想象力只能在自然世界的基础上进行构建。
◆"The Emperor of Ice-Cream"	◆《冰激凌皇帝》
(1) The interpretation of *The Emperor of Ice-Cream* varies. One view emphasizes "Let be be finale of seem," suggesting accepting reality—the woman is dead. However, this might not explain the title, "The only emperor is the emperor of ice-cream."	(1)《冰激凌皇帝》存在不同解读。其中一种认为重点在于"让它成为似乎的终曲"，暗示接受现实——女人已死。但这或不能解释标题"唯一的皇帝是冰淇淋之皇帝"。
(2) Another interpretation praises hedonism, evident in the title and "The only emperor is the emperor of ice-cream." The term "ice-cream" implies enjoying life to the fullest despite inevitable death.	(2)另一解读称赞享乐主义，标题及"唯一的皇帝是冰淇淋之皇帝"支持这解释。即使死亡不可避免，也要尽情享受生活。
◆"Sunday Morning"	◆《星期天的早晨》
The poem expresses contemplation of nature and acceptance of reality, demonstrates the contrast between Christian	这首诗表达了对自然的沉思和接受现实的态度，展现了基督教信

beliefs and pagan views, and shows the worship of nature and the sun, as well as the need to experience the interdependence of human beings and nature, human beings and the environment, and the belief in the understanding of absolute values.

仰和异教观点之间的对比，表现了对自然和太阳的崇拜，以及体验人与自然、人与环境相互依存的需求和对绝对价值理解的信仰。

Through the perspective of a female character, the poem demonstrates a yearning for the infinite beauty of time, as well as an obsession with the concept of death, ultimately accepting the world as a reference for her life and soul. The female character in the poem realizes that Jesus himself is mortal and must accept the fact of death, without which there can be no rebirth. The poem ends with the descent of the dove, which demonstrates a sublime attitude towards fate.

诗歌通过女性角色的视角，展现了对时间无穷美丽的向往，以及对死亡概念的困扰，最终接受这个世界作为她生命和灵魂的参照。诗中女性角色意识到耶稣本身是凡人，必须接受死亡的事实，而没有死亡就不会有重生。诗歌以鸽子的降临为结束，表现了对命运的崇高态度。

Ⅲ. William Carlos Williams (1883 – 1963)

Ⅲ. 威廉·卡洛斯·威廉斯

1. Life

1. 生平

William Carlos Williams was friends with Bond. He received the National Book Award in 1950. Williams had his own independent view of literary creation. He had his own unique views on the nature of poetry, the role of the poet, and the creation of poetry, which differed greatly from Eliot's views. He did not write poetry because he had to, but because he wanted to. He did not think he had to be recognized by the giants of the poetry world, such as Eliot, Pound and Yeats.

威廉·卡洛斯·威廉斯跟庞德是朋友。他于 1950 年获得国家图书奖。威廉斯对文学创作有自己的独立见解。在诗歌的性质、诗人的作用，以及诗歌的创作方面他有自己独到的见解，与艾略特的观点大相径庭。他之所以进行诗歌创作并不是他不得不写而是因为他想写诗。他认为自己不必非得得到当时诗坛的巨擘如艾略特、庞德以及叶芝等人的承认。

2. Williams' Aesthetics

2. 美学观点

(1) Williams strongly disapproved of Pound Eliot's "international", literate poetry. He asserted that American poetry must be rooted in American soil, which was the source of the poet's creative inspiration, material and creative subject.

(1)威廉斯极不赞同庞德－艾略特式的“国际的”、文人味十足的诗歌。他主张美国诗歌必须根植于美国本土，这是诗人创作灵感、素材和创作主体的来源。

(2) He argued that poets should not write about arcane and vague things. The poet should start from the concrete and the particular, find the universal in the particular, and discover the relationship between the real world and the spiritual world, the relationship between the ancient and the modern. Creative ideas should be expressed in their own unique way.

(2)他主张，诗人不应写玄妙模糊的东西，应当从具体和特殊出发，在特殊中发现普遍，发现现实世界与精神世界的关系、古和今的关系，用自己独特的方法表达有创见的思想。

(3) For Williams, life is the beginning and the end of the poet's creation. Life with all its details and rhythms, carefully observed and fully understood by the poet, is itself simple and pure poetry.

(3)对威廉斯来说，生活是诗人创作的起点和终点。经过诗人仔细观察和充分理解的具有各种细节和节奏的生活本身就是简单纯粹的诗歌。

3. The Basic Features of Williams Poetry

(1) Williams' poetic power comes from his clear vision of the real world, evident in the clarity of his imagery and devotion to capturing speech rhythms.

(2) He emphasized the peculiarity of objects, avoiding stereotyping through sentimentality and presenting everyday objects with uniqueness and wonder.

(3) He firmly asserted that poetry must be based on everyday life, using the language of ordinary people and the rhythms of this living language.

4. Major works

"The Red Wheelbarrow"

The Tempers

"Spring and All"

In the American Grain

Paterson

5. Analysis of major works

◆"The Red Wheelbarrow"

(1) This poem embodies the poetic theory of the Imagist poet Williams and is often regarded as his masterpiece.

(2) The poem fully expresses Williams' fidelity to life through the use of simple words and imagery from everyday life.

(3) The poem's style uses the traditional British rereading form to create the typical "American" image.

◆*Paterson*

①This work of Williams' poetry is in five volumes. He initially planned to write four volumes: the first to introduce "the natural features of the native land", the second to depict modern landscapes, the third to seek a language that would give voice to them, and the fourth to write about "the river below the falls".

②This poem reflects Williams' aesthetic view. By writing this long poem, he wanted to find an imagery that could embody the intelligible world around him.

③This long poem is innovative in terms of writing technique. It naturally uses poetry at times and prose at others, naturally adding confessions, dialogues and letters, faithfully

3. 诗歌观点

(1)威廉斯的诗歌力量来自于他对现实世界的清晰洞察，这一点从他清晰的意象和对语言节奏的专注捕捉中可见一斑。

(2)他强调事物的特殊性，避免因感伤而刻板印象，呈现出日常事物的独特性和奇妙性。

(3)他坚决主张诗歌必须以日常生活为基础，使用普通人的语言以及这种生活语言的韵律。诗歌必须摒弃一切的虚华粉饰。

4. 主要作品

《红色手推车》

《气质》

《春天及一切》

《美国性格》

《佩特森》

5. 主要作品解析

◆《红色手推车》

(1)这首诗体现了意象派诗人威廉斯的诗学理论，常被认为是他的代表作。

(2)这首诗通过日常生活中的简洁词汇和意象的运用充分表现了威廉斯对生活的忠实。

(3)这首诗的文体采用传统的英国重读形式来创作典型的"美国"形象。

◆《佩特森》

①威廉斯的这部诗作共5卷。他最初计划写四卷：第一卷介绍"本土的自然特点"，第二卷描绘现代风景，第三卷寻求一种使之发出声音的语言，第四卷写"瀑布下的河流"。

②这首诗体现威廉斯的美学观点。他通过写这首长诗，希冀寻觅一种可以体现他周围的可知世界的意象。

③这首长诗在写作技法上具有创新性。它自然地时而运用诗歌，时而运用散文，自然地加进自白、

reproducing the quiet rhythm of life itself with its fresh and airy style. It also includes, in its extremely flexible form, many of the themes he presents. ◆"Spring and All" (1) "Spring and All" is a poem depicting the passing of winter and the coming of spring, emphasizing on perception and observation, and presenting a captivating spring atmosphere through vivid visual images. (2) The poem conveys the imagery of life nourishing in death through the waning of winter and the awakening of spring, which is not yet fully arrived but the first signs of new life. (3) The poet shows the beginning of the whole natural cycle with beautiful expressions, especially the awakening of spring, which highlights his keen insight into nature. **6. Reputation** (1) Williams lived under T. S. Eliot's shadow, but his influence rose in the 1950s and 1960s, gaining long-overdue recognition after four decades of poetic work. (2) As a major voice in modern American poetry, Williams' poems began to impact contemporary poetry's development. *Paterson* with its focus on American themes and innovative writing style, attracted younger poets. (3) Williams became a prophetic figure of the new age, and his literary theories influenced major poetry schools like Confessional, Black Mountain, and New York schools.	对话和书信，以其清新、飘逸的风格忠实再现出生活自身恬静的节奏。这首诗也以其极为灵活的形式包括了他所表现的诸多主题。 ◆《春天及一切》 (1)《春天及一切》是一首描绘冬去春来的诗歌，强调感知和观察，通过生动的视觉形象展现迷人的春天氛围。 (2)诗中通过冬天的凋零和春天的苏醒，传递生命在死亡中滋生的意象，春天虽未完全来临，但新生命已初露端倪。 (3)诗人以优美的表达展现整个自然周期的开始，尤其春天的苏醒，突显了其对自然的敏锐洞察。 **6. 历史声誉** (1)威廉斯长期在艾略特的阴影下生活，直到1950年代和1960年代，他的影响力开始崭露头角，经过近40年的诗歌创作，终于得到了应有的认可。 (2)作为现代美国诗歌的重要代表，威廉斯的诗歌开始影响当代诗歌的发展。《帕特森》以其关注美国主题和创新的写作风格吸引了年轻诗人。 (3)威廉斯成为了新时代的先知性人物，他的文学理论影响了重要的诗歌流派，如忏悔派、黑山派和纽约派。

12.2 考研真题与典型题详解

I. Fill in the blanks.

1. In 1927, T. S. Eliot announced that he was a royalist in __________, a classicist in __________, and an Anglo-Catholic in __________. (国际关系学院2007研；首师大2008研)
2. Eliot's __________ is a morality play in verse dealing with the assassination of Archbishop Thomas Becket by knights of Henry II. (人大2006研)
3. __________ was successful in two fields of activity which did not seem compatible with one another: he was a very successful businessman and a very remarkable contemporary poet at the same time. (人大2006研)
4. *The Waste Land* was written by __________. (大连外国语学院2008研)

5. Taking the form of soliloquy, ________ by T. S. Eliot depicts a timid middle-aged man going (or thinking of going) to propose marriage to a lady but hesitating all the time. (天津外国语学院 2007 研)

6. T. S. Eliot's poem *The Waste Land* is divided into ________ sections. The waste land here stands for ________. (国际关系学院 2009 研)

7. Winner of the National Book Award in 1950 and the Pulitzer Prize in 1963, ________ is the author of the five-volume epic *Paterson* which is a lucid statement of the author's aesthetics.

8. At the age of 44, Wallace Stevens was finally persuaded to publish a book of poems, entitled ________.

9. After his death, Wallace Stevens's previously uncollected works appeared under the title ________.

10. In 1920, Thomas Stearns Eliot published his ________, containing, among other essays, "Tradition and the Individual Talent", the earliest statement of his aesthetics.

11. As Thomas Stearns Eliot declared, he followed strictly the advice of his close friend ________ in cutting and concentrating *The Waste Land*.

12. Thomas Stearns Eliot's later poetry took a positive turn toward faith in life. This was demonstrated by ________, a poem of mystical conflict between faith and doubt.

13. In his work ________, Thomas Stearns Eliot satirized the straw men, the Guy Fawkes men, whose world would end "not with a bang, but a whimper".

14. Few men of letters have been more fully honored in their own day than ________, and even those who strongly disagree with him seemed content with his selection for the Nobel Prize in 1948.

15. Thomas Stearns Eliot's last important work was ________, a profound meditation on time and timelessness, written in four parts.

II. Multiple Choice

1. ________ once declared himself a "classicist in literature, royalist in politics, and Anglo-Catholic in religion". (首师大 2008 研)

A. Walt Whitman　　B. Emily Dickinson

C. Wallace Stevens　　D. T. S. Eliot

2. ________ are not only poets but also literary critics. (北二外 2007 研)

① Edgar Allan Poe ② Carl Sandburg ③ T. S. Eliot ④ Ezra Pound

A. ①③④　　B. ①②③　　C. ①②④　　D. ①②③④

3. The central character J. Alfred Prufrock in T. S. Eliot's famous poem "The Love Song of J. Alfred Prufrock" is ________. (天津外国语学院 2009 研)

A. an old man　　B. a godlike figure

C. a restless young man　　D. a muse

III. Read the following quotations and answer the questions.

Passage 1 (首师大 2009 研)

And I have known the arms already, known them all—
Arms that are braceleted and white and bare

(But in the lamplight, downed with light brown hair!)
Is it perfume from a dress
That makes me so digress?
Arms that lie along a table, or wrap about a shawl.
And should I then presume?
And how should I begin?

Questions:

(1) What is the name of the narrator?

(2) What is he going to do and why does he fail to achieve his goal?

Passage 2(南开大学 2008 研)

Anecdote of the Jar

I placed a jar in Tennessee,
And round it was, upon a hill.
It made the slovenly wilderness
Surround that hill.
The wilderness rose up to it,
And sprawled around, no longer wild.
The jar was round upon the ground
And tall and of a port in air.
It took dominion every where.
The jar was gray and bare.
It did not give of bird or bush
Like nothing else in Tennessee.

Questions:

(1) What shape is the jar? Where does the speaker place it?

(2) According to the second stanza, what happens to the wilderness around the jar?

(3) What does the jar "take" everywhere? Of what does it "not give"?

(4) Explain in your own words the effect of the jar on the Tennessee wilderness. Does its effect seem positive in the first two stanzas? In the third? Why is jar an appropriate word?

(5) How is a jar different from the wilderness? What might the jar represent?

(6) Do you think ambiguity makes a poem more memorable? More effective?

Passage 3

Let us go then, you and I,
When the evening is spread out against the sky
Like a patient etherized upon a table;
Let us go, through certain half-deserted streets,
The muttering retreats
Of restless nights in one-night cheap hotels
And sawdust restaurants with oyster-shells:
Streets that follow like a tedious argument

Of insidious intent
To lead you to an overwhelming question...
Oh, do not ask, "What is it?"
Let us go and make our visit.
In the room the women come and go
Talking of Michelangelo.

Questions:

(1) This is the first 14 lines of a famous poem "The love Song of J. Alfred Prufrock." What is the name of the poet who wrote it?

(2) What image is created in this passage?

(3) Do you think Prufrock is a tragic figure? Why?

(4) Is this poem a dramatic monologue? Why?

Passage 4

The Burial of the Dead

April is the cruellest month, breeding
Lilacs out of the dead land, mixing
Memory and desire stirring
Duil roots with spring rain.
Winter kept us warm, covering
Earth in forgetful snow, feeding
A little life with dried tubers.

Questions:

(1) This is the first seven lines of a masterpiece poem. What is the name of this masterpiece?

(2) Who is the author of this masterpiece?

(3) What theme can you get from these lines?

Ⅳ. Short answer questions

1. How many parts are there in *The Waste Land*? (国际关系学院2007研)
2. Discuss the concept of Wasteland in relation to the works of those writers in the 20th century American literature.

Ⅴ. Essay questions

1. Analysis of Wallace Stevens *Anecdote of the Jar*.
2. Brief summary of Thomas Sterns Eliot's *The Waste Land*.
3. What is the subject of T. S. Eliot's masterpiece *The Waste Land*? What is the significance of the poem? Point out some of the features and innovations that you particularly appreciate in it. Who was T. S. Eliot probably influenced by in creating the poem? (人大2006研)
4. Analyze "The Love Song of J. Alfred Prufrock". (北航2008研)

参考答案及解析

Ⅰ. Fill in the blanks

1. politics; literature; religion

（艾略特宣称自己在政治上是个保皇派，文学上是古典主义者，宗教上是英国天主教徒。）

2. *Murder in the Cathedral*

（艾略特的《大教堂的谋杀案》是一部道德剧，讲述了亨利二世的骑士暗杀托马斯·贝克特大主教的故事。）

3. Wallace Stevens

（华莱士·史蒂文斯(Wallace Stevens)是美国20世纪的著名诗人。他集企业家和诗人于一身。）

4. T. S. Eliot

（艾略特，美国著名现代派诗人和文艺评论家，《荒原》是其代表作。）

5. *The Love Song of J. Alfred Prufrock*

（艾略特在《J·阿尔弗雷德·普鲁弗洛克的情歌》中，采用独白的方式，讲述了一个中年男人去(或者想去)向一位女士求婚，但一直犹豫不决的故事。）

6. five; the spiritual ruins in Europe

（艾略特最著名的长诗《荒原》分为五部分：《死者葬礼》《对弈》《火诫》《水里的死亡》和《雷霆的话》，将一战后的欧洲描写为一片人欲横流、精神堕落的荒原，折射出现代西方人的幻灭感和精神危机。）

7. William Carlos Williams

（威廉·卡洛斯·威廉斯的代表作是《佩特森》，它清晰地表达了诗人的美学观点。）

8. *Harmonium*

（1923年，44岁的华莱士·史蒂文斯出版了他的第一部诗集《风琴》(*Harmonium*)。）

9. *Opus Posthumous*

（华莱士·史蒂文斯死后，其之前未收集的诗作集合成册于1957年发表，名为《遗作》(*Opus Posthumous*)。）

10. *The Sacred Wood*

（1920年，T. S. 艾略特的批评文集《圣林》(*The Sacred Wood*)的出版奠定了他在20世纪文学理论和批评界的重要地位。其中《传统与个人才能》("Tradition and the Individual Talent")这篇论文最早阐释了他的美学观点。）

11. Ezra Pound

（埃兹拉·庞德(Ezra Pound)，帮助T. S. 艾略特整理删节了《荒原》(*The Waste Land*)的初稿，并向出版社推荐出版。

12. *Ash Wednesday*

（T. S. 艾略特在1930年出版的《圣灰节》(*Ash Wednesday*)鼓吹服从上帝旨意和悔罪的基督教教义，是艾略特创作中对文学和宗教认识发生转变的标志。）

13. *The Hollow Men*

（艾略特其他重要诗作如《空心人》(*The Hollow Men*)(1925)，绝望情绪更明显：人只是死亡国土上的一个空架子，一个填满了稻草的人。）

14. Thomas Stearns Eliot

（T·S·艾略特(Thomas Stearns Eliot)作为诗人、评论家、剧作家，其作品在二十世纪乃至今日的文学史上影响极为深远。1948年，60岁的艾略特迎来了他一生中最大的荣誉——诺贝尔文学奖。）

15. *Four Quartets*

(《四个四重奏》(*Four Quartets*))是一组由四部分组成的宗教冥想诗，它探索了超越时间的宗教启示，充满了《圣经》以及宗教仪式方面的典故，与早期的作品迥然不同。

II. Multiple Choice

1. D 艾略特曾宣称自己是文学上的古典主义者，政治上的保皇派，宗教上的国教徒。

2. A 爱伦·坡、艾略特和庞德都既是诗人，又是文学评论家，只有桑德堡只是诗人。

3. C 艾略特在《普鲁弗洛克的情诗》中描写了一位焦躁不安的上层社会年轻人求爱的矛盾心理。模仿了法国象征派诗人儒尔·拉夫格的风格，具有很浓的讽刺意味，刻画了当时社会背景下的人对于爱情对于生活的复杂心理。

III. Read the following quotations and answer the questions.

Passage 1

(1) The name of the narrator is J. Alfred Prufrock.

(2) He is going to propose marriage to a lady. Prufrock is a kind of tragic figure caught in a sense of defeated idealism and tortured by unsatisfied desire. His tragic flaw is timidity; his "curse" is his idealism. Knowing everything, but not being able to do everything, he lives in an area of life and death; and caught between the two worlds, so he belongs to neither. He craves love but has no courage to declare him.

Passage 2

(1) The jar is round. The speaker places it in Tennessee, upon a hill.

(2) The wilderness rose up to the jar, and sprawled around, no longer wild.

(3) The jar takes dominion everywhere. It does not give of bird and bush.

(4) In the first two stanzas, the effect seems positive. When "I" put the jar in the wilderness, it controls the whole disorderly landscape. The world of nature, shapeless and slovenly, takes shape and order from the presence of the jar. The world of art and imagination gives form and meaning to that of nature and reality. But in the third stanza, it seems that the world of reality exists to determine the limits of art, and that imagination can construct only on the basis of the world of nature.

"Jar" is an appropriate word because a jar is a man-made object, and, similar to the urn in the "Ode on a Grecian Urn", it is the fruit of human art and imagination.

(5) The jar differs from the wilderness in that it is an artificial thing. "It did not give of bird or bush / Like nothing else in Tennessee". The Tennessee wilderness is a symbol of the chaos and formlessness of nature. The jar suggests a world of art and imagination.

(6) Yes, I do think ambiguity can be effective in increasing the memorability of a poem. Great poems such as "The Waste Land" and "Anecdotes from the Altar" are usually not very explicable. Stevens has said that what comes from the imagination, or emotion, is usually vague and uncertain, so it is difficult to understand the rational implications without destroying the inherent vagueness and uncertainty of the imagination and emotion. I agree with Eliot's view that poetry is an autonomous structure that can be interpreted in many ways.

Passage 3

(1) Thomas Stearns Eliot

(2) A patient etherized upon a table

(3) Yes, Prufrock is the image of an ineffectual, sorrowful, tragic twentieth-century Western man divided between passion and timidity, between desire and impotence. His tragic flaw is timidity; his curse is his idealism. Knowing everything, but able to do nothing, he lives in an area of life and death. He despairs of life. He discovers its emptiness and yet finds nothing to replace it. Thus the poem develops a theme of frustration and emotional conflict.

(4) Yes, it is a dramatic monologue. He is a character created by Eliot, and he speaks directly to us. He tells us his thoughts in leaps and bounds, jumping from one image to another, just as a human mind does.

Passage 4

(1) *The Waste Land*

(2) Thomas Stearns Eliot

(3) The theme of the poem is the barrenness of the modern spirit, a reaction to the despair and depression of people after the First World War, the sterility and turmoil of the modern world. It also reflects the regret that in the face of the decline and collapse of Western culture, modern people are powerless to do anything about it.

Ⅳ. Short answer questions

1. *The Waste Land* is a great long poem written by T. S. Eliot. It consists of five parts, which are entitled as "The Burial of the Dead", "A Game of Chess", "The Fire Sermon", "Death by Water" and "What the Thunder Said".

2. *The Waste Land* is a poem written by T. S. Eliot on the theme of the sterility and chaos of the contemporary world. This most widely known expression of the despair in the postwar era has appeared over and over again in the works of those writers in the 20th century American literature. Faulkner exemplified T. S. Eliot's concept of modern society as a wasteland in a dramatic way he condemned the mechanized, industrialized society that has dehumanized man by forcing him to cultivate false values and decrease those essential human values such as courage, fortitude, honesty and goodness. Fitzgerald sought to portray a spiritual wasteland of the Jazz Age. Beneath the masks of relaxation and joviality, there was only sterility, meaninglessness and futility amid the grandeur and extravagance, and there was a hint of decadence and moral decay. Hemingway, the leading spokesman of the Lost Generation, though disillusioned in the post war period, strove to bring about man's "grace under pressure". He tried to bring out the idea that man can be physically destroyed but never defeated spiritually.

V. Essay questions

1. "Anecdote of the Jar" is a strange poem in some ways and not very easy to interpret. Wallace Stevens seems to agree with T. S. Eliot's notion of poetry as an autonomous construction capable of more than one interpretation.

   We can only decipher the meaning of "Anecdote of the Jar" by placing it in the larger context of his aesthetic credo and thematic concerns. Here lies the wildand chaotic and formless-rural

Tennessee, which let us assume is a symbol of the world of nature. Then the "I" of the poem places in it a tall, round jar, a manmade object, which is suggestive of the world of art, and by extension, the world of imagination. What happens when the jar is standing there is almost a miracle: it controls the whole disorderly landscape, so that "The wilderness rose up to it, /And sprawled around, no longer wild."

The poem seems to be talking about the relationship between art and nature. The natural world, though formless and massless, takes shape and order by the presence of the jar. The world of art and imagination gives meaning to the natural and real world, so the author may be suggesting that any society without art would be disorderly. Stevens is convinced that the poet is the archetype of human understanding of some creative force. His poets are the "necessary angels of the earth" in whose sight mankind re-examines the world. In other words, the poet is the instrument that helps mankind see life in its entirety again.

2. *The Waste Land* is 433 lines long. The whole poem is divided into five parts: I. "The Burial of the Dead", Ⅱ. "The Game of Chess", Ⅲ. "The Fire Sermon", Ⅳ. "Death by Water", Ⅴ. "What the Thunder Said". There is no sufficient formal connection between them. Things stop and begin without explicate shift. This radical disconnectedness is true even of the transition between the different sections within any one part of the poem, and between the different ideas within any one section. Through gap, absence of connective tissues, and discordance juxtaposition, the poet intends the reader to see and feel the fragmentary nature of life.

The Waste Land reveals its author's strong historical sense. To T. S. Eliot the past is of great significance to writers. The past should be altered by the present as much as the present is directed by the past. In *The Waste Land* Eliot uses the past as a yardstick to measure the present and underscore what is missing from the present. In a word, he is trying to throw into relief the negative qualities of the present by contrasting them with the positive ones of the past, and shock the reader into a recognition of the dismal truth about modern life.

The theme of the poem is the barrenness of the modern spirit, the despair and depression after the First World War, the turmoil of the modern world, and the decline and collapse of Western culture. The poem is notable for its varying lengths and rhythms. The poem conveys the author's central ideas in coordinated thematic variations, rhyme-free lines, and borrows heavily from various writers, employing material from Grail legends, Fraser's anthropological work The Golden Bough, and popular songs; as a result, the poem is obscure and logically lacking in continuity. T. S. Eliot's *The Waste Land*, however, is widely regarded as one of the most well-known landmarks of modernism.

3. (1) The subject: *The Waste Land*, Eliot's most important single poem, has been hailed as a landmark and a model of the 20th-century English poetry, comparable to Wordsworth's *Lyrical Ballads.* With bold technical innovations in versification and style, the poem not only presents a panorama of physical disorder and spiritual desolation in the modern Western world, but also reflects the prevalent mood of disillusionment and despair of a whole post-war generation.

(2) A poem concerned with the spiritual rupture of modern civilization and the loss of meaning in human life, *The Waste Land* has developed a set of historical, cultural and religious

themes. However, it is often thought of as primarily a reflection of the disillusionment and frustration of people in society in the 20th century. The horror and menace, the pain and disillusionment expressed in his poetry have been tormenting all sensitive people in the post-war generation. More importantly, his poetry used new styles, such as drawing extensively from other cultures and classics, that inspired many later writers. This poem is considered a landmark of modern poetry.

(3) Feature Appreciation: The style of the work in part grows out of Eliot's interest in exploring the possibilities of dramatic monologue. Eliot also enjoyed the music hall, and something of the flavor of this popular form of entertainment gets into the poem. It follows the pattern of the musical fugue, in which many voices enter throughout the piece re-stating the themes. Above all perhaps it is the disjointed nature of the poem, the way it jumps from one adopted manner to another, the way it moves between different voices and makes use of phrases in foreign languages, that is the most distinctive feature of the poem's style.

(4) Maybe Eliot was influenced by Homer, Sophocles, Petronius, Virgil, Dante Alighieri, William Shakespeare, Edmund Spenser, Geoffrey Chaucer, Thomas Middleton, John Milton, Andrew Marvell, and Walt Whitman for pieces of their works are frequently seen from this poem.

4. "The Love Song of J. Alfred Prufrock" is Eliot's most striking early achievement. The poem is a sort of dramatic monologue, suggesting an ironic contrast between a pretended "love song" and a confession of his incapability of facing up to love and to life in a sterile upper-class world. The poem presents the meditation of an aging young man over the business of proposing marriage. Prufrock, the protagonist of the poem, is mentally ill, neurotic, self-important, illogical and incapable of action. He is a figure representative of frustrations in modern bourgeois society.

Human predicament is the theme. Prufrock is a kind of tragic figure caught in a sense of defeated idealism and tortured by unsatisfied desire. The action of the poem consists of the interplay of impressions in the protagonist's mind.

The poem is extremely anti-romantic, with visual images of hard, rough and elusive hellish atmosphere. The surface appears to be anxiety about over-civilization, but the underlying mood is one of fear and malice. Individual words and phrases are borrowed from past works, bringing a richness of meaning to this poem. Within traditional English poetry, the rhyme scheme is varied and rhymes superbly.

第13章 弗罗斯特·桑德堡·卡明斯·哈特·克兰·穆尔

13.1 复习笔记

I. Robert Frost (1874 –1963)

1. Life

Robert Frost was born in San Francisco and spent his early childhood in the western United States. His father died when Frost was eleven, and the family moved to New Hampshire. After graduating from high school, he entered Dartmouth College. In 1913, his first collection of poems *A boy's Will* came out in London. His second volume *North of Boston* was published in 1914. The next year, Frost came back to the United States. At that time, he was already recognized as a great poet. He won the Pulitzer Prize four times and received awards from the American Academy of Arts and Letters and the Poetry Society of America respectively in 1938 and 1941. He received honorary titles from forty-four institutions. He became the nation's unofficial Poet Laureate when invited to read his poem at President Kennedy's inauguration in 1961.

2. Features of Frost's poems

(1) His poems are full of tact and wisdom, calmness and harmony, serenity and pleasure, making people temporarily away from confusion.

(2) Frost's poems have something to do with nature. Nature has the role of interpretation and regulation, which can be used as a standard for human behavior.

(3) Most of his poems are set in New England, and are based on ordinary people's daily life.

(4) Frost's poems are written in the traditional form. He shows little interest in experimentation in form.

(5) Frost's works demonstrate dark and terrifying facts. He is deeply aware of the fragmentation of modern life. His poems focus on the experiences of abnormal people.

I. 罗伯特·弗罗斯特

1. 生平

罗伯特·弗罗斯特出生于旧金山，在美国西部度过了童年。他11岁时父亲去世，全家迁往新罕布什尔。中学毕业后，他进入达特茅斯学院。1913年他的第一部诗集《少年的意志》在伦敦出版。1914年第二部诗集《波士顿以北》发表。第二年弗罗斯特返回美国时，他已经被公认为大诗人。他曾四次获得普利策诗歌奖，并于1938年和1941年分别获得美国艺术与文学院和美国诗歌协会的嘉奖。他一生获得44个机构授予的荣誉称号。1961年他应邀在约翰·肯尼迪总统的就职典礼上朗诵诗歌，从此成为美国非官方的“桂冠诗人”。

2. 诗歌特点

(1) 他的诗歌中充满着机敏与智慧，平静与和谐，祥和与愉悦，使人暂时地远离困惑。

(2) 弗罗斯特的诗歌很多都与自然有关。自然具有解释和调节的作用，它可作为人类行为的参考标准。

(3) 他的很多诗歌多以新英格兰为背景，取材于普通人的日常生活。

(4)弗罗斯特的诗歌一般都遵从传统诗歌的形式。他并不热衷于实验新的诗歌形式。

(5) 弗罗斯特的诗歌也描绘了一些黑暗、恐怖的事实。他深切地意识到现代生活的支离破碎。他的诗歌描绘了很多畸形人的经历。

3. Major works

A Boy's Will

North of Boston

"The Road Not Taken"

"Mending Wall"

"After Apple-Picking"

"Birches"

"Stopping by Woods on a Snowy Evening"

"The Wood Piles"

"Design"

"Desert Places"

"Home Burial"

"A Servant to Servants"

"The Black Cottage"

3. 主要作品

《少年的意志》

《波士顿以北》

《未选择的路》

《补墙》

《摘苹果之后》

《白桦树》

《雪夜驻足在林边》

《木堆》

《意图》

《沙漠地方》

《家里的埋葬》

《仆人之仆》

《黑屋》

4. Analysis of major poems

◆"The Road Not Taken"

The poem presents a common and typical life situation, where man is faced with the dilemma of making choices. What the speaker seems to express is that ultimately life would end in a circle and any taken roads lead to similar results. In addition, the poem conveys a kind of complaint that life offers people limited choices.

◆"Mending Wall"

One possible interpretation of the poem could be that the poem talks about the inherent alienation of life and human nature. The "I" in the poem feels that he is wiser as he no longer lives in the darkness, while his neighbor is still groping. Nevertheless, the neighbor is the wiser one because his experience taught him the paradox of life and human nature: distance makes people more intimate, which echoes Benjamin Franklin's famous saying that "Fish and visitors stink in three days."

4. 主要诗歌分析

◆《未选择的路》

该诗呈现了一个典型的人生境遇，即作抉择所面临的难处。诗人似乎在说人生在世诸事皆归于循环，任何选择的结果大概都相去不远。此外，诗传达出对人生选择余地太少的抱怨。

◆《补墙》

关于这首诗的解读之一是，它描写了生活和人性内在的疏远特性。诗中的"我"自我感觉更智慧，因为他已不再生活在黑暗之中，而他的邻人仍在黑暗中摸索。然而，恐怕还是邻人更智慧，因为他的经验教给他生活和人性的悖论：保持距离使人更为亲密，它令人记起富兰克林"朋友与鱼三日腥"的至理名言。

II. Carl Sandburg (1878 – 1967)

Carl Sandburg was one of the Mid-western poets well-known in the Chicago Renaissance (1912 – 1925). Other famous Chicago poets include Vachel Lindsay and Edgar Lee Masters.

II. 卡尔·桑德堡

卡尔·桑德堡是在"芝加哥文艺复兴"运动中闻名的美国中西部诗人之一。其他著名的芝加哥文艺复兴诗人有林赛和马斯特斯。

1. Features of Sandburg's poems

(1) Sandburg's ideal was to express "the voice of the people." He realized the importance of the people. There are the thoughts, feelings and wishes of ordinary people in his poems.

(2) Sandburg was an optimist. He had an insight of America in the future. He held a positive attitude toward American industrial civilization.

(3) He was involved in the poetic revolution. His long poems showed the influence of Imagist poetry. He wrote in free verse and his works are full of spontaneous slang. He made outstanding contributions to the colloquial style in American literature.

2. Major works

In Reckless Ecstasy
Chicago Poems
Cornhuskers
Smoke and Steel
Good Morning, America
The People, Yes.
Collected Poems
"Fog"
"Lost—"
"The Harbor"
"Cool Tombs"
"I am the People, the Mob"
The American Songbag
The Prairie Years
The War Years

Ⅲ. E. E. Cummings (1894 –1963)

E. E. Cummings was a representative of modern pioneering spirit in the history of modern American literature.

1. Features of Cummings' poems

(1) He disliked science and technology, believing they were inhumane and dehumanizing.

(2) The prevailing rebellious spirit in the art and literature of the time inspired Cummings, who has a dynamic personality to challenge tradition and fully express his unique style in his daring experiments.

(3) He attaches great importance to vitality, celebrates individualism and opposes collectivism. The usual themes on love and lust recur; an increasing number of nature poems reveal the poet's love for the world, especially a child's world. The simplicity, innocence and spontaneous happiness of this world are vividly shown in his poems.

1. 诗歌的特点

（1）桑德堡的理想是成为"人民之声"，在同代人中，他最了解人民大众的重要性。他的诗歌表现了普通人的思想、情感和理想抱负。

（2）桑德堡是乐观主义者，他洞察美国未来的状况。他对美国工业文明持肯定的态度。

（3）他参与了诗歌改革运动。他的长诗体现了意象主义诗歌的影响。他运用自由体写诗，作品中充满着活力充沛的俚语。他对美国文学中口语风格的发展做出了卓越的贡献。

2. 主要作品

《心醉神迷》
《芝加哥诗集》
《剥玉米机》
《烟与钢》
《早安，美国》
《人民，是的》
《诗集》
《雾》
《失落—》
《港口》
《清冷的墓》
《我是人民群众》
《美国歌集》
《草原年代》
《战争年代》

Ⅲ. 卡明斯

卡明斯是美国现代文学史上现代开拓精神的代表。

1. 诗歌的特点

（1）他对科学技术十分反感，认为其极不人道并使人失去人性。

（2）当时弥漫在文学艺术界的时代叛逆精神激励了活力充沛的卡明斯向传统挑战，通过大胆的实验手法充分表现自己的独特风格。

（3）他珍视活力，歌咏个人主义，反对集体主义。他描写爱情和性欲；他的自然诗表明他对世界，特别是对儿童世界的热爱。儿童世界的朴实、纯真和自发的快乐在他的诗歌中表现得淋漓尽致。

2. Major works *The Enormous Room* "Chanson Innocenter" "O sweet spontaneous"	**2. 主要作品** 《巨大的房间》 《单纯之歌》 《啊甜蜜的自发的》
Ⅳ. Hart Crane (1899 – 1932)	**Ⅳ. 哈特·克兰**
1. Life Hart Crane was born in Ohio. He began writing poetry when he was a teenager, and published his first poem at 17. His early work, published in *Little Review*, showed the characteristics of Elizabethan literature and French symbolism and recorded his nervous state of mind and homosexual orientation. His first collection of poems *White Building* came out in 1926, and was received with mixed comments. His major work, *The Bridge*, was published in 1930, which was not unanimously appreciated. His unstable life, his father's death, the estrangement from his mother and later from many friends and the Depression of the 1930s—all these brought great pressure on his increasingly fragile nerves. In 1930, he traveled to Mexico. In 1932, he jumped into the sea on his way back to New York.	**1. 生平** 哈特·克兰出生于俄亥俄州。十几岁时就开始写诗，17 岁时发表了第一首诗。他发表在《小杂志》上的早期诗歌，表现出伊丽莎白时期文学和法国象征主义的特点，记录了他紧张的精神状态和同性恋倾向。1926 年他的第一部诗集《白色的楼房》问世，评论界贬褒不一。他的主要作品《桥》于 1930 年出版，同样未获得一致的认可。不稳定的生活，父亲的去世，他与母亲及后来与许多朋友的疏远，20 世纪 30 年代的大萧条，都给他渐趋脆弱的神经带来压力。1930 年克兰赴墨西哥旅行。1932 年他在返回纽约的途中投海自尽。
2. Major works *White Buildings* *The Bridge* "For the Marriage of Faustus and Helen" "Voyages" "At Melville's Tomb" *Collected Poems* *Complete Poems and Selected Letters and Prose*	**2. 主要作品** 《白色的楼房》 《桥》 《为浮士德和海伦的婚姻而作》 《旅行》 《凭吊梅尔维尔墓》 《诗集》 《哈特·克兰诗作全集及书信与散文选》
3. Analysis of major work ◆*The Bridge* *The Bridge* consists of "To Brooklyn Bridge" as a preface, eight sections and a total of 15 poems. *The Bridge* is one of the long poems in the twentieth-century American modern epic tradition. The poem is the most majestic since *The Waste Land*. It answers to the pessimism in *The Waste Land*. What Crane tried to accomplish was to create a modern and mythological synthesis of the American experience in order to make sense of the experience and point out the close relationship between the present and the past and show hope for the future. He considers the Brooklyn Bridge as a symbol of America's future and its unique identity. He sees hope in the mechanical civilization which was criticized by his contemporary writers. Obviously, Crane was writing about the American myth in "an epic of modern consciousness".	**3. 主要作品分析** ◆《桥》 《桥》由一首序诗和八部分，共 15 首诗组成。 《桥》是 20 世纪美国现代史诗传统中的著名长诗之一。这首诗可以说是《荒原》问世以来用意最雄壮的诗作。诗歌回应了《荒原》中的悲观主义。克兰希望通过此诗对美国经历进行一种现代性、神话性的综合，以期彻底了解这种经历，指出现在与过去的紧密关系同时表达对未来的希望。他把布鲁克林桥视为美国的未来和独特身份的象征。他从同时代作家所抨击的机械文明中看到了希望。显然，克兰以“现代意识史诗”的方式书写了美国神话。

<table>
<tr><td>

V. Marianne Moore (1887 – 1972)

1. Life

Marianne Moore was born in Missouri and graduated from Bryn Mawr where she met her classmate H. D. She began to publish poems in the *Poetry* magazine around 1915 and became known for the novelty and liveliness of her poems. For some time she was editor of the literary magazine, *The Dial*, and it published poems by many of the best poets at that time. In 1951 her *Collected Poems* came out and won the Pulitzer Prize, the Bollingen Prize, and the National Book Award. Her *Completed Poems* came out in print in 1967. Late in life Marianne Moore was also known for her love of baseball.

2. Views on Poetics

The value of poetry lies in its representation of the essence of life and reality. The understanding of the phenomena in life is vital for a good poet. As her poetry "Poetry" conveys, good poet demand the raw materials of poetry "in all its rawness" and which is also genuine.

3. Literary contributions

Moore was a very original poet born and raised in the United States. She did a couple of things worth remembering for future generations.

(1) First, she was one of the first "new" poets in the early 20th century along with William Carlos Williams and Wallace Stevens.

(2) Another thing is her careful observation and description of minute details, and her poetic insight of the mundane things around.

4. Major works

Collected Poems
Complete Poems
"Poetry"
"The Fish"
"Silence"
"The Students"

</td><td>

V. 玛利安·穆尔

1. 生平

玛利安·穆尔生于密苏里州，毕业于布林茅尔学院，大学时和诗人希尔达·杜利特尔是同窗。她在1915年左右开始在《诗歌》杂志上发表诗作，她的诗歌以新颖和活泼见长。后来她担任《日晷》杂志的主编，刊出了当时不少优秀诗人的作品。1951年她的《诗歌选集》问世，获得了普利策奖、伯林根诗歌奖及美国国家图书奖。1967年她的《诗歌全集》出版。晚年的她还以对棒球的热爱而闻名。

2. 诗学观点

诗歌的价值在于它对生活和现实本质的反映。对生活现象的理解对一个好诗人来说是至关重要的。正如她的诗歌《诗歌》所传达的那样，好的诗人要求诗歌的原材料既是"原汁原味的"，又是真实的。

3. 文学贡献

穆尔是美国土生土长的颇具独创力的诗人。她有几件事值得后人铭记。

(1) 一是她和威廉姆斯及史蒂文斯同是20世纪初叶最初几位新诗人。

(2) 二是她对大小事务的细腻观察和描绘，以及她对周围平常事物的诗意洞察。

4. 主要作品

《诗歌选集》
《诗歌全集》
《诗歌》
《鱼》
《沉静》
《学生》

</td></tr>
</table>

13.2 考研真题与典型题详解

I. Fill in the blanks.

1. Author __________ Title __________（南京大学 2009 研）

   I shall be telling this with a sigh
   Somewhere ages and ages hence:
   Tow roads diverged in a wood, and I—
   I took the one less traveled by,
   And that has made all the difference.

2. "After Apple-Picking" is a well-known poem written by __________.
3. __________ combined traditional verse forms with a clear American local speech rhythm, forming his own characteristic.
4. At one time, Sandburg's reputation mainly rested on a multi-volume biography of __________ including *The Prairie Years* and *The War Years*.

II. Multiple Choice

1. __________ was regarded as America's poet laureate and invited to read his poem at the inauguration of President kennedy.（首师大 2009 研）

   A. T. S. Eliot　　B. E. E. Cummings
   C. Robert Frost　　D. Ezra Pound

2. Which of the following was not written by Robert Frost?

   A. "Tilbury Town"　　B. "A Witness Tree"
   C. "Steeple Bush"　　D. "In the Clearing"

3. Robert Frost is famous for his lyric poems. Which of the following lyric poems was not written by Robert Frost?

   A. "Richard Cory"　　B. "Stopping by Woods on a Snowy Evening"
   C. "After Apple-Picking"　　D. "The Road Not Taken"

4. "Two roads diverged in a yellow wood and sorry I could not travel both "In the above two lines of Robert Frost's "The Road Not Taken", the poet, by implication, was referring to __________.

   A. a travel experience　　B. a marriage decision
   C. a middle-age crisis　　D. one's course of life

5. To many who read "Fog"(1916), "I Am the People, the Mob" (1916), *Grass* (1918), and the 21 sections of *Good Morning, America*, __________ was successor to 19th-century poet Walt Whitman as the proclaimer of the American spirit.

   A. T. S. Eliot　　B. Ezra Pound
   C. Robert Frost　　D. Carl Sandburg

6. Carl Sandburg had also taken interest in folk songs which he tried to collect and sing during his travels. These folk songs appeared eventually in print in his well-known __________.

   A. *Good Morning, America*　　B. *The People, Yes*
   C. *In Reckless Ecstasy*　　D. *The American Songbag*

7. The three poets Ezra Pound, T. S. Eliot and __________ opened the way to Modern poetry.

A. O. Henry

B. Henry David Thoreau

C. E. E. Cummings

D. Robert Frost

III. Read the following quotations and answer the questions.

Passage 1（北外 2009 研）

"Stopping by Woods on a Snowy Evening"

Robert Frost

Whose woods these are I think I know.
His house is in the village, though;
He will not see me stopping here
To watch his woods fill up with snow.
My little horse must think it queer
To stop without a farmhouse near
Between the woods and frozen lake
The darkest evening of the year.
He gives his harness bells a shake
To ask if there is some mistake.
The only other sound's the sweep
Of easy wind and downy flake.
The woods are lovely, dark, and deep.
But I have promise to keep,
And miles to go before I sleep.
And miles to go before I sleep.

Question:

Try to analyze the poem.

Passage 2（北师大 2008 研）

The Road Not Taken

Two roads diverged in a yellow wood,
And sorry I could not travel both
And be one traveler, long I stood
And looked down one as far as I could
To where it bent in the undergrowth;
Then took the other, as just as fair,
And having perhaps the better claim,
Because it was grassy and wanted wear;
Though as for that the passing there
Had worn them really about the same.
And both that morning equally lay
In leaves no step had trodden black.
Oh, I kept the first for another day!
Yet knowing how way leads to way,

I doubted if I should ever come back.
I shall be telling this with a sigh
Somewhere ages and ages hence:
Two roads diverged in a wood, and I –
I took the one less traveled by,
And that has made all the difference.

Questions:

(1) Please analyze the symbolic meanings of this poem with your understanding of the theme implied in it;

(2) Please point out one or two artistic features of the poem with the examples in the text.

Passage 3

Some say the world will end in fire,
Some say in ice.
From what I've tasted of fire.
I hold with those who favor fire.
But if it had to perish twice,
I think I know enough of hate
To say that for destruction ice
Is also great and would suffice.

Questions:

(1) What is the title of the poem?

(2) What is the name of the poet?

(3) What do fire and ice respectively symbolize?

(4) What does the poet think the world will end in?

Ⅳ. Essay questions

1. Discuss Robert Frost's poetic style.
2. Analysis of Robert Frost's "The Road Not Taken".

参考答案及解析

I. Fill in the blanks.

1. Robert Frost; "The Road Not Taken"

(题目节选自罗伯特·弗罗斯特的"The Road Not Taken"(《未选择的路》)中的最后一节。《未选择的路》是美国著名诗人罗伯特·弗罗斯特的著名诗篇。罗伯特·弗罗斯特堪称美国20世纪最受欢迎的诗人之一，是美国非官方的桂冠诗人。)

2. Robert Frost

(《摘苹果之后》是罗伯特·弗罗斯特(Robert Frost)的名诗。)

3. Robert Frost

(弗罗斯特将传统诗歌形式与美国本土口语体结合起来，形成了独特的诗歌特点。)

4. Abraham Lincoln

(卡尔·桑德堡(Carl Sandburg)美国现代诗人及传记作家。20世纪20和30年代，他创作并出版了林肯的传记《草原年代》(*The Prairie Years*)和《战争年代》(*The War Years*)。)

II. Multiple Choice

1. C 罗伯特·弗罗斯特是美国的桂冠诗人，多次获普利策奖，1961 年 87 岁高龄的弗罗斯特应邀在约翰·肯尼迪总统(John . F. Kennedy)的就职典礼上朗诵自己的诗作。

2. A 选项 A“Tilbury Town”是埃德温·阿灵顿·罗宾逊的诗。其余三个选项“A Witness Tree”,“Steeple Bush”,“In the Clearing”都是罗伯特·弗罗斯特的作品。

3. A 罗伯特·弗罗斯特以抒情诗著称,《雪夜林边小驻》(“Stopping by Woods on a Snowy Evening”),《摘苹果之后》(“After Apple-Picking”), 和《未选择的路》(“The Road Not Taken”)都是弗罗斯特著名的抒情诗。而选项 A“Richard Cory”的作者是埃德温·阿灵顿·罗宾逊。

4. D 在《未选择的路》一诗中，作者想要表达的实际是人生的境遇。

5. D 桑德堡的理想是成为“人民之声”，在同代人中，他最了解人民大众的重要性。他的诗歌表现了普通人的思想、情感和理想抱负。

6. D 美国诗人及传记作家卡尔·桑德堡 Carl Sandburg)对民歌很感兴趣，他在旅途中收集和吟唱民歌。这些民歌后来出版名为《美国歌袋》(*The American Songbag*)。

7. C 庞德、艾略特和卡明斯在诗歌方面都具有创新精神，他们开启了现代派诗歌之门。

III. Read the following quotations and answer the questions.

Passage 1

“Stopping by Woods on a Snowy Evening” is a poem written in 1922 by Robert Frost, and came out in 1923 in his New Hampshire volume.

The poem is written in iambic tetrameter in the Rubaiyat stanza created by Edward Fitzgerald. Each verse (save the last) follows an a-a-b-a rhyming scheme, with the following verse's a rhyming with that verse's b, which is a chain rhyme. Overall, the rhyme scheme is AABA-BBCB-CCDC-DDDD.

The poet expresses a mixed feeling about mingling with the beautiful and quite nature and the responsibility which the speaker bears in the real world.

In the poem, the speaker is impressed by the snowy woods on a winter evening. Although the woods may have owner, , now it is part of the nature and it only belongs to the speaker. The little horse shows its puzzle when the speaker is indulging in the beautiful snowy woods, so “He gave his harness bells a shake to ask if there is any mistake”. Here, the personification is used. Although the woods are lovely and quiet, the speaker has to continue his journey. “Sleep” also indicates “death”. It is not the time for him to “sleep” for he has to fulfill his responsibility.

The poem shows the typical features of Robert Frost's poems. The language of his poems is coconcise, but he always tries to express some sensitive feeling toward the life and people's innermind. He attaches importance to the natural scene and ordinary thing. Imagery and personification are used skillfully in the poem.

Passage 2

(1) The poem seems to be about the poet, who is walking in the woods in autumn, and choosing which road he should follow on his way. In the poem, the poet hesitates for a long time, wondering which road to take, because they look both good. In the end, he follows the one which

seems to have fewer travelers on it. Symbolically, he chooses to follow an unusual, solitary life; perhaps he is talking about his choice to become a poet rather than some ordinary profession. But he always remembers the road which he might have taken, and which would have given him a differentlife.

In reality, it is about the important decisions which one must make in life, when one must give up a desirable thing in order to pursue another. Then, whatever the outcome, one must accept the consequences of one's choice for it is not possible to go back or have another chance to make a different choice. The different road one takes, the different kind of life one will have.

(2) In addition to the symbols used in this poem, other artistic features are employed in the rhythm aspects. This poem is written in classic five-line stanzas, with the rhyme scheme a-b-a-a-b and conversational rhythm. Alliteration is also employed in this poem. For example, "wanted wear" in the third line of the second stanza.

Passage 3

(1) The title of the poem is "Fire and Ice".

(2) The poet is Robert Frost.

(3) Fire symbolizes human desires while ice symbolizes hatred between people.

(4) The poet think desires are more dangerous than hatred because he says "I hold with those who favor fire." though he admits that hatred is also very destructive.

Ⅳ. Essay questions

1. Frost used concise language, a graceful style and traditional poetic form. He achieved an internal dynamics in his poetry by applying the rhythms of everyday language instead of the formal pattern of line and stanza. He often used regular iambic meter. Sometimes he used blank verse. He tends to be simple, but he explores complexity through triviality. He used symbols from everyday life to imply profound ideas. He made his poems seem effortless by using colloquial and direct expression and conversational rhythms. His success mainly includes two aspects: he combined traditional poetic forms with American vocabulary and language rhythms; he composed individual poems into a larger whole by presenting in them a recurrent "persona" in the image of a wise country man.

2. This poem is written in classic five-line stanzas, with an a-b-a-a-b rhyme and dialogue rhythm. The poem seems to be about the poet, who is walking in the woods in autumn, and choosing which road he should follow on his way. In reality, it is related to the important decisions which a person must make in life, when a person must give up one desirable thing in order to have another. Then, regardless of the outcome, one must accept the consequences of his choice, because it is not possible to go back and have another chance to make a different choice.

   In the poem, the poet hesitates for a long time, not knowing which way to go, because they are both good. In the end, he follows the one which seems to have fewer travelers on it. Symbolically, he chose to follow an unusual and lonely life; perhaps he was talking about his choice to become a poet rather than some ordinary profession. But he always remembers the road which he might have taken, and which would have given him a differentlife.

第 14 章　菲茨杰拉德 · 海明威

14.1　复习笔记

I. F. Scott Fitzgerald (1896 – 1940)

Fitzgerald was essentially a 1920s American novelist. His *Tales of the Jazz* portrays this crucial period in the cultural history of America. He was best known for his works depicting the flamboyance and excess of the Jazz Age.

I. 弗 · 司各特 · 菲茨杰拉德

菲茨杰拉德是20 世纪 20 年代最具代表性的美国作家。他的短篇小说集《爵士乐时代的故事》描绘了 20 年代的美国，他也因许多刻画了“爵士乐时代”的浮华与奢侈的作品而闻名。

1. Life

Fitzgerald was born into a middle-class family in St. Paul, Minnesota. He had education first in private schools and then at Princeton. He dropped out of university in 1917 to join the Army. But he never went to the war abroad. During the period of 15 months of service in the army, when stationed in Alabama, he fell in love with Zelda Sayre, the daughter of a judge. Zelda promised that she would marry him only if he could succeed in the literary circle. In 1920 Fitzgerald's *This Side of Paradise* was published and became immensely popular, which earned Zelda for him. In the 1920s, Fitzgerald frequented Europe, where he was influenced by the modernist writers and artists of the “Lost Generation”. Fitzgerald suffered from an unhappy marriage. The couple were also fighting each other all the time. Zelda began to have breakdowns and had to be put in a mental institution. Loneliness, alcohol and the awareness that he was dissipating his talent eventually combined to break the talent down. In the last year of his life, he began to write one very interesting novel, *The Last Tycoon*, which he never finished. In 1940, he died at the age of 44.

1. 生平

菲茨杰拉德出生于明尼苏达州首府圣保罗的一个中产阶级家庭。他被送进私立学校学习。后进入普林斯顿大学。1917 年他离校入伍，但未出国参战。在部队服役的 15 个月期间，他在驻扎阿拉巴马爱上了一位法官的女儿，泽尔达 · 赛尔。泽尔达告诉菲茨杰拉德只有他飞黄腾达才能娶到她。1920 年菲茨杰拉德的第一部小说《人间天堂》一经出版即大获成功。这部小说的成功还使得他赢得了泽尔达。随后菲茨杰拉德常到访欧洲，他也受到了被称为“迷惘的一代”的现代主义作家及艺术家的影响。菲茨杰拉德夫妇婚后生活并不幸福，他们之间的争吵不断。后来泽尔达开始出现精神崩溃，被送进了精神病院。孤独寂寞，常借酒消愁，再加上菲茨杰拉德感到自己在浪费才华，这些最终压垮了这位才子。在生命的最后一年，菲茨杰拉德开始写一部很有意思的小说《最后的大亨》，可惜作品未完成便在 1940 年与世长辞，年仅 44 岁。

2. Major works

This Side of Paradise
Flappers and Philosophers
Tales of the Jazz Age
The Beautiful and the Damned.
The Great Gatsby

2. 主要作品

《人间天堂》
《轻佻女郎与哲学家》
《爵士乐时代的故事》
《美丽与诅咒》
《了不起的盖茨比》

Tender is the Night
All the Sad Young Men
"The Rich Boy"
Taps at Reveille
The Last Tycoon
The Crack-Up

《夜色温柔》
《那些忧伤的年轻人》
《富家子》
《清晨起床号》
《最后的大亨》
《崩溃》

3. Analysis of major work

◆*The Great Gatsby* (1925)

(1) Gatsby's personal experience reflects the predicament of the Americans in the first few decades of the twentieth century. Modern men lives in sterility, futility and the excess of life, as best illustrated by Gatsby's essentially pointless parties. Thus, Gatsby's personal life has assumed a magnitude as a "cultural-historical allegory" for the nation. The novel is widely considered to be a literary masterwork and nominated for the title of the Great American Novel.

(2) The very rich attracted and repelled Fitzgerald at the same time. On the whole, Fitzgerald critiques the rich in that wealth emotionally weakens them. In *The Great Gatsby*, Tom and Daisy are completely dehumanized by wealth and both of them corrupt others.

(3) Fitzgerald's craftsmanship is impeccable in this novel. The use of a dramatic narrator, through whose consciousness everything filters, ensures the integration of the work. Carraway's limited perspective determines the facts that he deals with the information in such a manner that he seems to withhold it first, thus creating a mysterious effect of suspense.

(4) Fitzgerald was one of the great stylists in American literature. Fitzgerald's prose is smooth, penetrating, and completely original in its diction and metaphors. His language style features both simplicity and gracefulness, showing skill of manipulating the relationship between the general and the specific. Bold use of colors is a component of the novel's impressionism. The counter-realism in the novel can be seen in the uncertain boundaries between the animate and the inanimate. These techniques portray characters' personalities and convey the authorial vision, revealing Fitzgerald's consummate artistry.

3. 主要作品分析

◆《了不起的盖茨比》

（1）盖茨比的个人经历反映出20世纪前几十年美国整个国家的困境。现代人生活在物欲横流的精神荒原之上，生活已失去目的和意义，看看盖茨比豪华但毫无意义的宴会便可略知一二。因此，作为整个国家"文化历史层面的寓言"，盖茨比的私人生活也具备了重要意义。《了不起的盖茨比》被视为文学名著，且被提名为最伟大的美国小说。

（2）菲茨杰拉德对富人和富贵的态度有羡慕，但总体而言，菲茨杰拉德批判了富人，原因在于财富使他们的情感产生缺陷。在《了不起的盖茨比》中汤姆和黛西这两个人物因财富而堕落，同时也诱使他人堕落。

（3）在这部小说中，菲茨杰拉德的写作技巧无可挑剔。他选择了卡拉韦这一戏剧化的叙述者，通过其意识一切事件得以被筛选和过滤，因而保证了整个故事结构上的统一性。卡拉韦的有限视角确定了一个事实，即起初他对信息似乎有所保留，这制造了一种神秘的悬念效果。

（4）菲茨杰拉德是美国文学史上一位伟大的文体家。菲茨杰拉德的语言通顺流畅，观察细致入微，措辞和比喻极具独创性。他的文章质朴、雅致，较好地把握了整体与细节之间的关系。作者对色彩的大胆运用体现了小说的印象主义手法。而小说对动静态界限的模糊则体现了反现实主义色彩。这些技巧展现了人物的特质并传达了作者的观点，显示了菲茨杰拉德高超的艺术才能。

Ⅱ. Ernest Hemingway (1899 –1961)

1. Life

Born in Oak park, Illinois, Hemingway grew up in an nearly affluent family with his father being a physician and his mother a music teacher. At the age of 17, he tried to enlist in the army but was rejected because of his injured eye. He then became a reporter in the *Kansas City Star*. Then he went to Europe and served as an ambulance driver for the Red Cross. His war experience was so shocking and horrifying that his life and writings were affected for good. He was a world traveler. In 1920s, Hemingway lived in Europe as a crucial member of the expatriate artists of the "Lost Generation". After the Spanish Civil War, from 1939 to 1960, he lived in Cuba where he wrote many important novels such as *The Old Man and the Sea* (1952).

The modernist writer Hemingway was a myth in American literature. He was publicly acclaimed and his style of writing probably influenced other writers. His public image was one of a tough guy. He won the Nobel Prize for literature in 1954. In his later years, he often behaved in an odd manner and looked much older than his true age. Possibly due to the loss of writing talent, the failure of acting out his code, or both, adding to his ill health, he shot himself dead on July 2, 1961. The world was shocked by his death. His death marked that an era had come to an end in American literary history.

2. The Hemingway Hero

Throughout his life, Hemingway explores one theme, which is summed up in the famous phrase "grace under pressure". He shapes a Hemingway hero to demonstrate the theme. Hemingway's world is essentially chaotic and meaningless, in which man fights a solitary struggle against the unfathomable force. A sense of despair arose from the awareness that he must end in defeat, no matter how hard he strives against it. But the Hemingway hero possesses the despairing courage. This courage is a code of honor that allows a man to keep humanity and behave like a man to assert his dignity in face of adversity. Hemingway's characters, Nick Adams, Jake Barnes,

Ⅱ. 欧内斯特·海明威

1. 生平

海明威出生于伊利诺州的奥克帕克。父亲是内科医生，母亲是音乐教师。他17岁时曾试图参军，但因眼疾而未能成行，遂到《堪萨斯城星报》任记者。后海明威前往欧洲战场担任红十字会组织的救护车司机。这段令人震惊和恐惧的战争经历对海明威的生活和写作产生了终生的影响。20世纪20年代，海明威作为“迷惘的一代”的代表作家旅居欧洲。西班牙内战结束后，自1939到1960年他都居住在古巴，并创作出了《老人与海》等脍炙人口的作品。

现代主义作家海明威是美国文学中的一个神话。他获得了公众的认可，而他的写作风格可能影响了许多其他作家。在公众眼里，他是个十足的硬汉子。1954年，海明威获得了诺贝尔文学奖。晚年海明威行为古怪，看起来比实际年龄苍老许多。或许因为其文思枯竭，或许因为他不能实践自己的行为准则，又或许二者皆有之，再加上他疾病缠身，他于1961年7月2日开枪自杀，举世为之震惊。海明威的逝世标志着美国文学史上一个时代的结束。

2. 海明威式英雄

海明威的一生都在描写一个主题，即“重压下的优雅”。他同时塑造了典型的海明威式英雄。海明威笔下的世界在本质上混乱不堪，毫无意义可言。在这样的世界里，人单枪匹马地去抵抗他自己都无法理解的力量。人物最终意识到无论自己多么努力，最终还是会以失败告终，这必然招致失望的情绪。但是海明威式英雄表现出一种绝望中的勇气。这种勇气是一种荣誉准则，使他表现出大丈夫气概，在逆境中保持尊严。海明威小说中的人

Frederic Henry, and Santiago are all typical Hemingway heroes.

物，尼克·亚当斯、杰克·巴恩斯、弗瑞德里克·亨利、圣地亚哥等都是典型的海明威式英雄。

3. Writing style

In his declining years, Hemingway came to be known as "Papa Hemingway". This compliment refers generally to his contribution to the development of the new colloquial style of writing in America. Hemingway's prose is simple and apparently natural. It has the effect of directness, clarity and freshness. His words always carry connotations.

3. 写作风格

海明威晚年被称作"爸爸海明威"，这一赞誉主要指他为美国文学史上的新的口语写作风格做出了突出的贡献。海明威的文章简朴、自然，直截了当，清晰易懂，新颖活泼，而且意蕴丰富。

4. Major works

The Torrents of Spring
Three Stories and Ten Poems
In Our Times
Men Without Women
Winner Take Nothing
"Indian Camp"
The Sun Also Rises
A Farewell to Arms
Death in the Afternoon
Green Hills of Africa
To Have and Have not
The Fifth Column
For Whom the Bell Tolls
Across the River and into the Trees
The Old Man and the Sea

4. 主要作品

《春潮》
《三个故事和十首诗》
《我们的时代》
《没有女人的男人们》
《赢家一无所有》
《印第安人营地》
《太阳照常升起》
《永别了，武器》
《死在午后》
《非洲的青山》
《有钱人与没钱人》
《第五纵队》
《丧钟为谁而鸣》
《过河入林》
《老人与海》

5. Analysis of major works

◆*The Sun Also Rises*

The Sun Also Rises (1926) is Hemingway's first important novel, portraying the image of the "Lost Generation". People were trapped in the war trauma and cut off from the old value. Yet they were unable to come to terms with the new era when civilization had gone mad. The characters in the novel are seen wandering pointlessly and restless and impotent. They are absorbed in the material enjoyment of fishing, swimming, bull-fight and sightseeing but are fully aware all the while that the world is meaningless and futile. The protagonist's sense of loss is a symbol of modern man's spiritual impotence.

5. 主要作品分析

◆《太阳照常升起》

《太阳照常升起》是海明威第一部重要的小说。该书描绘了"迷惘的一代"的形象。这一代人处于战后的尴尬年代，旧的价值观业已过时，而新的时代文明已经近乎疯狂，无法与之和解。小说中的人物迷惘、无能为力，逃避现实，沉湎于垂钓、游泳、斗牛和欣赏自然美景中，但他们时刻意识到这个世界已变得疯狂和毫无意义。主人公的迷茫象征着现代人精神上的无能。

◆*A Farewell to Arms*

A Farewell to Arms can be read as a footnote to *The Sun Also Rises*. Set in Spain during the Civil War, the novel shapes the character Frederic Henry who has been to the war field but ironically found out that it was like a horrible slaughterhouse without sacredness and glory. Henry fights single-handedly against overwhelming odds as a typical Hemingway hero of action and few words. He is alone even with other people, somewhat an outsider, who keeps emotion under control. *A Farewell to Arms* reflects the despairing mood of the post-war generation who had lost hope and brings international fame to Hemingway.

◆《永别了，武器》

《永别了，武器》在某种意义上是《太阳照常升起》的注脚。弗瑞德里克·亨利亲历战争，却发现战争毫无神圣光荣可言，而是活生生的屠宰场。亨利孤军奋战，他是典型的海明威式英雄，少言寡语，行动果断。即使与他人在一起，通常表现的是个局外人，善于控制自己的感情。《永别了，武器》反映了一战后普遍存在于西方的失望情绪，为海明威带来了国际声誉。

◆*For Whom the Bell Tolls*

The title of *For Whom the Bell Tolls* come from John Donne's "Meditation XVIII": "Any man's death diminishes me, because I am involved in mankind, and therefore never send to know for whom the bell tolls; it tolls for thee." In this novel, the protagonist Robert Jordan is no longer alone but having a respected career and a cooperating group. More importantly, he has someone to love and die for. The war he is fighting is, for him, a metaphor for a struggle for freedom. It is for democracy that he sacrifices himself. Hemingway foregrounds the theme of human brotherhood in this novel.

◆《丧钟为谁而鸣》

《丧钟为谁而鸣》的标题来自约翰·多恩的《祈祷文集》第18章，"无论谁死了，都是我的一部分在死去，因为我包含在人类这个概念里。因此，不要问丧钟为谁而鸣，丧钟为你而鸣。"在这部小说里，海明威塑造了一个崭新的艺术形象。主人公罗伯特已经不是孑然一身，有了愿为之奋斗的事业，有了可以并肩作战的团队，最重要的是有了他珍爱且愿为之牺牲的爱人。战争对他而言象征了为自由而战。为了民主事业他愿意牺牲自己。在这部小说里海明威突出地反映出人与人之间兄弟情义的主题。

◆*The Old Man and the Sea*

The Old Man and the Sea is a novella about an old Cuban fisherman Santiago and his battle with a great marlin. Santiago represents the spirit of Hemingwayesque individualism, contending with a force which he knows is futile to rebel against. He keeps on fighting because he believes that "a man is not made for defeat. A man can be destroyed but not defeated." However, the old man eventually realizes that he has met his doom because he goes far out alone "beyond all the people in the world". He starts to miss being one of the human group and the natural world. His love for his fellowmen and nature testifies that Hemingway's vision of the world has undergone a profound change.

◆《老人与海》

《老人与海》是海明威著名的中篇小说，它描写了古巴老渔翁圣地亚哥与一条大马林鱼作斗争的故事。在圣地亚哥身上我们看到了海明威式的个人主义。他明知道徒劳无益，但是还是勇于斗争。他奋斗不懈，因为他坚信"人不是注定要失败的，人可以被毁灭，但不能被打败。"但是，老人最终意识到，他独自一人出海，"脱离了世界上所有的人"，于是才遇到厄运。他开始怀念作为人类群体和自然世界中的一员。他开始对人类及自然界的生物产生友爱之情，这充分表明了海明威的世界观发生了重大的变化。

14.2 考研真题与典型题详解

I. Fill in the blanks.

1. Set in Spain during the Civil War, the novel ________ stated again Hemingway's view of love found and lost, and described the indomitable spirit of the common people. (人大2006研)
2. F. Scott Fitzgerald's first novel ________, with its portrayal of casual dissipations of "flaming youth", was an immediate commercial success.
3. F. Scott Fitzgerald summarized the experiences and attitudes of the 1920s decade in his masterpiece novel ________.
4. F. Scott Fitzgerald's second novel ________ describes a handsome young man and his beautiful wife, undoubtedly modelled after himself and Zelda.
5. The hero in F. Scott Fitzgerald's novel ________ is a psychiatrist who marries a rich patient. The author condemns the wasted energy of misguided youth.
6. American writers of the first postwar era self-consciously acknowledged that they were a "________", devoid of faith and alienated from a civilization.
7. In the same way that F. Scott Fitzgerald's *Tales of the Jazz Age* became the symbol for an age, Ernest Hemingway's novel ________ painted the image of a whole generation, the Lost Generation.
8. Ernest Hemingway's stature as a writer was confirmed with the publication of his novel ________ in 1929. The novel portrayed a farewell both to war and to love.
9. In the story *The Old Man and the Sea*, Ernest Hemingway portrayed an old fisherman named ________, who is triumphant even in defeat.
10. In 1954, Ernest Hemingway was awarded a ________ for his "mastery of the art of modern narration".

II. Multiple Choice

1. Which of the following novels is a good illustration of the "Roaring 20s" and hence serves as a "cultural-history allegory" for the America? (首师大2007研)

   A. *A Farewell to Arms*　　B. *The Great Gatsby*
   C. *A Lost Lady*　　D. *The Portrait of a Young Lady*

2. In *The Great Gatsby*, Nick is the narrator who belongs to the type of ________. (首师大2008研)

   A. participant　　B. non-participant
   C. unreliable　　D. innocent eye

3. The following selection is taken from ________. (大连外国语学院2007研)

   A. *Sister Carrie*　　B. *Treasure Island*
   C. *The Great Gatsby*　　D. *Heart of Darkness*

   In my younger and more vulnerable years my father gave me some advice that I've been turning over in my mind ever since. "Whenever you feel like criticizing anyone," he told me, "just remember that all the people in this world haven't had the advantages that you've had."

4. "The lost generation" refers to the writers who relocated to Paris in the post WWI years to reject

the values of American materialism. All the following but ________ are involved in this group.（北二外 2007 研）

A. F. S. Fitzgerald B. Ernest Hemingway

C. Theodore Dreiser D. John Dos Passos

5. Ernest Hemingway is noted for the following EXCEPT ________.（首师大 2008 研）

A. Lost Generation B. iceberg theory

C. American Dream D. "grace under pressure"

6. Among the following writers, who is often acclaimed literary spokesman of the Jazz Age?

A. William Faulkner B. F. Scott Fitzgerald

C. Henry James D. Eugene O'Neill

7. "There was music from my neighbor's house through the summer nights. In his blue gardens men and girls came and went like moths among the whisperings and the champagne and the stars..." This quotation is taken from ________.

A. *Moby Dick* by Herman Melville B. *Daisy Miller* by Henry James

C. *Sister Carrie* by Theodore Dreiser D. *The Great Gatsby* by F. Scott Fitzgerald

8. Which of the following figures does not belong to "The Lost Generation"?

A. Ezra Pound B. William Carlos Williams

C. Robert Frost D. Theodore Dreiser

9. Nick's night trip to the Indian village and his experience inside the hut can be taken as ________.

A. an initiation to pain and suffering B. a confrontation with evil and sin

C. an essential lesson about Indian tribes D. a learning process of human connections

10. Ernest Hemingway was badly wounded in Italy and sent to a hospital where he fell in love with a nurse. These two persons later became the characters of his novel ________.

A. *The old Man and the Sea* B. *For Whom the Bell Tolls*

C. *The Sun Also Rises* D. *A Farewell to Arms*

Ⅲ. Explain the following terms.

1. the Jazz Age（北二外 2009 研；国际关系学院 2007 研；首师大 2009 研）
2. The Lost Generation（浙江大学 2023 研，四川大学 2010 研，北航 2007 研）
3. "Hemingway Heroes"（武汉大学 2008 年）
4. Santiago（北航 2009 研）

Ⅳ. Read the following quotations and answer the questions.

Passage 1（北航 2007 研）

Most of the big shore places were closed now and there were hardly any lights except the shadowy, moving glow of a ferryboat across the Sound. And as the moon rose higher the inessential houses began to melt away until gradually I became aware of the old island here that flowered once for Dutch sailors' eyes-a fresh, green breast of the new world. Its vanished trees, the trees that had made way for Gatsby's house, had once pandered in whispers to the last and greatest of all human dreams; for a transitory enchanted moment man must have held his breath in the presence of this continent, compelled into all aesthetic contemplation he neither understood nor desired, face to face for the last time in history with something commensurate to his capacity for wonder.

And as I sat there brooding on the old, unknown world, I thought of Gatsby's wonder when he first picked out the green light at the end of Daisy's dock. He had come a long way to this blue lawn, and his dream must have seemed so close that he could hardly fail to grasp it. He did not know that it was already behind him, somewhere back in that vast obscurity beyond the city, where the dark fields of the republic rolled on under the night.

Gatsby believed in the green light, the orgiastic future that year by year recedes before us. It eluded us then, but that's no matter-tomorrow we will run faster, stretch out our arms farther And one fine morning—

So we beat on, boats against the current, borne back ceaselessly in to the past.

Questions:

(1) Which fiction is this excerpt from? Who is the author of the novel?

(2) What does "Daisy's dock" stand for?

(3) Why are the Dutch sailors mentioned here? In what way does it contribute to the novel?

Passage 2（北航 2008 研）

In the later summer of that year we lived in a house in a village that looked across the river and the plain to the mountains. In the bed of the river there were pebbles and boulders, dry and white in the sun, and the water was clear and swiftly moving and blue in the channels. Troops went by the house and down the road and the dust they raised powdered the leaves of the trees. The trunks of the trees too were dusty and the leaves fell early that year and we saw the troops marching along the road and the dust rising and leaves, stirred by the breeze, falling and the soldiers marching and afterward the road bare and white except for the leaves.

…

Poor, poor dear Cat. And this was the price you paid for sleeping together. This was the end of the trap. This was what people got for loving each other. Thank God for gas, anyway. What must it have been like before there were anesthetics? Once it started, they were in the mill-race. Catherine had a good time in the time of pregnancy. It wasn't bad. She was hardly ever sick. She was not awfully uncomfortable until toward the last. So now they got her in the end. You never got away with anything, Get away hell! It would have been the same if we had been married fifty times. And what if she should die? She won't die. People don't die in childbirth nowadays. That was what all husbands thought. Yes, but what if she should die? She won't die. She's just having a bad time. Afterward we'd say what a bad time and Catherine would say it wasn't really so bad. But what if she should die.

Questions:

(1) Identify the author and the work from which the passage is selected.

(2) What is the symbolic meaning of the title?

(3) How do you understand the features of heroes in the author's works?

(4) Comment on author's writing style and philosophy underlying all his works?

Passage 3(中山大学 2018 研)

That's my middle west—not the wheat or the prairies or the lost Swede towns but the thrilling, returning trains of my youth and the street lamps and sleigh bells in the frosty dark and, the shadows of holly wreaths thrown by lighted windows on the snow. I am part of that, a little solemn with the feel of those long winters, a little complacent from growing up in the Carraway house in a city where dwellings are still called through decades by a family's name. I see now that this has been a story of the West, after all—Tom and Gatsby, Daisy and Jordan and I, were all Westerners, and perhaps we possessed some deficiency in common which made us subtly unadaptable to Eastern life.

Questions:

(1) Identify the title and the author of the novel from which the above excerpt is taken. Who is the narrator? (3%)

(2) What do "west" and "east" refer to respectively in the excerpt? Explain their symbolic meaning with respect to the social and cultural context of 1920's America. (15%)

V. Short answer questions

1. Why did F. Scott Fitzgerald use "great" to modify the protagonist's name Gatsby in the title of his novel *The Great Gatsby*?（南京大学2009研；人大2006研）
2. What are the most striking features of Hemingway's writing style?（国际关系学院2007研）
3. Why was Fitzgerald regarded as spokesman of the "Jazz Age"?
4. What are the artistic characteristics in Hemingway's novels?

VI. Essay questions

1. The relationship between man and nature is a recurrent theme, and perhaps one of the most important themes, in American literature. Write a short essay on it by contrasting two or three American literary works, or two or three American literary movements, to tell what you know about their different views of nature.（武汉大学2009研）
2. Hemingway's war novel ends with a scene in a maternity hospital. How does this final topic, the death of a woman and a child in childbirth, force us to enlarge or reconsider what we took to be the central subject of the novel? In what sense is the novel a war novel? What is its subject if it is not war, battle, engagement with the enemy, strategy, etc.? Sufficient textual information is required to illustrate your viewpoints.（南京大学2007研）
3. Irving Howe considers *The Great Gatsby* as a prose version of *The Waste Land*. What do you think of this view?（天津外国语学院2009研）

参考答案及解析

I. Fill in the blanks.

1. *For Whom the Bell Tolls*

（海明威的小说《丧钟为谁而鸣》(*For Whom the Bell Tolls*)以西班牙内战为背景，该小说陈述了海明威对爱与失去的观点，描写了普通人不屈不挠的精神。）

2. *This Side of Paradise*

（1920菲茨杰拉德发表第一部长篇小说《人间天堂》，一举成名。书中描写了一战后年轻一代的精神面貌和生活方式。）

3. *The Great Gatsby*

（《了不起的盖茨比》(*The Great Gatsby*)是美国作家弗朗西斯·司各特·菲茨杰拉德所写的

一部以20世纪20年代的纽约市及长岛为背景的小说，被视为美国文学“爵士时代”的象征。该书敏锐地抓住了当代社会生活的主题，并以象征手法展现了“美国梦”传奇之下的嘲讽及悲怅。）

4. *The Beautiful and the Damned*

（1922年菲茨杰拉德的第二部小说《美丽与诅咒》（*The Beautiful and the Damned*）出版。这部小说讲了一个年轻的有钱人，由于婚姻的不幸而导致感情和精神崩溃的故事。书中男女主角无疑是以菲茨杰拉德及其妻子泽尔达为原型而塑造的。）

5. *Tender is the Night*

（菲茨杰拉德的小说《夜色温柔》（*Tender is the Night*）讲述了一个美国精神病医生与一位美丽而又富有的病人结合终遭失败的故事。该小说反映了强烈的怀旧情绪、悔恨心理、失落的希望、破灭的幻想、人格的分裂。）

6. Lost Generation

（第一次世界大战后以海明威为代表的一些美国作家自称是“迷惘的一代”。所谓“迷惘”，是指他们共有的彷徨和失望情绪。这些作家中，大多数人亲身经历过第一次世界大战。在战场上，他们目睹了战争给人类带来的巨大灾难，经历了战争的折磨。）

7. *The Sun also Rises*

（菲茨杰拉德的短篇小说集《爵士乐时代的故事》（*Tales of the Jazz Age*）是爵士时代的标志，而海明威的小说《太阳照样升起》（*The Sun Also Rises*）则刻画了整个“迷惘的一代”的形象。）

8. *A Farewell to Arms*

（海明威的第二部力作是1929年出版的《永别了，武器》（*A Farewell to Arms*）。此书以爱情与战争两条主线，阐述了作者对战争及人生的看法和态度。）

9. Santiago

（《老人与海》（*The Old Man and the Sea*）是海明威最著名的作品之一，小说讲述了一位老年古巴渔夫圣地亚哥（Santiago），与一条巨大的马林鱼在离岸很远的湾流中搏斗的故事，表明了人可以被毁灭，但不能被打败的人生态度。）

10. Nobel Prize

（1954年海明威获诺贝尔文学奖。获奖理由：“因为他精通于叙事艺术，突出地表现在其近著《老人与海》之中；同时也因为他对当代文体风格之影响”。）

II. Multiple Choice

1. B 《了不起的盖茨比》既反映了20世纪20年代美国的精神面貌，也是关于美国的一种文化—历史性的寓言。

2. A 在《了不起的盖茨比》中，尼克既是一个叙述者，又是小说中的一个参与者。

3. C 题中片段选自美国著名小说家Francis Scott Fitzgerald的代表作《了不起的盖茨比》，是小说的开头部分，参考译文为：我年纪还轻，阅历不深的时候，我父亲教导过我一句话，我至今还念念不忘。“每逢你想要批评任何人的时候，”他对我说，“你就记住，这个世界上所有的人，并不是个个都有过你拥有的那些优越条件。”

4. C 菲茨杰拉德、海明威和帕索斯都属于“迷惘的一代”，选项C德莱塞则是一位自然主义作家。

5. C 海明威既是“迷惘的一代”的代表，也是“冰山理论”的提出者，其作品主题不少是关于

"压力之下的优雅"，但他并非"美国梦"的代表作家。

6. B　菲茨杰拉德是爵士乐时代的发言人。

7. D　这段话选自菲茨杰拉德的《了不起的盖茨比》，描写了盖茨比家举办晚会的情景。

8. D　西奥多·德莱赛是自然主义作家，他不属于"迷惘的一代"。

9. A　在《印第安营寨》中尼克开始了解到了人生的痛苦。

10. D　一战期间，海明威在意大利身受重伤，被送进医院。在那里他爱上了一个护士。海明威本人和这个护士日后成为小说《永别了，武器》(*A Farewell to Arms*)主人公人物的原型。

Ⅲ. Explain the following terms.

1. The Jazz Age refers to a period in American history following the end of World War I, continuing through the Roaring Twenties, and ending with the onset of the Great Depression. It marked a period of changing values alongside a soaring stock market. From the vantage point of historical and cultural studies it contrasts with the parallel Roaring Twenties descriptor with its greater emphasis on Modernism in its many forms. The age takes its name from jazz, which saw a tremendous surge in popularity among many segments of society. Among the prominent concerns and trends of the period are the public embrace of technological developments (typically seen as progress)—cars, air travel and the telephone—as well as new modernist trends in social behavior, the arts, and culture. One of the most representative literary works of the Jazz age is American writer F. Scott Fitzgerald's *The Great Gatsby* (1925).

2. The Lost Generation: The "Lost Generation" is a term used to characterize a general motif of disillusionment of American literary notables who lived in Europe, most notably Paris, after the First World War. Figures identified with the "Lost Generation" included authors and artists such as Ernest Hemingway, F. Scott Fitzgerald, Ezra Pound, Sherwood Anderson, Waldo Peirce, John Dos Passos, John Steinbeck, and Cole Porter.

3. "Hemingway Heroes": The works of Ernest Hemingway generally center on the concept of heroism. Each of his novels contains a "Hemingway hero"—a man of honor and integrity who expresses himself with actions rather than words. The Hemingway hero is a noble but tragic hero fighting alone with the overwhelming and unfathomable force; though he knows that he will be defeated at last, he decides to act like a hero.

   A Hemingway hero is not a Godlike figure, but an ordinary, often flawed mortal who must look to himself for strength. The Hemingway hero is actually a mirror image of the author himself. Frederic Henry in *A Farewell to Arms* and Santiago in *The Old Man and the Sea* are typical Hemingway heroes.

4. Santiago is the protagonist of *The Old Man and the Sea*, written by American novelist Ernest Hemingway. He is an old man who hasn't caught any fishes for eighty-four days. On the final journey he has a fight with sharks. This character depicted by Hemingway is a typical "tough guy". Santiago embodies Hemingway's definition of courage as "grace under pressure". He never loses dignity in the face of death. The glory and honor Santiago accrues comes not from his battle itself but from his pride and determination to fight. His famous words are "A man is not made for defeat... a man can be destroyed but not defeated."

Ⅳ. Read the following quotations and answer the questions.

Passage 1

(1) This excerpt is from *The Great Gatsby* by F. S. Fitzgerald.

(2) The green light at the end of Daisy's dock represents Gatsby's hopes and dreams about Daisy. Thus, "Daisy's dock" stands for Daisy and also the American Dream.

(3) The Dutch sailors are connected to the early settlement of the New York area. To the Dutch sailors, America is a place full of wonder and promise where they may fulfill their dreams. The same is for Gatsby who newly becomes a millionaire and wants to gain Daisy's love with his wealth. The Dutch sailors can be taken as an allegory in the novel.

Passage 2

(1) The passage is selected from *A Farewell to Arms* by Ernest Hemingway.

(2) The title has two symbolic meanings: First, it means Henry says goodbye to the war, for the word "arms" has the meaning of "weapon". The second meaning is that Henry says goodbye to his dear wife Catherine Berkley who dies in the hospital. The "arms" also symbolizes Catherine's arms.

(3) Hemingway's world is a world essentially chaotic and meaningless, in which man fights a solitary struggle against an unfathomable force. The Hemingway hero possesses "despairing courage." It is this courage that enables a man to behave like a man, to assert his dignity in face of adversity. The typical Hemingway hero is one who, wounded but strong, enjoys the pleasures of life in face of ruin and death and maintains, through some notion of a code, an ideal of himself. A Hemingway code hero can be destroyed but not defeated.

(4) Hemingway uses short sentences and paragraphs and vigorous and positive language. He always manages to choose words concrete, specific, more commonly found, more Anglo-Saxon, casual and conventional, and employ them often in syntax of short, simple sentences, which are orderly and patterned, conversational, and sometimes ungrammatical. The philosophy underlying his works is Iceberg Principle. Hemingway said: "If a writer of prose knows enough about what he is writing about he may omit things that will have a feeling of those things as strongly as though the writer had stated them. The dignity of movement of an iceberg is due to only one-eighth of it being above water. A good writer does not need to reveal every detail of a character or action."

Passage 3

(1) The title of this novel is *The Great Gatsby* and the author is Fitzgerald. The narrator is Nick.

(2) "East" represents a world of wealth and emptiness. "West" represents traditional ideas and values of American. Nick himself came from a wealthy family in the Midwest. After the war, he returned home from the battlefield. He felt that the Midwest was no longer like the west. So he went to the east to study bond business to make money. However, in less than a year in the east, after witnessing the tragedy of Gatsby and the hypocrisy and fraud of the rich in the east, he felt the east is a cold place. So he returned from the fashionable and corrupt eastern to the boring and chaotic but simple and natural west. This dislocation of ideals indicates the inevitability of the failure of the American dream. The ideal can only be realized in the west. It's im-

possible to realize it in the east. Then the so-called "American dream" has entered a dead end.

V. Short answer questions

1. Gatsby is great because he is able to create a new identity for himself when he needs to be someone else. His determination and audacity are amazing since he focuses on a goal of winning Daisy and he does whatever is necessary to attain it. He establishes that he needs wealth to keep Daisy in the manner she is accustomed to, and so he attains a "business" that gives him financial wealth. What is more, he studies mannerisms and expressions he thinks is what the social elite says and does.

   That Gatsby is great is also because of his unworldly love for Daisy. He takes the blame for Daisy when she commits a crime and that takes a great man.

   Gatsby is great because he is a mythical figure whose personal experience approximates a state of mind that embodies America. Gatsby is the last of the romantic hero, whose energy and sense of commitment take him in search of his personal grail.
2. Hemingway once said, "The dignity of movement of an iceberg is due to only one-eighth of it being above water." He adopts "Iceberg" theory in his own writing. He always manages to choose words concrete, specific, more commonly found, more Anglo-Saxon, casual and conversational, and employ them often in syntax of short, simple sentences, which are orderly and patterned, conversational, and sometimes ungrammatical. But it is good to note that Hemingway's style is also deliberate and polished and is never natural as it seems to be, and its simplicity can be disastrously deceptive, as it is highly suggestive and connotative and capable of offering layers of undercurrents of meaning.
3. Fitzgerald was a representative figure of the 1920s. He never failed to remain detached and foresee the tragedy of the "Dollar Decade." His works mirror the exciting age in almost every way. Through the glittering world of his fiction run the themes of moral waste and decay and necessity of personal responsibility. *The Great Gatsby*, a book about the Jazz Age, is a case study in people's pursuit of an elusive American Dream. It is also a powerful criticism of American society. Thus he is often acclaimed literary spokesman of the Jazz Age.
4. Hemingway's characterization is typical of the "iceberg" analogy in psychoanalysis. According to Hemingway, good literary writing should be able to make readers feel the emotion of the characters directly and the best way to produce the effect is to observe every particular kind of feeling without any authorial comments or conventionally emotive language but with a bare minimum of adjectives and adverbs. Seemingly simply and natural, Hemingway's language style is actually polished and tightly controlled. The outward physical events and sensations express the meaning of the story and convey the complex emotions of his characters with a considerable range and astonishing intensity of feeling. Besides, Hemingway develops the style of colloquialism initiated by Mark Twain. The accents and mannerisms of human speech are so well presented that the characters are full of flesh and blood. The use of short, simple and conversational words and sentences has an effect of clearness, terseness and great care.

Ⅵ. Essay questions

1. American literature can be called a young literature, but American writers take the relationship between man and nature as an important theme with changing views of nature. We can see the subtle change from two literary works: Melville's *Moby Dick* and Hemingway's *The Old Man and the Sea.*

   In *Moby Dick*, the captain Ahab is driven by a monomaniacal desire to kill Moby Dick, the whale that maimed him on the previous whaling voyage. The white whale has also been seen as a symbol for nature and those elements of life that are out of human control. To Ahab, killing the whale becomes the ultimate goal in his life, and this observation can also be expanded allegorically so that the whale represents everyone's goals. Furthermore, his vengeance against the whale is analogous to man's struggle against nature.

   The Old Man and the Sea recounts a battle between an aging Cuban fisherman Santiago and a giant marlin, when he straps the marlin to the side of his skiff and heads home, he finds that sharks are attracted by the marlin's blood and he has to fight against the sharks. In this novel, although Santiago kills fishes to make money and survive, he is friendly and grateful to the creatures in the sea.

   The relationship between man and nature in American literature has changed from conquering nature to making proper use of nature, from taking nature as an enemy to regarding it as a friend. People are realizing that man needs to exist harmoniously with nature.

2. *A Farewell to Arms* is considered to be the greatest war novels of all time, because it reveals the nature of the war. In the novel, the war is not glamorized; instead, it is presented in a very real and horrifying fashion from the perspective of the ambulance driver. At some moments, war is derided as a game for the ruling classes in which the poor suffer. War is only rarely viewed in a patriotic fight and more often seen as tiresome.

   As a nurse, Catherine is able to transfer herself to the hospital where Frederic is recovering. Then, she flees with him to Switzerland where she dies from internal bleeding resulting from a difficult childbirth. In her death she is the picture of heroism and her statements are full of dark humor. "I am not afraid. I just hate it." Concerning this, we can conclude that this novel is also a tragic love story, in which man is doomed to be trapped in difficult situations and in misery.

   Besides the subject of war, the novel also explores the searching of identity. Frederick Henry represents the experience of a whole nation, who is wounded in war and disillusioned with the insanity and futility of the universe. This subject is important to the story because it expresses the general question of the individual in the postwar world. Frederic represents this questioning of what is the force that can cause such awful destruction and human suffering. Frederic's identity is displaced by the late introduction of his name to the reader, the fact of his being an American in an Italian army, and his constant play with words. He speaks Italian, but not well enough. All these examples try to show Frederic does not know who he is.

3. Both *The Great Gatsby* and *The Waste Land* both reflect the loss of an ideal and the disillusionment that people's incorruptible dream is smashed into pieces by the relentless reality. Both of them reflect a world in which desires are filled with, spirits fall down, moral is lost and life is

corrupt. Through the two works, the general disappointment toward reality, world and human civilization are shown. So *The Great Gatsby* interprets *The Waste Land's* theme by the story of Gatsby.

But in another respect, the artistic feature of *The Great Gatsby* is that the language manifests the poetic quality. The style of F. Scott Fitzgerald, closely related to his themes, is explicit and chilly. His accurate dialogues and his sensitive styles provide the reader with a vivid sense of reality. He uses the scenic method in his chapters, each one of which consists of one or more dramatic scenes. Sometimes he intervenes passages of narration, leaving the tedious process of transition to the readers' imagination. He also skillfully chooses a dramatic narrator through whose "central consciousness" everything is delivered to organize the wholeness of the work. The accurate details, the completely original diction and metaphors, the bold impressionistic and colorful quality have all revealed his consummate artistry. His words are like pieces of poems, provoking reader's imagination and placing them in the beauty of poetry. In this sense, *The Great Gatsby* is a prose version of *The Waste Land*.

第 15 章　南方文艺复兴·威廉姆·福克纳

15.1　复习笔记

I. The Southern Renaissance	I. 南方文艺复兴
1. Historical background	**1. 历史背景**
The American south has always been a unique region. Different to the Hamiltonian north, the Jeffersonian south is of its own history and customs, which remind us of the conflict between the two regions in the history. The Civil War is a crucial historical point. After the war, the agricultural south became more subordinate to the industrial north, and the long-existing glaring gap in culture and thinking mode between the two parts contributes even more to the intensity of the north-south relationship. Measures were taken to develop the south so that economic improvements slowly came about. Although the south in many aspects remained conservative, in the field of literature, there glittered a visible spark of revolution. Efforts were taken to reassess the past and the present and self-exploration was carried out. Thus the blooming of southern literature in the 1920s and 1930s was given rise to.	美国南方一直是一个独特的地区。不同于杰斐逊式的北方，哈米尔顿式南方有着自己的历史和风俗，这也提醒我们在美国历史上两个地区间存在的冲突。美国内战是一个关键的历史节点，战后，农业式的南方越发地从属于工业化的北方。这两个地区之间在文化和思维方式上长期存在的显著差距使得南北关系更加紧张。国家采取措施以促进南方发展，其经济方面缓慢地取得了进展。尽管南方在许多方面仍旧保守，在文学上却闪现出了变革的火花，人们努力重新评估过去和现在，并且进行自我探索。这样就推动了 19 世纪二三十年代南方文学的繁荣。
2. Major writers of the South Renaissance	**2. 南方文艺复兴主要作家**
Ellen Glasgow, whose series of novels are featured by the Virginia setting, concentrated more on future rather than keeping casting eyes on the old times. In her novels, such as *Virginia* and *Barren Ground*, the builders of the future of Virginia are depicted in elaboration. Glasgow made her unique contribution to the emergence of William Faulkner.	埃伦·格拉斯高的一系列小说以弗吉尼亚为背景，她更多地关注明天而不是不停地回顾旧时光。在其小说如，《弗吉尼亚》和《不毛之地》中，弗吉尼亚未来的建设者们得到了细致的描绘。格拉斯高为威廉姆·福克纳的出现做出了独有的贡献。
As the most important figure among the Southern Renaissance writers, Faulkner, with altogether 19 novels and countless short stories elaborating on the American south, provided profound scrutiny of the problems deep-rooted in the south. Historically speaking, Faulkner contributed to the Southern Renaissance in the 1920s and helped usher in a whole new group of southern authors of the 1930s such as Katherine Anne Porter, Eudora Welty, and Carson McCullers.	作为南方文艺复兴中最重要的作家，福克纳的 19 部长篇小说和众多短篇小说都与南方息息相关。这些作品详细考察了南方所面临的困境。福克纳竭力为 20 年代南方文艺复兴做出了贡献，并且引领了 30 年代一群新的南方作家。如凯瑟琳·安·波特，尤多拉·韦尔蒂和卡森·麦卡勒斯。

After the WWII, there were a number of younger writers continuing probing into the southern tradition, among whom Flannery O'Connor, William Styron, and Walker Percy are representatives. These writers have endeavored to write about the southern theme and made it evergreen in American literature.

二战后出现了许多继续探索南方文学传统的作家，如弗兰纳里·奥康纳，威廉姆·史泰伦，沃克·珀西等。这些作家保持了南方主题的连续性，使得南方主题在美国文学中常青。

Ⅱ. William Faulkner (1897 – 1962)

Ⅱ. 威廉姆·福克纳

1. Life

1. 生平

Faulkner was born as the eldest of the four sons in a Southern family with a fairly long tradition. The town of Oxford where he was brought up became the prototype for his fictional Jefferson. His own family history was also written into his novels. Faulkner joined the Royal Flying Corps in Canada and was still under training when the war was over. After the military service, he went back home and attended the University of Mississippi for a year, maintaining himself with several odd jobs. His first two novels were not very promising, but *Sartoris* (1929) showed Faulkner's growth and maturity as a promising writer. His next book, *The Sound and the Fury*, was definitely the mature work of a major work, especially for its technical sophistication. In the following years, his major works appeared one after another. In 1946, Malcolm Cowley edited *The Viking Portable Faulkner* with a detailed introduction of his works. Faulkner was gradually seen as the center of critical attention. He won the Nobel Price for literature in 1949.

福克纳出生于一个历史悠久的南方家庭，是家中四个孩子中的长子。他在牛津镇长大，该镇后来成为其小说中虚构的杰斐逊镇的原型。他的家族史也被写进了他的小说中。一战早期他曾在加拿大参加英国陆军航空队，训练未完一战就已结束了。回国后他在密西西比大学就读一年，后做过多种杂工。他的前两部小说并未引起注意，而1929年出版的《沙特里斯》却表现出作为一名前途光明的作家其创作已渐臻成熟。他的下一部《喧哗与骚动》是一部较为成熟的作品，尤其是它复杂的技巧。尔后，他的主要作品陆续出版。1946年文学批评家马尔科姆·考利编辑了他的作品选集《福克纳读本》，并详细介绍他的著作。福克纳成为文学批评界的焦点。福克纳于1949年获得诺贝尔文学奖。

2. Subject matter

2. 创作题材

The Faulkner's oeuvre include altogether 19 novels and three volumes of short stories. In these works the Deep South is depicted in great details. An important part of Faulkner's works has been termed the Yoknapatawpha saga, which tells the histories of a number of southern aristocratic families. In the very rise of these family fortunes, Faulkner already foresees their inevitable fall for the displacement of the Indians

福克纳共创作了19部长篇小说和3本短篇小说集。在这些作品里，福克纳极为细致地刻画了美国南方。福克纳作品中最重要的一部分被称为"约克纳帕特发世家小说"。在这些作品里福克纳描写了许多南方贵族的家族史。在这些家族发迹时福克纳就预示到他们必然的衰落。

and the enslavement of the black race, thus putting a curse upon the land as well as their own fate. When the same narration on the tragic ebb and flow of these families continues to occur novel after novel, it assumes symbolic proportion. Evidently, Faulkner talks about the American south as much as the universal human situation. He conveys the message that the typical spiritual deterioration in modern life derives directly from the loss of love and the unquenchable desire for emotional response.

因为他们剥夺了印第安人的土地，奴役了黑人，使得他们的土地和自己的命运都受到了诅咒。当悲壮的兴衰史在一部部小说中不断呈现时，它就具有了象征性的意义。很显然，福克纳想要表达的不仅仅涉及美国南方，也包括人类普遍的生活状况。福克纳传递了这样的信息：现代生活中典型的精神堕落直接源于爱的缺乏和无法得到满足的对情感回应的欲望。

3. Characteristics of Faulkner's writings

Faulkner was a daring formal experimentalist. He kept evolving his literary strategies so as to be better able to communicate his ideas.

(1) Characterization was, to Faulkner, an essential medium to reveal the multifaceted nature of man. His characterization allowed the characters a maximum degree of autonomy and independence. One of the most important devices to achieve such effect is authorial transcendence, which means the author makes himself invisible by employing a fallible narrator or multiple narrators.

(2) Faulkner is a difficult writer to understand. His novels consist of a large number of interior monologues, many of which are composed through the stream of consciousness technique. Faulkner's words breaks the graphological rules, which are seen running together, lacking capitalization and proper punctuation. As for sentences, they are not always clearly indicated and many long ones are pushed together in peculiar ways. Besides, the pronouns are blurred in reference, causing the texts' perplexity.

(3) Faulkner's prose style ranges from colloquial, regional dialects to highly charged courtroom rhetoric, covering a variety of "registers" of the English language.

(4) Faulkner's power of imagination is extraordinary. Rooting his works in the Deep South, he manages to create a literary milieu of his own through which he tries to transcend the limits of particularity to reach universality. In his works, Faulkner manifests a tendency toward the rhetoric power and vitality of myth and succeeds eventually in elevating plain, down-to-earth stories of human life to the plane of an elaborate mythology.

3. 写作特点

福克纳在形式上大胆地进行创新实验，他不断发展文学策略以更好地表达他的观点。

（1）福克纳极重视人物的塑造，这是他表现人的多面性的关键所在。他给予角色最大程度的自主和独立。为达到这种效果，最重要的一种手段是借助于“作者的超脱”，即通过不可靠的叙事者和多位叙事者的手法使作者本人隐身。

（2）要读懂福克纳是很吃力的事。他的作品里有很多的内心独白，且多用现代意识流技巧来呈现。福克纳的词语打破了语相规则，单词常挤到一块，没有大写和标点符号。在句子层面上，句子意义指代不明，长句子奇怪地堆积到一起。此外，代词的模糊指代加重了其文章的复杂性。

（3）福克纳散文的语言风格包含日常口语，地方方言，又有规范的文学语言，涵盖了英语语言的多个语域。

（4）福克纳的想象力异常丰富。他把作品植根于美国南部历史，创造出一种独特的文学氛围，最终超越具体的人或事的局限而触及普遍性的问题。在其作品中福克纳展现了逐步向神话的修辞力量和生命力运动的趋势，他成功地把人生的简单却真实的故事提高到神话的高度。

4. Major works

The Marble Faun
Soldier's Pay
Mosquitoes
Sartoris
The Sound and Fury
Sanctuary
Light in August
Absalom, Absalom!
Go Down, Moses
"A Rose for Emily"
The Unvanquished
Knight's Gambit
As I Lay Dying
The Wild Palms
Requiem for a Nun
The Hamlet

5. Analysis of major work

◆*The Sound and the Fury*

The Sound and the Fury (1929) is Faulkner's fourth novel. The title is taken from Macbeth's lines in Shakespeare's *Macbeth* "It (life) is a tale / Told by an idiot, full of sound and fury, / Signifying nothing." The novel details the destruction and downfall of the aristocratic Compson family from four different points of view. There is enough despair and nihilism but not much love and emotion in this sad story of the Compsons. The whole novel is divided into four sections. The first three are presented from the perspectives of the three Compson sons: Benjamin ("Benjy"), the "idiot"; Quentin, the suicidal student; and Jason, the failed businessman. The fourth section has a third-person omniscient narrator. All but the second section are set in fictional Yoknapatawpha County, Mississippi, in April 1928.

It is a story of deterioration from the past to the present. The past is idealized to form a striking contrast with the loveless present. There is in the book an acute feeling of nostalgia toward the happy past. Through Benjy' narration Faulkner highlights the theme of loss. Quentin's suicide could be regarded as an example of a thorough negation of the present. To some extent, Quentin's value system may reflect Faulkner's own view towards an ideal way of life, that of an antebellum society. Through the selfish and heartless individual Jason, the triumph of rationalism over feeling and compassion is best illustrated.

4. 主要作品

《玉石雕像》
《士兵的报酬》
《蚊群》
《沙特里斯》
《喧哗与骚动》
《圣殿》
《八月之光》
《押沙龙，押沙龙!》
《去吧，摩西》
《献给艾米丽的玫瑰花》
《不败者》
《马弃兵》
《我弥留之际》
《野棕榈》
《修女安魂曲》
《村子》

5. 主要作品分析

◆《喧哗与骚动》

《喧哗与骚动》是福克纳的第四本小说。标题选自莎士比亚的《麦克白》中麦克白的台词，"人生如痴人说梦，充满着喧哗与躁动，却没有任何意义。"小说从四个不同的视角详细讲述了贵族康普生家族的毁灭和衰落。在康普生一家悲剧性的故事里没有爱与情感，弥漫着绝望情绪和虚无主义。整部小说分为四个部分。前三部分是从康普生家族三个儿子的角度呈现的：本杰明("班吉")，"白痴"；昆汀，自杀的学生；杰森，失败的商人。第四部分出现了第三人称全知叙述者。除了第二部分之外，其余部分都以 1928 年 4 月密西西比的约克纳帕塔法县为背景。

故事讲述了从过去到现在的堕落。过去被人为地理想化了，与现在的冷酷无情形成了强烈的对比。书中充满了强烈的怀旧之情。通过班吉的叙述作者渲染了"失去"这一主题。昆丁的自杀可被视作对现在的完全否定的一个例证。在某种程度上，昆丁的价值体系折射了福克纳本人关于理想生活方式，即战前社会的看法。在自私自利的杰生的身上，我们看到理性战胜了情感与同情之心。

15.2 考研真题与典型题详解

I. Fill in the blanks.

1. __________ wrote about the disintegration of the old social system in the American Southern States and its effect on the lives of modern people, both black and white.（人大 2006 研）
2. In his novel, William Faulkner has invented a county named __________ and the seat of the county __________.（国际关系学院 2009 研）
3. The works written by __________ may be viewed as a culmination of the development of twentieth-century southern fiction.
4. Quentin is a character in William Faulkner's novel __________.
5. Joe Christmas is a character in William Faulkner's novel __________.

II. Multiple Choice

1. William Faulkner is NOT the writer of __________.（北二外 2008 研）
   A. *Herzog*　　B. *A Rose for Emily*
   C. *As I Lay Dying*　　D. *Go Down, Moses*
2. The author of *The Sound and the Fury* also wrote __________.（大连外国语学院 2008 研）
   A. *Billy Budd*　　B. *As I Lay Dying*　　C. *Sea Wolf*　　D. *Dangling Man*
3. Of the four Compson Children, __________'s life embodies all the vices of the modern world.（天津外国语学院 2009 研）
   A. Quentin　　B. Caddy　　C. Jason　　D. Benjy
4. Among the many novels written by William Faulkner, the title of __________ is associated with the Bible.（首师大 2008 研）
   A. *The Sound and the Fury*　　B. *Absalom, Absalom!*
   C. *As I Lay Dying*　　D. *Light in August*
5. Which of the following is not written by William Faulkner?（首师大 2007 研）
   A. *The Sound and the Fury*　　B. *For Whom the Bell Tolls*
   C. *Light in August*　　D. *Hamlet*
6. The fictional place that bears marked similarities to the town where __________ had been raised was called by himself his "little postage stamp of native soil".
   A. William Styron　　B. Mark Twain
   C. William Faulkner　　D. John Barth
7. Which of the following is not a theme of *The Sound and the Fury*?
   A. The decline of a family　　B. The South vs. the North
   C. The past vs. the present　　D. racial problems
8. Thomas Sutpen is a character in William Faulkner's novel __________.
   A. *Absalom, Absalom!*　　B. *Light in August*
   C. *Go Down, Moses*　　D. *The Sound and the Fury*
9. __________ is about Thomas Sutpen's attempt to found a Southern dynasty.
   A. *Soldier's Pay*　　B. *Absalom, Absalom!*
   C. *The Sound and the Fury*　　D. *Light in August*

10. ________ is said to be a "historical novel" by Faulkner.

A. *Go Down, Moses*　　B. *Light in August*

C. *The Sound and the Fun*　　D. *Absalom, Absalom*

Ⅲ. Explain the following terms.

1. Southern Renaissance（北二外 2010 研；北航 2008 研）
2. Yoknapatawpha（四川外国语大学 2023 研；北航 2007 研）
3. Multiple point of view

Ⅳ. Read the following quotations and answer the questions.

Passage 1（首师大 2009 研）

So she vanquished them, horse and foot, just as she had vanquished their fathers thirty years before about the smell. That was two years after her father's death and a short time after her sweet-heart—the one we believed would marry her—had deserted her. After her father's death she went out very little; after her sweetheart went away, people hardly saw her at all. A few of the ladies had the temerity to call, but were not received, and the only sign of life about the place was the Negro man—a young man then—going in and out with a market basket.

Questions:

(1) What is the title of this work?

(2) What is the theme of the whole work?

Passage 2

Then we noticed that in the second pillow was the indentation of a head. One of us lifted something from it, and leaning forward, that faint and invisible dust dry and acrid in the nostrils, we saw a long strand of iron-gray hair.

Questions:

(1) Which short story is this passage taken from?

(2) What is the identity of the narrator "us"?

(3) Whose is the iron-gray hair?

(4) What causes the indentation in the pillow?

(5) Is the story a tragedy or a comedy?

V. Short answer questions

1. Which of William Faulkner's works impresses you most? Why?（国际关系学院 2007 研）
2. Where did William Faulkner usually locate his stories? What does the place stand for?
3. In what way is William Faulkner called a Southern writer?
4. Discuss William Faulkner's style.

Ⅵ. Essay questions

1. In what way is Emily Grierson a monument of tradition?（天津外国语学院 2009 研）
2. William Faulkner once said, "she [Caddy Compson] was the beautiful one", "She was my heart's darling. That's what I wrote the book about and I used the tools which seemed to me the proper tools to try to tell, try to draw the picture of Caddy." How do you understand Faulkner's appraisal of Caddy?（天津外国语学院 2007 研）
3. Analysis of William Faulkner's *The Sound and the Fury*.

参考答案及解析

I. Fill in the blanks.

1. William Faulkner

（福克纳的作品主要是关于美国南方的沉浮。在这中间，黑人和白人，南方与北方，农业和工业之间发生剧烈的摩擦和冲动。结果是腐朽的古老传统被新兴的资本势力所击败，急剧的演变过程中形形色色的人物终不免成为客观势力和主观弱点的牺牲品。）

2. Yoknapatawpha；the town of Jefferson

（福克纳在自己的一系列著作中虚构了位于密西西比州北部的约克纳帕塔法县，这个县的中心是杰斐逊镇。）

3. William Faulkner

（威廉·福克纳的作品可以看做是20世纪美国南方小说发展的巅峰之作。）

4. *The Sound and the Fury*

（昆丁（Quentin）是威廉·福克纳小说《喧哗与骚动》（*The Sound and the Fury*）中的人物，同时也是该小说第三部分的叙述者。）

5. *Light in August*

（《八月之光》（*Light in August*）是威廉·福克纳写的一部批判种族主义的小说。乔·克里斯默斯（Joe Christmas）是该小说的主人公。

II. Multiple Choice

1. A　*Herzog*（《赫索格》）的作者是Saul Bellow（索尔·贝娄），其余选项都是福克纳的作品。

2. B　《喧嚣与骚动》的作者是美国作家威廉·福克纳，他其他的重要作品还有：*As I Lay Dying*（《我弥留之际》），*Light in August*（《八月之光》）、*Absalom, Absalom*!（《押沙龙！押沙龙》），*Go Down, Moses*（《去吧，摩西》）等。*Billy Budd*（《比利·巴德》）是Herman Melville（赫尔曼·梅尔维尔）的作品；*Sea Wolf*（《海狼》）的作者是Jack London（杰克·伦敦）；*Dangling Man*（《晃来晃去的人》）是Saul Bellow（索尔·贝娄）的小说。

3. C　《喧哗与骚动》是福克纳第一部成熟的作品，讲述的是南方没落地主康普生一家的家族悲剧。长子昆丁绝望地抱住南方所谓的旧传统不放，因妹妹凯蒂风流成性、有辱南方淑女身份而恨疚交加，竟至溺水自杀。次子杰生冷酷贪婪，三子班吉则是个白痴，三十三岁时只有三岁小儿的智能。本书通过这三个儿子的内心独白，围绕凯蒂的堕落展开，最后则由黑人女佣迪尔西对前三部分的"有限视角"作补充，归结全书。小说大量运用多视角叙述方法及意识流手法，是意识流小说乃至整个现代派小说的经典名著。

4. B　在福克纳的小说中，《押沙龙，押沙龙！》的题目是和圣经有关的，因为押沙龙是旧约里的一个人物，是大卫的儿子。

5. B　《丧钟为谁而鸣》的作者是海明威。选项D《村子》是福克纳的斯诺普斯三部曲的第一部。

6. C　福克纳小说中虚构的地方与他长大的地方有很多相似之处，被他称为"乡土的微型邮票"。

7. D　《喧哗与骚动》中涉及到了家族的衰落、南方与北方、过去与现在的主题，但是种族主义不是主要方面。

8. A　托马斯·塞德潘（Thomas Sutpen）是威廉·福克纳小说《押沙龙，押沙龙！》中的主人公。

9. B 《押沙龙，押沙龙!》是最复杂、深奥，最具史诗风格的一部作品。它讲述的是美国南方一个家族从1860年到1910年左右所经历的激烈的分崩离析的故事，深刻地表现了人与人、人与自己内心的种种冲突，触及与人类境遇有关的诸多普遍性的问题。

10. D 福克纳称《押沙龙，押沙龙!》是一部历史小说。

Ⅲ. Explain the following terms.

1. The Southern Renaissance (also known as Southern Renascence) was the reinvigoration of American Southern literature that began in the 1920s and 1930s with the appearance of writers such as William Faulkner, Caroline Gordon, Elizabeth Madox Roberts, Katherine Anne Porter, Allen Tate, Tennessee Williams, and Robert Penn Warren, among others. The major themes in their works are: the South's conservative culture; the South's troubled history in regards to racial issues and the burden of history in a place where many people still remembered slavery, Reconstruction, and a devastating military defeat. These writers also brought new modernistic techniques such as stream of consciousness and complex narrative techniques to their works.
2. Yoknapatawpha is a fictional county created by American author William Faulkner as a setting for many of his novels. It is widely believed by scholars that Lafayette County, Mississippi is the basis for Yoknapatawpha County. Faulkner would often refer to it as "my apocryphal county." Yoknapatawpha is located in northwestern Mississippi and its seat is the town of Jefferson. This fictional county is bounded on the north by the Tallahatchie River and on the south by the Yoknapatawpha River.
3. Point of view is the vantage point from which a narrative is told. Novels sometimes, but infrequently, mix point of views. The American writer William Faulkner is a master at presenting multiple points of view, showing within the same story how characters react differently to the center and various points of view radiating from it. This technique makes it difficult for the reader to see the truth of the story.

Ⅳ. Read the following quotations and answer the questions.

Passage 1

(1) The title of the work is "A Rose for Emily".

(2) The main theme of "A Rose for Emily" is the decline of the Old South after the Civil War. Emily was treated as the monument of the tradition. After the Civil War, the south began to crumble under the crash of northern industrialization. The old buildings were torn and the old social system collapsed. The most important was that people's ideas were changed. Another theme of this story is community vs. isolation which is related to the relationship between Emily and the town people. Emily's seemingly eccentric behaviors were actually evidence that she was alienated by the whole town.

Passage 2

(1) The passage is taken from "A Rose for Emily" by William Faulkner.

(2) "us" in this passage refers to the townspeople in Jefferson.

(3) The iron-gray hair is Emily's.

(4) Emily sleeps every night besides Homer—her lover's corpse. It is her head that causes the indentation in the pillow.

(5) The story is a tragedy.

V. Short answer questions

1. In my opinion, *The Sound and the Fury* is the most impressing novel of William Faulkner. It tells a story of deterioration from the past to the present. The past is idealized to form a striking contrast with the loveless present. There is enough despair and nihilism but not much love and emotion in this novel.
2. Faulkner usually located his stories in a fictional town called Jefferson in the fictional Yoknapatawpha County.
   With his imagination, Faulkner turned the land, the people and the history of the place into a literary creation and a mythical kingdom, which stands for the American South. The Yoknapatawpha County fiction has an overall pattern in which Faulkner's protagonists collide with the twentieth century society. Most of the major themes are directly related to this confrontation in Faulkner's fiction.
3. Faulkner is called a Southern writer in that most of Faulkner's works are set in the South. His works have managed to show a panorama of the experience and consciousness of the whole Southern society both before and after the Civil War. Though Faulkner set his works in the South, his concern was always with the general human situation.
4. William Faulkner is among the most challenging American writers of the twentieth century. He is known as a novelist of great importance. His novels are exclusively celebrated for the narrative technique he has employed in his works. He always structures his stories in his original fashion and is proficient in employing a distinctive narrative method of gradually fitting in and withholding or even giving confusing information. Gradually confusions vanish as context and periphery are defined and the center is revealed. Faulkner also used a naturalistic or more conventional prose form as well for much of his work. Most of his novels and stories offer a combination between naturalistic prose and stream-of-consciousness. There are a lot of interior-monologues; the modern stream of consciousness technique is frequently and skillfully used. Words often run together, with no capitalization and no proper punctuation. Faulkner is well-known for his stylistically complex sentence structure. The complicity of sentence structures parallels the complexity of the thoughts of his characters. Sentences are not always clearly indicates; many long ones are pushed together in peculiar ways. One fragment runs into another without proper notice, and added to all this, is the use of pronouns which often causes irritating perplexity. For his handling of language, Faulkner's prose ranges from colloquial, regional dialects to highly charged courtroom rhetoric, covering a variety of registers of the English language. Faulkner was a master of his own particular style of writing.

VI. Essay questions

1. Emily Grierson, the main character in "A Rose for Emily" by William Faulkner, represents the tradition of the south. Firstly, she is the representative of the high class of southern society which is crumbling. Social class is the typical production of southern tradition and her family is a typical upper-class family. Her father did a special contribution to the town during the war which gained respects of government. Her family members have eccentric temper which is thought understanda-

ble for royal family. Standing in the garages and cotton gins, her house is the only building of the old time. Secondly, she is living in a traditional way which is worshiped by old men in the town. She lived with a black servant, having no tax to the town. Thirdly, she has the hereditary obligation upon this town which is the spirit core of the southern tradition. According to her obligation, she can't marry man from north and low class, which buried her love at last. This is the root of her tragedy. Fourthly, she rejects advance of society, new life value and locks herself in her big, old house as the only rejection in the whole town. Though people all begin to live in a new way ignoring the old tradition, they sent Emily as their representative of the vanishing past. Faulkner saw the north industrialization eroding the south tradition day after day and set Emily as the monument to fight against it which is in vain finally.

2. According to Faulkner, Caddy Compson is the true hero of *The Sound and the Fury*. She is the second Compson child, a strong-willed yet caring woman. She is Benjy's only real caregiver and Quentin's best friend. Caddy never develops a voice, but rather allows her brothers' emotions towards her to develop her character.

   The first section of the novel is narrated by Benjamin Compson, a source of shame to the family due to his mental retardation; the only characters who evidence a genuine care for him are Caddy, his older sister; and Dilsey, a matriarchal servant. From Benjy's memory we know that Caddy is very kind and caring.

   In the second section, we understand Quentin's feeling about Caddy. He is obsessed with southern ideals of chivalry and is strongly protective of women, especially his sister Caddy. He could protect his sister by joining her in whatever punishment she might have to endure. He is depressed on hearing the sexual affairs of Caddy, and finally kills himself.

   Through the memories of her brothers, the voice of Caddy becomes clear. In fact, the whole story is told by different people, all around Caddy. She is the most active and attractive one of the Compson family, as well as the favorite character of Faulkner in the novel.

3. *The Sound and the Fury* is William Faulkner's best novel. The title is taken from Macbeth's lines in Shakespeare's *Macbeth* "It (life) is a tale / Told by an idiot, full of sound and fury, / Signifying nothing." There is enough despair and nihilism but not much love and emotion in this sad story of the Compsons. One of the overarching themes of the book is the decline of the Compson family, which also acts as a symbol of the decline of the South itself. Mr. Compson is disenchanted with life and the society he lives in. Unable to find meaning in the moral verities he was brought up with, he escapes into alcoholism and cynicism. Mrs. Compson is spiritually effete and has little love to spare for her children. Of the four children, Caddy is the only one capable of loving, but she loses her virginity. The youngest brother, Benjy, is an idiot, a curse on the family. Another, Quentin, lives in the ideal world of his youth with his dreams of love, honor, and integrity, and, when he fails to keep off the intrusion of the "loud, harsh world", he destroys himself. The life of the eldest brother, Jason, is empty and meaningless. Love is alien to him, and so are other traditional humanistic values.

   It is one of the first modernist works to apply the stream of consciousness and objective correlative literary techniques. The nonlinear story is told from the perspectives of the three Compson brothers between 1910 and 1928: Benjy, Jason, and Quentin. A fourth unnamed narrator gives a third-person account of the family's live-in maid, Dilsey. It is a story of deterioration from the past to the present. The past is idealized to form a striking contrast with the loveless present. There is in the book an acute feeling of nostalgia toward the happy past. Through Benjy' narration Faulkner highlights the theme of loss. Quentin's suicide could be regarded as an example of a thorough negation of the present. To some extent, Quentin's value system may reflect Faulkner's own view towards an ideal way of life, that of an antebellum society. It is through the selfish and heartless individual Jason, the triumph of rationalism over feeling and compassion is best illustrated.

第16章 安德森·斯坦·刘易斯·凯瑟·沃尔夫

16.1 复习笔记

I. Sherwood Anderson (1876 –1941)

1. Life

Sherwood Anderson was born in Ohio. At the age of 36, he had a successful career and a happy family. But he always felt uneasy and obsessed with literary creation. Therefore, he later engaged in business during the day and wrote in the evening. One day, he suddenly left the office in the middle of a dictation and never came back. People found him in a poor mental state and wandering around. He then was sent to the hospital. After that, he gave up business and started his literary career.

2. Literary contributions

(1) In terms of themes, Anderson showed the courage to explore the new material of novel creation, namely the psychological and emotional aspects of life in small American towns. He focused on low-level figures, such as losers, fallen ones, and people who were not good at expressing. His classic work *Winsburg, Ohio* is a good example.

(2) In terms of technique, Anderson was an original writer who relies on inspiration to create. He observed the grotesque behaviors of human beings from the perspective of Freudian psychoanalysis, thus trying to accurately reveal the abnormal psychological conditions of the characters.

(3) Anderson was probably the first writer who used oral language to create after Mark Twain. He believed that daily language was a reliable medium. His writing style was known for being clear, direct and deceptively simple. This style had a great influence on Hemingway and Faulkner.

I. 舍伍德·安德森

1. 生平

舍伍德·安德森出生于俄亥俄州。36岁时他已经事业成功，家庭幸福。但是他总觉内心不安，着迷于文学创作。故后来白天从事经营事业，晚上时间写作。一天，他在默写时，突然停下来离开了办公室，然后再也没有回来。人们发现他精神混乱、四处游荡，并把他送到了医院。之后，他永远地告别了商界，并开始了他的文学生涯。

2. 文学贡献

（1）在主题方面，安德森勇于挖掘小说创作的新素材，即美国小镇生活中的心理和情感层面。他着重关注底层人物，诸如失败者、堕落者和不善表达的人等。他的经典作品《小城畸人》就是很好的例证。

（2）技巧方面，安德森是原创性的作家，他依靠灵感进行创作。他从佛洛依德心理分析的角度观察人类的怪诞行为，从而试图准确地揭示人物反常的心理状况。

（3）安德森是继马克·吐温之后运用口头语言进行创作的首位作家。他认为日常用语是一种可靠的媒介。他的写作风格以清晰，直接和貌似简单著称。这种风格对后来的海明威和福克纳产生了很大影响。

3. Major works

Windy McPherson's Son

Marching Men

Winesburg, Ohio

The Triumph of the Egg

Horses and Men

Death in the Woods

Poor White

Many Marriages

Dark Laughter

Kit Brandon

A Story-Teller's Story

Tar: A Midwest Childhood

"Hands"

"Paper Pills"

"Mother"

"I Want to Know Why"

3. 主要作品

《饶舌的迈克逊的儿子》

《前进中的人们》

《小城畸人》

《鸡蛋的胜利》

《马和人》

《林中之死》

《穷白人》

《许多婚姻》

《暗笑》

《吉特·布兰登》

《讲故事人的故事》

《中西部的童年》

《双手》

《纸团》

《母亲》

《我想知道为什么》

Ⅱ. Gertrude Stein (1874–1946)

Gertrude Stein is famous in the history of literature firstly for her work, and secondly for being a patron of art and literature.

Ⅱ. 格特鲁德·斯坦

格特鲁德·斯坦在文学史上出名一是因为她的作品，二是因为她是艺术和文学的赞助人。

1. Life

Gertrude Stein was born in a well-to-do family. Relying on her inheritance, she was able to live a comfortable life in Paris. She graduated from Radcliffe College, and her amazing abstract thinking left a deep impression on her writing teachers. She also studied psychology courses offered by William James, the brother of novelist Henry James. She worked hard throughout her life and created more than 50 works. She often gave lectures on her literary theory at Cambridge University and Oxford University. In 1934 she returned to the United States to give a lecture tour.

1. 生平

格特鲁德·斯坦生于富贵之家。依靠继承的遗产她得以在巴黎过着舒适的生活。她毕业于拉德克利夫学院，大学时其惊人的抽象思维给写作老师留下很深的印象。她还听过小说家亨利·詹姆斯的哥哥威廉姆·詹姆斯开设的心理课程。她终生笔耕不辍，共著有50余部作品。她经常在剑桥大学和牛津大学举办讲座阐述她的文学理论。1934年她回美国做了一次巡回演讲。

2. Literary contributions

Stan did several things to make a name for herself in the history of American literature.

(1) She had a keen mind and was sensitive to the trend of the age and subtle changes. She believed that life after the First World War was different, in this way, art and literature should also make corresponding changes in the way of expressing life. She made many contributions in leading the new modern era of literature.

2. 文学贡献

斯坦做过的几件事情足以让她在美国文学史上留名。

(1) 她思想敏锐，意识到了时代趋势和微妙的变化。她认为一战后的生活与战前不一样了，因此艺术和文学在表现生活的方式上也应作出相应的改变。她在引领新的文学现代时期上做出了很多贡献。

(2) Another thing worthy of praise is her literary theory and practice. Her literary theories were well explained in her work *How to Write*. Her works show the spirit and modernity of her courage to experiment.	(2) 另一件值得称道的是她的文学理论与实践。她的文学理论在其作品《写作指南》上得到了很好地阐释。她的作品显示出其勇于尝试的精神和现代性。
3. Major works *Three lives* "The Good Anna" "The Gentle Lena" "Melanctha" *Tender Buttons* *The Making of Americans* *How to Write* *Four Saints in Three Acts* *The Autobiography of Alice b. Toklas* "Sacred Emily" "Picasso"	**3. 主要作品** 《三个女人》 《好人安娜》 《温和的丽娜》 《米兰克莎》 《温柔的纽扣》 《美国人的成长》 《写作指南》 《三幕剧里的四仙人》 《爱丽丝 · B. 托克拉斯的自传》 《神圣的艾米莉》 《毕加索》
Ⅲ. Sinclair Lewis (1885 – 1951)	**Ⅲ. 辛克莱 · 刘易斯**
1. Life Sinclair Lewis was the first American writer to win the Nobel Prize for literature. He was born in a middle-class family in central Sauk, Minnesota. Lewis has been ruthlessly satirizing this class all his life while at the same time affirming some of its virtues. He started writing when he was in college. After graduating from Yale University, he spent a few years in a row, during which he had been working hard to write and tried to publish novels. From 1912 to 1919, his five novels were published. It was not until the publication of his sixth novel *Main Street* in the summer of 1920. He then became famous all over the world. In the next ten years, Lewis was on the rise. He became famous in Europe and won the Nobel Prize in 1930. He reached the pinnacle of his literary career in 20 years. However, after that, he started to go downhill. He is now known as the worst important writer in the history of American literature.	**1. 生平** 辛克莱 · 刘易斯是第一位获得诺贝尔文学奖的美国作家。他出生在明尼苏达州索克中心镇一个中产阶级家庭。刘易斯一生都在对这个阶级进行无情的讽刺，同时又肯定它的某些美德。他在大学时便开始写作。他从耶鲁大学毕业以后，闯荡了一些年，然而他一直努力写作并试图发表小说。从 1912 年到 1919 年，他共发表了五部小说，直到 1920 年夏天他的第六部小说《大街》问世，他才得以闻名天下。此后十年间，刘易斯平步青云。他开始享誉欧洲，并于 1930 年获得诺贝尔奖。他在 20 年间爬到了文学生涯的顶峰。然而，在那以后，他就开始走下坡路。现在他被称作美国文学史上最差劲的重要作家。
2. Literary contribution Lewis is a sociological writer, and his works are an integral part of American social history. Lewis learned and introduced the American middle class in decades. He explained the American middle class to the world and coined a word, "Babbitt", which has been included in the English dictionary as a synonym for "vulgar and philistine businessman".	**2. 文学贡献** 刘易斯是位社会学型作家，他的作品是美国社会史的组成部分。刘易斯在几十年内了解和介绍了美国中产阶级。他向世人解释了美国中产阶级，并且创造了一个词，"巴比特"，这个词已经作为"庸俗低级的商人"的同义词而被列进英文字典里。

3. His limitations On the subject, he affirmed certain virtues of the middle class, which seems to be rather old-fashioned. In terms of style, his novels are too scattered, lacking order and artistry. In addition, his external description is very accurate, but lacks psychological exploration. In the atmosphere of post-war experimentalism, Lewis appeared to be too conservative and outdated. Even now, critics and readers still have the same impression of him.	**3. 局限性** 在主题方面，他肯定中产阶级的某些美德，这使他显得太过时。在风格上，他的小说过于散乱，缺乏秩序和艺术性。此外，他对外在的描写十分准确，但缺乏心理上的探究。在战后实验主义的氛围中，刘易斯显得过于守旧和过时。即便是现在，评论家和读者对他的印象仍是如此。
4. Major Works *Main Street* *Babbitt* *Arrowsmith* *Dodsworth* *Elmer Gantry*	**4. 主要作品** 《大街》 《巴比特》 《阿罗斯密斯》 《多兹沃斯》 《艾尔默·甘特里》
Ⅳ. Willa Cather (1873 – 1947) **1. Life** Willa Cather was born in Virginia. At the age of 9, she moved with her family to Nebraska and grew up in a western prairie town. In her later novels, the lifestyle in Old West became the moral judgment standard for measuring the current living conditions. She was a traditional writer who refused to accept the modern life. She once claimed that 1922 or thereabouts, the world broke into two. She seemed to live between the two worlds, trying to escape into the past. All her main works were portrayals of her ambivalence in life.	**Ⅳ. 薇拉·凯瑟** **1. 生平** 薇拉·凯瑟生于弗吉尼亚州，9岁时随家人移居到内布拉斯加州，在西部大草原乡镇里长大。在其后来的小说中大西部成为衡量现在生存状况的道德评判标准。薇拉是传统型的作家，她拒绝接受现代生活。她曾说过，在1922年前后，世界已一分为二，她似乎生活在两个世界之间，力图逃避到过去的日子里去。她的主要作品都是她在生活中这种矛盾心理的写照。
2. Major works *My Antonia* *The song of the Lark* *A Lost Lady* *The Professor's House* *Death Comes for the Archbishop* *Shadows on the Rock*	**2. 主要作品** 《我的安东妮亚》 《百灵鸟之歌》 《迷途的女人》 《教授的住宅》 《大教主之死》 《磐石上的阴影》
Ⅴ. Thomas Wolfe (1900 – 1938) **1. Characteristics** (1) Wolfe's works are mostly autobiographical, which reveal his personal emotions. Therefore, his writing art is close to confession.	**Ⅴ. 托马斯·沃尔夫** **1. 特点** (1) 沃尔夫的作品多是自传性质的，其中表露了他个人的情感，因而他的写作艺术接近于自白性质。

(2) He is an extremely aspiring writer. He takes every aspect of American life as his novel writing material. (3) He is an original writer, and the strengths and weaknesses in his writing are unique to him personally.	(2)他是一个极有抱负的作家，他把美国生活的方方面面都当做他的小说写作范畴。 (3)他是一位原创性的作家，他的写作中有力之处与薄弱之处都是属于他个人独有的。
2. Major works *Look Homeward, Angel* *Of Time and the River* *The web and The Rock* *You Can't Go Home Again*	**2. 主要作品** 《天使望故乡》 《时间与河流》 《网与石》 《你不能再回家》

16.2 考研真题与典型题详解

I. Fill in the blanks.

1. *Winesburg*, *Ohio* was written by ________. (大连外国语学院 2007 研)
2. Two writers played important roles in making Faulkner what he later became. ________ helped him to write and publish his first novel *Soldier's Pay* and ________ was his idol and inspired him to write creatively.
3. The author of *Main Street* is ________.

II. Multiple Choice

1. Which of the following pairs concerning the writer and the main setting in his/her works is incorrect? (天津外国语学院 2009 研)
   A. Kate Chopin——Louisana　　B. Willa Cather——Georgia
   C. O Henry——New York　　D. Sherwood Anderson——Ohio
2. Among the following writers, ________ is best known for his sensitive depiction of the American small-town life. (首师大 2007 研)
   A. Henry James　　B. Sherwood Anderson
   C. Stephen Crane　　D. Ernest Hemingway
3. Which of the following techniques is NOT typical of Gertrude Stein's?
   A. Automatic writing
   B. Minimalist style
   C. Frequent use of repetition and reiteration
   D. Circular movement in story-telling
4. Sinclair Lewis' *Babbitt* presents a documentary picture of the narrow and limited ________.
   A. up-class mind　　B. middle-class mind
   C. proletarian　　D. ordinary people
5. The first American to win the Nobel Prize for Literature was a sharp social critic, whose name was ________.
   A. Sinclair Lewis　　B. Thomas Stearns Eliot
   C. Ernest Hemingway　　D. William Faulkner

6. Which of the following works is NOT written by Willa Cather?

A. *The Song of the Lark*　　B. *O Pioneers*

C. *House of Mirth*　　D. *Shadows on the Rock*

III. Essay questions

1. Comment briefly on the contribution Sherwood Anderson made to American literature.
2. Comment on the contribution of Gertrude Stein to American Literature.

参考答案及解析

I. Fill in the blanks.

1. Sherwood Anderson

(《俄亥俄州的温斯堡》(或译《小城畸人》)是美国二十世纪早期小说家舍伍德·安德森(Sherwood Anderson)的一部著名小说。)

2. Sherwood Anderson; James Joyce

(安德森和乔伊斯对福克纳的文学创作产生了很大影响。)

3. Sinclair Lewis

(《大街》的作者是辛克莱·刘易斯，他是第一个获得诺贝尔文学奖的美国人。)

II. Multiple Choice

1. B　薇拉·凯瑟是美国著名女作家，以自幼所熟悉的西部边疆生活为题材，创作富有地方特色的作品，而 Georgia 是美国东南部的州。凯特·肖邦是美国女作家，出生于美国圣路易斯，小说背景为路易斯安那。欧·亨利的作品构思新颖，语言诙谐，结局常常出人意外，善于描写美国社会尤其是纽约百姓的生活。舍伍德·安德森出生在中西部俄亥俄州克莱德镇的一个贫寒家庭，作品背景为自己所熟悉的俄亥俄州。

2. B　舍伍德·安德森擅长描写美国小镇的生活。

3. B　极简风格不是斯坦的写作技巧。

4. B　刘易斯的《巴比特》表现了中产阶级的狭隘性和局限性。

5. A　辛克莱·刘易斯(Sinclair Lewis)是第一位获得诺贝尔文学奖的美国作家。刘易斯不仅是小说家，还是一位敏锐的社会观察家和批评家。他以犀利的文笔触及 20 世纪上半叶美国社会的许多方面，成为当时最有影响力的人物之一。

6. C　《欢乐之家》的作者是伊迪斯·华顿。

III. Essay questions

1. Sherwood Anderson did a few things for which he is remembered today.

In terms of themes, Anderson showed the courage to explore the new material of novel creation, namely the psychological and emotional aspects of life in small American towns. He focuses on low-level figures, such as losers, fallen ones, and people who are not good at expressing. His classic work *Winsburg*, *Ohio* is a good example.

Technically, Anderson was an original writer who relies on inspiration to create. He observes the grotesque behaviors of human beings from the perspective of Freudian psychoanalysis, thus trying to accurately reveal the abnormal psychological conditions of the characters.

Then there is his style to consider. Anderson was probably the first writer who used oral language to create after Mark Twain. He believed that everyday language was a reliable medium.

His writing style was known for being clear, direct and deceptively simple. This style had a great influence on Hemingway and Faulkner.

2. Gertrude Stein is famous in the history of literature. First, because of her work, and second, because she was a patron of art and literature. She worked hard throughout her life and created more than 50 works. These include *Three Lives*, *Tender Buttons*, *The Making of Americans*, *How to Write and Four Saints in Three Acts.*

   Stan did several things to make her a name in the history of American literature. She had a keen mind and was aware of the trend of the age and subtle changes. She believed that life after the First World War was different, in this way, art and literature should also make corresponding changes in the way of expressing life. She made many contributions in leading the new modern era of literature.

   Another thing worthy of praise is her literary theory and practice. Her literary theories were well explained in her work How to Write. One of the hallmarks of her writing is her repetition of words. She believes that these words can eliminate their superficial meaning and reveal their practical meaning. Her work is full of obscure abstractions and cryptic language, which she believes will help describe reality. In most of her works, she breaks the conventional word order and coherence. She connects sounds to sounds, the taste, smell and rhythm of individual words. Her works show the spirit and modernity of her courage to experiment.

第17章　20世纪30年代·多斯·帕索斯·斯坦贝克

17.1　复习笔记

Ⅰ. The 1930s

1. Historical background

The social atmosphere in the 1930s was very depressing. On October 24, 1929 "the bottom dropped out of the stock market" and the Great Depression began. For the next ten years, Americans struggled in darkness. The situation did not change until the outbreak of World War II. The 1930s was a dark time. Banks and factories closed. Agriculture was also severely affected. Millions of unemployed people flocked to the streets, waiting in long lines for food. Extreme poverty became an indisputable fact. As the Great Depression spread further, for many people, survival became a cruel struggle.

American writers in the 1930s were concerned about their role in serving the country, and social involvement became a major theme in literature. The writers of the 1930s responded well to the turbulence of their times, producing abundant and forceful literary works in fiction, poetry, and drama.

2. Overview of literature in 1930s

If Eliot tries to express the spiritual wasteland in his famous poem *The Wasteland*, then the writers of the 1930s had to depict America's material wasteland. Obviously, social attention has become a top priority for most writers, and social participation has become the main feature of literature in the 1930s. The three branches of literature—novels, poetry and drama all did their best to face the challenges of history.

Ⅰ. 20世纪30年代

1. 历史背景

20世纪30年代的社会氛围十分压抑。1929年10月24日纽约华尔街证券交易所"掉穿了底盘"，大萧条至此开始。在其后长达十年间的时间里，美国人在黑暗中挣扎。直到二战爆发情况才有所改观。20世纪30年代是真正黑暗的时代，银行关门，工厂倒闭，农业凋敝。数百万失业者涌上街头，等待救济食物的队伍像长龙一般，极度贫困成为不争的事实。随着大萧条的进一步蔓延，对于许多人来是说生存本身成为一场不折不扣的搏斗。

面对困苦和绝望的现实，美国作家开始思考自己能为国家做些什么，社会关注成为他们的主要焦点。20世纪30年代的作家对时代的动荡做出了良好的回应，文学表达丰富而有力。

2. 20世纪30年代文学简介

如果艾略特试图在其著名诗歌《荒原》中表现精神上的荒原，那么20世纪30年代的作家则面临着描绘美国这个物质上的荒原。显然，对大多数作家来说，社会关注成为头等大事，社会参与成为30年代文学的主要特点。文学的三大分支——小说，诗歌，戏剧——都竭尽全力应对历史的挑战。

(1) The 1930s was a great era of novels. Dreiser's naturalistic style became the mainstream during the Great Depression. Neglected during their time, Henry Miller and Nathanael West experienced a resurgence in the postwar years. John Dos Passos and John Steinbeck became famous figures in the novel world. Dos Passos' *U. S. A*, Steinbeck's The *Grapes of Wrath*, and other writers' works together reflect American society during the Great Depression.

(2) The dramas in 1930s were also excellent. Although no one could match O'Neill during this period, many talented scholars tried their best to add luster to the stage of the times. These playwrights include Clifford Odets, Maxwell Anderson, Lillian Hellman, Thornton Wilder, etc. John Steinbeck successfully dramatized his novel *Of Mice and Men*.

(3) Possibly because there were many great masters such as Eliot, poetry in this period was not as prosperous as novels and dramas. There was no new great poet in this era.

The New Criticism held sway in the writing and criticism of poetry for about three decades, but its influence waned in the 1950s and 1960s with changing tastes and values. However, its impact extended beyond its period of dominance and left an imprint on literary history.

(1) 20 世纪 30 年代是小说的伟大时代。德莱赛的自然主义风格成为大萧条时期作家的典范。还有一些在当时被忽视但在战后得到"复活"的小说家，如亨利·米勒和纳撒尼尔·韦斯特。约翰·多斯·帕索斯和约翰·斯坦贝克成为这一成为小说界的著名人物。多斯·帕索斯的《美国》和斯坦贝克的《愤怒的葡萄》以及其他作家的作品真实地反映了大萧条时期美国的经历。

(2) 20 世纪 30 年代的戏剧也是丰富多彩的。诚然，这一时期没有人能与奥尼尔相媲美。但是许多有才学之士都竭尽全力，为时代的舞台添彩。这其中包括克利福德·奥德茨，马克斯威尔·安德森，莉莲·海尔曼，索顿·怀尔德等。约翰·斯坦贝克努力将他的小说《人鼠之间》改编成戏剧，这是一个成功的尝试。

(3) 可能是因为有诸如艾略特等大师们的掩盖之故，这一时期诗歌没有像小说和戏剧那样繁盛。诗歌舞台上没有出现新的大诗人。

新批评主义在诗歌创作和批评中占据约三十年的主导地位，但其影响力在 20 世纪 50 年代和 1960 年代随着品味和价值观的变化而减弱。然而，它的影响超越了它的统治时期，并在文学史上留下了印记。

Ⅱ. John Dos Passos (1896 – 1970)

1. Life

John Dos Passos was born in Chicago. He is a peculiar figure in the history of American literature in the 20th century. Among all the major writers who are closely related to the turbulent modern American life, he has shown a drastic change in political views from left to right. He began his writing career by depicting the situation of the lower class. In 1917, he proclaimed himself as a "red radical revolutionary". His works exhibited communist tendency for a long time. Not until the 1950s that he completely turned to conservatism. Dos Passos later showed his approving attitude towards large companies and supported the Vietnam War effort. He is best remembered today for his trilogy, *U. S. A*.

Ⅱ. 约翰·多斯·帕索斯

1. 生平

约翰·多斯·帕索斯生于芝加哥。他是 20 世纪美国文学史上的一位奇特人物，在所有与动荡的现代美国生活紧密联系的主要作家中，他的政治观点经历了从左向右的最突出的激烈转变。他是从描绘下层人的境遇开始他的写作生涯的。1917 年，他曾自称是"红色的激进的革命者"。他的作品在很长时间内具有共产主义倾向。直到 20 世纪 50 年代，他彻底转向保守主义。多斯·帕索斯后期对大企业表现出赞许态度，支持美国对越南的侵略战争。他如今主要因他的三部曲《美国》而被人们铭记。

2. Major works

U. S. A

The 42nd Parallel

1919

The Big Money

District of Columbia

Adventures of a Young Man

3. Analysis of major work

◆*U. S. A*

(1) The *U. S. A* trilogy includes *The 42nd Parallel*, *1919* and *The Big Money*. The first work depicts the formation process of the American capitalist "machine", as well as its dictatorial nature and its destructive impact on individuals. The second work provides a record of American life during World War I. It continues to describe the "depersonalizing" process mentioned in the first novel, laying the foundation for the next novel to describe the prosperity of the 1920s.

(2) The *U. S. A* trilogy is a "collective" novel, which describes the lives of 11 main characters and more than 30 minor characters. Its purpose is to expose the social reality of how capitalist "machines" influence the physical and mental development of individuals.

(3) In *U. S. A*, the author portrayed the lower class with a touching and sad tone.

(4) This trilogy shows the creative spirit of Dos Passos. In his novels, he cited techniques such as "Newsreels," the "Biographies," and the "Camera Eye".

(5) In addition, Dos Passos' language was concise with touching image and full rhythm. He used many parallel sentences. His language exhibits typical characteristics of the American colloquial style, contributing to his unique style as a writer.

Ⅲ. John Steinbeck (1902 –1968)

1. Life

John Steinbeck was born in Salinas, California. He loved literature since he was a child and read a lot of English and French literature at home. He later studied at Stanford University, but did not graduate. For a while, he felt confused and

2. 主要作品

《美国》

《北纬四十二度》

《一九一九年》

《赚大钱》

《哥伦比亚特区》

《一个年轻人的冒险》

3. 主要作品分析

◆《美国》

(1)《美国》由《北纬四十二度》、《一九一九年》和《赚大钱》组成。第一部《北纬四十二度》描绘了美国资本主义“机器”的形成过程以及它对个人的专制和摧残。第二部《一九一九年》是第一次世界大战中美国生活的记录，继续描写第一部小说中提到的“非人格化”过程，为下一部小说记述“繁荣”的20世纪20年代奠定了基础。

(2)《美国》是部“群体小说”，它描述了11位主要人物和30余位次要人物的生活。其中心意图在于揭露资本主义“机器”如何左右个人身心发展的社会现实。

(3) 在《美国》里作者对下层人民的刻画具有一种动人的伤感色调。

(4)《美国》三部曲表现了多斯·帕索斯勇于创新的精神。在其小说中，他引用了“新闻片”“人物传记”及“照相机镜头”等手法。

(5) 此外，多斯·帕索斯的语言简练，意象感人，句子富有节奏感，结构多排比句，其语言具有美国口语风格的一些典型特点，他是独具特点的文体家。

Ⅲ. 约翰·斯坦贝克

1. 生平

约翰·斯坦贝克出生于加利福尼亚州的萨利纳斯。他自幼喜爱文学，在家读了不少英国和法国文学作品。后来他就读于斯坦福大学，但未毕业。之后一段时间，他感到

didn't know what to do. He did a lot of work during this period. This experience was very helpful to him and became the basic material for his outstanding works in the future. Later, with the support of his father, he decided to specialize in literary creation. He wrote some romantic works. But none of these works produced any impact in the literary world.

迷茫，不知何去何从。这期间他做过很多零工。这段时间对他有教育意义，因为这成为他日后优秀作品的基本素材。后来在父亲的资助下，他决定专门从事文学创作。他写了一些浪漫主义作品。但这些作品在文坛上都未产生任何反响。

His masterpiece *The Grapes of Wrath* was published in 1939 and he won the Pulitzer Prize for Fiction. In his later years, Steinbeck became extremely conservative like Dos Passos. He won the Nobel Prize in Literature in 1962.

1939 年他的代表作《愤怒的葡萄》出版并获得了普利策小说奖。如同多斯·帕索斯，晚年的斯坦贝克变得极为保守。1962 年他获得了诺贝尔文学奖。

2. Major works

Cup of Gold

The Pastures of Heaven

To a God Unknown

Tortilla Flat

In Dubious Battle

Of Mice and Men

The Grapes of Wrath

The Moon is Down

East of Eden

The Winter of Our Discontent

Travels with Charley

2. 主要作品

《金杯》

《天堂里的牧地》

《致无名之神》

《薄饼坪》

《胜负未决的战斗》

《鼠与人》

《愤怒的葡萄》

《月落》

《伊甸园以东》

《我们的不满的冬天》

《查理和我》

3. Analysis of major work

◆*The Grapes of Wrath*

(1) *The Grapes of Wrath* is an important novel in the history of American literature. Its title is taken from a few lines in "The Battle Hymn of the Republic," a war song of the Civil War, "Mine eyes have seen the glory of the coming of the Lord, / He is tramping out the vintage where the grapes of wrath are stored."

(2) This novel depicts the process of the Joads and other families moving westward. What Steinbeck wants to say is that when most people are hungry and cold, they will resort to violence to get what they need. The days of anger are coming. The anger in people's souls is growing heavier and heavier. If no measures are taken to prevent them, the social revolution will occur.

(3) In terms of structure, this novel consists of two parts, the westward trek of the Joads and the dispossessed

3. 主要作品分析

◆《愤怒的葡萄》

(1)《愤怒的葡萄》是美国文学史上一部重要的小说。它的题目取自美国内战时期的《共和国战歌》中的几句“我的眼睛已看到了上帝到来的光环，/他在走遍储存愤怒葡萄的葡萄园。”

(2) 这部小说描绘了乔德等家庭西迁的过程。斯坦贝克想要说的是，当大多数的人们处于饥寒交迫的情况时，他们就会付诸暴力，取其所需。愤怒的日子正在到来，在人们的灵魂中愤怒的葡萄正在成长得越来越沉甸甸，倘不采取措施阻止，某种社会革命将会发生。

(3) 在结构上，这部小说由两部分材料组成，乔德一家和被迫迁

Oklahomans, and the general picture of the Great Depression. The inserted chapter provides the social and historical background for the character's activities. In addition, the structure of the novel draws on the outlines of the biblical story. There are many places in the novel that are obviously influenced by the Bible. (4) This novel shows the difference between Steinbeck and other writers who reflected on the economic crisis during the 1930s. Depression and defeatism permeated the works of that era. But in such an atmosphere, Steinbeck believed in human nature and thought that people would overcome difficulties in the future and the situation could get better. Despite the prevailing gloom and defeatism of the decade, Steinbeck's refreshing faith in humanity and the potential for a better life have contributed to his fame and enduring reputation.	移的俄克拉荷马人集体西迁的过程，以及大萧条的概貌。插入章节为人物活动提供了社会和历史背景。另外，小说的结构借鉴了圣经故事的构思轮廓。小说中有很多地方明显受到圣经的影响。 (4) 该小说显示了斯坦贝克和其他20世纪30年代反映经济危机的作家有不同之处。那个年代的作品中弥漫着沮丧与失败主义，但在这样的氛围之中，斯坦贝克相信人性，相信未来人们能克服困难，情况能有所好转。 能够超越眼前的困境，展望更美好的未来，正是斯坦贝克成为名人并获得永恒地位的原因之一。

17.2 考研真题与典型题详解

I. Fill in the blanks.

1. The novel, set in the American Dust Bowl region, that shows the social significance of the migrant labor problem was written by ________ and the title is ________.（大连外国语学院2007研）
2. The ________ of the 1930s greatly weakened the American nation's self-confidence.
3. In the short novel ________, John Steinbeck portrayed the tragic friendship between two migrant workers.
4. ________ is generally regarded as John Steinbeck's masterpiece.
5. In 1935, John Steinbeck published ________, a collection of short stories which vividly described the life of poor Mexican-Americans with affection and humor.
6. John Steinbeck's post-war novel ________ reflected his bitter feelings against those greedy, rapacious elements of society which made the war possible.
7. ________ was the foremost novelist of the American Depression of the 1930s.

II. Multiple Choice

1. The American social upheavals and the literary concerns of the Great Depression years ended with the prosperity and turmoil brought by the ________.

   A. First Word War　　B. Second World War

   C. Civil War　　D. War of Independence

2. ________ tells the Joad family's life from the time they were evicted from their farm in Oklahoma until their first winter in California.

   A. *Of Mice and Men*　　B. *The Grapes of Wrath*

C. *The Great Gatsby*　　D. *For Whom the Bell Tolls*

Ⅲ. Explain the following term.

1. Camera eye

Ⅳ. Essay questions

1. What are the major artistic features of John Steinbeck?（北航 2007 研）
2. Analysis of John Steinbeck's *The Grapes of Wrath*.

参考答案及解析

I. Fill in the blanks.

1. John Steinbeck, *The Grapes of Wrath*

（20 世纪 30 年代中期，由于受到沙尘暴的侵袭，美国中部大平原地区变成“尘谷”（Dust Bowl)，受此影响，大批居民迁徙到加利福尼亚州，被称为“沙尘暴移民”，美国小说家 John Steinbeck 的小说《愤怒的葡萄》正是以此为背景。）

2. Great Depression

（20 世纪 30 年代的经济危机 Great Depression 极大地削弱了美国整个民族的自信心。）

3. *Of Mice and Men*

（约翰·斯坦贝克在 1937 年发表小说《鼠与人》(*Of Mice and Men*)，描写了两个无家可归、无地可耕、相依为命的流动农业工人的悲惨遭遇。）

4. *The Grapes of Wrath*

（《愤怒的葡萄》(*The Grapes of Wrath*)是约翰·斯坦贝克的代表小说。该小说通过乔德一家从俄克拉荷马向西迁徙的过程，描绘了在 30 年代经济危机和特大旱灾影响下大批农民破产的真实面貌，揭示了人们在苦难历程中精神上的变化。）

5. *Tortilla Flat*

（1935 年约翰·斯坦贝克发表了小说《煎饼坪》(*Tortilla Flat*)。在这部小说里斯坦贝克用幽默的语言善意地描写了居住在蒙特雷城郊煎饼坪的一群贫穷墨西哥裔美国人的生活。）

6. *The Pearl*

（1947 年约翰·斯坦贝克的著名中篇小说《珍珠》出版。这部小说文字洗练，寓意深刻，无情地鞭挞了人世间有钱人的贪婪和凶恶。）

7. John Steinbeck

（约翰·斯坦贝克是 20 世纪 30 年代美国文坛上最活跃、最引人瞩目的作家之一，也是经济大萧条期间最重要的小说家。他的小说《愤怒的葡萄》(*The Grapes of Wrath*)以大萧条为背景，具有史诗般的规模和气魄。）

II. Multiple Choice

1. B　第二次世界大战结束了大萧条带来的美国的社会动荡和文学对这方面的关注。
2. B　《愤怒的葡萄》(*The Grapes of Wrath*)通过乔德一家从俄克拉荷马州向西迁至加利福尼亚州的过程，描绘了在 30 年代经济危机和特大旱灾影响下大批农民破产的真实面貌，揭示了人们在苦难历程中精神上的变化。

Ⅲ. Explain the following term.

1. ①Dos Passos developed the literary device. Corresponding to the time of the narrative, the novel shows his life autobiography. ②With the stream-of-consciousness style, the author's activities

and thinking are reflected while the fictional narrative takes place. ③These narratives which show his changing mood in the chaotic era indicate that his private experience is part of the complexity of social culture.

Ⅳ. Essay questions

1. John Steinbeck was a significant Depression writer. He did all kinds of jobs when he was young. This experience was very helpful to him and became the basic material for his outstanding works in the future. He gives a vivid picture of his time. His works examined the lives of the working class and migrant workers during the Dust Bowl and the Great Depression.

   His novels showed the difference between Steinbeck and other writers who reflected on the economic crisis in the 1930s. Depression and defeatism permeated the works of that era. But in such an atmosphere, Steinbeck believed in human nature and thought that people would overcome difficulties in the future and the situation could get better.

   Steinbeck uses many literary devices such as metaphors, similes, symbols and imagery to develop his characters and describe the scenes. The structures of Steinbeck's novels are well-arranged. For example, there is an inherent unity in his *The Grape of Wrath.* Its structure is dictated by the Bible. The 30 chapters fall neatly into three sections, which correspond to "The Exodus" story in the Old Testament.

2. John Steinbeck's *The Grapes of Wrath* is one of the major American books. The title of the book comes from "The Battle Hymn of the Republic", a war song of the Civil War. The implication of the title is that as injustice is building up and up, something is going to explode into violence.

   The Grapes of Wrath is a crisis novel. It is Steinbeck's clear expression of sympathy with the dispossessed and the wretched. This novel depicts the process of Joads and other families moving westward. What Steinbeck wants to say is that when most people are hungry and cold, they will resort to violence to get what they need. The days of anger are coming. The anger in people's souls is growing more and more heavy. If no measures are taken to prevent them, the social revolution will occur. In terms of structure, this novel consists of two parts, the westward trek of the Joads and the dispossessed Oklahomans, and the general picture of the Great Depression. The inserted chapter provides the social and historical background for the character's activities.

   The novel is structurally interesting for another, perhaps more important, reason, that its structure is dictated by the Bible. There are suggestions that the author was thinking about the Bible when writing the novel. Steinbeck is not stating this very explicitly, but the suggestion is very strong, and is supported by symbols such as that of the grapes.

   This novel shows the difference between Steinbeck and other writers who reflected on the economic crisis in the 1930s. Depression and defeatism permeated the works of that era. But in such an atmosphere, Steinbeck believed in human nature and thought that people would overcome difficulties in the future and the situation could get better.

第 18 章　波特·韦尔蒂·麦卡勒斯·韦斯特·新批评

18.1　复习笔记

Ⅰ. Katherine Anne Porter (1890 – 1980)

1. Life

Born in India Greek, Texas, Katherine Anne Porter had worked as a news reporter, an actress and a ballad singer before starting her writing career. Later she traveled to Europe and Mexico, which proved to be very useful for her later writing. Her only novel, *Ship of Fools*, which she started in the 1930s, was published in 1962 and was considered a significant publishing event but did not stand the test of time well.

Her major works are short stories, among which *Collected Stories* helped her to win a Pulitzer Prize, as well as a National Book Award. She was awarded honorary doctorates, and she also gave lectures at many universities, with her works selected and collected as standard textbooks for college students. From 1950 to 1952, she served as the vice president of the National Institute of Arts and Letters.

2. Major works

Flowering Judas
"The Flowering Judas"
"The Jilting of Granny Weatherall"
Pale Horse, Pale Rider
Leaning Tower and Other Stories
Ships Of Fools

3. Analysis of major work

◆*Ships Of Fools*

This novel originated from her travel trip from Mexico to Europe in 1931. She believed that her novel is a true reflection of the gradual decline of Western civilization. The novel is divided into three parts: "Embarkation", "High Sea" and "The Harbours". Here the boat represents the entirety of human life and the world. What we can learn from the novel is

Ⅰ. 凯瑟琳·安·波特

1. 生平

凯瑟琳·安·波特出生于德克萨斯州印第安河市。她曾做过报社记者，演员和民谣歌手。后来她到过欧洲和墨西哥。这段经历对她日后的写作很有帮助。她唯一一部小说《愚人船》始于20世纪30年代，最终在1962年问世，并被称为“有史以来的出版事件”。然而，它在经受时间考验方面表现不佳。

她主要是短篇小说家。她的《短篇小说集》获得了普利策奖和全国图书奖。她曾到许多大学做讲座，收到了许多机构授予的荣誉博士学位，作品也被节选为大学的标准教材。从1950年到1952年她担任美国国家艺术与文学协会副主席。

2. 主要作品

《开花的犹大树》
《开花的犹大树》
《风霜老奶奶的婚变》
《灰色骑士灰色马》
《斜塔及其他》
《愚人船》

3. 主要作品分析

◆《愚人船》

该小说是作者根据1931年从墨西哥到欧洲的航行经历写成的。她曾说她的小说讲的是西方文明逐渐衰落的情况。小说分为三部分，即《上船》《海上》和《港口》。船本身便是人类世界的缩影。小说讲述

the bleak reality of our lives. In this novel, man is depicted as a foolish being with numerous shortcomings, and his behavior is truly repulsive. Life is cold, lonely and disgusting, and human beings are living without any aims or targets. The final destination of humanity's voyage lies in a dark and cold place. It is evident from the novel that the author holds misanthropic views.	了关于人及人生的真谛，但是这真谛确实令人感到憋闷。小说描述了人类的缺点不足以致其显得像个十足的傻子。他们的行为令人沮丧的。而人生则苍凉、落寞、病态，人活着毫无意义。人们的航行最终驶向黑暗、阴冷之地。读这本小说很容易看出作者的厌世情绪。
Ⅱ. Eudora Welty (1909 –2001)	**Ⅱ. 尤多拉 · 韦尔蒂**
1. Life	**1. 生平**
Eudora Welty was born into a rich family in Jackson, Mississippi. She received a good education and was exposed to a wide range of social life, and her first short story "Death of a Traveling Salesman" helped her gain a good reputation. Later she kept her writing habit and produced many pieces of short stories, novellas and novels, thus she won various kinds of awards including the Pulitzer Prize. She was well-known for her short stories.	尤多拉 · 韦尔蒂生于密西西比州杰克逊市一个较富裕的家庭。她受过良好的教育，并且广泛地接触社会生活。1936 年她发表了第一篇短篇小说《旅行推销员之死》，这使得她声名鹊起。这之后她笔耕不辍，创作了多篇短篇小说、中篇小说和长篇小说，并获得了普利策奖等奖项。她因短篇小说方面的成就而知名。
2. Literary theory	**2. 文学理论**
Great significance has been given to the place where the works are produced. In her *Place in Fiction*, Welty has emphasized that "place" is a treasure house of an author's emotions, enabling them to focus on details, depict everything accurately, and explore the nature of life. She thinks that only if the art is molded clearly, directly and passionately from its original place can it be remained and understood forever. She is known for her loyalty to the South and for presenting a broader picture of America to readers. Welty's characters come from different social backgrounds and engage in self-searching, seeking meaning in their existence.	韦尔蒂强调文学创作中地点的重要性。她在《小说里的地点》一文中指出：地点是作者情感的宝库，能使他们关注细节，确切地描绘事物，并且能使他们看清事物的本质。她认为出自其发源地，并以清晰、明确、直接和热情的方式所表达的艺术最能长久地为人们所理解。她以忠于美国南方、并在更普遍的层面上触及读者。她的角色涵盖了从贵族到农民的各种人物，他们通过内心独白展示出他们生活的情感基调。
3. Major themes	**3. 主题**
Welty's major themes revolve around traditional family relationships in the South, focusing on the inner world of characters, their interactions, and the power of love instead of describing the ups of downs of a family. In some pieces, she focuses on the theme of loneliness, estragement and other sides of family life. Her story "Death of a Traveling Salesman" is particularly famous as an example of her work.	韦尔蒂作品的主要主题是传统南方社会家庭关系。她的重点并不在于描述家族的兴衰、变化无常，而在于探索人物的内心世界，人际关系以及爱的力量等。她的一些作品强调孤立、疏远及其他家庭生活方面等主题。她最著名的故事《旅行推销员之死》就是一个例证。

4. Major works "Death of a Traveling Salesman" "Place in Fiction" *Delta Wedding* "A Worn Path" "Why I Live at the P. O." "Lily Draw and Three Ladies" "The key" "The Whistle" "Flowers for Marjorie"	**4. 主要作品** 《旅行推销员之死》 《小说里的地点》 《三角洲婚礼》 《熟路》 《我为什么住在邮局》 《莉莉和三位女士》 《钥匙》 《哨子》 《送给玛朱莉的花》
5. Analysis of major work ◆"Death of a Traveling Salesman" The significance of family has been emphasized in the short story "Death of a Traveling Salesman". Alienation has been depicted in this short story though Bowman's lonely life. Without love and a sense of belonging, Bowman lives alone and cannot find the meaning of life, while the farmer and his wife love each other and enjoy mutual trust. Poverty has not eroded their positive attitude towards life and expectation for the future. Their life has illustrated the coordination of the inside and outside world, as well as the balance between sense and sensibility. These are exactly what are lacking in the bleak life of the salesman. Stricken by illness and loneliness, he longs for love and warmth but lacks them. Ultimately, he dies on a long and desolate night road.	**5. 主要作品分析** ◆《旅行推销员之死》 《旅行推销员之死》生动地表达了家庭的重要性。在这篇短篇小说中韦尔蒂通过对鲍曼的刻画描绘了一幅孤立的画面。鲍曼与世隔绝，生活中没有爱，没有意义，没有归属感。与此相反，农夫和他的妻子珍爱彼此、互相信任。他们尽管贫穷，但是思想积极，行动积极。总是憧憬着美好的未来。他们阐释了内心与外界、理智与情感的协调一致，而这些正好是推销员鲍曼凄凉的生活中所缺乏的，他生病孤独，渴望爱和温暖，却一无所有，在眼前无尽的长夜道路上离世。
Ⅲ. Carson McCullers (1917 – 1967)	**Ⅲ. 卡森·麦卡勒斯**
1. Life Carson McCullers was born in Columbus, Georgia, with astonishing talent, strong character but few friends. The themes of isolation, violence and terror in her later works were probably related to her intense feeling of loneliness. She was imaginative and wanted to be an author. She was an omnivorous reader and once attended the fiction-writing class at Columbus University. Her glorious writing career began with her first novel *The Heart Is a Lonely Hunter* being published. Before her mentally exhaustion led to her death at the age of 50, she had written several bestsellers and gained both fame and wealth. Although she was weak and sickly, she was versatile and perseverant, which was very impressive.	**1. 生平** 卡森·麦卡勒斯生于佐治亚州的哥伦布市，幼时天资过人，性格坚定，但朋友不多。强烈的孤立感和她日后作品中经常写疏远、暴力和恐怖等主题有关。她想象力丰富并立志成为作家。她阅读广泛，曾在哥伦比亚大学上过小说创作课。1940 年她的第一部小说《心是孤独的猎手》出版，她辉煌的文学创作生涯自此开始。她写了一些畅销书，名利双收，但后来精神起伏不定，在 50 岁时去世。麦卡勒斯多才多艺多产，虽然体弱多病，但坚持创作，颇令人叹服。

2. Major themes Carson McCullers holds a Gothic view of human life, which is described as "sense of awful" by her friend Tennessee Williams. She seems to believe that some people are bound to live a horrible and isolated life. And the existence of these people with physical and spiritual problems represents the power that will destroy lives of human beings. She has shown a special preference for the incongruity in life. Loneliness, the outcast and the lack of belonging are the focus of her novel. She believes love is significant, but it also leads to pain and death when it creates problems. Her fictional world depicted hunchbacks, deaf mutes, and adolescents struggling to love and lead normal lives, with many characters being bisexual or asexual.	**2. 主题** 卡森·麦卡勒斯对生活持有一种"哥特式"的观点，他的好友田纳西·威廉姆斯称之为"对可怕事物的感知"。她似乎认为，世上有些人注定要过可怕、与世隔绝的生活。这些身心方面的怪异人物的存在代表了摧毁人类生活的力量。她对生活中的怪异、奇特、不协调的现象情有独钟。她的小说重点描绘孤独、遗弃和没有归属感。她认为爱情是重要的，但它带来无法解决的问题，导致痛苦甚至死亡。麦卡勒斯的虚构世界中居住着驼背、聋哑人，或者很难爱和过正常生活的青少年。他们中的许多人是双性恋或无性的。
3. Major works *The heart Is a Lonely Hunter* *Reflections in a Golden Eye* *The Ballad of the Sad Café* *The Member of the Wedding* *Clock Without Hands*	**3. 主要作品** 《心是孤独的猎手》 《金眼里的映像》 《伤心咖啡馆之歌》 《婚礼的成员》 《没有指针的钟》
4. Analysis of major work ◆*The Ballad of the Sad Café* Love and pain are the main themes of the whole story *The Ballad of the Sad Café*, which reflects the life and people's behavior in McCullers' works. The story can be divided into three parts, and in the second section, she declared that love is bound to bring pain to both sides due to the insoluble conflicts between them. Hate emerges when the lover and the beloved have different experiences and comprehension about love, and the hate will lead to violence, death and pain. The love-hate complex exists in the relationships of the three couples, among whom the character Lyman perfectly explains the author's notion of love.	**4. 主要作品分析** ◆《伤心咖啡馆之歌》 《伤心咖啡馆之歌》反映出麦卡勒斯作品里生活的基调和人物的行为模式。爱情与痛苦这一主题贯穿着整个故事。这个故事分为三个部分，麦卡勒斯在第二部分中解释到，爱情必定给双方都带来痛苦，因为他们之间的矛盾无法解决。爱与被爱者对爱的体会不同，结果必然产生仇恨。仇恨导致暴力、死亡和痛苦。在这部小说中爱恨情结存在于三对恋爱关系中，其中里曼这个人物代表了作者对爱的理解。
Ⅳ. Nathanael West (1903 – 1940) **1. Life** Nathanael West, born to a wealthy New York family, was one of the most important figures in American literature in the 1930s. He was familiar with the classics of world literature and	**Ⅳ. 纳撒尼尔·韦斯特** **1. 生平** 纳撒尼尔·韦斯特出生于纽约一个富有之家，是20世纪30年代出现在美国文坛上的重要人物之一。他熟读世界文学经典作品，竭

tried his best to introduce the avant-garde of European literature and art to America. He went to Paris in the 1920s, where he came into contact with French symbolism, aestheticism and surrealism, and he also got acquainted with several modernists writers. During the Great Depression of the 1930s, he met left-wing writers and expressed his support for the Spanish people in their struggle against fascism, later he died in a car crash in 1940.

力把当时欧洲文艺界的前卫主义介绍到美国。他在20世纪20年代去了巴黎，在那结识了一些现代派作家，并他接触到法国象征主义、唯美主义和超现实主义。在30年代的大萧条时期，他结识了左翼作家，并对西班牙人民的反法西斯斗争表示支持。他在1940年死于车祸。

2. Major themes

While Nathanael West considered his works to be "moral satires," there are evident signs of immorality and spiritual decay. He enjoyed scandalizing his readers through his writing and his works often involve brutal violence, presented in a surreal manner, with grotesque and dehumanized characters, and also convey a bleak and absurd vision. He was relatively unknown during his lifetime but gained recognition posthumously, especially in the postwar years when there was a surge of interest in his works.

2. 主题

虽然纳撒尼尔·韦斯特认为他的作品是"道德讽刺"，但其中有明显的不道德和精神堕落的迹象。他喜欢通过自己的写作来震惊读者，他的作品经常涉及残酷的暴力，以超现实的方式呈现，人物怪诞且非人性化，也传达出一种凄凉荒诞的景象。他生前相对默默无闻，但死后获得了认可，尤其是在战后人们对他的作品兴趣高涨的时期。

3. Major works

The Complete Works of Nathanael West
The Dream Life of Balso-Snell
Miss Lonelyhearts
A Cool Million: The Dismantling of Lemuel Pitkin
The Day of the Locust

3. 主要作品

《纳撒尼尔·韦斯特全集》
《巴尔索·斯乃尔的梦幻生活》
《孤心小姐》
《整一百万：莱缪尔·皮特金的肢解》
《蝗灾日》

V. The new Criticism

As a school of poetry writing and literary criticism, New Criticism became an orthodox school in American academic circles in the 1940s. Until today, it still has a great influence in the literary world and college teaching. The new Criticism emerged in the early 1920s, and was acknowledged in the 1930s and 1940s, establishing itself as the dominant school in poetry writing and literary criticism. However, it faced rebellion in the 1950s and 1960s, leading to its gradual decline as a school.

V. 新批评

20世纪40年代新批评作为诗歌创作和文学批评的一个流派，在美国成为学术界的正统学派。时至今日，它仍然在文学界和大学教学中有重要影响。这个学派在20年代开始兴起，通过20年的时间，于30年代和40年代获得认可，在诗歌创作和文学批评中占统治地位。它在50年代和60年代遭到反对，渐渐失去作为正统学派的地位。

1. Features of the New Criticism

The New Criticism emerged as a reaction against the prevailing tendency in criticism to focus on the theme rather than the form of a work. The New Criticism is a school of formalist criticism, famous for its outstanding features:

1. 新批评的特点

新批评主义是对传统批评倾向的反应，传统批评过于关注作品的主题而忽视形式。新批评作为形式主义的一个流派，因其突出特点而著称。

(1) It emphasizes the text itself instead of analyzing the external factors such as its social background and influence, as well as the writer's intention and political attitude. (2) It tries to find out the structure of the work instead of the framework of writer's mind or the reader's reaction. (3) It emphasizes the careful reading of the texture and regards a literary piece as an organic entity with the text itself being the focus of critical reading and analysis. Notably, the New Criticism exhibited a distinct feature from the beginning, namely its tendency to separate criticism from social and moral concerns.	(1) 它集中分析文本本身，而不关注诸如社会背景、作者的意图和政治态度、其对社会的影响力等外部因素。 (2) 它挖掘作品本身的艺术结构，而不是作者的思想框架及读者的反应。 (3) 它把文学作品视为一个有机的实体，是内容和形式的统一。并且强调细读文本，将其成为批评性阅读和分析的焦点。 值得注意的是，新批评从一开始就展示了一个显著特点，即它倾向于将批评与社会和道德关切分离开来。
2. Features of the New Critical poem Many writers, especially poets, were influenced by the values of New Criticism, and their works became an important part of contemporary American poetry. (1) The new critical poem retained the basic characteristics of Modernist, such as concision, irony, humor, impersonality and the usage of antiphrasis, while other features like fragmentation, parallel sentences, ellipsis, symbolism and myth are being abandoned or weakened. (2) The new critical poem represents the cohesion of attitude and views, with the forms, images, quotations, rhymes and stanzas being regulated and combined together.	**2. 新批评诗歌的特点** 许多作家，尤其是诗人，接受了新批评的价值观，并且他们的作品构成了当代美国诗歌的重要部分。 (1) 新批评诗歌保留了现代派的基本特点，如简练、幽默、运用反语、非个人化、注重形式等。但同时摈弃或弱化了现代派的一些其他特征，如凌乱、并连句式、省略、象征与神话的运用、跨文化多语言的出现以及通篇用典等。 (2) 新批评诗歌体现了态度和观点的凝聚，形式、意象、典故、韵律、诗节等整齐而连贯，也有非人格化的特点。
3. Major New Critics **(1) John Crowe Ransom (1888 – 1974)** **◆Major works** *Poems about God* *Chills and Fever* *Two Gentlemen in Bonds* *God without Thunder* *I'll Take My Stand* *The New Criticism* **(2) Allen Tate (1899 – 1979)** **◆Major works** *I'll Take My Stand*	**3. 主要的新批评家** **(1) 约翰·克劳·兰塞姆** **◆主要作品** 《关于上帝的诗歌》 《发冷与发烧》 《契约中的两个绅士》 《没有雷声的上帝》 《我要坚持我的立场》 《新批评》 **(2) 艾伦·塔特** **◆主要作品** 《我要坚持我的立场》

Mr. Pope and Others *Three Poems* *Collected Poems*: *1922 – 1947* *Collected Poems* "Ode to the Confederate Dead"	《蒲柏先生及其他诗篇》 《三首诗》 《诗集：1922 – 1947》 《诗集》 《南方同盟烈士颂》

18.2 考研真题与典型题详解

I. Fill in the blanks.

1. In her essay "Place in Fiction", Eudora Welty emphasizes the importance of ________ for literary creations. She is noted for her fidelity to the American South, so her major theme relates to ________.
2. Carson McCullers was said to touch William Faulkner in writing, and her well-known novels are ________ and ________.
3. One of the important figures in the 1930s who tried to adapt European avant-gardism to American writing is ________.
4. The New Criticism first emerged in 1920s as a reaction against the prevailing time-honored critical tendency to focus on the theme often in disregard of the form of the work. The name is given by John Crowe Ransom's collection of critical essays ________.

II. Multiple Choice

1. Which of the following works by Katherine Anne Porter is a novel?

A. *Pale Horse*, *Pale Rider* B. *The Leaning Tower*
C. *Ship of Fools* D. *The Big Tree*

III. Explain the following term.

1. new criticism (厦门大学 2008 研)

参考答案及解析

I. Fill in the blanks.

1. place, traditional southern family relationships
(美国女作家尤多拉·韦尔蒂(Eudora Welty)在其论文《小说中的地点》中强调地点在文学创作中的重要性。她以对美国社会的忠诚而著称，其作品主要的主题是传统南方社会的家族观念和家庭关系。)
2. *The Heart Is a Lonely Hunter*, *The Ballad of the Sad Café.*
(卡森·麦卡勒斯(Carson McCullers)，20 世纪美国最重要的女作家之一，重要作品是《心是孤独的猎手》(*The Heart Is a Lonely Hunter*)和《伤心咖啡馆之歌》(*The Ballad of the Sad Café*)。)
3. Nathanael West
(纳撒内尔·韦斯特(Nathanael West)是 20 世纪 30 年代美国文学上的重要人物。他试图将欧洲的新潮主义引入美国文学。)
4. *The New Criticism*

(“新批评”一词，源于美国文艺批评家约翰·克劳·兰塞姆(John Crowe Ransom)1941 年出版的《新批评》(*The New Criticism*)一书。新批评于二十世纪二十年代在英国发端，三十年代在美国形成，并于四五十年代在美国蔚成大势。它反对只关注文学作品主题而忽视文本本身的批评倾向。)

Ⅱ. Multiple Choice

1. C 《愚人船》是凯瑟琳·安·波特根据 1931 年从墨西哥到欧洲的航行经历写成的小说。

Ⅲ. Explain the following term.

1. It's an approach to literature made popular between the 1940s and the 1960s that evolved out of formalist criticism. New Critics suggest that detailed analysis of the language of a literary text can uncover important layers of meaning in that work. Critics such as John Crown Ransom, I. A. Richards, and Robert Penn Warren are commonly associated with New Criticism.

第 19 章　美国戏剧

19.1　复习笔记

Ⅰ. Overview of American drama

American drama emerged in the late 19th century, and in the 1920s, a group of playwrights made efforts to contribute to its rise, including William Vaughn Moody, Eugene Walter, and Percy Mackaye.

(1) The 1920s were an exciting period for American drama, with the emergence of experimental theaters and the introduction of works by European playwrights. Modern American playwrights began to attract attention. During the Great Depression, theater remained vibrant by addressing social issues.

(2) Although theatrical productions experienced a temporary decline in the late 1950s, the subsequent decade saw a rejuvenation of American drama with the active participation of playwrights such as Edward Albee, Arthur Kopit, David Mamet, and Sam Shepard.

(3) In the late 1960s, American theater entered a new era characterized by diversity and inclusivity. Since the 1980s, numerous talented playwrights have created remarkable plays, continuing the rich tradition of American drama.

Ⅱ. Eugene O'Neill (1888 – 1953)

1. Life

Eugene O'Neill was America's greatest playwright. He was born in New York. His father was a well-known actor, which made O'Neill travel around with his father's group a lot. O'Neill's early years involved traveling with his father's theater group, being expelled from Princeton, and working odd jobs. These experiences exposed him to various aspects of life and influenced his creative work. O'Neill got tuberculosis and was sent to a sanitarium in the winter of 1912 – 1913, During his recovery, he immersed himself in reading and was particularly

Ⅰ. 美国戏剧概述

美国戏剧于19世纪末出现，20世纪20年代有一批剧作家为其崛起做出了努力，包括威廉·沃恩·穆迪、尤金·沃尔特和珀西·麦凯。

(1)20世纪20年代是美国戏剧的重要时期，代表性剧院涌现，欧洲剧作家的作品开始在舞台上演出，现代美国剧作家开始吸引人们的关注。大萧条时期的戏剧并不沉闷，它关注社会问题。

(2)20世纪50年代末戏剧制作出现了暂时的下滑，但在接下来的十年里，爱德华·阿尔比、阿瑟·科皮特、大卫·马梅特和萨姆·谢泼德等人的活跃使美国戏剧焕发了新的活力。

(3)20世纪60年代末，美国戏剧进入了一个多样化发展的新时期，包容多元成为其显著特点。自20世纪80年代以来，许多优秀的剧作家创作了许多优秀的戏剧作品。

Ⅱ. 尤金·奥尼尔

1. 生平

尤金·奥尼尔是美国最伟大的剧作家。他出生于纽约市，他的父亲是当时有名的演员。奥尼尔的早年经历包括跟随父亲的剧团旅行、被普林斯顿大学开除以及从事零散的工作。这些经历让他接触到生活的各个方面，并影响了他的创作。1912年到1913年冬天奥尼尔因肺结核不得不疗养治病。在康复期间，他钟爱易卜生和斯特林伯格的

drawn to the works of Ibsen and Strindberg. In 1916 his one-act play *Bound East for Cardiff* was staged, which marked the beginning of O'Neill's long-lasting and successful career as a playwright, as well as the coming of American Theater modernization. O'Neill obtained a number of prizes as a playwright. For example, he was awarded the Pulitzer Prize during 1920 – 1922 for his *Beyond the Horizon* and *Anna Christie* and was honored with the Nobel Prize in Literature in the year 1936.

2. Artistic characteristics

(1) O'Neill was disgusted with the melodramatic and disconnected nature of the American theater at the time. He liberated drama from the traditional shackles of the 19th century and made it deeply rooted in real life. He was the first who introduced realism or even naturalism into the American theater. His writing style is known for its diversity and proficiency.

(2) The spirit of innovation in him allowed him to borrow from the best traditions of European drama, such as Greek tragedies, Ibsen's realism, or Strindberg's expressionism and integrated them into the art of his own in an organic manner. He also borrowed from modernist literary techniques such as the stream-of-consciousness, which helped him better reveal the emotional and psychological complexities of modern people.

(3) Moreover, he paid much attention to the use of setting and stage property in his dramatic representation. O'Neill's unremitting experimentation enriched American drama and left a lasting impact on subsequent playwrights, such as Tennessee Williams, William Inge, and Edward Albee. He was regarded as the American Shakespeare.

3. Major works

Bound East for Cardiff
Beyond the Horizon
The Emperor Jones
Anna Christie
The Hairy Ape
Desire under the Elms
All God's Chillun God Wings
The Great God Brown
Lazarus Laughed
Strange Interlude

作品。1916年他的独幕剧《东航卡迪夫》上演。这标志着奥尼尔漫长且成功的戏剧生涯的开始，也标志着美国戏剧现代化时代的到来。奥尼尔的一生赢得了众多奖项。1920年到1922年间，他的《天边外》和《安娜·克里斯蒂》分别获得普利策奖，1936年他获得了诺贝尔文学奖。

2. 艺术特点

（1）奥尼尔批判当时美国戏剧夸张和脱离现实的性质，他把戏剧从19世纪的传统束缚中解放出来，使之深深地扎根于现实生活。第一次把现实主义乃至自然主义的手法引进美国戏剧中，他的艺术以多样化及精深圆熟而著称。

（2）他大胆借鉴欧洲戏剧传统中的精华，诸如希腊悲剧、易卜生现实主义及斯特林堡表现主义等，并把它们融入到自己的艺术中。他还大胆借鉴现代派文学技巧，如意识流手法，这有助于他揭露现代人情感及心理上的复杂性。

（3）此外，他还特别重视布景和道具的使用。奥尼尔不懈的创新丰富了美国戏剧、影响了后来的剧作家，如田纳西·威廉斯、威廉·英吉和爱德华·阿尔比。他被誉为“美国的莎士比亚”。

3. 主要作品

《东航卡迪夫》
《天边外》
《琼斯皇帝》
《安娜·克里斯蒂》
《毛猿》
《榆树下的欲望》
《上帝的儿女都有翅膀》
《大神布朗》
《拉萨路笑了》
《奇异的插曲》

Marco Millions	《马可百万》
Dynamo	《发电机》
Morning Becomes Electra	《悲悼》
Ah, Wilderness	《啊，荒野》
Days without End	《日子没有尽头》
The Iceman cometh	《送冰的人来了》
Long Day's Journey into Night	《进入黑夜的漫长旅途》
A Moon For the Misbegotten	《月照不幸人》
A Touch of the Poet	《诗人的气质》
Ⅲ. Elmer Rice (1892 -1967)	**Ⅲ. 艾尔默·赖斯**
◆Major works	**◆主要作品**
The Adding Machine	《计算器》
On Trial	《审判》
Street Scene	《街景》
Left Bank	《左岸》
Judgment Day	《审判日》
Dream Girl	《梦幻女孩》
The Grand Tour	《周游》
The Winner	《获胜者》
A Voyage Purilia	《小溪之旅》
Ⅳ. Susan Glaspell (1882 -1948)	**Ⅳ. 苏珊·格拉斯伯尔**
◆Major works	**◆主要作品**
The Verge	《边缘》
Alison's House	《爱丽森之家》
Fidelity	《忠贞不贰》
The Morning Is Near Us	《清晨在靠近我们》
Trifles	《琐事》
Ⅴ. Clifford Odets (1906 -1963)	**Ⅴ. 克里夫德·奥德茨**
◆Major works	**◆主要作品**
Waiting For Lefty	《等待老左》
Till the Day I Die	《到我死之时》
Paradise Lost	《失乐园》
Awake and Sing!	《觉醒而唱歌》
I Can't Sleep	《我睡不着》
Golden Boy	《金孩子》
Rocket to the Moon	《飞往月球》
Night Music	《夜里的音乐》
Clash by Night	《夜冲突》
The Big Knife	《大刀》

VI. Tennessee Williams (1911 –1983)

1. Life

Tennessee Williams was one of the greatest American playwrights. His original name was Thomas Lanier Williams, but was then changed to "Tennessee" in 1939. His first play, *Battle of Angels*, proved to be a fiasco that kept him unknown to the world until 1945 when *The Glass Menagerie* won him international recognition. After that, he released new work for an average of two years and enjoyed popularity all along. He was also a novelist and a poet. He wrote a novel, two volumes of poetry, and six volumes of prose, including three collections of short stories. Williams was a typical product of the post-O'Neill era. While O'Neill continued to lead American theater even in the postwar period, the bold endeavors of his generation paved the way for new figures like Williams, who were daring enough to tackle themes such as violence.

2. Major works

American Blues
Battle of Angels
A Streetcar Named Desire
Summer and Smoke
The Rose Tattoo
Cat on a Hot Tin Roof
Suddenly Last Summer
Sweet Bird of Youth
Period of Adjustment
Night of the Iguana
The Milk Train Does Not Stop Here Anymore
Red Battery Sign
Vieux Carre
The Glass Menagerie

VII. Arthur Miller (1915 –2005)

1. Life

Arthur Miller was a great playwright in the 1940s. He was born in New York. He grew up during the Depression when he witnessed his father's business failure. In the mid-1930s he studied journalism at Michigan University, where he began to write plays and radio scripts. His first play, *The Man*

VI. 田纳西·威廉斯

1. 生平

田纳西·威廉斯是美国最伟大的剧作家之一。他的原名是托马斯·拉尼尔·威廉斯，1939 年他把"托马斯"改为"田纳西"。他的第一部剧本《天使之战》遭遇惨败。直到 1945 年《玻璃动物园》的上演，他才得以扬名世界。这之后，他平均两年推出一部新作并且一直广受欢迎。他同时还是小说家和诗人。他著有一本长篇小说，两本诗集，六本散文集，其中包括 3 本短篇小说集。威廉斯是奥尼尔时代后的典型作家。尽管奥尼尔在战后时期仍然在美国戏剧中居于主导地位，但新生代的努力使得公众能够接受像威廉斯这样大胆处理暴力、性和同性恋等主题的新人。

2. 主要作品

《美国布鲁斯》
《天使之战》
《欲望号街车》
《夏日烟云》
《玫瑰纹身》
《热铁皮屋顶上的猫》
《夏天的突变》
《可爱的青春小鸟》
《调整时期》
《鬣蜥之夜》
《牛奶车不再在此停留》
《红色的炮台信号》
《维厄·卡雷》
《玻璃动物园》

VII. 阿瑟·米勒

1. 生平

阿瑟·米勒是 40 年代出现的伟大剧作家。他出生于纽约市，成长于经济大萧条时期。他目睹了父亲生意上的失败。30 年代中期他就读于密西根大学，并开始写剧本

Who Had All the Luck, was completed in 1944, and his first important work, *All My Sons*, helped him acquire his reputation as an Ibsenian playwright. The staging of *Death of a Salesman*, helped him win the Tony Award and the Pulitzer Prize and strengthened his position as a genius playwright. In 1965 he was elected the president of the international P. E. N. It was the first time for a writer from America who got this position. Arthur Miller is a friend of the Chinese people. He once visited China in 1978 and in 1983 to help stage his Death of Salesman, and its stage finally acquired a big success around the country.	和广播剧脚本。第一个剧作《鸿运高照的人》创作于1944年。他的第一个意义重大的剧作,《全是我的儿子》为其赢得"易卜生式剧作家"的美名。《推销员之死》公演后,为其赢得了托尼奖和普利策奖,并坚定了其戏剧界天才作家的地位。1965年他当选为国际笔会的首任美国主席。阿瑟·米勒是中国人民的朋友。他曾在1978年访问中国,1983年他又亲自到中国指导话剧《推销员之死》,该剧在中国大获成功。
2. Major themes	**2. 主题**
A typical theme of Arthur Miller's work is the plight of modern individuals in their family and work. In his plays, the protagonist often finds himself under pressure from his society and moral norms. He finds himself trapped in a mental and material predicament, striving to escape, but realizing that all his efforts are in vain. He believes that only through suicide, either mentally or physically, can he save himself. The world is harsh. There is no choice for the protagonist. Either he submits to the impossible demands of society, or he rejects them. He dies in either case. Miller is, however, not completely pessimistic. Reading his plays, one feels a faith in human and in life, however vague it may be, there is a sense of faith in humanity and life, albeit sometimes overshadowed by gloom.	阿瑟·米勒作品典型的主题是现代人在家庭与工作方面的困境。在他的剧作中,主人公经常处于社会及其道德规范的压力之下。他陷入了精神及物质上的困境,他竭力摆脱却发现一切只是徒劳,真实或精神上的自杀才能使之解脱。主人公别无选择,对于社会的需求,他要么服从要么拒绝,两种情况下都是死亡。然而,米勒并不是完全悲观的。虽然他的剧本中阴郁多过希冀,但是我们能感受到一种对人类、对生活的信念,尽管这种信念可能不太明确。
3. Major works	**3. 主要作品**
The Man Who Had All the Luck *All My Sons* *Death of a Salesman* *The Crucible* *A View from the Bridge* *Collected Plays* *After the Fall* *Incident at Vicky* *The Price* *The Creation of the World and Other Business* *The Archbishop's Ceiling* *The Last Yankee* *Broken Glass*	《鸿运高照的人》 《全是我的儿子》 《推销员之死》 《炼狱》 《桥头眺望》 《戏剧集》 《堕落之后》 《维希事件》 《代价》 《创世纪及其他》 《大主教的天花板》 《最后一个美国佬》 《破碎的镜子》

Ⅷ. Edward Albee (1928 –2016)

1. The Theater of the Absurd

Albee was closely tied with the tradition of the Theater of the Absurd which prevailed in the 1950s and 1960s. The theater of the absurd refers to those plays focusing on the theme such as the meaninglessness of life with its pain and sufferings that looks ridiculous. The typical works includes Samuel Becket's *Waiting for Godot and Endgame*. In these works the playwright tries to force the audience to face up to the human condition as it is, instead of making false depictions in order to satisfy the needs of the public. Edward Albee has written in this spirit. His plays seem to only focus solely on one problem, namely, the absurdity of human life based on a fragile illusion and spiritual emptiness. *Who is Afraid of Virginia Woolf ?* is a good example.

2. Major works

The Zoo Story
The Death of Bessie Smith
The Sandbox
The American Dream
Who's Afraid of Virginia Woolf ?
The Ballad of the Sad Cafe
A Delicate Balance
Box and Quotations from Chairman Mao TSe-Tung
All Over
Seascape
The Lady from Dubuque
The Man Who Had 3 Arms
Three Tall Women

Ⅸ. Sam Shepard (1943 –2017)

The two eminent playwrights that have impacted contemporary American theater are Sam Shepard and David Mamet.

◆Major works

Buried Child
Fool for Love
A Lie of the Mind
Paris, Texas

Ⅷ. 爱德华·阿尔比

1. 荒诞派戏剧

阿尔比与20世纪五、六十年代盛行的荒诞派戏剧的传统紧密相关。荒诞派戏剧是指一些集中反映人生的虚无、痛苦及折磨是滑稽、荒谬的等主题的剧作。典型的例子是塞缪尔·贝克特的《等待戈多》和《终局》。在这些作品里作者试图迫使观众正视人类的生活状况，而不是为迎合公众需要而进行虚假描绘。爱德华·阿尔比正是在这种精神下进行创作的。他的作品似乎只集中反映一个问题，即建筑在脆弱的幻想及精神的空虚之上的人类生活的荒诞性。《谁害怕弗吉尼亚·伍尔夫?》就是很好的例证。

2. 主要作品

《动物园的故事》
《贝西·史密斯之死》
《沙盒》
《美国梦》
《谁害怕弗吉尼亚·伍尔夫?》
《伤心咖啡馆之歌》
《脆弱的平衡》
《匣子和毛主席语录》
《一切皆已过去》
《海景》
《杜布克的女人》
《三臂人》
《三个高个女人》

Ⅸ. 塞姆·谢泼德

当代美国戏剧界富有影响力的两位剧作家是塞姆·谢泼德和大卫·马麦特。

◆主要作品

《被埋葬的孩子》
《爱情傻瓜》
《心之谎》
《德州巴黎》

Motel Chronicles *Geography of a Horse Dreamer* *States of Shock*	《旅店纪实》 《马塞梦测者的地理》 《震动》
X. David Mamet (1947 –) **◆Major works** *House of Games* *Sexual Perversity in Chicago* *American Buffalo* *Glengarry Glen Ross* *The Woods* *The Shawl* *Speed the Plow*	**X. 大卫·马麦特** **◆主要作品** 《娱乐之家》 《芝加哥的性变态》 《美国水牛》 《拜金一族》 《树林》 《披肩》 《快耕》

19.2 考研真题与典型题详解

I. Fill in the blanks.

1. Early in the 1920s, the most prominent of the new American playwrights, whose name is __________, established an international reputation. (人大 2006 研)
2. Eugene O'Neill borrowed freely from the best traditions of __________ drama, be it Greek __________, or the __________ of Ibsen, or the __________ of Strindberg. (国际关系学院 2010 研)
3. __________ is the first master in the American history of drama.
4. The magic of Eugene O'Neill's power lies in his never ceasing attempt to improve his art in step with the spirit of the times. He began writing in a __________ vein, then, he moved on and became obsessed with devices such as __________ and __________. During the 1940s, he turned back to what he had started with. Thus, his career came full circle.
5. Of all the plays that O'Neill wrote, most of them are __________, dealing with the basic issues of human existence and predicament such as life and death.
6. __________ is the one who dares to deal with themes such as violence, sex, and homosexuality on the stage in the postwar period.
7. __________ in the 1950s and 1960s refers to some plays, some of which center on the meaninglessness of life with its pain and suffering that seems funny, even ridiculous, __________ is one of the representatives.

II. Multiple Choice

1. __________ is NOT written by Eugene O'Neill. (首师大 2009 研)

   A. *Beyond the Horizon*　　B. *The Iceman Cometh*

   C. *Long Day's Journey into Night*　　D. *The Crucible*

2. The author of *Long Day's Journey into Night* also wrote __________. (北二外 2010 研)

   A. *Death of a Salesman*　　B. *The Hairy Ape*

   C. *A Streetcar Named Desire*　　D. *Looking Back in Anger*

3. "American Shakespeare" refers to __________.

A. Elmer Rice | B. Edward Albee
C. Eugene O'Neill | D. Tennessee Williams

4. "He got me, aw fight. I'm trou. Even him didn't rink I belonged." In these sentences taken from *The Hairy Ape*, the words "he" and "him" both refer to __________

A. Yank
B. God
C. The ape in the zoo
D. A person unnamed

5. Which of the following works is NOT written by Tennessee Williams?

A. *The Class Menagerie*
B. *A Streetcar Named Desire*
C. *Cat on a Hot Tin Roof*
D. *A Moon for the Misbegotten*

6. Which of the following statements concerning Tennessee Williams is NOT correct?

A. He has been influenced by Anton Chekhov, D. H. Lawrence and Hart Crane.
B. His last Broadway play is named *Clothes for a Summer Hotel.*
C. The recurrent themes in many of his plays are loneliness and desire.
D. He was awarded Nobel Prize for his brilliance as a dramatist.

7. *Death of a Salesman* is written by __________.

A. Tennessee Williams
B. Arthur Miller
C. Elmer Rice
D. Clifford Odets

Ⅲ. Explain the following terms.

1. Theatre of Absurdity
2. Monodrama
3. Parody
4. Tragic hero
5. Willy Loman

Ⅳ. Short answer questions

1. Which play of Eugene O' Neill's is autobiographical?（国际关系学院 2007 研）
2. Analyze the character of Willy Loman in *Death of a Salesman* by Arthur Miller.（南京大学 2008 研；厦门大学 2010 研）
3. What is Yank struggling for in Eugene O'Neill's *The Hairy Ape*? And how does his struggle reflect the universal dilemma of the modern man?

Ⅴ. Essay question

1. Highlight Nobel Prize Laureate Eugene O'Neill.（北航 2010 研）

参考答案及解析

Ⅰ. Fill in the blanks.

1. Eugene O'Neill

（美国文学史上最伟大的戏剧家尤金·奥尼尔在 20 世纪 20 年代确立了国际声望。）

2. European; tragedies; realism; expressionism

（尤金·奥尼尔被称为"美国戏剧之父"，其戏剧融合欧洲戏剧传统的精华，包括希腊的悲剧，易卜生现实主义剧作和斯特林堡的表现主义。）

3. Eugene O'Neill

(尤金·奥尼尔(Eugene O'Neill)是美国最伟大的剧作家，他在1936年获得诺贝尔文学奖，被誉为"美国戏剧之父"。)

4. naturalistic, symbolism, expressionism

(尤金·奥尼尔是一位不断创新的剧作家，创作初期他倾向于自然主义风格，而后转向运用象征主义和表现主义的手法。)

5. tragedies

(奥尼尔大部分剧作是悲剧，探讨人类生存及生与死等困境。)

6. Tennessee Williams

(田纳西·威廉姆斯(Tennessee Williams)的戏剧勇于探讨暴力、性和同性恋等主题。)

7. The Theater of the Absurd, Edward Albee

(20世纪五、六十年代的荒诞派戏剧(The Theater of the Absurd))集中表现现实的丑恶与恐怖、人生的痛苦与绝望，达到一种抽象的荒诞效果。爱德华·阿尔比(Edward Albee)是荒诞派戏剧的代表作家之一。)

II. Multiple Choice

1. D *The Crucible* 的作者是 Arthur Miller(阿瑟·米勒)，其余都是奥尼尔的作品。
2. B 《进入黑夜的漫长旅程》是美国伟大剧作家 Eugene O'Neill(尤金·奥尼尔)的代表作，他的其他作品有 *The Emperor Jones*(《琼斯皇帝》), *The Hairy Ape*(《毛猿》), *Desire Under the Elms*(《榆树下的欲望》), *The Great God Brown*(《大神布朗》)。
3. C 尤金·奥尼尔(Eugene O'Neill)是美国最伟大的剧作家，他被誉为"美国的莎士比亚"("American Shakespeare")。
4. B 这句话选自奥尼尔的《毛猿》，其中"他"指代上帝。
5. D D项《月照不幸人》是奥尼尔的作品。
6. D 田纳西·威廉斯并未获得诺贝尔奖。
7. B 《推销员之死》(*Death of a Salesman*)是阿瑟·米勒(Arthur Miller)的代表作，该剧获得了纽约剧评奖和普利策奖。

III. Explain the following terms.

1. Theatre of Absurdity referred to a kind of plays written mainly in France from the mid-1940s to the whole 1950s. These works usually employ illogical facts, unconventional dialogues, and very simple plots to express the obvious absurdity of human society. This term was first used, in 1961, by British scholar Martin Esslin. Samuel Beckett and Eugene Ionesco are two of the leading figures of Theatre of Absurdity movement.
2. monodrama, a play or a scene in which only one character speaks; or a series of dramatic monologues all made by one single character. Many plays written by Samuel Beckett, including *Krapp's Last Tape* (first performed 1958) and *Happy Days* (1961), are monodramas. Monodrama also refers to a dramatic expression of what a person's thought in his or her mind, or refers to a musical drama in which there is only one solo performer.
3. Parody is a mocking imitation of the style of literary works, ridiculing the typical writing style of an author or school by exaggerated imitation. Henry Fielding and James Joyce are two of the leading parodists in English literature. Poets in the 19th century, especially William Wordsworth and

Robert Browning suffered lots of parodies of their works.

4. A privileged, heroic character of high repute, who, by virtue of tragic flaws and destiny, ultimately suffers a downfall from glory into suffering. A tragic hero is usually a protagonist. Sophocles' Oedipus is an example.
5. Willy Lowman is the protagonist of Arthur Miller's play *Death of a Salesman*, which is a sad representation of the American dream. Willy Lowman, the salesman of the title, is as "phony" as Mark Twain's Colonel Sellers but more diligent and honest. He is as tragic as F. Scott Fitzgerald's Great Gatsby but not as successful and "great". It seems that Willy has never been aware of how suffocating the modern world he's living and never stopping on dreaming of success. He is all the time governed by the desire for success. His dreaming is certainly a symptom of his illusion and craziness. The mind of Willy eventually falls apart under too much pressure.

Ⅳ. Short answer questions

1. *Long Day's Journey into Night* is regarded as Eugene O'Neill's autobiographical play. the drama written in 1956 is widely welcomed, leading to O'Neill's winning of the 1957 Pulitzer Prize. The action depicts a fateful, heart-rending day from about 8:30 in the morning to midnight, in August 1912, at the seaside Connecticut home of the Tyrones—the autobiographical representations of O'Neill himself, his older brother, and their parents at their home, Monte Cristo Cottage.
2. In the play, Willy Loman keeps on dreaming of success and living in illusions and lies. He desires to build up his own business and own a big house. He dreams of a "big" future for his children. The success in his mind is something that can be measured only in terms of dollars. In fact, the dreaminess of Willy is a symptom of the craziness which is absorbing him. The mind of Willy is finally falling apart under the pressure of this much. All he can think of day and night is his global success, thus making him mentally unprepared for the impending tragedy. Willy never came to realize that it was the problematic social system that had made it impossible for him to achieve success and that the American obsession with financial success had ruined him. Willy is a typical example of a tragic hero.
3. Throughout the play, Yank is struggling to find the place where he belongs. However, he is rejected by the whole society. He attempts to make friends with the ape and calls him brother, but finally crushed by the gorillas and dies in the cage. Identity is what Yank has been struggling with, but no matter how he struggles, he can only finds himself an outsider, a freak.

Ⅴ. Essay question

1. Eugene O'Neill was considered the greatest American playwright of the first half of the 20th century, and was called "founder of the American drama". Some of his famous plays are: *Beyond the Horizon*, *The Emperor Jones*, *The Hairy Ape*, *Desire Under the Elms*, *The Great God Brown*, *Long Day's Journey Into Night.* His plays have been translated and staged all over the world.

   He was the first playwright to touch serious themes in the theater and to carry out his constant and bold experiments with theatrical traditions. Most of his works are tragedies, dealing with human existence and predicament: life and death, illusion and disillusion, alienation and communication, dream and reality, self and society, desire and frustration, etc.

   As the nation's first important playwright with forty nine published plays, he did a great deal to establish the modes of the modern theatre in the country. He employed sets, lighting and sound to enhance emotion rather than to represent a real place. He often ignored normal play divisions of scenes and acts, paid little attention to the expected length of plays, made his character wear masks, split one character between two actors, reintroduced ghosts, chorus, monologue and direct addresses to audience.

He successfully introduced the European theatrical trends of realism, naturalism, and expressionism to the American stage as devices to express his comprehensive interest in life and humanity. He grounded his works in personal experience and reflected the life of his country and his time.

第 20 章　二战后诗歌·20 世纪 40 年代的诗人

20.1　复习笔记

Ⅰ. The Postwar Scene The world after the war has undergone tremendous changes. The new experience in the new stage makes the way of literary expression more unique. The great changes include the threat of nuclear weapons, the madness of McCarthyism, the upsurge of the civil rights movement, the outrage caused by the Vietnam War, the feminist movement and sexual liberation, the contemporary information explosion, the improvement of self-awareness, as well as economic development and social abundance. The younger generation of poets in the 1950s and 1960s felt the need to break away from the inadequate heritage of the previous period. The rumblings of rebellion were heard in the early 1950s when Charles Olson, Allen Ginsberg, Robert Lowell, and others decided to explore a new direction in their creative endeavors. The era of Postmodernism had arrived. **Ⅱ. Postmodernism** Postmodernism shows a new way of understanding and creation. In terms of poetry, it tries its best to maintain opposition to the new critical poetry fashion and modernism decades ago. In terms of creative themes, postmodernism sees the world as formless and unpredictable, rather than something to be shaped. Postmodernism does not strive to exert influence on life and reality. It tends to accept life and reality for what they are. It often uses topics and objects which reflect personal nature or even forbidden nature to create. In terms of form, postmodernism seeks freedom of literary expression. For example, it tends to use colloquial and informal language rather than always pursuing the grammatical correctness and coherence of sentences. Various unconventional elements, such as Dada gestures and surrealistic associations, gained popularity in the	**Ⅰ. 社会背景** 战后的世界发生了重大的变化。新阶段的新的经历使得文学表达方式更具独特性：核武器的威胁，麦卡锡主义的疯狂，民权运动的高涨，越战所引起的民情激愤，女权运动及性解放，当代信息大爆炸以及人们自我意识的提高，加上经济的发展和社会的富足等等，20 世纪 50 年代和 20 世纪 60 年代的年轻诗人们认为前期的传统已经无法满足他们面对的独特问题，因此决定突破。20 世纪 50 年代早期就能听到反叛的声音，查尔斯·奥尔森、艾伦·金斯伯格和罗伯特·洛威尔等人决定在创作上探索新的方向。后现代主义时代已经到来。 **Ⅱ. 后现代主义** 后现代主义代表了一种新的感知模式和创作方法。在诗歌方面，它尽量与新批评诗歌的风尚及几十年前的现代主义保持对立。在创作主题方面，后现代主义将世界看成是无形的、不可预知的，而非有待塑造的。后现代主义并不竭力对生活和现实施加影响，而是乐于接受生活和现实本来面貌。它往往使用反映个人本性甚至是被禁止的本性的话题和对象进行创作。形式方面，后现代主义寻求文学表达上的自由。例如，它更倾向于使用口语和非正式用语，而并不总是追求句子的语法正确和连贯性。在战后几十年中，独特的表达方式如达达主义手势、藏传佛教咏唱、超现实主

postwar decades. Postmodern novels show their unique characteristics including metafiction, black humor and avant-garde forms. Postmodernism is still evolving as the dominant literary form.

义联想、荣格的原型、玛雅和埃及神祇的顿悟等逐渐流行起来。后现代小说展示了它独有的特点，如超小说、黑色幽默和先锋派的形式。现在仍作为主导的文学形式发展着。

III. Elizabeth Bishop (1911 –1979)

1. Life

Elizabeth Bishop was born in Worcester, Massachusetts. When she was eight months old, her father died. When she was five years old, her mother was sent to a mental hospital. So she was raised by her grandparents. She graduated from Vassar College. She won many awards, including the Pulitzer Prize for poetry and the National Book Award.

2. The features of her poems

Bishop's poems mostly portray her personal experience. For example, the loss of her parents in her childhood, her travels in Europe, South America and her home country, and the encounters with Marianne Moore and T. S. Eliot, all these events are reflected in her works. She is a postmodernist who not only accepts life as it is, but also pursues the openness of poetry themes and forms. Her poetry portrays the material aspects of life while suggesting deeper meanings. It also captures the ongoing process of life, embracing its openness and reflecting on the interplay between experiences and perspectives.

3. Major Works

Questions of Travel
Geography III
"Sestina"
"One Art"
"Over 2000 Illustrations and a Complete Concordance"
"The Fish"
"At the Fish House"

4. Analysis of major work

◆"The Fish"

The poem can be divided into several sections. The poet describes catching a big fish. The first 20 lines describe its

Ⅲ. 伊丽莎白·毕肖普

1. 生平

伊丽莎白·毕肖普出生于马萨诸塞州的伍斯特。在她八个月大的时候，父亲去世了。而在她五岁时，母亲又被送进了精神病院。所以她先后由外祖父母和祖父母抚养。她毕业于瓦萨学院。她曾获得过很多奖项，其中包括普利策诗歌奖和国家图书奖。

2. 诗歌特点

毕肖普的诗歌大多是她个人经历的写照。比如她童年时代失去双亲，她在欧洲、南美洲和自己祖国的旅行，以及与玛丽安·穆尔与T.S. 艾略特的相遇，所有这些事件都被浓缩在她的作品中。她是一位后现代主义者，不仅对生活的坦然接受，而且追求诗歌主题与形式的开放。她的诗歌描绘生活实质的同时也提供了超越物质的暗示，展现出她对生活的广泛而包容的视野，能够捕捉到生命的持续过程，拥抱其开放性，并反映了经历和观点之间的相互作用。

3. 主要作品

《旅行的问题》
《地理Ⅲ》
《六行诗》
《一种艺术》
《两千多幅图解》
《鱼》
《渔屋》

4. 主要作品分析

◆《鱼》

这首诗可以分为几节，诗人说她钓到一条大鱼，前20行向读者

appearance to the reader objectively and informatively. The next 25 lines involve emotional intervention and delve into specific subjective emotions. The poet gradually developed admiration and awe, and ultimately releases the fish back into the water. The poet initially admires the wisdom and heroism of fish. After that, she felt immensely proud and happy, because she felt that she was the same as the fish. The reason why the poet released the fish is that she had a sense of identity with the fish either consciously or subconsciously, the concept of "Heroes love heroes". She protected the dignity of the fish out of respect and sympathy. This poem shows people's gradual process of understanding reality, and reflects the poet's idea of "the perpetually changing integration of what has been written with what is being written."

Ⅳ. Richard Wilbur (1921 –2017)

1. Life

Richard Wilbur is an American poet and literary translator. He was born in New York. He then attended Amherst College and Harvard University. He participated in World War II in Europe. He was a prolific and award-winning author, writing and publishing throughout his life. Despite occasional criticism of elitism and conservatism, Wilbur was undoubtedly a Postmodernist poet.

2. Writing style

The question of what art can do for life has been a lifelong concern for Wilbur. Wilbur was one of the most elegant poets of the New Criticism era. He paid attention to pace and rhythm. His poems possess a beautiful rhythm and leave a very pleasant impression on the readers. Wilbur is devoted to the details of life and the world, even the seemingly insignificant ones. In terms of form, Wilbur accepted any form which is conducive to creation. Although his style is always witty and elegant, his form is flexible. He rejected dogma and extremist models. His language style is casual and relaxing. He was appointed US Poet Laureate in 1988.

客观而翔实地描绘它的外观，在接下来的25行有情感上的介入和进一步具体的主观情感上的描述，诗人逐渐产生敬佩之情，肃然起敬，最后把鱼又放回水中。诗人首先钦佩鱼的智慧和英雄主义，之后她感到莫大的自豪和快乐，觉得自己和鱼是一样的。诗人为什么将鱼放生是因为意识中或者潜意识中与鱼有认同感，"英雄惜英雄"，出于尊重和同情来保全对手的尊严。这首诗显示出人对现实的循序渐进的认识过程，体现出诗人的写作是"对已有的作品和创作中的作品所进行的不断变化的整合"的思想。

Ⅳ. 理查德·威尔伯

1. 生平

理查德·威尔伯是美国诗人和文学翻译。他生于纽约，在艾姆赫斯特学院和哈佛大学接受过教育。二战期间在欧洲参战。他是一位多产且屡获殊荣的作家，一生都奉献于写作和出版工作。尽管在形式上的优雅和魅力使其有时会被人们贴上"精英主义"和"保守"的标签，但毫无疑问，他是一位后现代主义诗人。

2. 写作风格

艺术对生活能做些什么？这一直是威尔伯的终身关注点。作为新批评时代文风最优雅的诗人，他注重步格和韵律。他的诗韵律优美，给读者留下了很愉悦的印象。威尔伯关注现实，忠于生活和世界的细节，无论它们看起来多么微不足道，他的奉献是坚定不移的。在形式上，威尔伯对任何有助于创作的形式都采取开放的态度。尽管他的风格总是机智、优雅的，形式总是灵活的，但他拒绝教条和极端主义的模式。语言风格很随意轻松。他于1988年被任命为美国桂冠诗人。

3. Major works

The Beautiful Changes and Other Poems

Ceremony and Other Poems

Things of This World

Complaint

The Mind-Reader: New Poems

Verses on The Times

New and Collected Poems

Bone Key and Other Poems

V. John Berryman (1914 –1972)

1. Life

John Berryman was an American poet. He was the main representative of American poetry in the second half of the 20th century. He was regarded as the originator of confessional poetry. When he was 12 years old, his father committed suicide by shooting himself. He attempted to use his life and career in poetry creation to escape the shadow but was unsuccessful. When he couldn't bear the great despair and pain, he finally suffered a nervous breakdown and committed suicide.

2. Themes

The theme of Berryman's poems was largely related to his father's suicide. Whether consciously or unconsciously, he was always tortured by this event. He could not overcome his guilt, nor could he escape the pain and anger in his heart. He constantly struggled with his despair. His inner conflicts were also exacerbated by the chaos of his personal life: his desire for the meaning of love, sexual guilt, alcoholism, etc. In addition, he was anxious because of his desire for the recognition of his work. In short, he must always face his naked inner world. So his poems were full of details of his life, or the heavy cargo.

The Dream Songs represents his frenzied self-dissection as he seeks a way out of the complexities of his life but finds none.

In "Love and Fame", he delves into his innermost world to confront potential horrors and find salvation in God, only to confront a vast void that characterizes his life. His life and struggle come full circle in his literary creations.

3. 主要作品

《美好的变化及其他诗》

《礼仪及其他诗》

《世事的诗歌》

《抱怨》

《知心人：新诗》

《时代之歌》

《诗集》

《骨头钥匙及其他诗》

V. 约翰·贝里曼

1. 生平

约翰·贝里曼是美国诗人。他是20世纪下半叶美国诗歌的主要代表人物。他被视作“自白诗的鼻祖”。当他12岁时他父亲饮弹自尽。这件事对他造成极大的伤害。他试图用一生的时间和诗歌创作生涯来摆脱阴影，但没成功。当无法忍受巨大的绝望和痛苦之时，他最终精神崩溃自尽身亡。

2. 主题

贝里曼诗歌的主题大体和他父亲的自杀有关。无论是有意识或无意识地，他总是受到这个事件的折磨，不能克服自己的负罪感，也摆脱不了内心的痛苦和气愤，他不断地与自己的绝望情绪做斗争。他的内心矛盾也由于他个人生活的混乱而加剧了：他对爱情的渴望、性方面的负罪感、酗酒成性等，此外还有他在艺术上渴求承认的忧虑。总之他必须时刻面对他的赤裸裸的内心世界。所以他的诗充满了他生活的细节，或者说沉重的负荷。

在《梦之歌》中，他疯狂地进行自我剖析，试图找到一条走出生活迷宫的出路。

在他的后期作品《爱和名望》中，他多次深入内心世界，面对其中可能存在的恐怖，以寻求救赎的上帝，但只看到了与他一生相伴的巨大虚无。他的生活和奋斗在他的文学创作中得到圆满呈现。

3. Major Works

The Dream Songs

77 Dream Songs

His Toy, His Dream, His Rest

Ⅵ. Randall Jarrell (1914 –1965)

1. Life

Randall Jarrell was born in Nashville, Tennessee, in 1914. He received bachelor's and master's degrees from Vanderbilt University. From 1937 to 1939 he taught at Kenyon College, where he met John Crowe Ransom and Robert Lowell. He joined the navy in 1942. Then he joined the army as a control tower operator. This experience provided him with a lot of material for his poetry creation.

2. Theme

Jarrell's poetry creation can be roughly divided into three stages: early childhood emotional frustrations, wartime poems about war, and similar themes of his early poems after the war. The content of his poems is always related to childhood. His poems all contain his memories, or the meaning of thinking about mother or looking for his mother. His best works often feature memories of his childhood.

3. Major Works

Blood for a Stranger

Little Friend, Little Friend

The Woman at the Washington Zoo

The Lost World

Ⅶ. James Merrill (1926 –1995)

1. Life

James Merrill grew up under the influence of New Criticism. In his career as a poet, he insisted on using these concept to create. His parents divorced when he was young, and this event cast a heavy shadow over his life. He consistently wrote about this in his poetry creation. Many of his poems directly or indirectly addressed this topic.

2. Major features of his works

He focuses on writing about romantic love, family, memories of the past, and treats science as a potential threat to human life. He also pays attention to form and believes that art

3. 主要作品

《梦之歌》

《77 首梦之歌》

《他的玩具,他的梦想,他的安息》

Ⅵ. 兰德尔·贾雷尔

1. 生平

兰德尔·贾雷尔于 1914 年在田纳西州的纳什维尔出生。在范德堡大学获得学士和硕士学位。1937 年至 1939 年间在肯尼恩学院执教，在那儿遇见约翰·克劳·兰塞姆和罗伯特·洛威尔。1942 年加入空军。不久又加入陆军，做控制塔操作员，这一经历给他的诗歌创作提供了大量的素材。

2. 主题

贾雷尔的诗歌创作大体可以分作三个阶段：早期儿时感情受挫，战时关于战争的诗歌，战后又返回早期诗作的主题。他的诗歌内容总和幼儿时期有关。他的诗作都有某种回首往事，或思母或寻母的意味。他最好的作品总是有关于他的童年及对幼时的回忆。

3. 主要作品

《给陌生人的血》

《小朋友，小朋友》

《华盛顿动物园的女人》

《失去的世界》

Ⅶ. 詹姆斯·梅里尔

1. 生平

詹姆斯·梅里尔在新批评观念的影响下成长。在他的诗人生涯中也坚持用这种观念进行创作。幼时父母离异，这件事在他的一生中留下浓重的阴影挥之不去。在他的诗歌创作中，常常情不自禁地写到此事，他的不少诗作直接或间接地触及这个题目。

2. 作品的主要特点

他注重写浪漫的爱情，家庭，回忆往昔以及科学是人类生活的潜在威胁等题材。他也注重形式，认

itself is form. He can be described as versatile and adept in the use of traditional poetry forms, such as sonnets, six-section poems, plain-style poems, and three-line rhyming poems. Merrill's puns, overtones, word games, and sense of humor are all well-known.	为艺术就是形式。他在运用传统诗歌形式方面可谓多才多艺，精深圆熟，比如十四行诗，六节诗，素体诗，三行隔句押韵诗等。梅里尔的双关语、弦外音、文字游戏及幽默感等都相当闻明。
3. Major Works *First Poems* *The Country of a Thousand Years of Peace* *Nights and Days* *Braving the Elements* *Changing Lights at Sandover*	**3. 主要作品** 《处女作》 《千年和平之国》 《夜与日》 《搏击风雨》 《桑多弗变化的光》

20.2 考研真题与典型题详解

I. Essay questions

1. Write a short essay (in no more than 200 words) about the basic features of Postmodernism. (上海交大 2007 研)

参考答案

1. Postmodernism is a disputed term that has occupied much recent debate about contemporary culture since the early 1980s. As applied to literature and other arts, the term is notoriously ambiguous, implying either that modernism has been superseded or that it has continued into a new phase. Postmodernism shows a new way of understanding and creation. In terms of poetry, it tries its best to maintain opposition to the new critical poetry fashion and modernism decades ago. In terms of creative themes, postmodernism sees the world as invisible and unpredictable, rather than something to be shaped. Postmodernism does not strive to exert influence on life and reality. It tends to accept life and reality as it is. It often uses topics and objects which reflect personal nature or even forbidden nature to create. In terms of form, postmodernism seeks freedom of literary expression. For example, it tends to use colloquial and informal language rather than always pursuing the grammatical correctness and coherence of sentences. Postmodern novels show its unique characteristics including metafiction, black humor and avant-garde forms. Postmodernism is still developing as the dominant literary form.

第21章　自白派·垮掉的一代

21.1　复习笔记

Ⅰ. The Confessional School The term is usually used to designate certain poets of the United States from the late 1950s to the late 1960s. Broadly, the poetry of this group of poets shares common features such as a merciless, painful self-analysis of one's own history, one's own most secret desires and illusions, etc., and the urgent "I'll-tell-it-all-to-you" impulse. In a sense, Lowell's merciless dissection regenerated Confessional poetry and made it more fashionable than ever before. Representatives of the Confessional School include Robert Lowell, Anne Sexton and Sylvia Plath. Lowell's *Life Studies* revitalized Confessional poetry with its harsh self-examination.	**Ⅰ. 自白派** 这一术语用来指20世界50年代末到60年代末的一些美国诗人。广义上讲，这些诗人的诗歌具有以下共同特点，如对自己的历史，内心深处的欲望和幻想等进行无情的、令人痛苦的自我分析，以及一种急切的"我将告诉你一切"的冲动。从某种程度上讲，洛威尔无情的自我剖析使自白诗获得新生也使其成为新时尚，并远超以往。 自白派代表人物是罗伯特·洛威尔、安妮·塞克斯顿、西尔维娅·普拉斯。洛威尔的《生命研究》以其严厉的自我剖析为"告解派"诗歌注入了新的生命和史无前例的流行度。
Ⅱ. Robert Lowell (1917–1977) **1. Life** Lowell came from a distinguished New England family. This background endowed him with culture and taste in his poetic nature, and meanwhile enabled him to examine and dissect the decline of his New England tradition. He received an excellent education at Harvard and then at Kenyon College, Ohio under the famous New Critical poet and critic John Crowe Ransom. Lowell's poetic career peaked when he won the 1946 Pulitzer for his second volume of poetry, *Lord Weary's Castle*. In 1959 his *Life Studies* came out. At that time his poetic style was no longer the New Critical but embraced an open form, and had unintentionally started a new school of poetry, Confessional poetry. He won the National Book Award for *Life Studies*. In 1967 he was arrested for his part in the march on the Pentagon against the Vietnam War.	**Ⅱ. 罗伯特·洛威尔** **1. 生平** 洛威尔来自显赫的新英格兰家族。这样的家族背景赋予了他文化和品味上的诗人气质，同时也使得他能审视新英格兰传统衰败与剖析其衰败的原因。他接受了良好的教育。先在哈佛大学就读，后又进入俄亥俄州的肯尼恩学院师从著名的新批评主义诗人、评论家约翰·克洛·兰森。1946年洛威尔因其第二部诗集《威尔利老爷的城堡》获得普利策奖，他的诗歌生涯达到顶峰。1959年他的新作《生命研究》问世。那时他的诗作风格已不再是新批评主义，而是开放自由的了，他也在不经意间开创了一个新的诗歌流派，自白派。他也因为这部新作而获得国家图书奖。1967年，他曾因为参与在五角大楼举行的反越战游行而被捕。

2. Comments on Lowell

(1) Lowell at first strictly adhered to the New Critical school in the 1940s. His poetry before *Life Studies* had a regular form, witty, tight, and delicate . Stunned at "all the horrors of this age," Lowell was constantly concerned with human's existence and salvation and turned to more secular subjects like society and individual life stories, exploring the potential for secular stability through supra-personal forms of belief or meditation.

(2) However, at the end of the 1950s Lowell started his painful introspection. He left his "City of God" and set foot in the "City of Man" of which he was a member. He examined his social and family background and the potential of art as a means to his own salvation.

(3) What made Lowell great is that he dissected his national culture. It seems that a sense of historic mission always inspires Lowell and endows his poetry with an epic quality.

Robert Lowell desired to be a part of his time and candidly discussed himself, which led to an examination of his nation's culture. His prophetic denunciations, injunctions, and his passionate commitment were morally uplifting. Lowell was one of the finest poets in postwar America.

3. Major works

Land of Unlikeness
Lord Weary's Castle
The Mills of the Kavanaughs
Life Studies
For the Union Dead
History
Day by Day

4. Analysis of major work

◆*Life of Studies*

(1) It is regarded as the masterpiece of Confessional poetry, consisting of four parts.

2. 对洛威尔的评价

(1)起初，洛威尔在20世纪40年代的时候是新批评主义的严格形式主义者。出版《生命研究》之前，他的诗歌形式规整，不失机智、紧凑、精美。惊讶于“这个时代的所有令人惊恐的事情”，洛威尔一直对人类的生存和救赎感兴趣，并将目光从宗教热情转向了更加世俗的素材，如社会和个人生活故事，并探索人们通过超个人形式的信仰神话或冥想来找到世俗稳定的可能性。

(2)然而，20世纪50年代末，洛威尔转向内心世界，开始他痛苦的自我反省。他离开“上帝之城”，进入自己也是其中一员的“人类之城”。他分析了自己的社会和家庭背景，及将艺术作为自我救赎的可能性。

(3)洛威尔之所以伟大在于他剖析了自己国家的文化。似乎总有一种历时使命感激励洛威尔去创作，他的诗歌也因此具有了史诗的品质。

罗伯特·洛威尔渴望成为这个时代的一部分，并且真诚地谈论自己，从而审视了他所处的国家文化。他的预言式谴责、命令和他对诗歌的执着使人们在道德上得到提升。洛威尔是战后美国最杰出的诗人之一。

3. 主要作品

《不一样的国度》
《威尔利老爷的城堡》
《卡瓦纳家族的磨坊》
《生命研究》
《为联邦军阵亡将士而作》
《历史》
《日复一日》

4. 主要作品分析

◆《生命研究》

(1) 这首诗被看作是自白派诗歌的代表作，由四个部分组成。

(2) Part one, four poems, defines the situation of human behavior and offers a reference framework for ensuing revelations. Part two is the book's prose section, entitled "91 Revere Street." Strictly speaking, it is an autobiography, disclosing the poet's concern over the declining New England culture. The third part, consisting of four poems, aims to explore whether aesthetic redemption is possible. Part four, entitled "Life Studies," consists of two parts, altogether containing 15 poems. Section one is a series of 11 poems related to failure. The first 7 poems are centered on the Lowell family's failure. The later 4 poems are centered on his own failure.

(3) *Life Studies* concludes with "Skunk Hour", which may be his most well-known one. The poem's title is interesting. The hour of skunks' out eating is the hour when humans realize their embarrassments and predicaments, when the poet is at the lowest circle of hell, and achieves self-realization and prophetically appeals humankind to follow.

（2）第一部分由四首诗组成，给人类行为划定了界限，并为同时带来的启示提供了参照框架。第二部分是散文，题目为《里维尔街91号》。严格来说，这部分属于自传，它反映出诗人为衰败的新英格兰文化深深忧虑。诗歌的第三部分有四首诗组成，旨在探索艺术救赎是否可能。第四部分标题为《生命研究》，包括两部分，共15首诗。其中，开始的7首诗全都讲述了洛威尔家族的失败。之后的4首诗讲述了自己的失败。

（3）《臭鼬时刻》是《生命研究》的最后一首诗，也可能是洛威尔最为著名的一首诗。诗的题名也很有意思。臭鼬外出觅食的时刻是人类意识到自己卑微与自身困境的时刻。诗人意识到自己处于地狱的底层，并获得自我认识，同时向人类发出先知般的呼吁，呼吁大家认识自我。

Ⅲ. Sylvia Plath (1932 –1963)

1. Brief introduction on Sylvia Plath's writing

For Sylvia Plath writing was a relief, a process of removing her keen "existential anxiety," caused by her self-consciousness of being a German descendant, her father's death, her fierce subconscious distaste for her mother, and the hurt of her husband's infidelity which she failed to ease for herself. Unable to alleviate her own agony, she became obsessed with death and suicide. Thus, death along with suffering and agony became central themes in her major works. Her poetic art transmutes her individual experience to made it accessible to most people. This is where her excellent art lies.

2. Major works

A Winter Ship

The Colossus and Other Poems

Ariel

Crystal Gazer and Other Poems

Winter Trees

Ⅲ. 西尔维娅·普拉斯

1. 创作简介

对西尔维娅·普拉斯来说，创作是减轻痛苦的过程，是驱除她剧烈的“生存焦虑”的过程。这焦虑源于她是德国后裔的自我意识、父亲之死、潜意识里对母亲的厌恶以及丈夫不忠带给她的无法缓解的伤害。由于她未能为自己减轻痛苦，她对死亡和自杀产生了困扰。因此死亡和痛苦、苦恼一并成为她重要作品中的主题。她的诗歌艺术再创了其个人经历，尽力使得更多的人明白诗歌的内容。这就是她诗歌艺术高明之所在。

2. 主要作品

《冬天的船》

《巨人及其他诗歌》

《爱丽尔》

《水晶球占卜师及其他》

《冬天的树》

Fiesta Melons
Crossing the Water
Lyonesse: Hitherto Uncollected Poems
Pursuit
The Bell Jar

《瓜果节》
《渡河》
《莱昂尼斯：迄今为止未收录的诗歌》
《追求》
《钟形坛》

Ⅳ. Anne Sexton (1928 –1974)

1. Brief introduction about Anne Sexton's writing

Anne Sexton was a prominent figure among Confessional poet. Her urgent desire to unleash her suppressed inner turmoil is clearly shown in her poetry. Madness, victimization, a sense of engulfing chaos, fascination with suicide and death, incest, adultery, illegitimacy, guilt, and addiction constitute her fundamental themes.

Her work represents her emotionally dramatic life journey where she struggled for survival and reached no salvation. Her poetry is emotionally intense and possesses a contagious power. She was one of the most sensitive, hurt, and eloquent voices representing the dilemma of modern women.

2. Major works

Live or Die
To Bedlam and Part Way Back
All My Pretty Ones
Transformations
The Death of Notebooks
The Awful Rowing toward God
"Her Kind"
"Housewife"
"Young"
"The Farmer's Wife"
"Death Baby"

Ⅳ. 安妮·塞克斯顿

1. 创作简介

安妮·塞克斯顿是一位非常重要的自白派诗人。她的诗歌生动展示了她急迫地想要倾泻自己的情感以释放内心的压抑。她创作的基本主题包括精神错乱、欺骗、吞噬一切的混乱感、迷恋自杀和死亡、乱伦、通奸、私生、罪恶和吸毒。

她的作品代表了她所经历的生命历程，一个诸多情感变故的历程，一个她奋力生存最终却没得到救赎的经历。她的诗歌充满了情感强度，因此具有一种具有感染力的力量。她代表了那些受伤害最深、在困境中表达最为雄辩的现代女性之一。

2. 主要作品

《生或死》
《去精神病院中途返回》
《所有我可爱的人》
《变形》
《死亡笔记》
《庄重地划向上帝》
《她那一类》
《家庭主妇》
《年幼》
《农夫的妻子》
《死亡宝贝》

Ⅴ. The Beat Generation

The 1950s witnessed a sweeping discontentment among the postwar generation, who protested against all the American mainstream culture. They have become known as the Beat Generation. Ginsberg and his friend Jack Kerouac picked "beat" from one of their junkie friends. The word "beat" represented a rebellious attitude related to traditional values toward sex, religion, the arts, and the American way of life.

Ⅴ. "垮掉的一代"

20 世纪 50 年代，二战后一代人中普遍存在着一种不满情绪，他们反对美国的一切主流文化。他们被认为是"垮掉的一代"。金斯堡和他的朋友杰克·凯鲁亚克从一个吸毒的朋友那儿听来了"垮掉"一词，它代表了一种不遵从传统价值

Depression, despair, and the desire to flee into an unconventional, sometimes communal, living mode shaped this rebellious attitude.

"Beat" literature refreshed the prose and poetry of the 1950s and 1960s. The evaluation of the Beat Generation and the San Francisco Poetry Renaissance should be based on historical perspective rather than solely on the works of a few authors.

观的叛逆态度，有关性、宗教、艺术和美国的生活方式。沮丧和厌倦感，想逃入一种非传统的、有时是团体的生活方式的需求塑造了这种反叛的态度。

"垮掉派"文学在20世纪50年代和60年代是诗歌和散文界刮起一阵新的强风。对于"垮掉的一代"和旧金山诗歌复兴运动的评价应该从历史的角度来看，而不仅仅局限于其中个别作家的作品。

Ⅵ. Allen Ginsberg (1926 –1997)

1. Brief Introduction

A rebel, a trailblazer, and an explorer of the unknown, and the poet laureate of the Beat Generation may best conclude Allen Ginsberg. He was born in Newark, New Jersey. Both of his parents influenced his literary career. Ginsberg attended to Columbia University where he met Lucien Carr, William Burroughs, and Jack Kerouac, forming the heart of the Beat Generation. Kerouac and Burroughs introduced him to the use of drugs and the illusion of drugs exceeding human consciousness. Columbia suspended him for his graffiti on classroom windows.

Ginsberg has achieved international acclaim. His ideas developed into a unique system that had a significant influence on postwar thinking. He continued writing and publishing works, remaining attractive to critical circles.

2. Ginsberg's Literary Points of View

To Ginsberg, the fullest art, the most individual, uninfluenced, unrepressed, uninhibited expression of art, is true expression and true art, thus having a clear vision of writing anti-mainstream poetry in a natural, spontaneous style. William Carlos Williams' literary doctrine of portraying contemporary life in daily speech was advocated and practiced by Allen Ginsberg.

3. Major works

Howl

"America"

The Fall of America

Ⅵ. 艾伦·金斯堡

1. 简介

叛逆者、开拓者和对未知的探索者，"垮掉的一代"的桂冠诗人这些名号也许最能概括艾伦·金斯堡其人。他出生于新泽西州的纽瓦克。父母对他的文学生涯有一定的影响。金斯堡就读于哥伦比亚大学，在那里遇到了卢辛·卡尔、威廉·巴罗斯、杰克·凯鲁亚克，组成了"垮掉的一代"的核心。凯鲁亚克和巴罗斯带着他吸毒，给了他超越人类正常意识的幻象。他由于在教室窗户上涂鸦而被哥伦比亚大学勒令退学。

金斯堡赢得了国际声誉，其思想逐渐形成了一套独特的体系，在战后思维中产生了相当大的影响。他写作并出版了更多作品，并一直受到评论界的关注。

2. 文学观点

对金斯堡来说，最完美的艺术，最个人的、不受影响的、不受压抑的、不受限制的艺术表达才是真实的艺术表达、真实的艺术。由此他的文学未来有了清晰的愿景：他将以一种自然、自发的措辞写一种反主流的诗歌。他崇尚威廉·卡洛斯·威廉斯用生活语言再现当代生活的原则。

3. 主要作品

《嚎叫》

《美国》

《美国的衰落》

4. Analysis of major work	**4. 主要作品分析**
◆*Howl*	◆《嚎叫》
(1) *Howl* is typical of Ginsberg's life. It consists of three sections. Section one sums up and glorifies the Beat Generation with all its features: its anti-mainstream way of living, its vision and its power, its ambition and a sense of historical mission and the depth of their despair in face of the threat of failure. Section two digs into the root cause of their plight and their nightmarish experience. This section mainly attacks America's mechanical civilization. The last section is at once an elegy about the possible defeat at the hands of fate and an effort to brace for the future.	(1)《嚎叫》整体上以金斯堡的生活为原型，由三部分组成。第一部分勾勒了"垮掉的一代"显著且不可磨灭的特征：他们反主流的生活方式、他们的视野和力量、他们的雄心壮志和使命感和他们面对失败时那极度失望的感受。第二部分深入挖掘了带给他们困境和噩梦般经历的根本原因，这一部分集中抨击了机械化的美国文明。最后一部分既是命运手中可能出现的失败的挽歌，又是支持未来的努力。
(2) In formal terms, Ginsberg imitated the cataloging form of Whitman's prose poetry and William Carlos Williams's tone and rhythm.	(2) 在形式上，金斯堡借鉴了惠特曼散文诗中的列举形式和威廉·卡洛斯·威廉斯的音调和节奏。
Ⅶ. Gary Snyder (1930 –)	**Ⅶ. 加里·斯奈达**
In the mid-1950s and early 1960s, the "Beats" included Snyder among whom he was only second to Ginsberg in reputation. Snyder believes that nature will leave an imprint on history for him.	在20世纪50年代中期和60年代早期，斯奈达是跨掉派中的一员。在这派中，他的名声仅次于金斯堡。他相信自然将在历史上留下他的印记。
1. Snyder's literary points of view	**1. 文学观点**
(1) For Snyder, the wilderness can always stimulate humanity. He tries to hold history and wilderness in his mind so that his poetry may approach the true measure of things and stand against the imbalance and ignorance of his time.	(1) 对于斯奈达来讲，荒野总是人类的兴奋剂。他总是将历史和荒野牢记脑海以使他的诗歌接近事物的真实面貌，并使之与他那个时代的紊乱和无知作对。
(2) The "stillness" among the dynamic universe is fundamental to Snyder's poetic concern.	(2)"静止"是斯奈达诗歌关注的中心。他试图在变动不居的雨中中寻找"静止"之物。
(3) Snyder believes the mission of the poet is to find poetry which is exclusive to nature.	(3) 斯奈达似乎认为诗人的职责就是要看到诗歌的哲学，而诗学就蕴藏于自然界。
2. Major works	**2. 主要作品**
"Mid-August at Sourdough Mountain Lookout" "Stillness" "Straight-Creek—Great Burn" "Riprap" "It Was When" "Song of the Taste"	《八月中旬的苏德尔山瞭望点》 《静止》 《笔直的小溪——伟大的燃烧》 《砌石》 《就在那时》 《品味之歌》

Ⅷ. Other poets **1. W. S. Merwin (1927 –2019)** The theme of Merwin's poetry is generally concerned with the dilemmas of humankind and the wholesome effect of the natural world. **◆Major works** "The Asians Dying" "For a Coming Extinction" "Summer Doorway" "The Drunk in the Furnace" **2. Robert Bly (1926 –2021)** Aside from surrealism, he thinks that the poet should liberate himself from reason and reveal the subconscious mind. Also, modern poetry should capture the flowing spiritual power. His opinion on imagery is "Deep image". Bly's poetry is generally sad. **◆Major works** *Silence in the Snowfields* *The Light around the Body* *This Tree Will be Here for a Thousand Years* **3. James Wright (1927 –1980)** Wright began writing poems in traditional forms. But later he abandoned it, and turned to a new poetry of leaping images and free verse of American colloquial speech. **◆Major works** *The Green Wall* *Saint Judas* *To a Blossoming Pear Tree* *This Journey*	**Ⅷ. 其他诗人** **1. W. S. 默温** 默温诗歌的主题通常是关于人类的困境和大自然有益健康的功效。 **◆主要作品** 《亚洲人正在死亡》 《为即将到来的灭亡而作》 《夏天的门洞里》 《炉边醉汉》 **2. 罗伯特·布莱** 关于布莱的诗学，除了他对超现实主义的观点外，他还认为诗人必须将自己从理性的自我中解放出来，释放出潜藏在脑海中的思想。现代诗也要抓住流动的精神力量。他对意象的观点被称为"深层意象"。布莱的诗歌通常比较忧郁。 **◆主要作品** 《雪地里的寂静》 《身体周围的光》 《此树在此待千年》 **3. 詹姆斯·赖特** 赖特开始是以传统的方式创作诗歌。后来他放弃了以前的写作方式，创作了具有跳动意象的新诗和美国口语化的自由诗。 **◆主要作品** 《绿墙》 《圣犹大》 《致鲜花盛开的梨树》 《此行》

21.2 考研真题与典型题详解

I. Fill in the blanks.

1. In the 1950s, there was a widespread discontentment among the postwar generation, whose voice was one of protest against all the mainstream culture that America had come to represent. This generation was known as the ________ generation.（天津外国语学院 2009 研）
2. Author ________ Title ________（南京大学 2009 研）
What thoughts I have of you tonight, Walt Whitman, for I walked down the sidestreets under the trees with a headache self-conscious looking at the full moon.

3. The publication of Robert Lowell's *Life Studies* marked the coming of the age of ________, which represents a new mode of perception and a way of writing.
4. ________ is the spokesman of postwar Beat Generation in American literary history.
5. Gary Snyder has been placed next to Allen Ginsberg among the Beat Generation. He seems to think that the job of the poet is to catch sight of ________, which resides nowhere but in ________.

II. Multiple Choice

1. Of the following poets, who is NOT remembered as a confessional poet?

A. Anne Sexton B. Sylvia Plath
C. Robert Lowell D. Elizabeth Bishop

III. Explain the following terms.

1. confessional poetry（厦门大学 2009 研）
2. The Beat Generation（北航 2007 研；北二外 2010 研）

参考答案及解析

I. Fill in the blanks.

1. beat

（垮掉的一代：第二次世界大战后风行于美国的文学流派。该流派的作家都是性格粗犷豪放、落拓不羁的男女青年，他们生活简单、不修边幅，喜穿奇装异服，厌弃工作和学业，拒绝承担任何社会义务，以浪迹天涯为乐，反对一切世俗陈规和垄断资本统治，抵制对外侵略和种族隔离，讨厌机器文明，他们永远寻求新的刺激，寻求绝对自由，纵欲、吸毒、沉沦，以此向体面的传统价值标准进行挑战，因此被称作“垮掉的一代”。代表作家有金斯堡及其作品《嚎叫》。）

2. Allen Ginsberg；*A Supermarket in California*

（题目选自金斯堡的 *A Supermarket in California*。）

3. Postmodernism

（罗伯特·洛威尔（Robert Lowell）《人生探索》（*Life Studies*）是一部里程碑式的诗集，它的发表标志着后现代主义（Postmodernism）时代的到来。）

4. Allen Ginsberg

（美国当代诗人艾伦·金斯堡是 20 世纪 50 年代末美国“垮掉派”文学运动的中心人物。他的代表作是《嚎叫》（*Howl*）。）

5. the poetic, the natural world

（加里·斯奈德（Gary Snyder），二十世纪美国著名诗人、“垮掉派”代表人物之一。所以喜欢沉浸于自然，在大自然中，他既是劳动者也是思考者，因此他的诗“更加接近于事物的本色以对抗我们时代的失衡、紊乱及愚昧无知”。）

II. Multiple Choice

1. D 伊丽莎白·毕肖普属于 20 世纪 40 年代的诗人，她不是自白派诗人。

III. Explain the following terms.

1. Confessional poetry traffics in intimate, and sometimes unflattering, information about details of the poet's personal life, such as in poems about illness, sexuality, and despondence. The confes-

sionalist label was applied to a number of poets of the 1950s and 1960s. John Berryman, Allen Ginsberg, Robert Lowell and Anne Sexton have all been called "Confessional Poets".

2. The Beat Generation is a group of American writers in the late 1950s, led by the poet Allen Ginsberg and the novelist Jack Kerouac. Writers of the "beat generation" dropped out of middle-class society in search of "beatific" ecstasy through drugs, sex, and Zen Buddhism. Their loose styles favor spontaneous self-expression and recitation to jazz accompaniment. The principal works of the group are Ginsberg's *Howl* (1956) and Kerouac's *On the Road* (1957).

第22章 纽约派诗人·沉思型诗歌·黑山派诗人

22.1 复习笔记

Ⅰ. The New York School

1. Features of the New York School

The so-called New York School became famous with Donald Allen's anthology published in 1960. The New York School poets have different pursuits, but their poems all share the same characteristics.

(1) First, they each strongly oppose the dominant New Critical values such as the presentation of objective imagery, and both seek to express their individual poetic characteristics.

(2) They also introduced popular, more populist features of life, such as popular songs, cartoon comic strips and Hollywood movies, into their poetry.

(3) Third, they each display a strong sense of humor, and their works are not without their vulgar and sentimental elements.

(4) Finally, they each experimented with surrealism during the 1960s.

2. Representatives of the New York School

Frank O'Hara
Kenneth Koch
John Ashbery
James Schuyler

Ⅱ. Frank O'Hara (1926 –1966)

1. Features of O'Hara's poetry

(1) A large part of O'Hara's work is of the "occasional" variety, such as birthday tributes and thank-yous. His poems are full of names of people, places, and works, with no particular commentary.

(2) Much of O'Hara's early poetry is surrealistic. Although quite Zen, it is usually obscure and difficult to understand.

Ⅰ. 纽约派诗人

1. 纽约派诗歌的特点

所谓的纽约派是随着唐纳德·艾伦1960年发表的文集而出名的。纽约派诗人的追求各异，但他们的诗歌都有相同的特点。

(1)首先，他们都强烈反对占主导的新批评价值观如客观意象的展现，都力图表达个人的诗歌特点。

(2)他们也把大众化的，比较低俗的生活特色，如通俗歌曲，卡通连环画和好莱坞电影等引入诗歌中。

(3)第三，他们都展现了浓郁的幽默感，他们的作品中也不乏粗俗和伤感成分。

(4)最后，他们都在20世纪60年代内尝试过超现实主义。

2. 纽约派代表诗人

弗兰克·奥哈拉
肯尼斯·科克
约翰·阿什贝里
詹姆斯·舒伊勒

Ⅱ. 弗兰克·奥哈拉

1. 奥哈拉诗作的特点

(1) 奥哈拉的很大一部分作品都是"即景生情"类，例如致生日、致谢等。他的诗满是人名、地名、作品名，没有特别的注释。

(2) 奥哈拉早期的诗歌大部分都是超现实主义的。因此虽颇有禅机，却通常晦涩难懂。

(3) In his poetry, O'Hara expresses a sense of tragedy.

(4) His poetry is famous for its colloquial, leisurely, casual, and unrefined language, making it perfectly in tune with the anti-literary and anti-art tradition.

2. Major works

The Lunch Poems

"Second Avenue"

"Why I Am Not a Painter"

"The Day Lady Died"

"Joe's Jacket"

III. John Ashbery (1927 –2017)

For a long time, John Ashbery was seen as a member of the New York School. But as he reached a mature stage in his career, his poetry increasingly showed the prominent characteristics of contemplative thought. Today Ashbery is one of the most contemplative contemporary American poets.

He benefited from his association with painting and painters, experimented with collage and fragmentation structures, and wrote expansive poems.

1. Features of his poems

(1) Ashbery is probably the most obscure and unknown poet of our time. When reading his poetry, the reader does not need to make much effort to understand its literal meaning; it is the underlying meaning represented by the structure of the words that is difficult.

(2) Ashbery's poetry reflects on mistakes and makes a record of these indulgent "spiritual acts". His ideas operate in a unique and distinctive way, often breaking with widely accepted logical principles. Ashbery's poetic mind seems to include everything without selecting or filtering from its raw materials.

(3) His poems, no matter how long or short, are generally recorded in a stream-of-consciousness style. His poetry observes anything temporarily appealing while engaging in a great deal of commentary, using its own imagery and language, and thus appears to be drawn out, irrelevant, uninformative and mysterious. They are a combination of reason and fallacy.

(3) 在其诗歌中，奥哈拉表达一种悲剧的感受。

(4) 他因其诗歌中语言通俗、闲适、随意、不经雕琢的特点而著名，因此他与反文学反艺术的传统绝对搭调。

2. 主要作品

《午餐诗》

《第二大街》

《我为何不是一个画家》

《黛女士死的那天》

《乔的夹克》

Ⅲ. 约翰·阿什伯利

很长一段时间以来，约翰·阿什伯利被看作是纽约派的成员。但当他在事业上走向成熟阶段，他的诗歌越来越显示了沉思型思想的突出特征。如今阿什伯利已成为当代美国最有沉思型特色的诗人。

他受益于与绘画和画家的交往，尝试了拼贴和碎片化的结构，并创作了广阔的诗歌作品。

1. 诗歌特点

(1) 阿什伯利可能是当代最隐晦不明的诗人。读他的诗歌，读者并不需费大力去理解它的字面意思，困难的是文字结构所代表的潜在意义。

(2) 阿什伯利的诗歌对错误进行反思，做这些放纵的"精神行为"记录。他的思想运作方式独特，别具一格，通常会打破广为接受的逻辑原则。阿什伯利的诗歌涵盖了各种主题和材料，不进行选择和筛选。

(3) 他的诗歌，无论长短，一般都是意识流式的记录，观察任何暂时吸引人的东西，同时进行大量的评论，运用自身意象和语言，因此显得东拉西扯，毫不相干，寓意不明，神秘莫测，是理性和谬误的结合。

2. **Major works**

Some Trees

The Tennis Court Oath

Rivers and Mountains

The Double Dream of Spring

Self-Portrait in a Convex Mirror

The Vermont Notebook

Houseboat Days

As You Know

Shadow Train

A Wave

Selected Poems

April Galleons

Flow Chart

Hotel L'Autreamont

Can You Hear, Bird

Ⅳ. A. R. Ammons (1926 – 2001)

1. Features of his poems

(1) Ammons is another major contemporary poet of the contemplative type. He often writes in the Romantic tradition. Ammons was well read in Wordsworth, Emerson, Whitman, and Indian and Chinese philosophy, and wrote often in the Romantic tradition.

(2) Ammons is highly aware of the natural world and its multiple significance, seeing nature and life in various forms ranging from the infinitesimal to the infinite.

(3) He also seeks to perceive and understand the outline of a larger design, a mystery probably unknown to man, and believes that his art should strive to present his vision as accurately as possible.

2. Major works

"Corson Inlet"

"Mountain Talk"

"So I Said I am Ezra"

Ⅴ. The Black Mountain Poets

The Black Mountain School refers to a group of poets active in the contemporary era, including Charles Olson, Denis Levertov, Robert Duncan, and Robert Creeley. These people were either associated with Black Mountain College or with the *Black Mountain Review* magazine, and were therefore called "Black Mountain Poets".

2. 主要作品

《一些树》

《网球场誓言》

《河与山》

《双重春梦》

《凸镜中的自画像》

《佛蒙特笔记本》

《船家日子》

《如你所知》

《影子列车》

《波浪》

《诗选》

《四月的古帆船》

《流程图》

《洛特雷阿蒙酒店》

《鸟儿，你能否听见》

Ⅳ. A. R. 阿蒙斯

1. 诗歌特点

（1）阿蒙斯是当代另一位主要的沉思型诗人。他常以浪漫主义的传统方式写作。他熟读华兹华斯、爱默生、惠特曼以及印度和中国哲学，常常在浪漫主义传统中创作。

（2）阿蒙斯高度关注自然界及其多重意义，将自然和生命视为各种存在形式的总和，从无限小到无限大。

（3）他试图洞察并理解一个更大设计的轮廓，这可能是人类所不知道的神秘之处，并认为他的艺术应该尽可能准确地呈现他的视觉。

2. 主要作品

《科尔森水湾》

《山地语言》

《我说我是艾兹拉》

Ⅴ. 黑山派诗人

黑山派指的是活跃在当代的一群诗人，包括查尔斯·奥尔森、丹尼斯·莱弗托夫、罗伯特·邓肯和罗伯特·克瑞里。他们这些人要么与黑山学院有关，要么与《黑山评论》杂志有关，因此被称为“黑山派诗人”。

The Black Mountain poets have left a brilliant page in contemporary American literature. Although the college closed in 1956, it actively supported the growth of postwar art and literature, and the Black Mountain poets made a significant contribution to American literature.

黑山派诗人在当代美国文坛留下了辉煌的一页。尽管黑山学院在1956年关闭，该流派仍尽力促进战后艺术和文学的发展，而黑山诗人们对美国文学做出了重要贡献。

VI. Charles Olson (1910 –1970)

VI. 查尔斯·奥尔森

1. Brief Introduction about Olson

1. 奥尔森简介

Charles Olson was born and raised in Worcester, Massachusetts, and did his doctoral research at Harvard University. He is a distinguishing scholar in the fields of archaeology, education and anthropology. As a poet and critic, his writing contributed greatly to moving American poetry away from the traditions of T. S. Eliot and New Criticism and to elevating the status of Williams and Pound's poetry. Olson had a strong sense of mission. He was almost alone in his fighting to resist the New Criticism's monopoly on the publishing world and to promote the birth of new poetry. He was the first American poet to call for a new poetic style after World War II and remains highly influential in the contemporary American poetry scene.

查尔斯·奥尔森出生并成长于马萨诸塞州的沃斯特在哈佛大学做了博士研究。他是考古学、教育学和人类学领域的杰出学者。作为诗人和批评家，他的写作对促使美国诗歌脱离T. S. 艾略特和新批评的传统，对提升威廉斯和庞德诗歌的地位作出了极大贡献。奥尔森有种强烈的使命感。为了反抗新批评对出版界的垄断，促进新诗的诞生他几乎是孤军奋战。他是二战后呼唤新诗体的美国诗歌第一人，在当代美国诗坛仍有很大的影响力。

2. Major Works

"Projective Verse"
In Cold Hell, In Thicket
The Distances
The Maximus Poems
Call me Ishmael
"Human Universe"

2. 主要作品

《投射体诗》
《在冰冷的地狱中，在灌木丛中》
《距离》
《马克西姆诗集》
《叫我以实玛利吧》
《人类的宇宙》

VII. Robert Creeley (1926 – 2005)

VII. 罗伯特·克瑞里

Robert Creeley was born in West Acton, Massachusetts. He published extensively in the 1950s, gained fame in the 1960s, and taught at various universities.

罗伯特·克瑞里出生于马萨诸塞州的西阿克顿，在20世纪50年代广泛发表作品，在60年代成名，并在一些大学任教。

1. Literary points of view

1. 文学观点

(1) In terms of content, he fully subscribes to Williams' idea of "no ideas but in things". He also agrees with Pound's stance that "any tendency to abstract general statement is a greased slide."

（1）在内容方面，他完全赞同威廉斯"没有观点，只有事实"的思想，也认同庞德"任何抽象概括陈述的倾向就如爬一个油滑的斜坡。"

(2) In terms of form, Creeley feels that the criterion of "form" should not be seen as a necessary criterion anymore, since form is an extension of content. His literary criteria are clearly open-ended.

（2）在形式方面，克瑞里觉得"形式"的准则不该继续被看作是必要标准，形式不过是内容的延伸。克瑞里的文学标准显然是开放式的。

(3) The themes of Creeley's poetry usually around love, marriage, complex human relationships and the connection between individuals of both sexes.	(3) 克瑞里诗歌的主题通常是爱情、婚姻、复杂的人际关系和两性个体之间的联系。
2. Major works	**2. 主要作品**
For Love: Poems 1950 – 1960 *Words* *The Charm: Early and Uncollected Poems* *Pieces* *A Day Book* *Thirty Things* *Away* *Later* *The Collected Poems 1945 – 1975* *Mirrors* *The Memory Gardens* *Windows*	《致爱情：1950 – 1960》 《文字》 《早期杂诗的魅力》 《碎片》 《一日记》 《三十件事》 《离开》 《后来》 《1945 – 1975 诗选》 《镜子》 《记忆花园》 《窗》
Ⅷ. Denise Levertov (1923 – 1997)	**Ⅷ. 丹尼斯·莱弗托夫**
Denise Levertov was born and raised in England and published her first book of poetry, *The Double Image*, using traditional English rhymes and meters. She is considered one of the most respected poets of her generation.	丹尼斯·莱弗托夫在英国出生并长大，在那里出版了她的第一本诗集《双重形象》，该诗集采用传统的英文韵律和格律，她被认为是那一代中最受尊敬的诗人之一。
1. Features of Levertov's Poetry	**1. 莱弗托夫诗歌的特点**
(1) Over the years Levertov has developed her own poetic views and aesthetic. As a poet, she has a strong sense of a mission. Her works have a significant religious dimension.	(1) 多年来莱弗托夫形成了自己的诗学观点和审美。作为一名诗人，她有种强烈的使命感。她的作品中有浓厚的宗教色彩。
(2) Levertov's poetry demonstrates a clear social purposefulness. She has always been interested in humanitarian politics. Her passion responds to a wide variety of issues, such as the status of women, marriage, eroticism, war etc.	(2) 莱弗托夫的诗歌展现了一种明确的社会目的性。她一直都对人道主义感兴趣。她的热情体现在各种议题，如女性的地位，婚姻，情欲，战争等。
(3) Many of her poems focus on subjects that are more personal and directly related to nature.	(3) 她的许多诗歌聚焦于更个人化、更直接贴近自然的题材。
(4) Levertov's differences in the perception of men and women are also very interesting and worth mentioning. This perceptions is not quite feminist in nature, but very close.	(4) 莱弗托夫对男女认知的差异也是非常有趣值得一提的。这种感知本质上讲不太像女权主义，却很接近。
2. Major works	**2. 主要作品**
The Double Image *Here and Now* *The Jacob's Ladder* *Overland to Islands* *With Eyes at the Back of Our Heads*	《双重形象》 《此时此地》 《雅各的梯子》 《群岛之路》 《追随的目光》

O Taste and See *The Sorrow Dance* *Relearning the Alphabet* *To Stay Alive* *Footprints* *The Freeing of the Dust* *Life in the Forest* *Candles in Babylon* *Oblique Prayers* *Breathing the Water* *A Door in the Hive* *Evening Train*	《哦，尝尝看看吧》 《悲伤之舞》 《重学字母表》 《活着》 《足迹》 《解放灰尘》 《林中生活》 《巴比伦之烛》 《不虔诚的祷告》 《水中呼吸》 《闹市中的门》 《晚间列车》
IX. Robert Duncan (1919 –1988)	**IX. 罗伯特·邓肯**
1. Literary Points of View	**1. 文学观点**
(1) Duncan argues that poetry comes from life and that language is capable of renewal and reordering because of its regenerative power. He was a devoted supporter of Olson's ideas and became a distinctive poet of "projective verse."	(1) 邓肯认为，诗歌来源于生活，语言因其再生能力能够进行更新，重列新秩序。他是奥尔森观点的积极支持者，成为了"投射诗歌"独特的诗人。
(2) Duncan is a love poet. He points out that poetry is the soul of life, a way to give and receive love, and that the most perfect form of life is love. Love is divine.	(2) 邓肯是位爱情诗人。他指出诗歌是生命的灵魂，是给予和获得爱的方式，生命最完美的形式就是爱。爱是神圣的。
(3) Throughout his writing career, Duncan believed in the reality of myth and used it to define his role as a poet and the nature of poetry.	(3) 在他整个写作生涯，邓肯相信神话的真实性，并用神话来定义自己作为诗人的作用和诗歌的本质。
2. Major works	**2. 主要作品**
Heavenly City Earthly City *The Opening of the Field* *Passages* *Roots and Branches* *Bending the Bow* *Ground Work: Before the War* *Ground Work II: In the Dark* "A Poem Beginning with a Line by Pindar" "Often I am Permitted to a Meadow" "Dove"	《天国之城与世俗之城》 《开垦土地》 《路》 《根与枝》 《开弓》 《地基：战前》 《地基 II：黑暗中》 《以品达诗行开始的诗》 《我常回到草地》 《鸽子》

22.2 考研真题与典型题详解

I. Fill in the blanks.

1. The Black Mountain Poets are so called because these poets are associated with ___________, or

with ___________.

II. Multiple Choice

1. Which of the following poets is NOT a member of the New York School?

A. William Burroughs　　B. John Ashbery

C. Frank O'Hara　　D. Kenneth Koch

2. Which of the following poets is NOT member of the Black Mountain poets?

A. Robert Creeley　B. Robert Duncan　C. Theodore Roethke　D. Charles Olson

Ⅲ. Explain the following terms.

1. Black Mountain poets
2. The New York School

参考答案及解析

I. Fill in the blanks.

1. Black Mountain College; Black Mountain Review

(黑山派诗歌是美国当代的一个诗歌流派。20世纪50年代初，在马萨诸塞州黑山学院任教的查·奥尔逊、罗·邓肯、罗·克瑞利等人创办《黑山评论》杂志，提倡与40年代流行的传统格律体相反的"放射体"诗歌，逐步形成一个流派。)

II. Multiple Choice

1. A　威廉·勃洛斯是垮掉派作家之一。

2. C　西奥多·罗特克是自白派诗人之一。

Ⅲ. Explain the following terms.

1. A loosely associated group of poets that formed an important part of the avant-garde of American poetry in the 1950s, publishing innovative yet disciplined verse in the Black Mountain Review (1954 –57), which became a leading forum of experimental verse. Their experimental yet disciplined style took its impetus from the essay "Projective Verse" (1950) by Charles Olson. The Black Mountain School is linked with Charles Olson's theory of "projective verse," which insisted on an open form based on the spontaneity of the breath pause in speech and the typewriter line in writing. The group grew up around the poets Robert Creeley, Robert Duncan, and Charles Olson while they were teaching at Black Mountain.

2. Unlike the Beat and San Franciso poets, the poets of the New York School are not interested in overtly moral questions, and, in general, they steer clear of political issues. They have the best formal educations of any group. The major figures of the New York School are John Ashbery, Frank O'Hara, and Kenneth Koch. They are quintessentially urban, cool, nonreligious, witty with a poignant, pastel sophistication. Their poems are fast moving, full of urban detail, incongruity, and an almost palpable sense of suspended belief. New York City is the fine arts center of America and the birthplace of Abstract Expressionism, a major inspiration of this poetry. Most of the poets worked as art reviewers or museum curators, or collaborated with painters. Perhaps because of their feeling for abstract art, which distrusts figurative shapes and obvious meanings, their work is often difficult to comprehend, as in the later work of John Ashbery (1927 –), perhaps the most influential poet writing today.

第23章　二战后美国小说(1)

23.1　复习笔记

Ⅰ. Overview of postwar novel **1. Historical Background** The optimism in the post-World War II generation was quickly eroded by the Cold War between the great powers. McCarthyism fundamentally poisoned people's lives in the 1950s. The civil rights movement, the emergence of a counter-culture, and the rise of feminism greatly enriched life in the 1960s. And the Vietnam War weighed heavily on people's minds. Life has been complicated by political or radical acts of violence, such as the assassinations of John. F. Kennedy and Martin Luther King, Jr. Everything is caught up in being skeptical. Advances in science and technology have made people feel empowered, but they have also taken the mystery out of life.	**Ⅰ. 二战后小说简介** **1. 历史背景** 在二战后的一代中的乐观情绪，很快就被大国之间的冷战削弱了。麦卡锡主义从根本上毒害了人们的50年代的生活。民权运动，反主流文化的出现，女权主义的风起云涌则极大地丰富了60年代的生活。而越南战争使人们的思想沉重。生活因政治上的或激进的暴力行径而变得错综复杂，例如，肯尼迪和马丁·路德·金的遇刺身亡。一切都陷入被质疑中。科学技术方面的进步使人们感觉到力量，但同时也使生活失去了神秘感。
2. Features of postwar novels Between the end of the war and the end of 1960, war novel, Southern novel, Jewish novel, the Beat novel, the Black novel, satire and secular fiction, attracted a great deal of attention. This was followed by fantastic and surrealist fiction, nonfiction, science fiction, dark or absurd humor, parody and popular novel, and experimental novel-writing techniques. Themes included social tyranny, the subjugation of the individual, the search for personal identity, and the writer's self-indulgence in a self-imposed environment.	**2. 战后小说特点** 战末至1960年末期间，战争小说、南方小说、犹太小说、垮掉派小说、黑人小说、讽刺与世俗小说，引起了人们的广泛关注。这之后，又有梦幻与超现实主义小说、非虚构小说、科幻小说、黑色或荒诞幽默小说、模仿与通俗小说、试验小说等。主题则包括社会专制，个人被征服，寻求个人认同，作家在自我环境下的自我放纵等。
3. Features of postwar writers The new generation of writers has demonstrated their novelty and competence through a wide range of experiments, impressing even their brilliant predecessors like Faulkner and Hemingway. Themes such as societal tyranny, individual subjugation, the quest for self-identity, and the writer's self-indulgence in relation to the environment have become the concerns of many contemporary authors.	**3. 战后作家特点** 新一代作家通过广泛的实验展示了他们的新颖性和能力，甚至给福克纳和海明威等杰出的前辈留下了深刻的印象。社会暴政、个人征服、自我认同的追求以及作家对环境的自我放纵等主题已成为许多当代作家关注的话题。

Ⅱ. Saul Bellow (1915 – 2005)

1. Life

Saul Bellow is one of the most famous contemporary American novelists. He was born in Canada to a family of Russian Jewish immigrants and grew up in Chicago. He published his first book, *Dangling Man* in 1944. Over the next half century or so, he wrote a large number of full-length novels, short stories and plays, winning numerous awards. His creative career reached its peak in 1976 when he was awarded both the Pulitzer Prize and the Nobel Prize for Literature.

2. His Themes

Saul Bellow's themes are divided into three main areas. First, he believes that contemporary society is a threat to people's lives and independent personalities. As a result, people living in this environment are prone to paranoia, nervousness, weakness and incompetence to the point of losing their minds. Finally, there is always the theme of the search for truth and values in his works. The process of the search is difficult and painful, but the end result is successful.

3. Major works

Dangling Man
The Victim
The Adventures of Augie March
Seize the Day
Henderson the Rain King
Herzog
Mosby's Memoirs
Mr. Sammler's Planet
Humboldt's Gift
The Dean's December
More Die of Heartbreak
The Bellarosa Connection
A Theft
Something to Remember Me
The Last Analysis

4. Difference Between Modernism and Postmodernism

(1) Transformation in literature

The 1950s and 1960s witnessed a shift from modernism to postmodernism in the literary scene.

Ⅱ. 索尔·贝洛

1. 生平

索尔·贝洛是当代美国最著名的小说家。他出生于加拿大一个俄国犹太移民家庭。他在芝加哥长大。他的第一部小说《摇来晃去的人》发表于1944年。在接下来的半个多世纪，他创作了大量的长篇小说、短篇小说和剧本，赢得了众多的奖项。1976年他的创作事业到达巅峰，他同时被授予普利策奖和诺贝尔文学奖。

2. 主题

索尔·贝洛的主题主要是如下三方面：首先，他认为当代社会对人们的生活和独立人格是个威胁。因此，生活在这种环境中，人们容易偏执多疑、精神紧张、虚弱无能以至失去理智。最后，他的作品中总会有追寻真理及价值观的主题，追寻的过程是困难的、痛苦的，但最终结果却是成功的。

3. 主要作品

《摇来晃去的人》
《受害者》
《奥吉·马奇历险记》
《只争朝夕》
《雨王汉德森》
《赫索格》
《莫斯比的回忆》
《塞姆勒先生的行星》
《洪堡的礼物》
《院长的十二月》
《更多的人死于伤心》
《贝拉罗莎暗道》
《偷窃》
《以此记住我》
《最后的分析》

4. 现代主义与后现代主义的对比

(1)文学界的转变

20世纪50年代和60年代见证了从现代主义到后现代主义的转变。

(2) Difference in themes

Modernists try to impose shape and significance on life, while postmodernists accept life's chaos and contingency and try to make sense of it for survival.

(3) Difference in form

Modernist writings tend to be retrospectively heavy, often featuring interior monologues or stream of consciousness, with story interest taking a secondary place. Postmodernist writings, on the other hand, freely borrow technically from modernist works and from various other writing modes to serve their purpose in addition to their own unique creative features.

Ⅲ. Norman Mailer (1923 – 2007)

1. Introduction

Norman Mailer was a multifaceted genius. In addition to being a novelist, he was a metaphysical philosopher, poet, playwright, filmmaker, journalist, politician, and actor. His best-known work is *The Naked and the Dead*.

2. Major works

The Naked and the Dead
Barbary Shore
The Deer Park
The Armies of the Night
Marilyn: A Novel Biography
The Execution's Song
Ancient Evening
Tough Guys Don't Dance
Harlot's Ghost
The Gospel According to the son
Advertisement for Myself
An American Dream
Why Are We in Vietnam?
Miami and the Siege of Chicago
Existential Errands
Genies and Lust
"The White Negro"

3. Analysis of major work

◆ *The Naked and the Dead*

"The Naked and the Dead" is Norman Mailer's first and most acclaimed book. It takes place on a barren beach of

(2)主题方面的差异

现代主义作品试图对生活赋予形式和意义，而后现代主义作品接受生活的混乱和偶然性，并试图为了生存而理解它。

(3)形式方面的差异

现代主义作品常常沉重地回顾过去，经常包含内心独白或意识流的特征，并将故事兴趣放在次要位置。后现代主义作品则在技术上可以借鉴现代主义作品，同时也可以自由地借鉴其他各种写作方式，以满足自己的目的。

Ⅲ. 诺曼·梅勒

1. 简介

诺曼·梅勒是多方面的天才。除了是小说家之外，他还是形而上学哲学家、诗人、剧作家、电影制作人、记者、政治家、演员。他最知名的作品是《裸者与死者》。

2. 主要作品

《裸者与死者》
《北非之岸》
《鹿园》
《夜幕下的大军》
《玛莉琳：小说体传记》
《刽子手之歌》
《古老的夜晚》
《硬汉不跳舞》
《哈洛特的鬼影》
《圣子福音》
《我自己的广告》
《美国梦》
《我们为什么在越南?》
《迈阿密和芝加哥之围》
《存在主义的使命》
《天才与欲望》
《白色黑人》

3. 主要作品分析

◆《裸者与死者》

《裸者与死者》是诺曼·梅勒的第一部作品，也是他最杰出的作品之一。故事发生在南太平洋一座

Anopopei, a small Japanese-held island in the South Pacific. The story follows a fourteen-man platoon as they land on the island and engage in combat with the enemy. This platoon is part of a larger force of six thousand soldiers deployed to capture the island and pave the way for an American offensive into the Philippines. The characters in the novel are diverse, representing various regions and social backgrounds, Through these characters, Mailer aims to portray a microcosm of American society.

Ⅳ. J. D. Salinger (1919 – 2010)

1. Life

J. D. Salinger was born in New York City to a Jewish middle-class family. Shy and unsociable as a child, he entered the Valle Foch Military Academy at the age of 15, where he felt uncomfortable. This school later became the model for *The Catcher in the Rye*. Many aspects of the protagonist Holden's life replicate Salinger's experiences at this school. Salinger is a unique writer. He has written only one full-length novel, for which he has become famous. For decades afterward, he lived in seclusion in his New Hampshire home, refusing interviews and other means of contact with the media and the outside world. He died on January 27th, 2010, at the age of 91.

2. Major works

The Catcher in the Rye
"The Young Folks"
"Slight Rebellion off Madison"
"I'm Crazy"
Nine Story
Franny and Zooey
Raise High the Roof Beam, Carpenters; and Seymour: An Introduction

3. Analysis of major work

◆*The Catcher in the Rye*

Salinger's only novel, *The Catcher in the Rye*, is a highly influential book from the postwar era. The novel tells the painful story of a high school boy growing up in a decadent New York, which may symbolize the larger Western society. The book's success is partly due to its superb handling of language. He demonstrates thoughtful and sympathetic insight into adolescence and adulthood. All these factors significantly contribute to the novel's remarkable achievement.

被日本占领的小岛安诺波贝的贫瘠海滩上。故事主要讲述了一个由十四人组成的军队登陆该岛并与敌人作战的经历。这个军队是一个六千人部队中的一部分，目标是夺取岛屿控制权，并为美军进攻菲律宾做准备。小说中的角色多样性很大，包括来自不同地区和社会背景的人物，通过这些角色，梅勒试图呈现美国社会的微缩画面。

Ⅳ. 杰罗姆·大卫·塞林格

1. 生平

塞林格出生于纽约市一个犹太中产阶级家庭。他幼时腼腆、不爱交际。15岁时进入瓦利福奇军校，在这里他感觉不能适应。这所学校后来成为《麦田里的守望者》的原型。主人公霍尔顿生活的诸多方面复制了塞林格在这所学校的经历。塞林格是一位独特的作家。他只写过一部长篇小说，并因此而扬名。之后数十年，他隐居在新罕布什尔的家中，拒绝采访和其他与媒体及外界联系的方式。他死于2010年1月27日，享年91岁。

2. 主要作品

《麦田里的守望者》
《年轻人》
《麦迪逊街边的小乱子》
《我疯了》
《九篇故事》
《弗拉尼和佐伊》
《木工们，升高顶梁；及西摩介绍》

3. 主要作品分析

◆《麦田里的守望者》

《麦田里的守望者》是塞林格创作的唯一一部小说，对战后时期产生了很大的影响。小说讲述了一个在腐朽的纽约成长的高中生的痛苦故事，可能是对整个西方社会的缩影。该书成功的原因之一是对语言的精彩处理。他对青春期和成年期的思考和同情是深入而富有洞察力的。所有这些因素都极大地增加了这部小说的壮丽成就。

V. Bernard Malamud (1914 -1986)

1. Introduction

Bernard Malamud is considered one of the major Jewish writers of the postwar period. Most of his works are about Jews and their lives.

2. Major works

The Natural
The Assistant
A New Life
The Fixer
The Tenants
Pictures of Fidelman
Dubin's Lives
God's Grace
The People
The Magic Barrel
Idiots First
Rembrandt's Hat

3. Analysis of major work

◆*The Assistant*

The Assistant is a typical Malamud narrative, telling a heartwarming story. The story is set in Brooklyn, New York City, with Morris Bober as the protagonist, a Jewish immigrant. Morris embodies the belief that love is a moral responsibility and perseveres through suffering, maintaining hope and faith in adversity.

Ⅵ. John Updike (1932 -2009)

1. Introduction

Updike's portrayal of the social landscape is authentic. He is deeply engaged in character development. He wrestles with experience to unveil its essence and establish a sense of direction. He is a dedicated literary artist.

2. Major works

The Centaur
Couples
Marry Me
Gertrude & Claudius
Rabbit, Run
Rabbit Redux
Rabbit Is Rich
Rabbit at Rest
Licks of Love

V. 伯纳德·马拉穆德

1. 简介

伯纳德·马拉穆德被认为是战后时期主要的犹太作家之一。他的大多数作品都是关于犹太人及其生活。

2. 主要作品

《天生有才能的人》
《店员》
《新生活》
《基辅怨》
《房客》
《费德尔曼写照》
《杜宾的生活》
《上帝的恩惠》
《人们》
《魔桶》
《白痴第一》
《拉姆布兰特的帽子》

3. 主要作品分析

◆《店员》

《店员》是一部典型的马拉默德作品，讲述了一个温馨的故事。故事背景设定在纽约市布鲁克林区，主人公莫里斯·博伯是一位犹太移民。莫里斯坚信爱是一种道德责任，在苦难中坚持不懈，在逆境中保持希望和信念。

Ⅵ. 约翰·厄普代克

1. 简介

厄普代克描绘社会景观具有真实性。他专注于人物刻画，努力探索经历，以揭示其本质并获得定向感，是一个认真的文学艺术家。

2. 主要作品

《半人半马》
《夫妻们》
《同我结婚》
《格特鲁德与克劳迪斯》
《兔子快跑》
《兔子归来》
《兔子阔了》
《兔子歇了》
《怀念兔子》

3. Analysis of major work	**3. 主要作品分析**
◆*Rabbit*, *Run*	◆《兔子快跑》
Rabbit, *Run* is the first book in a series. The main character, Harry (known as Rabbit), is a young man in his mid-twenties who feels empty and depressed. Unable to cope with the situation, Harry runs away for good. Rabbit keeps running from job to job, seeking advice and relationships with different women. He is unstoppable. John Updike portrays an individual abandoned to fend for himself in a society characterized by callousness and a lack of hope.	《兔子快跑》是系列小说的第一部。故事情节简单。主人公哈里(兔子)是一个二十多岁的年轻人，已经感到内心空虚和沮丧。因不能处理这样的情况，他选择了逃跑，而兔子一直在奔跑，从工作到工作，寻找着人生的答案，从一个女人到另一个女人。他不停地奔跑，没有什么可以阻止他。约翰·厄普代克描绘了一个人被自己抛弃在一个充满冷酷和缺乏希望的社会中。
Ⅶ. John Cheever (1912 – 1982)	**Ⅶ. 约翰·契弗**
1. Introduction	**1. 简介**
John Cheever is a notable short-story writer. Cheever's works primarily revolve around the lives of suburban middle-class individuals. His works have faced some critical neglect, as he writes in a more conservative style of mannered realism.	约翰·契弗是一位著名的短篇小说作家。他的作品主要围绕郊区中产阶级的生活，受到了一些批评家的忽视，因为他以一种更为保守的矫揉造作的现实主义风格写作。
2. Major works	**2. 主要作品**
The Stories of John Cheever	《约翰·契弗短篇小说集》
The Wapshot Chronicle	《维普肖特记事》
The Wapshot Scandal	《维普肖特丑闻》
Bullet Park	《布里特公园》
Falconer	《猎鹰者》
Oh What a Paradise It Seems	《啊，那多么像天堂》
"The Swimmer"	《游泳者》
Ⅷ. Flannery O'Connor (1925 – 1964)	**Ⅷ. 弗兰纳里·奥康纳**
1. Southern Literature	**1. 南方文学**
O'Connor is described as a representative of southern, Catholic, and grotesque literature, but she encompasses more than just these labels. Southern literature flourished during this period due to the dedicated efforts of writers like Flannery O'Connor and William Styron.	奥康纳被描述为南方文学、天主教和怪诞文学的代表。她不仅具备这些特点，还更加多样化。南方文学在此期间得以发展，主要归功于弗兰纳利·奥康纳和威廉·斯泰龙等作家的辛勤努力。
2. Literature Style	**2. 文学风格**
Growing up in the South, O'Connor focused on what she knew best as her main subject matter. Her works were influenced by the mid-century Catholic revival, evident in her religious perspective. Furthermore, O'Connor believes in the use of violence as a means to awaken people to the need for grace.	奥康纳在南方长大，将自己最熟悉的事物作为主要创作题材。她的作品中世纪天主教复兴时期的影响，并在她的所有作品中展现出宗教的视角。此外，奥康纳相信暴力可以作为唤醒人们对恩典需求的手段。

3. **Major works**

Wise Blood

A Good Man Is Hard to Find

The Violent Bear It Away

Everything That Rises Must Converge

4. **Analysis of major work**

◆*A Good Man Is Hard to Find*

A Good Man Is Hard to Find is O'Connor's most famous work, embodying the notable ingredients of her stories. The story revolves around a family of six who are killed by an escaped convict known as the Misfit during their vacation. The main character is the Grandmother, while the Misfit is a cold-blooded criminal with strong views on religion and society.

Ⅸ. William Styron (1925–2006)

1. **Introduction**

William Styron, born in Newport News, Virginia, was a prominent southern writer. Throughout his career, he received several prestigious awards, such as the Prix de Rome from the American Academy of Arts and Letters, the Pulitzer Prize, and the National Book Award.

2. **Major works**

Lie Down in Darkness

Set This House on Fire

The Confessions of Nat Turner

Sophie's Choice

The Long March

3. **Analysis of major work**

◆*Sophie's Choice*

The novel is a complex narrative that combines fact and autobiography, comedy and pathos, and history and fiction. Its aim is to universalize the Holocaust and delve into the depths of human evil. The story was adapted into a successful film starring Meryl Streep and Kevin Kline, winning the Oscar Award in 1983.

Ⅹ. Truman Capote (1924–1984)

1. **Introduction**

Truman Capote, born in New York, was a southern writer by theme. Most of his work is set in the Louisiana-Mississippi-Alabama area. The world he depicts in his works is a Gothic

3. **主要作品**

《慧血》

《好人难寻》

《暴力得逞》

《水到渠成》

4. **主要作品分析**

◆《好人难寻》

《好人难寻》是奥康纳最著名的作品，故事中体现了她作品的显著特点。故事描述了一个六口之家在度假期间被名为“不合群者”的逃犯杀害。故事的主要人物是祖母，而不合群者是一个冷血的罪犯，对宗教和社会有强烈的观点。

Ⅸ. 威廉·史泰伦

1. **简介**

威廉·史泰伦是美国南方作家之一，出生于弗吉尼亚州纽波特纽斯。他赢得了许多奖项，包括美国艺术与文学学院的罗马奖、普利策奖和国家图书奖。

2. **主要作品**

《在黑暗中躺下》

《放火烧屋》

《奈特·特纳的自白》

《索菲的选择》

《长途行军》

3. **主要作品分析**

◆《索菲的选择》

这部小说是一部复杂的叙事作品，融合了事实与自传、喜剧与悲剧、历史与虚构。它试图将大屠杀普遍化，并探索人类邪恶的程度。这个故事被改编成了一部成功的电影，由梅丽尔·斯特里普和凯文·克莱因主演，获得了1983年奥斯卡奖。

Ⅹ. 杜鲁门·卡波特

1. **简介**

杜鲁门·卡波特是纽约出生的作家，主题上属于南方作家。他的大部分作品设定在路易斯安那州、密西西比州和阿拉巴马州的地区。

and violent one. Capote was an autobiographical writer, with some motifs in his works reflecting his own life experience.

他描绘的世界充满哥特式和暴力元素。卡波特是一位自传性作家，他的作品中有一些基本的主题重复展现了他自己的生活经历。

2. Major works

Other Voices, Other Rooms

The Grass Harp

A Christmas Memory

Breakfast at Tiffany's

In Cold Blood

2. 主要作品

《其他声音，其他房间》

《草竖琴》

《圣诞回忆》

《蒂凡尼早餐》

《冷血》

XI. Philip Roth (1933 – 2018)

1. Introduction

Philip Roth, a major American Jewish writer, incorporated his personal Jewish experience into his fiction. His childhood in Newark, New Jersey, college education, brief military career, marriage, college teaching, psychoanalysis, and travel all influenced his works. He wrote over 20 volumes of work and was essentially a novelist of manners.

2. Major works

Goodbye, Columbus and Five Short Story

Portnoy's Complaint

XI. 菲利普·罗斯

1. 简介

菲利普·罗斯是一位重要的美国犹太作家，他在自己的小说中大量描写了自己的犹太人经历。他的童年在新泽西州纽瓦克度过，大学教育、短暂的军旅生涯、婚姻、大学教学、心理分析和旅行等经历都出现在他的作品中。罗斯创作了20多部作品，本质上是一位风俗小说家。

2. 主要作品

《再见，哥伦布，及五个短篇故事》

《波特诺伊的抱怨》

XII. Joyce Carol Oates (1938 –)

1. Introduction

Oates is a social novelist in the realist tradition. She focuses on common people and portrays their lives. Her works include characters such as students, merchants, teachers, clergymen, and workers, depicting their fears, anxieties, misfortunes, joys, and laughter. Oates excels at representing the inner complexities and sufferings of her characters when faced with overwhelming pressures from society, fate, or emotional inadequacies.

2. Major works

Them

Wonderland

Do with Me What You Will

XII. 乔伊斯·卡罗尔·欧茨

1. 简介

欧茨是一位现实主义传统的社会小说家。她关注普通人，描绘他们的生活。她的作品包括学生、商人、教师、牧师、工人等人物，描绘他们的恐惧、焦虑、不幸、欢乐和欢笑。奥茨擅长表现人物在面临来自社会、命运或情感不足的巨大压力时的内心复杂性和痛苦。

2. 主要作品

《他们》

《奇境》

《对我爱怎样就怎样》

XIII. Ann Beattie (1947 –)

1. Introduction

Ann Beattie is described as a minimalist writer. She abstracts and simplifies life to present a spare and dull social

XIII. 安·比蒂

1. 简介

安·比蒂被描述为一位极简主义作家。她将生活抽象化、简单化，

reality. She acknowledges Hemingway as a major stylistic influence, and her language, like his, is concise, suggestive, and connotative. Beattie's stories may appear realistic, but they lack realism in essence. She has already developed her own distinctive writing style.	呈现出闲适而沉闷的社会现实。她承认海明威对她的风格产生了重大影响，她的语言和他的语言一样简洁、富有启发性和内涵。比蒂的故事看似现实，但本质上缺乏现实主义。她已经形成了自己独特的写作风格。
2. Major works *Chilly Scenes of Winter* *Falling In Place* *Love Always* *Picturing Will* *Another You* *The Doctor's House* *Mrs. Nixon: A Novelist Imagines A Life* *A Wonderful Stroke of Luck*	**2. 主要作品** 《冬天的寒冷景象》 《到位》 《一直爱》 《想象意志》 《另一个你》 《医生之家》 《尼克松夫人：小说家想象的生活》 《奇妙的运气》

23.2 考研真题与典型题详解

I. Fill in the blanks.

1. *Seize the Day* was written by __________. （大连外国语学院2008研）
2. A very influential book to come out of the post-war world is a novel by J. D. Salinger entitled __________. （南开大学2008研）
3. John Cheever has written some of the finest short stories, and he wrote mainly about the __________ people.
4. The post-World War Ⅱ period wasn't a peaceful one for America. The life of the 1950s was poisoned at the root by __________, and that of the sixties enriched by __________. Whereas __________ weighted all the time on the consciousness of the people, life was complicated by violence, political or racial, including the assassination of __________ and __________.
5. The experimental feature of *The Naked and the Dead* merits attention. In it, Norman Mailer wedges __________ and __________ into otherwise normal narrative.

II. Multiple Choice

1. The title of J. D. Salinger's novel *The Catcher in the Rye* comes from __________ poem "if a body catch a body coming from the rye".

   A. William Wordsworth　　B. William Black
   C. Alfred Tennyson　　D. Robert Burns

2. Which of the following is NOT a southern writer in the USA?

   A. Saul Bellow　　B. Tennessee Williams
   C. Eudora Welty　　D. Flannery O'Connor

Ⅲ. Explain the following term.

1. Modernism

Ⅳ. Short answer question

1. Comment briefly on Saul Bellow's theme.

参考答案及解析

I. Fill in the blanks.

1. Saul Bellow

（索尔·贝洛，美国作家，1976 年荣获诺贝尔文学奖，瑞典皇家学会授奖时特别提及他的小说《只争朝夕》，认为是现代典型作品之一。）

2. *The Catcher in the Rye*

（《麦田里的守望者》是塞林格最著名的作品，描写的是一个叛逆的中学生霍尔顿。）

3. suburban middle class

（约翰·契弗(John Cheever)当代美国著名的短篇小说家，其小说主要描写郊区中产阶级生活。其最著名的短篇小说为《游泳者》"The Swimmer"。）

4. McCarthyism；the Civil Rights Movement；the Vietnam War；John F. Kennedy；Martin Luther King

（二战后美国并不太平。50 年代麦卡锡主义(McCarthyism)，60 年代的民权运动(the Civil Rights Movement)，越战(the Vietnam War)，及约翰·肯尼迪(John F. Kennedy)和马丁·路德·金(Martin Luther King)的遇刺都使美国人的思想不断经历着冲击。）

5. "chorus"；"the time machine"

（诺曼·梅勒(Norman Mailer)的作品《裸者与死者》(*The Naked and the Dead*)成为美国战争小说史上里程碑式的作品，其主题在于表现兽性与理想在人类心灵中的搏斗。该小说中诺曼·梅勒成功地运用了"副歌"("chorus")和"时间机器"("the time machine")的手法。）

II. Multiple Choice

1. D　J. D. 赛林格代表作是《麦田里的守望者》(*The Catcher in the Rye*)。这部小说的题目选自于罗伯特·彭斯的诗句"if a body catch a body coming from the rye"。

2. A　索尔·贝洛是著名的犹太作家，他出生于加拿大，在芝加哥长大，因而不是南方作家。

Ⅲ. Explain the following term

1. It's a general term applied to the wide range of experimental and avant-garde trends in literature of the early 20th century, including Symbolism, Futurism, Expressionism, Imagism, Vorticism, Dada, and Surrealism. Modernist literature is characterized chiefly by a rejection of 19th century traditions: the conventions of realism, for instance, were abandoned by Franz Kafka and other novelists, and by expressionist drama, while several poets rejected traditional meters in favor of free verse. Modernist writers tended to see themselves as an avant-garde disengaged from bourgeois values, and disturbed their readers by adopting complex and difficult new forms and styles. In fiction, the accepted continuity of chronological development was upset by Joseph Conrad, and William Faulkner, while James Joyce and Virginia Woolf attempted new ways of tracing the flow of characters' thoughts in their stream-of-consciousness styles. In poetry, Ezra Pound and T. S. Eliot replaced the logical exposition of thoughts with collages of fragmentary images and complex

allusions. Modernist writing is predominantly cosmopolitan, and often expresses a sense of urban cultural dislocation, along with an awareness of new anthropological and psychological theories. Its favored techniques of juxtaposition and multiple point of view challenge the reader to reestablish a coherence of meaning from fragmentary forms.

Ⅳ. Short answer question

1. Saul Bellow's themes are divided into three main areas. First, he believes that contemporary society is a threat to people's lives and independent personalities. Modern civilization tends to dehumanize, making people lose their distinction and turning them into what he calls "fat goods". Material abundance distracts people and separates them from each other. As a result, people living in this environment are prone to paranoia, nervousness, weakness and incompetence to the point of losing their minds. Bellow's characters are most likely to suffer from certain psychosis. They go through a phase before they regain their mental balance and serenity. F Finally, there is always the theme of the search for truth and values in his works. The process of the search is difficult and painful, but the end result is successful. To Saul Bellow, human's search for affirmation should have a happy ending, and people should see light in the end. The emotions of his characters are a mixture of sadness and joy, but in the end, they are all happy. He is indeed a very human writer.

第 24 章　二战后美国小说(2)

24.1　复习笔记

<table>
<tr>
<td>

Ⅰ. The Postmodernist Novel

1. Historical Background

Social, political, and artistic life in America were in turmoil when America moved into the 1960s. A wide range of social, political and artistic restlessness disturbed the thinking minds in the decades of 1960s and 1970s (It is necessary to remember a few things listed in the book such as the Vietnam war). Americans are more concerned about their society with the help of flooding information from various channels. The principles of democracy, individualism, and the credibility of the government all changed evidently in nature. So does popular awareness. It is noted that there is only a faint line or none between fact and fiction.

2. Postmodernist Novel

There was the novel of the absurd, metafiction, and avant-gardism.

(1) Old-fashioned novelistic devices are usually satirized by the novelists of the absurd. They believe it is impossible to grasp a certain truth and reality and that it is invalid for any traditional literary form to be faithful to reality. Their works often portray the tragic absurdity of the human condition as a huge joke. Therefore, their works share some common devices such as black humor or black comedy. It is probable to see a feeling of frustration and dilemma as well as a sense of suffering comes through laughter.

(2) Metafiction is fiction about fiction. It opposes realism but makes readers aware of fiction is fiction and makes readers to shape a reality for themselves. Text within text, authorial personae, and undecidability with no real story are among a series of metafictional approaches.

</td>
<td>

Ⅰ. 后现代主义小说

1. 历史背景

自美国步入 20 世纪 60 年代，美国社会、政治和艺术生活都处在不安动荡之中。一系列动荡不安的社会，政治和艺术生活现象强烈冲击着人们的思想(有必要识记书中列举的几种事件，比如越战)。信息通过各种渠道涌来，这使得大众对社会的关注更加强烈。民权主义、个人主义、政府的可信度等都发生了质的变化，公众的意识也发生了相似的改变。人们发现事实和虚幻之间的界限不再那么明显，甚至是不再存在了。

2. 后现代小说

后现代主义出现了荒诞小说，元小说和先驱小说。

(1) 荒诞主义小说家常常嘲弄传统小说技巧。他们认为真理和现实都是多样的、捉摸不透的、不稳定的；他们觉得任何自称能真实展现现实的传统形式都是不合逻辑、具有误导性的。人类境况的悲剧荒诞性在他们的作品中经常表现为特大笑话。小说家多采用的黑色幽默或是黑色喜剧。通常笑声传递出的更多的是悲哀和痛苦，苦恼和被困的感觉。

(2) 元小说以小说形式写作，又是一种有关小说的写作形式。它反对现实主义，使用小说的叙述风格，力图告诉读者小说就是小说，让读者自己去找到一种现实。重要的元小说技巧包括互为文本、原著者人物和没有真实故事的不可判定性。

</td>
</tr>
</table>

(3) Avant-gardism is a usual term for postwar writing which possesses forefront literary techniques. An avant-garde novel departs from novelistic norms, often not readable, even insulting to middlebrow taste.

Ⅱ. Joseph Heller (1923 – 1999)

The most important American novelist of the absurd after the Second World War is Joseph Heller. His famous *Catch-22* is based on his war experience, the title of which now is an English phrase.

1. Major Works

Catch-22

Something Happened

We Bombed in New Haven

Good as Gold

God Knows

2. Analysis of major work

◆*Catch-22*

(1) *Catch-22* was the first book in America to employ absurdist techniques to portray absurdity. The military power structure in the book is an objection to the absurdity of modern America.

(2) The protagonist, Yossarian, is afraid of death. He is no longer faithful to God, and feels insecure. The sight of death and absurdity frightens him and his fellow pilots.

(3) The world of Yossarian is absurd. The way Heller reveals it is through parody. Three major features satirize fully the military unreason: the structured turmoil of the military organization, the military logic (the typical symbol is the rule "Catch-22"), and the ubiquitous absurdity.

(4) The absurd depth of the modern world is reflected by Joseph Heller's absurd linguistic superficial appearance. The absurdity of the mad world is exposed deftly by the following devices: "circular conversations", constructions with their

(3) 先驱主义被用来指具有先驱位置的战后作品。先驱小说代表着与普通小说标准的完全脱离，通常很少或几乎没有故事趣味性，不仅枯燥无味，而且不为受过一般教育的读者所喜欢，大都没有可读性。

Ⅱ. 约瑟夫·海勒

约瑟夫·海勒是美国二战后最杰出的荒诞派小说家。著名的《第二十二条军规》是以其战争经历为基础写就的，其标题已经成为英语语言中的一个新的词汇。

1. 主要作品

《第二十二条军规》

《出了毛病》

《我们轰炸纽黑文》

《好的不得了》

《上帝知道》

2. 主要作品分析

◆《第二十二条军规》

(1)《第二十二条军规》是美国第一部以荒诞技巧表现荒诞主题的著作，它以对军队情景的具体描述抗议现代美国社会的荒诞性。

(2) 故事的主人公，飞行员尤索林，害怕自己会死去，他对上帝失去了信仰，再也没有了安全感。他和其他伙伴一起惊恐地目睹了发生在身边的死亡和荒诞事件。

(3) 尤索林所在的是一个荒诞的世界，通过三个特点，海勒对军队的荒谬性进行了残酷讽刺：即军队结构中的组织混乱，军事逻辑（其象征之一就是"第二十二条军规"）和各个层面上分布的荒诞性。

(4) 约瑟夫海勒运用了荒诞的语言表象来反映现代社会的荒诞程度之深。许多文学手法，如"循环式对话"问答极其幽默并出人意料；"套语"的运用，即把俗语中关键字眼换成能产生荒谬效果的字词；谈话语气的突然变化，即由严肃话

funny, unexpected responses, the "wrenched cliché" which is a consequence of the change of "a key word in an otherwise hackneyed expression," juxtaposed incongruities, sudden tonal changes from seriousness to triviality.

题到琐细话题的突然跳跃和转换等等诸如此类的文学修辞手法。这些手法的巧妙结合，使小说的文字呈现一种荒诞状貌，有力地表现了一个疯狂世界缺乏理智和逻辑以及不可预料的特点。

Ⅲ. Kurt Vonnegut (1922 –2007)

Vonnegut is basically a science fiction writer. His short stories are also famous where he skillfully combines black humor with science fiction.

Ⅲ. 库尔特·冯内古特

冯内古特基本上是一位科幻作家。他同时也是一位短篇小说家。他善于在短篇作品中将黑色幽默和科幻相结合。

1. Major Works

Player Piano
Mother Night
Cat's Cradle
Slaughterhouse-Five
Breakfast of Champions
Slapsticks
Jailbird
Deadeye Dick
Galapagos
Bluebird
Hocus Pocus
Canary in a Cathouse
Welcome to the Monkey House

1. 主要作品

《自动钢琴》
《黑夜母亲》
《猫的摇篮》
《第五号屠宰场》
《冠军的早餐》
《滑稽剧》
《囚鸟》
《神枪手迪克》
《加拉帕戈斯群岛》
《蓝鸟》
《咒语》
《猫舍里的金丝雀》
《欢迎来到猴子屋》

2. Analysis of major work

◆*Slaughterhouse-Five*

(1) *Slaughterhouse-Five* is an antiwar novel. It not only delineates life and history but also disapproves of human's brutality against human during the war, which is the root cause of life's misery.

(2) Death is a common phenomenon in the novel and is always concluded by "So it goes", a phrase that mixes so many emotional shades such as anger, agony, apathy, helplessness, and cynical distaste at life and history. He implies that history is either meaningless or purposeless, and the human dilemma does not bother God. Life is so absurd that the people's attitude toward life is nihilistic.

2. 主要作品分析

◆《第五号屠宰场》

(1)《第五号屠场》是一部反战小说。它不仅描述了生活和历史如何如何，也谴责了战争中人类对彼此的野蛮残酷。后者使得生活变得悲惨。

(2) 小说中一百次提到了死亡，而且每次都伴随着"就这么回事"的语句，这个短语包含了对生活和历史的愤怒、痛苦、冷漠、无助、愤世嫉俗的厌恶这样多种感情色彩。作者暗示着历史既没有意义，也没有目的，上帝对人类的困境丝毫没有兴趣。生命是荒诞的，偶然的和尴尬的，所以人们似乎不在意它的结束。

(3) The structure of the book confirms the absurdity in the book. The stream of consciousness dealing with time strengthens the absurdity.	(3) 生活的荒诞主题通过其结构得到加强，处理时间的方式是使用了意识流。
(4) Black humor also strengthens the absurdity in the book.	(4) 黑色幽默使得这部作品的荒诞特点得到加强。
Ⅳ. Ken Kesey (1935 – 2001)	**Ⅳ. 肯·克西**
Ken Kesey was another well-known novelist of the absurd.	肯·克西是另一位著名的荒诞派小说家。
1. Major Works	**1. 主要作品**
One Flew Over the Cuckoo's Nest *Sometimes a Great Notion* *Demon Box* *Sailor Song*	《飞越疯人院》 《永不让步》 《恶魔的盒子》 《水手之歌》
2. Analysis of major work	**2. 主要作品分析**
◆*One Flew Over the Cuckoo's Nest*	◆《飞越疯人院》
(1) Theme of the book	(1)主题概要
The mental hospital ward symbolizes a microcosm of the larger world, the world people live in. It suggests that crazy individuals live in a crazy world. The story describes a cold ruler, known as "the Combine," who controls a system of control. This ruler is Big Nurse, who establishes rules and enforces them, disregarding human worth and rights.	精神病院病房象征着整个世界的缩影，人们生活的世界。这意味着疯狂的人生活在一个疯狂的世界中。这个故事描述了一位被称为“联合体”的冷酷统治者，他控制着一个控制系统。这位统治者是大护士，他制定规则并执行它们，无视人类的价值和权利。
(2) McMurphy's Tragedy	(2)麦克墨菲的悲剧
There are two basic reasons for McMurphy's personal tragedy: one personal and one social. In terms of his personal conduct, McMurphy has a tendency to resent and resist all rules and regulations. McMurphy lacks self-control, allowing his anger to overpower him and putting himself and his friends at unnecessary risk of danger and death.	麦克墨菲的个人悲剧有两个基本原因：一个是个人原因，一个是社会原因。从个人行为来看，麦克墨菲的性格存在一些缺点，即他倾向于对所有规则和法规产生怨恨和抵制。麦克墨菲并不以自我控制著称，他允许愤怒压倒自己，并使自己和他的朋友们暴露在不必要的危险和死亡之中。
(3) Absurdist techniques of the book	(3)荒诞主义技巧
One Flew Over the Cuckoo's Nest portrays an absurd world where a fog-generating machine creates a surreal atmosphere and blurs the line between reality and unreality, leading to uncertainty.	《飞越疯人院》刻画了一个荒谬的世界，通过雾机器制造出超现实的印象，使现实与虚幻交织，产生不确定性。
Ⅴ. John Barth (1930 –)	**Ⅴ. 约翰·巴思**
He is a highly significant writer of the period. His credited 1967 essay "The Literature of Exhaustion" marked the beginning of postmodern and metafictional fiction in America and also claimed the end of conventional realism.	他是这一时期重要的作家。其为人称道的一件事是，他在 1967 年写了一篇文章《枯竭的文学》，这篇文章标志着美国后现代和超小说的开端，也宣布了传统现实主义的死亡。

1. Major works *The Floating Opera* *The End of the Road* *The Scot-Weed Factor* *Lost in the Funhouse* *Letters: A Novel* *Sabbatical: A Romance* *The Tidewater Tales* *The Friday Book* *Giles Goat-Boy*	**1. 主要作品** 《浮动的歌剧》 《路的尽头》 《烟草代理商》 《迷失在娱乐场中》 《书信集》 《假日浪漫史》 《湖边的故事》 《星期五札记》 《羊孩贾尔思》
2. View of "The Literature of Exhaustion" In 1967, Barth wrote an essay declaring the death of the traditional realist novel. Barth believed that the novel as a genre had reached its limits and exhausted all available plots.	**2.《枯竭的文学》观点概述** 巴思在 1967 年写了一篇文章，宣布传统现实主义小说的死亡。他认为小说其形式的可能性已经用尽，所有可用的情节都已经被使用过。
3. New way of writing John Barth's early novels mark the beginning of his attempt to establish a new approach to fiction writing. While still following traditional models, these works introduce changes in theme and technique. Barth presents an absurd and meaningless world, which becomes a central theme in his later works. He also seeks to revitalize exhausted literary forms by incorporating parody and framing into his own structures. Parody and framing later become significant features of his postmodern writing.	**3. 写作创新** 巴思的早期小说标志着他尝试建立小说写作新方法的开始。这些作品在沿袭传统模式的同时，在主题和技法上也发生了变化。巴特呈现了一个荒诞无意义的世界，这成为他后期作品的中心主题。他还试图通过将戏仿和框架融入自己的结构中来复兴枯竭的文学形式。戏仿和框架后来成为他后现代写作的重要特征。
Ⅵ. Donald Barthelme (1931 – 1989) Barthelme was a short story writer, a novelist, and a writer of children's literature.	**Ⅵ. 唐纳德·巴塞尔姆** 巴塞尔姆是一位短篇故事家、小说家、儿童文学作家。
1. Major Works *Come Back, Dr. Caligarri* *Unspeakable Practices, Unnatural Acts* *City Life* *Sadness* *Guilty Pleasures* *Amateurs* *Great Days* *Overnight to Many Distant Cities* *Snow White* *The Dead Father* *The King* *The Slightly Irregular Fire Engine*	**1. 主要作品** 《回来吧，卡里加利博士》 《不可言说的做法，不自然的行为》 《城市生活》 《悲伤》 《心感内疚的娱乐》 《业余爱好者》 《美好的日子》 《通宵畅游许多遥远的城市》 《白雪公主》 《亡父》 《国王》 《不太规则的消防车》

2. As an anti-novelist

Barthelme is known as an anti-novelist, with his short stories exemplifying this characteristic. He wrote over 150 short stories that offer new perspectives on life and artistic presentations. His writing style includes language and tonal overtones, unique sentences, crosscutting, collage and avant-garde techniques, and surrealism, making his works not always easily readable. However, his enjoyable black humor helps dispel depression and gloom.

2. 反小说家

巴塞尔姆被称为反小说家，主要在他的短篇小说中展现了这一特点。他写了一百五十多篇短篇小说，让人们以新的角度看待生活和艺术呈现。他的写作风格包括语言和意义的暗示、独特的句子、交叉剪辑、拼贴和前卫技巧以及超现实主义，这些使他的作品并非总是易于阅读。然而，他愉快的黑色幽默能够消除沮丧和忧郁。

Ⅶ. Thomas Pynchon (1937 –)

Thomas Pynchon is a contemporary writer with his life unknown. The publication of the *Gravity's Rainbow* won him the National Book Award and has since received enormous critical attention. It ensured Pynchon's prominence in American postmodern fiction.

Ⅶ. 托马斯·品钦

托马斯·品钦是当代作家中生平鲜为人所知的一个。他的作品《万有引力之虹》获得了国家图书奖并吸引了评论界的关注，这奠定了他在美国后现代小说界的杰出地位。

1. Literary theories

Scientific and technologic theories, which help to explain Pynchon's thematic worries, play a principal role through Pynchon's writing career. These include entropy and the quantum theory. Entropy is a physics term, denoting the tendency of the universe toward uniformity. Quantum theory thinks that uncertainty is immanent in everything, and that human's knowledge is false. His entropic vision sees the mechanical civilization puts humans at risk. It leads to dehumanization of humans and reduces them into "inanimate automation".

1. 文学理论

品钦在写作生涯中借鉴了科学技术理论，并将它们作为作品中传递消息的原理，包括熵和量子理论。熵是物理名词，指示着宇宙走向统一的趋势。品钦也同样对量子理论着迷，根据该理论，所有的事物包含一定程度的不确定性，扩充来说，人类的知识是不准确的。这些理论很好地反映了品钦的主题思想。在他关于熵的看法里，机械文明的威胁会使人们失去人性，将他们变为灰暗的"死气沉沉的自动机器"。

2. Major Works

V.

The Crying of Lot 49

Gravity's Rainbow

Vineland

Mason & Dixon

Slow Learner: *Early Stories*

2. 主要作品

《V.》

《第四十九组拍卖邮票的呼唤》

《万有引力之虹》

《葡萄园》

《梅森和迪克森》

《笨鸟集》

Ⅷ. William Burroughs (1914 –1997)

William Burroughs was the oldest of the Beat writers.

Ⅷ. 威廉·勃洛斯

威廉·勃洛斯是"垮掉的一代"作家中最为年长的一位。

1. Features of his works

Drugs, perverse ways of living, violence, and homosexuality

1. 作品特点

他只写毒品、变态生活、暴力

are the themes of his works which are devoted to portraying life in its oddest form. He likes to think and communicate distinctly from accepted standards. Burroughs enjoyed shocking his readers out of their accustomed perceptive patterns and delighted in distracting them from their self-satisfaction.

和同性恋题材，总之，就是关于生活最奇异和古怪的形式。他的作品展示了不同于普通标准的思考和交流状态。博罗斯喜欢使读者震惊，脱离他们的常规理解方式，他非常着迷于将让他们从舒适自得中转移注意力。

2. Major works

Junkie

The Exterminator

The Wild Boys

Cities of the Red Light

Queer

Mind Wars

The Naked Lunch

Place of Dead Roads

2. 主要作品

《吸毒者》

《灭虫者》

《放荡的人们》

《红夜城》

《同性恋》

《思想战争》

《裸露午餐》

《死路之地》

Ⅸ. Jack Kerouac (1922 –1969)

Jack Kerouac was, along with Ginsberg and Burroughs, representative of the Beat generation of the 1950s.

Ⅸ. 杰克·凯鲁瓦克

杰克·凯鲁瓦克和金斯堡、勃洛斯一起，是20世纪50年代年轻骚动一代的代表人物。

1. Writing style

Kerouac is famous for his "spontaneous prose", an experimental style that made him disregard accepted rules and restraints in writing. He declared that he found this style in 1951. It is rapid writing like jazz, emphasizing improvisation and neglecting steadiness. *On the Road* is a good example of "spontaneous prose".

1. 写作风格

克鲁亚克的实验性写作风格叫做"自发式散文"，这使得他能摆脱一般写作规则和局限，自由地写作。他宣称在1951年发现了这种方式。这种写作方式基本不用时间思考、较少进行修改，像爵士乐一样自由、快速，没有固定的音调。《在路上》是这种写作风格的典型例子。

2. Major Works

The Subterraneans

Maggie Cassady

The Lonesome Traveler

On the Road

2. 主要作品

《地下者》

《麦吉·凯萨迪》

《孤独的旅行者》

《在路上》

3. Analysis of major work

◆*On the Road*

Tensions, conflicts, and abnormal themes in the book are attractive to the imagination of the readers, though it has neither an obvious dramatic interest nor an obvious plot line. Alcoholics, junkies, and jazz musicians are common characters in the book. Although the two protagonists, Dean Moriarty

3. 主要作品分析

◆《在路上》

作品属于散文叙述体，没有多少戏剧性，也没有什么情节，有的只是悬而未决的紧张局面，让人身心疲惫的冲突，和非传统的主题，明显地吸引着读者的想象力。作品中许多角色都是酒鬼、瘾君子和爵

and Sal Paradise, are both depraved drug addicts they still grope for their truth. *On the Road* is a story immune to life pressure, featuring a sympathetic first-person narrator and a confessional style.	士音乐家等。迪恩莫里亚蒂和萨尔帕拉斯蒂两个主角都是吸毒成瘾者，虽然堕落却还仍在摸索着属于他们的真理。《在路上》由一位富有同情心的第一人称叙述者讲述，使用忏悔式风格，是一个关于从生活的重压下得到自由的故事。
X. Vladimir Nabokov(1899 –1977) He was from a wealthy family in St. Petersburg of Czarist Russia. He studied Romance languages and literature in Trinity College, Cambridge University. His immigration to America in 1940 indicated a turning point of his career. He was a classic postmodern and metafiction writer. **1. Major Works** *Lolita* *Dar, or the Gift* *Pale Fire* **2. Writing style** Nabokov is a typical postmodern and metafiction writer. He aimed to subvert the narrative strategies of traditional realism. He employed metafictional techniques, such as text within text. He told his stories in confusing ways, often destabilizing the narratives to confuse readers.	**X. 弗拉基米尔·纳博科夫** 弗拉基米尔·纳博科夫出生在沙皇俄国圣彼得堡的一个富有家庭。他在剑桥大学三一学院学习罗曼语言和文学。1940 年移居美国成为他事业的转折点。他是一位典型的后现代和超小说作家。 **1. 主要作品** 《洛丽塔》 《献礼，又名天赋》 《微暗的火》 **2. 写作风格** 纳博科夫是典型的后现代和元小说作家。他试图颠覆传统现实主义的叙事策略。他在作品中运用了元小说技巧，如文字中的文字。他以令人困惑的方式叙述故事，常常使叙述不稳定，以困惑读者。

24.2 考研真题与典型题详解

I. Fill in the blanks.

1. __________ by Joseph Heller is the representative novel of black humor. (南开大学 2008 研)
2. A great postmodern writer, __________ became the cult figure of the counterculture generation at that time, known as "a gum for the youth" in supporting the students in their anti-war movements.

II. Multiple Choice

1. __________ wrote the essay "The Literature of Exhaustion" and was the first to announce that the traditional novel is dead, and that traditional novelistic resources have been exhausted.
   A. Donald Barthelme　　B. John Barth
   C. Kurt Vonnegut　　D. Vladimir Nabokov
2. Out of the fifty-two paragraphs that make up the story of *Lost in the Funhouse* by John Barth, five consist wholly of the author's chat about fiction writing, which is the typical feature of __________.
   A. metafiction　　B. poststructuralist fiction

C. dystopian fiction D. black humor fiction

3. Which of the following is not Thomas Pynchon's works?

A. *V.* B. *The Crying of Lot* 49

C. *Gravity's Rainbow* D. *Letters*

4. William Burroughs and Jack Kerouac belong to ________.

A. the Confessional School B. the Black Mountain Poets

C. novelists of absurdity D. the Beat Writers

5. Which beat-poet wrote the work *On the Road*?

A. Allen Ginsberg. B. Jack Kerouac.

C. William Burroughs. D. Charles Bukowski.

Ⅲ. Explain the following terms.

1. Postmodernism（北航 2010 研）
2. Yossarian（from: *Catch-22*）（厦门大学 2008 研）
3. Surrealism
4. Expressionism
5. Black humor（厦门大学 2010 研）
6. Metafiction

Ⅳ. Short answer questions

1. What are the formal characteristics of postmodern writings（list at least three）.
2. What ideas does Thomas Pynchon want to express by the obscure identity of V in the novel *V.*?

Ⅴ. Essay questions

1. What brought the change from Modernism to Postmodernism in postwar American literature?
2. How do you understand the novel of the absurd of the 1960s?

参考答案及解析

Ⅰ. Fill in the blanks.

1. *Catch-22*

（《第二十二条军规》是约瑟夫·海勒的著名小说，也是黑色幽默的代表作。）

2. Kurt Vonnegut

（在上世纪 60－70 年代的美国大学里，年轻学生们常常把库尔特·冯内古特的书揣在牛仔裤兜里，他让前卫小说变得好读、有趣，成为美国黑色幽默文学代表人物。）

Ⅱ. Multiple Choice

1. B 约翰·巴斯在 1967 年写了一篇文章《枯竭的文学》，这篇文章标志着美国后现代和超小说的开端，也宣布了传统现实主义的死亡。

2. A 超小说（metafiction）是有关小说的小说：是关注小说的虚构身份及其创作过程的小说。小说的叙述往往在谈论正在进行的叙述本身，并使这种对叙述的叙述成为小说整体的一部分。

3. D D 项不是品钦的作品。

4. D 美国作家威廉·巴勒斯（William Burroughs）与艾伦·金斯堡（Allen Ginsberg）及杰克·

凯鲁亚克(Jack Kerouac)同为“垮掉的一代”文学运动的创始者。

5. B 《在路上》是“垮掉的一代”作家杰克·凯鲁亚克的代表作。

Ⅲ. Explain the following terms.

1. Postmodernism: Postmodernism is a disputed term that has occupied much recent debate about contemporary culture since the early 1980s. It is said to be a culture of fragmentary sensations, eclectic nostalgia, disposable simulacra, and promiscuous superficiality, in which the traditionally valued qualities of depth, coherence, meaning, originality, and authenticity are evacuated or dissolved amid the random swirl of empty signals. It seems to have no relevance to modern poetry, and little to drama, but is used widely in reference to fiction, notably to the novels (or anti-novels) and stories of Thomas Pynchon, Kurt Vonnegut, Italo Calvino, Vladimir Nabokov, William S. Burroughs, and Angela Carter.
2. In *Catch-22*, Yossarian is a 28-year-old Captain in the 256th squadron of the Army Air Forces where he serves as a B-25 bombardier stationed on the small island of Pianosa during World War II. Throughout the novel, Yossarian's main concern is the idea that people are trying to kill him, and he goes to great lengths to try to prevent his death.
3. Surrealism is a literary and art movement, influenced by Freudianism, dedicated to expressing the imagination as revealed in dreams, free of the conscious control of reason and convention. Founded in Paris by Andre Breton with his Manifesto of Surrealism, it can be traced back to Rimbaud, and Baudelaire. In literature, surrealism was confined almost exclusively to France, and was based on the associations and implications of words. Surrealism was a major intellectual force between the wars.
4. The term refers to a movement in Germany early in the 20th century, in which a number of painters sought to avoid the representation of external reality and instead, to project a highly personal vision of the world. The main principle involved is that expression determines form, and therefore imagery, punctuation, syntax, and so on. In belief, any of the formal rules and elements of writing can be bent or disjointed to suit the purpose. Theatrically, expressionism was a reaction against realism in that it tends to show inner psychological realities. O'Neill's plays are some of the best examples.
5. It is a kind of writing that places grotesque elements side by side with humorous ones in an attempt to shock the readers, forcing him or her to laugh at the horrifying reality of a disordered world. It is a humor out of despair and laughter out of tears. Black humor conveys anguish and fury at conditions in which institutionalized absurdity gets the upper hand. It intends to satirize hypocrisy, racial prejudice, and above all the dehumanization of the individual by a modern society. Black humor prevails in modern American Literature. Joseph Heller's Novel *Catch-22* is considered a superb example of the use of Black humor. Kurt Vonnegut's *Slaughterhouse Five* is also a case in point.
6. Metafiction is a literary term popularized by Robert Scholes to describe novels that specifically and self-consciously examine the nature and status of fiction itself and that often contain experiments to test fiction as a form in one way or another. Postmodernist writers tend to apply metafic-

tion in their works, for instance, John Barth's *Lost in the Funhouse* and John Fowles's *The French Lieutenant's Woman.*

Ⅳ. Short answer questions

1. Postmodern writers tend to (1) apply metafictional techniques; (2) use parody; (3) employ literary collage; (4) aim at the deconstruction of genres; (5) have fragmented narratives; (6) discontinuity, uncertainty, and disorder in time and plot, etc.
2. V is the person/thing that the protagonist wants to seek in the story. V seems to have many identities, which puzzles the protagonist. The author wants to show that the world is full of uncertainties and that it is impossible to gain access to the truth.

Ⅴ. Essay questions

1. In terms of the idea of art, in the 1890s and the first years of the 20th century art and poetry were regarded as the finished products of the creative process, closed in form, with rhymes and stanzas, coherent images and figures, and completed in plot enacted. While art and poetry of Postmodernism are seen as open, on-going, not as the end of thought, but as the process of the mind thinking, stressing motion, created on the impulse of the moment, and not previously well-planned. And there is not much of the finely metered Modernist poem in the new verse that, instead of aiming at an elite readership, endeavors to the common people as much as possible.

   Thematically, the new poetry normally portrays everyday experiences, events, and emotions. It envisions man as vulnerable and helpless and at the mercy of overwhelming odds. It accepts life for what it is, feeling resigned, painfully aware of its inability to control and contain life. Instead of trying to "give shape and significance to the immense panorama of futility and anarchy that is contemporaneous history" (as Eliot puts it), the new verse tries to represent life as it is with its strengths and weaknesses, as something inconsistent, ever changing, and never wholly knowable. The poets' job is, seen by some people, to seize the moment and make the best of it for themselves as well as for the world at large.

   As regards formal considerations, the new verse embraces open form, "the perfect, easy discipline of the swallow's dip and swoop, without east to west" (as Gary Snyder puts it). It repudiates the Eliotic, New Critical values of impersonality and objectivity as distancing art from life. It refuses to use "persona" as they feel it separates the writers from their readers. In the new verse, there is very often autobiographical; the tone is personal and emotional; the emotions are often intense though qualifies: there is ambivalence and humor amid remorse, disgust of anguish. The diction of the new verse is mostly from daily speech, its style is conversational, colloquial, discursive and meditative, and its mood generally casual and relaxed. It is necessary to note here that contemporary American poetry is not always easy to read. In fact, much of this poetry is very hard to understand. Possible reasons for this may include the private nature of the poet's thinking and expression, and their self-indulgence encouraged by the postmodern tendency of extreme individualization.
2. The notion that the universe is absurd was not really new to American authors. But the "absurd" novelists of the sixties tend to regard the conventional novel as "literature of exhaustion". To

them the old ways of presentation are no longer good enough, and even obsolete. To reflect the new, stupefying and sickening reality, these conventions must be updated, while at the same time new devices should be found. The 1960s and 1970s proved to be a period in which the common run of humanity had also come to sense absurdity existing on all conceivable levels of life, and it fell to the "absurd" novelists to discover a new rhetoric effective enough to voice that feeling in literature.

The novelists of the absurd tend to burlesque traditional novelistic devices. They parody other novels, other styles and forms and take them with highly equivocal attitudes: they want to prove the artificiality of any literary art which, by pretending to bring order to reality, falsifies it and keeps people from comprehending its absurdity. The universe is out of joint. It is a tragic place to live in. The response they intend to provoke in the reader to the blackness of modern life is laughter that is, laughing in face of a tragic situation. Hence black humor, or black comedy, is one of the commonly employed devices of the novelists of the absurd. What occurs oftener is a sense of grief and pain coming through the laughter, a feeling of frustration and being bottle up.

The writers of the absurd tend to accept the world as it is. They regard these features of modern existence as normal and locate themselves within the messiness of their world. They attempt to generate meaning in the face of, but without denying chaos and absurdity. For them uncertainty is the rule. Because they believe that the self constitutes part and parcel of the world, involvement, immersion, and participation become their ethic.

第 25 章　多种族文学(1)：非裔美国文学

25.1　复习笔记

I. Overview of African American Literature	**I. 非裔美国文学发展概貌**
1. General Introduction	**1. 概述**
Mainstream American literature distorted the portrayal of African Americans for a long time. Even well-intentioned writers like Mark Twain couldn't overcome their prejudices. African American literature, different in nature, centers on the myth of deliverance from slavery, akin to the biblical story of Moses leading the Jews to freedom. African American people often express their feelings and aspirations in biblical terms, reflecting the essential spirit of their literature.	美国主流文学长期以来扭曲了非裔美国人的形象，即使是马克·吐温这样善意的作家也无法克服他们的偏见。非裔美国文学性质不同，以摆脱奴隶制的神话为中心，类似于摩西带领犹太人走向自由的圣经故事。非裔美国人经常用圣经术语表达他们的感受和愿望，反映了他们文学的基本精神。
2. Literature Evolution	**2. 演变**
(1) African American literature is closely connected to the unique experiences of African Americans. African American literature develops from oral tradition in the form of songs, ballads, and spirituals. The folk literature in its various manifestations contributes to Afro-American literature.	(1)非裔美国文学与非裔美国人独特的经历紧密相连。非裔美国文学从口头传说发展而来，包括歌曲、民谣、圣歌等形式。各种各样表现形式的民间文学促进了非裔美国文学的发展。
(2) The 1960s turned out to be a chaotic period for the United States when the African Americans awoke to the pursuit for Black power. It also proved to be a period of spectacular growth in African American literature.	(2)20 世纪 60 年代是美国社会的动荡时期，这一时期美国黑人觉醒和黑人权利斗争。它同时也是美国非裔文学茁壮成长、颇受关注的时期。
(3) Contemporary writers such as Toni Morrison and Alice Walker contribute to the development of African American literature.	(3)当代作家托尼·莫里森和爱丽丝·沃克为非裔美国文学做出了突出的贡献。
3. The Great Migration	**3. 大迁徙**
The abolitionist movement and the Civil War inspired African American literature. After the Emancipation, the Great Migration occurred in full swing in the years between 1890 and 1920. Large numbers of sharecroppers moved from the south to the north and poured into the cities. Harlem New York City became the hub of black life after the Great Migration attracted artists and intellectuals.	废奴运动和美国内战为非裔美国文学注入了新活力。黑人奴隶解放后，1890 年到 1920 年间，大规模的迁移进行的如火如荼。大量的佃农从南向北迁移涌入城市。大迁徙吸引了大批黑人艺术家和知识分子，而纽约的哈莱姆区也成为黑人文化中心。

4. The Harlem Renaissance

The Harlem Renaissance was an intellectual and cultural revival of African American literature in the 1920s and 1930s. Shortly after the First World War, a new black intelligentsia appeared on the scene, rebelling against traditional values and embracing the influence of the modernist movement in Europe and the United States. They sought a better standard of living and relief from the institutionalized racism in the South. They began a search for a distinct tradition of their own lives and values and tried to solicit the attention of their African American people as well as the whites. The movement continued to be an important cultural force in the United States.

II. Frederick Douglass (1817 –1895)

Frederick Douglass was born a slave, who saw his own folks born enslaved and lived a brutal life himself.

◆Major work

My Bondage and My Freedom

The Life and Times of Frederick Douglass

III. W. E. B. Dubois (1868 –1963)

As the first African American intellectual to receive a Ph. D., Dubois helped to found the National Association for the Advancement of Colored People. His major works includes *The Souls of Black Folks: Essays and Sketches.*

IV. Jean Toomer (1894 –1967)

Jean Toomer, a leader of the Harlem Renaissance, wrote a significant novel *Cane* in 1923, which holds an important place in African American literature.

◆Analysis of major work

Cane is captivating due to its themes and experimental techniques, influenced by James Joyce, T. S. Eliot, and Ezra Pound, while remaining deeply connected to the African American community.

The novel is based on Toomer's experiences teaching at a school for African Americans in Georgia and is divided into three sections set in different locations. It has an autobiographical

4. 哈莱姆文艺复兴

"哈莱姆文艺复兴"是20世纪20和30年代的由非裔知识分子主导的美国非裔文学的复兴运动。一战后不久，出现了一个新的黑人知识分子阶层，他们反叛父辈的价值观和生活方式，并受到纽约市的艺术和文学创新中心以及欧美现代主义运动的影响。他们试图从南方奴隶制度的阴影中得到解脱，寻求更好的生活方式。他们开始追寻能确立非裔身份的传统生活与价值，并试图让美国黑人和白人都注意到这一点。哈莱姆文艺复兴作为一种文化力量持续影响着美国社会。

II. 弗雷德里克·道格拉斯

弗雷德里克·道格拉斯生来就是奴隶，他亲眼目睹了他的种族受奴役的生活，也亲身体验过那种残酷的生活。

◆主要作品

《我的枷锁和我的自由》

《弗雷德里克·道格拉斯的生平及时代》

III. W. E. B. 杜波依斯

杜波依斯是第一位获得博士学位的美国黑人。他还协助建立了"全国有色人种发展协会"。他的主要作品包括《黑人的灵魂》。

IV. 基恩·图默

基恩·图默是哈莱姆文艺复兴运动的领导者之一，他的小说《甘蔗》是非常重要的美国非裔文学作品之一。

◆主要作品分析

《甘蔗》的主题和实验性技巧都非常吸引人，显示出作者对詹姆斯·乔伊斯、T·S·艾略特和埃兹拉·庞德有意识的借鉴，同时与自己的族群紧密联系。

这部小说基于作者在乔治亚州一所非裔学校工作的经历。小说分为三个部分，第一部分和第三部分

element, recording the author's experiences as acting principal of the Sparta Agricultural and Industrial Institute in Georgia, where he rediscovered his African American heritage and folklore lost during the Great Migration.

Cane defies easy categorization, mixing different genres in a well-arranged and balanced manner, employing unique narrative strategies and shifting perspectives.

设定在乔治亚州，第二部分设定在芝加哥和华盛顿特区。其是自传性的，记录了作者在乔治亚州斯帕塔农业工业学院担任代理校长的个人经历，发现了自己的非裔美国人血统，并重新信仰了他认为在大迁徙中失去的种族民间传说。

这本书的形式难以定义，它融合了不同的文学体裁，安排得很好，平衡度高，具有独特的叙述策略和不断变换的视角。

V. Countee Cullen (1903 – 1946)

Countee Cullen was a well-educated poet, having studied at New York University and Harvard. At the time, he was likely the most popular African American poet and literary figure in America.

◆Major works

Color

Copper Sun

The Black Christ

The Ballad of the Brown Girl

V. 康提·库伦

康提·库伦是受过良好教育的诗人，曾在纽约大学和哈佛大学学习。在当时那个时期，他可能是美国最受欢迎的非裔美国诗人和文学家。

◆主要作品

《色彩》

《铜太阳》

《黑色基督》

《棕色女孩的歌谣》

Ⅵ. Langston Hughes (1902 – 1967)

Langston Hughes was a key figure in the Harlem Renaissance and known as African Americans' poet laureate. Hughes was an important speaker at the American Writers' Conference in 1935. As an influential writer, he wrote novels, poems, plays, and autobiography that encouraged writing of other African American writers. During the Depression, he helped the founding of the black theater in the Federal Theater Project. He was the editor of many literary anthologies of African American literature.

1. Features of his writing

(1) Hughes wrote in praise of the October Revolution and encouraged the Chinese in their revolutions. He visited Spain and wrote to support the Spanish people in their fight against the Fascist regime of Franco.

(2) In form, Hughes Hughes' poetry is famous for its fresh simplicity and its notable features of the free verse of Whitman, Sandburg, and Paul Dunbar.

Ⅵ. 兰斯顿·休斯

兰斯顿·休斯是哈莱姆文艺复兴运动的核心人物，也是众所周知的美国黑人桂冠诗人。1935 年成为美国作家协会的主要发言人之一。此后，作为一名有影响的作家，他的小说、诗歌、戏剧和自传鼓励了其他黑人作家的创作。他还是大萧条时期联邦剧院工程中黑人剧院的创始人之一。他也为许多美国黑人文学作品选集担任编辑。

1. 写作特点

(1)休斯在写作中歌颂十月革命，并对中国人民及其革命深表同情，他访问西班牙，发文支持西班牙人民反抗弗朗哥法西斯统治的斗争。

(2)在形式上，休斯的诗歌以其清新简约和运用惠特曼、桑德堡和保罗·顿巴的自由诗体的显著特征而著称。

2. Major works

The Weary Blues

The Ways of White Folks

Simple Speaks His Mind

Montage of a Dream Deferred

The Best of Simple

Simple's Uncle Sam

"The Negro Speaks of Rivers"

"As I Grew Older"

"Dream Variation"

Ⅶ. Richard Wright (1908 – 1960)

Wright was a power writer who appeared in the 1940s. Many of Wright's literary works concern racial themes, especially related to the plight of African Americans during the late 19th to mid-20th centuries. He exerted a great influence over subsequent African American writers. He began the contemporary African American literary tradition of violent self-assertion.

1. Major works

Uncle Tom's Children: Four Novellas

Native Son

Black Boy

2. Analysis of major work

◆*Native Son*

(1) Centering on an African American adolescent's growth, *Native Son* consists of three sections, subtitled respectively, "Fear," "Flight," and "Fate."

(2) *Native Son* is an extremely fascinating book. It deals with one of the thorniest problems with which American had been beleaguered, the racial question.

(3) The novel tells the story of 20-year-old Bigger Thomas, a black youth living in utter poverty in a poor area on Chicago's South Side in the 1930s. Bigger Thomas embodies a new type of African American personality and a higher level of African American racial awareness. Rebellious by nature, he is never able to feel at peace with the world in which he finds himself. His actions represent African American identity and the obligation of the whites. In the end, he committed violent crimes and was sentenced to death. The author denotes that there is no escape from this destiny for Bigger or any other black American since they are the product of the mainstream society that formed them.

2. 主要作品

《疲惫的布鲁斯》

《白人的行径》

《辛普尔倾诉衷情》

《缓梦蒙太奇》

《辛普尔集锦》

《辛普尔的山姆叔叔》

《黑人谈河》

《当我长大》

《梦的变奏》

Ⅶ. 理查德·赖特

赖特于20世纪40年代创作的文学作品主要围绕种族议题，尤其讲述了非裔美国人从19世纪末期到20世纪中叶期间所面临的困境。赖特对后来的黑人作家影响深远，他开启了现代美国文学极端彰显自我的传统。

1. 主要作品

《汤姆叔叔的孩子们》

《土生子》

《黑孩子》

2. 主要作品分析

◆《土生子》

(1)《土生子》是一个美国黑人青年成长的故事，由三部分组成，副标题分别为“恐惧”、“逃跑”和“命运”。

(2)《土生子》是一部极具吸引力的作品。它着手于美国最为苦恼和棘手的种族问题。

(3) 小说主人公比格·托马斯是一位20岁的美国黑人青年，成长于20世纪30年代芝加哥南部的贫穷地区。比格·托马斯展现了新非裔青年的特点和美国黑人更高层次的民族认知。他本性叛逆，在发现自我的世界里他感受不到安宁。他的行为代表了黑人自身的定位和白人的责任。他最终因犯下暴力罪行而被判死刑。作者借此指出比格及其他非裔美国人都难逃悲剧性命运，因为他们都是主流社会价值下的产物。

Ⅷ. Ralph Ellison (1914 –1994)

1. Major works

Invisible Man

Shadow and Act

Going to the Territory

2. Analysis of major work

◆*Invisible Man*

(1) *Invisible Man* tells an atypical modern existential story. The protagonist-narrator is nameless apparently because he is invisible. He was brought up in Deep South. As a teenager he attended a horrifying "battle royal" where black men were reduced to fighting animals. After he journeyed to the streets of Harlem, he joined a Communist rally where black men were elevated to the status of trophies. He had to hide in basements to avoid policemen.

(2) The novel's ending is significant, which can be particularly seen from the fact that the narrator constantly refers to "you", humanity at large. He transcends the physical limits of African American individuality and speaks for all men in the world. His dilemma, generalized and magnified, assumes a universal magnitude.

(3) In addition, the novel's writing style and techniques are amazing. Its language is more or less naturalistic in the beginning, then changes into something expressionistic, and ends with a surrealistic texture.

IX. James Baldwin (1924 –1987)

James Baldwin has been seen as Richard Wright's successor. Like Wright he stayed in Europe for some nine years to escape intolerable racial discrimination in America. Baldwin was a serious writer and an honest man. He criticized his country due to patriotism. He considered this his greatest responsibility in life.

1. Major works

Go Tell It on the Mountain

Notes of a Native Son

Giovanni's Room

Nobody Knows My Name

The Fire Next Time

Another Country

Blues for Mister Charlie

Tell Me How Long the Train Been Gone

Ⅷ. 拉尔夫·埃里森

1. 主要作品

《看不见的人》

《影子与行动》

《走向领域》

2. 主要作品分析

◆《看不见的人》

(1)《看不见的人》是一个典型的现代存在主义的典型故事。叙事者主人公无名无姓显然是因为人们对他视而不见。他生长于美国南方，在白人俱乐部里参与黑人少年之间残忍血腥的格斗，而后他流亡到纽约哈莱姆区，投身"兄弟会"牵头的激进政治运动，为警察的追捕隐居地下。

(2) 书的结尾十分重要，尤其是叙事者时常提及"你们"，这里的"你们"广泛指全人类。他叙事者由此超越了美国黑人个体身份的界限，骤然成为所有人的代表，他的困境推及到全人类，放大到了全世界的层面。

(3) 此外，这部小说的写作方式和技巧令人震撼。小说的语言开头多少有些自然主义的特征，后来转为表现主义，最后则是以超现实主义结尾。

IX. 詹姆斯·鲍德温

詹姆斯·鲍德温被看作是理查德·莱特的接班人。他与莱特一样，由于无法忍受美国的种族歧视逃到欧洲，并在那里生活了九年。鲍德温是位非常严肃的作家和诚实的人。他出于爱国主义精神而批判国家不合理的制度。他认为这是生命中最大的责任。

1. 主要作品

《向苍天呼吁》

《土生子札记》

《乔万尼的房间》

《没有人知道我的名字》

《下一次将是烈火》

《另一个国家》

《为查理先生唱的布鲁斯》

《告诉我火车已经开多久》

2. Analysis of major works

◆*Go Tell It on the Mountain*

Go Tell It on the Mountain revolves around a 14-year-old boy named John Grimes who struggles to find his identity amidst the influences of his father, church, and life's challenges. The book's style and language evoke the Old Testament, incorporating stream-of-consciousness techniques to gradually piece together the Grimes family's lives through church services and prayers.

X. Toni Morrison (1931 –2019)

Morrison inherited the legacy of African American literature. She has been recognized with the highest awards, including the National Book Award, the National Book Critical Circle Award, the Pulitzer Prize and the Nobel Prize in 1993.

1. Major works

The Bluest Eyes

Sula

Song of Solomon

Tar Baby

Beloved

Paradise

2. Analysis of major works

◆*Song of Solomon*

(1) Morrison won her literary position in contemporary American literature with the novel *Song of Solomon* (1977). This novel is seen as another great work in African American literature after *Native Son* and *Invisible Man*. It tells the story of an African American trying to recover his family roots.

(2) Morrison praises the history and civilization of the African Americans and expose the cruelty of racism. She uses folk myths, legends and magic realism to achieve her theme.

(3) The greatness of this novel lies in its interlocking plotlines, varieties of language, and colorful folktales, legends, magic, and fantasy.

◆*Beloved*

(1) *Beloved* is based on the true antebellum story of a slave mother, Margaret Garner, who killed her own children just to spare them from the tragedy of slavery. "Beloved" in Morrison's novel is the word inscribed on the tombstone of the child killed by its mother.

2. 主要作品分析

◆《向苍天呼吁》

《向苍天呼吁》围绕一个名叫约翰·格莱姆斯的14岁男孩展开，他在父亲、教会和生活挑战的影响下努力寻找自己的身份。这本书的风格和语言让人想起旧约，融入意识流技巧，通过教堂礼拜和祈祷逐渐拼凑出格莱姆斯一家的生活。

X. 托尼·莫里森

莫里森继承了非裔美国文学的传统。她曾摘得无数重要文学奖项，包括国家图书奖、国家图书批评奖、普利策奖以及1993年的诺贝尔文学奖。

1. 主要作品

《最蓝的眼睛》

《秀拉》

《所罗门之歌》

《柏油孩子》

《宠儿》

《天堂》

2. 主要作品分析

◆《所罗门之歌》

(1) 莫里森凭借《所罗门之歌》的发表奠定了在当代美国文坛的地位。这部小说被看作是继《土生子》和《隐形人》之后非裔美国文学的又一里程碑。它讲述了一个美国黑人试图寻找家族根源的故事。

(2) 在《所罗门之歌》中莫里森颂扬美国黑人文明及其悠久的历史，展现种族主义的罪恶可耻。她通过使用民间神话传奇和魔幻现实主义来点明主题。

(3) 这部作品的伟大之处在于它交错纵横的情节，多种多样的语言，以及丰富多彩的民间故事、传说、魔法和幻想。

◆《宠儿》

(1)《宠儿》根据内战前一个真实的故事创作而成。一个奴隶母亲，玛格丽特·加纳，杀死自己的孩子以免他们沦为奴隶。莫里森小说中的"宠儿"就是孩子母亲在墓碑上刻的文字。

(2) The novel reconstructs horrible slavery history through black folk culture and folk tales. It is a powerful book: it not only sympathize with African Americans but compels the white to face history.	(2) 这部小说通过黑人民俗文化和民间故事重建和再现可怕的奴隶历史。这是一部极具影响力的作品：它不仅与美国黑人的经历共情，也迫使白人面对历史。
XI. Alice Walker (1944 –)	**XI. 爱丽丝·沃克**
1. Major works	**1. 主要作品**
The Third Life of Grange Copeland *Meridian* *The Color Purple* *The Temple of My Familiar* *Possessing the Secret of Joy*	《格兰奇·科普兰德的第三次生命》 《子午线》 《紫色》 《殿堂》 《拥有快乐的秘密》
2. Analysis of major work	**2. 主要作品分析**
◆*The Color Purple*	◆《紫色》
(1) As an epistolary novel, *The Color Purple* consists of 90 letters, of which over two thirds are written to God by Celie, 14 to her sister Nettie, and 15 from Nettie to Celie. The story centers on Celie's life, with Nettie's African adventure as complementary.	(1)《紫色》是一部书信体小说，共有90封信，其中三分之二是希莉写给上帝的，14封是写给妹妹南蒂的，15封是南蒂写给希莉的。故事以希莉的生活为中心，以南蒂的非洲冒险为辅。
(2) *The Color Purple* describes African American women's growth against social and familial oppression. From the perspective of feminism, the book relates a story of solidarity between the oppressed women in a sexist, racist world.	(2) 从主题上来看，《紫色》第一次深入分析美国黑人女性在社会和家庭的双重压迫下的成长。从女性主义角度出发，这本书讲述了有关置身性别和种族歧视、压迫世界里的女性之间的团结互助。
(3) *The Color Purple* marks a new dawn in the growth of African American consciousness. It raises questions for the African Americans: they need to know themselves better and get ready for their own responsibility.	(3)《紫色》标志着美国黑人意识成长的新阶段。它提出了美国黑人需要思考的问题：他们得更了解自己，得为自己生活中的责任和义务做好准备。
(4) The title of the novel is symbolic. The purple color denotes self-dignity, love, human fellowship, and survival in spite of suffering and pain. It represents God's creation as well as common humanity.	(4) 小说的标题深含寓意。紫色象征尊严、爱、人类同胞之情，与痛苦和苦难时时相伴。它同时代表了上帝造物和普通人性。
XII. Maya Angelou (1928 – 2014)	**XII. 玛雅·安吉洛**
◆Major works	**◆主要作品**
I Know Why the Caged Bird Sing *Gather Together in My Name* *Swingin' and Swingin' Merry Like Christmas* *The Heart of a Woman* *All God's Children Need Traveling Shoes*	《我知道囚鸟为何歌唱》 《以我的名义集合》 《摇啊摇，像圣诞节一样快乐》 《女人心》 《上帝的孩子都需要旅行鞋》

XIII. Gloria Naylor (1950 –2016)	XIII. 格洛丽亚·奈勒
◆Major works *Linden Hills* *Mama Day* *Bailey's Café* *Sophhira Wade* *Women of Brewster Place* *Men of Brewster Place*	◆主要作品 《林顿山》 《母亲节》 《贝利的咖啡馆》 《索菲拉·韦德》 《布鲁斯特地的女人们》 《布鲁斯特地的男人们》

25.2 考研真题与典型题详解

I. Fill in the blanks.

1. Author ________ Title ________（南京大学 2007 研）

   It goes a long way back, some twenty years. All my life I had been looking for something, and everywhere I turned someone tried to tell me what it was. I accepted their answers too, though they were often in contradiction and even self-contradictory. I was naive. I was looking for myself and asking everyone except myself questions which I, and only could answer.

2. African American literature is patterned on a myth of ________ from slavery, that of the Hebrew prophet Moses leading the Jews in their flight from the bond age in Egypt.

3. African American literature has undergone a long process of evolution. Its early form was ________, including ________, ________ and ________, in short, folk literature in its various manifestations.

4. In the 1920s, there was a new upsurge of African American literature, which has come to be known as ________.

5. DuBois helped to found a movement and established the organization ________ which fought more than any other for civil right.

6. By far the most important person in the Harlem Renaissance was ________ known as African Americans' poet laureate, who ultimately outgrew the movement, and developed into one of the major African American authors to help make African American culture.

7. Alex Haley's ________ marked a new level of self-awareness of the African American people as a race.

8. In the 1940 Richard Wright's ________ came out as a watershed in the tradition of the African American novel.

9. Native Son by ________ is a story about an African American adolescent's growth of awareness. It consists of three sections, namely ________, ________ and ________.

10. African American literature attained a higher degree of maturity in 1952 when Ralph Ellison's ________ appeared in print.

11. In 1993, ________ became President Clinton's inaugural poet (the second person ever to do so for a president in history, the other being ________).

Ⅱ. Multiple Choice

1. The most popular and versatile of all the writers connected with the Harlem Renaissance is ________.（大连外国语学院 2008 研）

   A. Richard Wright　　B. W. E. B. Du Bois

   C. Langston Hughes　　D. James Baldwin

2. ________, Booker T. Washington, and Frederick Douglass are generally regarded as the three greatest African American writers in the 19th century.

   A. Ralph Ellison　　B. Langston Hughes

   C. Toni Morrison　　D. W. E. B. Du Bois

3. One of the most noticeable elements of Harlem Renaissance writing is its use of dialect and folklore and its identification with the spirit of ________.

   A. rap　　B. jazz　　C. blues　　D. R&B

4. Among the African American writers of the fist half of the 20th century, ________ was the most durable and versatile: he was a poet, playwright, novelist, song writer, biographer, editor, newspaper columnist, translator and lecturer.

   A. Countee Cullen　　B. Claude McKay

   C. Jean Toomer　　D. Langston Hughes

5. Which of the following is not said of Langston Hughes?

   A. The first African American to support himself as a professional writer.

   B. National Book Award winner.

   C. Poet Laureate of Harlem.

   D. O. Henry of Harlem.

III. Explain the following term.

1. Harlem Renaissance（北外 2009 研；北师大 2007 研；南开大学 2007 研；山东大学 2018 研）

Ⅳ. Read the following quotations and answer the questions.

Passage 1

I've known rivers:
I've known rivers ancient as the world and older than the
Flow of human blood in human veins.
My soul has grown deep like the rivers.
I bathed in the Euphrates when dawns were young.
I built my hut near the Congo and it lulled me to sleep.
I looked upon the Nile and raised the pyramids above it.
I heard the singing of Mississippi when Abe Lincoln
Went down to New Orleans, and I've seen its muddy bosom turn
All golden in the sunset.
I've known rivers.
Ancient, dusky rivers.
My soul has grown deep like the rivers.

Questions:

(1) What is the title of the poem?

(2) What is the name of the poet?

(3) What does "I" stand for in the poem?

(4) What is the theme of the poem?

Passage 2

I am an invisible man... I am invisible, understand, simply because people refuse to see me. Like the bodiless heads you see sometimes in circus sideshows, it is as though I have been surrounded by mirrors of hard, distorting glass. When they approach me they see only my surroundings, themselves. Or figments of their imagination—indeed, everything and anything except me... You often doubt if you really exist... You ache with the need to convince yourself that you do exist in the real world.

Questions:

(1) Which novel is this passage taken from?

(2) What is the name of the author?

(3) At the end of the novel, the author writes "even an invisible man has a socially responsible role to play.., who knows but that, on the lower frequencies, I speak for you?". What does "you" refer to here? What does the author want to convey by applying this pronoun?

V. Short answer question

1. What are the major themes of *Native Son* by Richard Wright (give at least three)?

VI. Essay questions

1. Discuss one significant Jewish writer or Black writer in American literature. (大连外国语学院 2007 研)
2. Searching for identity is always a dominant theme in African American literature. Discuss how this theme is developed in one specific African American book. (天津外国语学院 2007 研)
3. Toni Morrison is considered the best and the most representative of the contemporary African American writers. Discuss her art of fiction.

参考答案及解析

I. Fill in the blanks.

1. Ralph Waldo Ellison; *Invisible Man*

   (题目节选自埃利森的《看不见的人》，本书是当代美国黑人文学中的经典之作，具有西方当代小说的许多特点：思想内容上提出了个人在荒谬的宇宙里的处境问题并探索自我本质；艺术上大胆创新，现实主义与超现实主义相结合，在运用黑色幽默手法上开美国后现代派文学的先河。)

2. deliverance

   (美国黑人文学是建筑在摆脱奴役的神话之上的，即希伯来先知摩西率领犹太人反抗埃及的奴役和压迫。)

3. oral, songs, ballads, spirituals

   (美国黑人文学经历了长期的演变。其早期主要是口述形式的，包括：歌曲、民谣和圣歌。）

4. the Harlem Renaissance

（哈勒姆文艺复兴（the Harlem Renaissance）是20世纪20年代黑人文学充满活力和创造力的时期，其中心在纽约市哈勒姆黑人聚居区。）

5. the National Association for the Advancement of Colored People

（1910年5月，全国黑人委员会与杜波依斯领导尼亚加拉运动合并，定名为全国有色人种协进会(the National Association for the Advancement of Colored People)。协进会的目标，是通过改良的道路，使黑人享有完全的公民权、法庭公平裁判权。）

6. Langston Hughes

（兰斯顿·休斯(Langston Hughes)在美国文坛，尤其是黑人文学方面，是一个举足轻重的人物。他主要以诗歌著称，被誉为"黑人民族的桂冠诗人"。）

7. *Roots*

（1976年，美国出版了黑人作家亚历克斯·哈利(Alex Haley)所写的一部家史小说《根》(*Roots*)。该小说标志着美国黑人整个民族新的自我觉醒。）

8. *Native Son*

（1940年美国黑人作家理查德·赖特(Richard Wright)发表了小说《土生子》(*Native Son*)，该小说成为美国黑人文学的分水岭。）

9. Richard Wright，"Fear"，"Flight"，"Fate"

（美国黑人作家理查德·赖特(Richard Wright)的小说《土生子》(*Native Son*)讲述了一个美国黑人青年觉醒的过程。小说共分三部分：《恐惧》("Fear")、《逃跑》("Flight")和《命运》("Fate")。）

10. *Invisible Man*

（拉尔夫·艾里森(Ralph Ellison)的小说《看不见的人》(*Invisible Man*)是当代美国黑人文学中的经典之作。它的出版标志着美国黑人文学的成熟。）

11. Maya Angelou; Robert Frost

（1993年，黑人女作家玛娅·安杰洛(Maya Angelou)应总统比尔·克林顿的邀请，在其就职仪式上朗诵献诗《清晨的脉搏》("On the Pulse of the Morning")，成为美国历史上继罗伯特·弗罗斯特之后的官方诗人。）

II. Multiple Choice

1. C　兰斯顿·休斯，美国著名黑人诗人，"哈莱姆文艺复兴"的代表，《黑人谈河》是其最脍炙人口的作品。
2. D　杜波依斯、布克·华盛顿及弗雷德里克被认为是19世纪美国最伟大的3位非裔文学作家。
3. B　哈莱姆文艺复兴最突出的特点之一是运用方言及民歌，以及展现了爵士乐的精神。
4. D　兰斯顿·休斯是哈莱姆文艺复兴运动的核心人物，也是众所周知的美国黑人桂冠诗人。1935年成为美国作家协会的主要发言人之一。此后，作为作家他的影响力无处不在，作品产量惊人。小说、诗歌、戏剧、散文、译著、自传——他轻松地写出这一切。
5. B　休斯并未获得国家图书奖。

III. Explain the following term.

1. Harlem Renaissance: The Harlem Renaissance refers to the flowering of African American cultural and intellectual life during the 1920s and 1930s. At the time, it was known as the "New Negro Movement", named after the 1925 anthology The New Negro edited by Alain Locke. Centered in the Harlem neighborhood of New York City, the movement impacted urban centers throughout the United States. Challenging white paternalism and racism, African-American artists and intellectuals rejected imitating the styles of Europeans and white Americans and instead celebrated black dignity and creativity.

IV. Read the following quotations and answer the questions.

Passage 1

(1) The poem is entitled "The Negro Speaks of Rivers".

(2) The poet is Langston Hughes.

(3) "I" stands for the Blacks throughout history.

(4) The poem writes about the wisdom, courage and the powerful aspirations of a race suffering mistreatment and injustice throughout history.

Passage 2

(1) *Invisible Man*

(2) Ralph Ellison

(3) By using the pronoun "you", the author is addressing his readers. By doing so, he transcends the physical limits of an African American individuality. "You" in the novel refers to all the modern people, whether they are black or white. The author wanted his readers to realize that all the modern people with their aspirations for self-identity are suffering from alienation and frustration in a dehumanized society.

V. Short answer question

1. The major themes of *Native Son* by Richard Wright are racism, protest, alienation, frustration, and the mentality of African Americans.

VI. Essay questions

1. Toni Morrison is a great contemporary American writer, she won the Nobel Prize for Literature in 1993, the first African American writer who won this prize.

   Toni Morrison is known for "magical realism" in that she uses magic, folktales, and the supernatural in her novels. Her style combines unrealistic (supernatural) dements with a realistic presentation of life and characters.

   For Morrison, "all good art has been political" and the Black artist need to be responsible for the Black community. She aims at capturing "the something" that defines what makes a book "Black." All her fictions bear witness to the experience of the Black community. Sense of loss, roots, community, and identity of the Blacks are usual themes of her works. In her works Toni Morrison has shaped roles of black women in a racist and male dominated society. In the center of her complex and multilayered narratives is the unique cultural inheritance of African-Americans.

   Morrison's prose has the quality of speech. She deliberately strives for this effect, which she calls "aural literature." Morrison wants readers to participate in her novels, to be involved actively. Readers are encouraged to create the novel with her and to help construct meaning. She is known for her epic power, unerring ear for dialogue, and her poetically-charged and richly-expressive depictions of Black America.

2. Searching for identity is a dominant theme of *Invisible Man*, a novel written by Ralph Ellison. The novel addresses many of the social and intellectual issues facing African-Americans in the early twentieth century, as well as issues of individuality and personal identity.

   Invisible Man is narrated in the first person by the protagonist, an unnamed African American man who considers himself socially invisible. Speaking from the basement of Harlem which he says is "like a grave," he relates his bitter experience of having lived a horrible life for decades until he discovered his social invisibility. He tells readers how he held great expectations and won the approval of the whites who, satisfied with his docile character, sent him with a scholarship to a state college for Negroes. There he became the apprentice of Dr. Bledsoe, the black president, who, however, expelled him for having shown a white sponsor the dark secrets of the place. Next he went to New York where blacks are forced to be "invisible." What he tried to do was to be seen. At last, his dreams were failed and he had to hide in an underground cellar. It is from the basement that he narrates. The book ends with the narrator's awareness that "even an invisible man has a socially responsible role to play." The whole story is about a black man searching for his identity in a country dominated by the white.

3. Toni Morrison is a great contemporary American writer.

   Toni Morrison is known for "magical realism" in that she uses magic, folktales, and the supernatural in her novels. Her style combines unrealistic (supernatural) dements with a realistic presentation of life and characters.

   For Morrison, "all good art has been political" and the Black artist has a responsibility to the Black community. She aims at capturing "the something" that defines what makes a book "Black." All her fictions "bear witness" to the experience of the Black community. Sense of loss, roots, community, and identity of the Blacks are usual themes of her works. Her sympathy is especially given to the Black women who suffer from both the Whites and Black men.

   Morrison's prose has the quality of speech. She deliberately strives for this effect, which she calls "aural literature." Morrison wants readers to participate in her novels, to be involved actively. Readers are encouraged to create the novel with her and to help construct meaning.

第 26 章　多种族文学(2)：其他少数群体

26.1　复习笔记

Ⅰ. Other Minority Groups In recent decades, diversity has been highly valued as a strength of American culture and literature. Interest in multiculturalism has grown, leading to a strong enthusiasm for the literatures of various ethnic groups in America. The 1960s and 1970s witnessed a rise in multiracial awareness among different ethnic groups, with African Americans taking the lead and other minority groups like Hispanic Americans and Asian Americans following suit.	**Ⅰ. 其他少数群体** 近几十年来，美国文化和文学中的多样性备受重视，被认为是其优势之一。多元文化主义的兴起促进了对美国不同民族文学的热情追求。20 世纪 60 年代和 20 世纪 70 年代，各个民族间开始觉醒并强化多元文化意识，其中以非裔美国人为先导，其他少数族裔如西班牙裔美国人和亚裔美国人紧随其后。
Ⅱ. Native American Literature **1. Brief Introduction** For a long time, Indians in American literature have been a distorted image. No matter how they were portrayed in mainstream literature, their images were more or less distorted. As the American Indian writer N. Scott Momaday pointed out, "American Indians were once caught in a crisis in which the Indians left a rigid image in Americans' minds." So far, the Indians have been telling their stories from their own point of view for a long time, and they successfully changed the original image and made it a real and vivid existence. In 1968, N. Scott Momaday published *House Made of Dawn* and won the Pulitzer Prize, which inspired the well-known "Renaissance of Native American Literature" in the late 1960s. Nowadays, the works of American Indian writers flood the book market, and their literature has become a unique part of American literature.	**Ⅱ. 美国本土印第安文学** **1. 简介** 很长一段时期内，美国文学中的印第安人一直是一种被歪曲的形象。无论主流文学如何刻画，他们的形象都会或多或少有些失真。正如美国印第安作家 N. 司各特·莫玛戴所指出的，"美国印第安人曾一度陷入这样一种危机，即印第安人在美国人的脑海中留下的是一种僵化的形象。"迄今为止，印第安人长期以来一直从自己的角度出发讲述自己的故事，他们成功的改变了了原先的形象，使之成为一种真实鲜活的存在。1968 年 N. 司各特·莫玛戴发表了《黎明之屋》，获得普利策奖。这激发了 20 世纪 60 年代末众所周知的"美国本土印第安文学复兴"。如今美国印第安作家的作品充斥书市，他们的文学也已成为美国文学中独特的一部分。
2. D'Arcy McNickle (1904 –1977) McNickle devoted his whole life to improving the fortunes of his fellow American Indians.	**2. 德·安塞·麦克尼克** 麦克尼克一生都在致力于改善他的印第安同胞的命运。

◆**Major works**

Native American Tribalism: Indian Survivals and Renewal

The Surrounded

◆**Analysis of *The Surrounded***

The Surrounded is a milestone in the history of Native American literature. The novel tells a tragic story of cultural dislocation and identity division, and reveals the painful process of the disintegration of the Native American culture. It also directly accuses the invasion of Indian traditional life by the whites.

◆**主要作品**

《美国印第安部落文化：印第安的幸存者与再生代》

《被包围者》

◆**《被包围者》分析**

《被包围者》是美国本土印第安文学历史上的一个里程碑。小说讲述了一个文化错位、身份分裂的悲剧故事。它揭示了美国本土文化分崩离析的悲恸过程。它将控诉的矛头直指白人对印第安传统生活的入侵。

3. N. Scott Momaday (1934 –)

Momaday is one of the most influential Native American novelists and poets. He is a Kiowa Indian and received education at the University of New Mexico and Stanford University.

◆**Major works**

House Made of Dawn

Angle of Geese

The Names

The Gourd Dancer

The Ancient Child

In the Presence of the Sun: Stories and Poems

3. N. 司各特·莫玛戴

莫玛戴是最有影响力的美国原住民小说家和诗人之一。他是基奥瓦族印第安人，在新墨西哥大学和斯坦福大学接受教育。

◆**主要作品**

《黎明之屋》

《鹅的视角》

《名字》

《葫芦舞者》

《远古的孩子》

《在太阳面前：故事和诗歌》

4. James Welch (1940 – 2003)

Welch's narratives are usually not optimistic, conveying an element of desperation. Most of his stories are set on the Montana plains, focusing on the contrast between modern and traditional lifestyles.

◆**Major works**

Winter in the Blood

The Death of Jim Loney

Fools Crow

The Indian Lawyer

4. 詹姆斯·韦尔奇

韦尔奇的叙述通常并不乐观，传达出一种绝望的元素。他的大部分故事都以蒙大拿平原为背景，重点关注现代与传统生活方式的对比。

◆**主要作品**

《血中的冬天》

《吉姆·洛尼之死》

《伏厄斯·克洛》

《印第安律师》

5. Leslie Marmon Silko (1948 –)

Leslie Marmon Silko grew up in a cultural environment that highly valued oral traditions and was deeply fascinated and inspired by her great grandmother's stories from ancient times. Initially studying law at the University of New Mexico, she abandoned it due to the inherent injustice in the Anglo-American legal system. Turning to writing as her career, she sought justice through her work.

5. 莱斯利·马尔蒙·希尔科

希尔科成长在一个强调口头传统的文化环境中，曾听她的曾祖母讲述古老的故事，深感着迷和启发。她曾作为法律学生就读于新墨西哥大学，但看到盎格鲁-美国法律体系中的不公正后选择辍学。她转而将写作作为职业，追求正义与公平。

◆**Major works**

Laguna Women

Ceremony

Storyteller

Almanac of the Dead

Sacred Water

Yellow Women and a Beauty of the Spirit

◆**Analysis of Ceremony**

"Ceremony" is a story of profound philosophical significance, following the protagonist Tayo's quest for personal well-being, the welfare of his Indian nation, and the world in general. It is a remarkable work that blends Indian oral tradition, encompassing myths and legends.

Silko successfully draws attention to the greatness of her Indian heritage, shedding light on the overlooked greatness of minorities like Native Americans.

6. Louise Erdrich (1954 –)

Erdrich was born in Minnesota and raised in North Dakota. She is of mixed heritage and received her education at Dartmouth College and Johns Hopkins University. Erdrich focuses on aspects of her Ojibwa Indian heritage, while also sensitively exploring the universal significance of human nature.

◆**Major works**

Love Medicine

The Beet Queen

Tracks

The Bingo Palace

Tales of Burning Love

The Antelope Wife

Ⅲ. Native American Poetry

Native American poetry is remarkably diverse, with a wealth of uniqueness and variety. These poets aim to enrich the representation of the Native American experience, contributing to the development of Native American literature.

Through the hard work of these Native American writers, their works have emerged from obscurity and continue to be present in bookstores today.

◆**主要作品**

《拉姑纳妇女》

《典礼》

《说故事者》

《死者年鉴》

《圣水》

《黄皮肤的女人与神灵美人》

◆**《典礼》分析**

《典礼》是一个具有深刻哲学意义的故事。故事讲述了主人公塔佑追求个人健康、印第安族民族的福祉以及整个世界的过程，是一部杰出的作品，融合了印第安口头传统的神话和传说。

希尔科成功地引起了世界对她的印第安传统的关注，让人们注意到少数民族如美洲土著的伟大。

6. 路易斯·厄德里齐

厄德里齐在明尼苏达州出生，在北达科他州长大，是混血儿。她在达特茅斯学院和约翰霍普金斯大学接受教育。她关注自身的奥吉布瓦印第安传承的特征，但她对人性太敏感，不允许它使其普遍意义黯然失色。

◆**主要作品**

《爱药》

《土著皇后》

《痕迹》

《宾果宫》

《燃情故事集》

《羚羊妻》

Ⅲ. 美国本土印第安诗歌

美洲原住民诗歌非常多样化，具有丰富的独特性和多样性。这些诗人旨在丰富美洲原住民经历的表现，为美洲原住民文学的发展做出贡献。

通过这些美国原住民作家的辛勤工作，他们的作品从默默无闻中脱颖而出，并继续出现在今天的书店里。

Ⅳ. Asian American Literature

1. Brief Introduction

Asian American literature is usually subdivided into Chinese American literature, Japanese American literature, Indian American literature, Korean American literature, and Filipino American literature. Because these Asian American writers incorporate different cultural and historical backgrounds in their creations, Asian American literary works present a highly diverse feature. In the 1970s, Asian American literature began to receive attention as a branch of American literature. It was the civil rights movement of the 1960s that aroused the national independence spirit of the various minorities in the United States. Courses on university campuses become "ethnical" and Asian American academic research projects emerged. The Immigration Reform Act of 1965 brought a new round of highly educated immigrants to make the cultural atmosphere more oriented, leading Asian American writers to develop further.

2. Maxine Hong Kingston (1940 –)

Kingston was born and grew up in a dual cultural environment: during her growth, the conflict and integration of Chinese and American cultures were very obvious, which also made identity, race and ethnic issues the themes of her writing.

◆Major works

The Woman Warrior

China Men

Tripmaster Monkey: His Fake Book

3. Amy Tan (1952 –)

Amy Tan's first novel, *The Joy Luck Club*, has set off a lot of waves in contemporary American literary circles, enabling readers and critics to conduct a comprehensive review of Asian American literature.

◆Major works

The Joy Luck Club

The Kitchen God's Wife

The Bonesetter's Daughter

4. Bharati Mukherjee (1940 – 2017)

Mukherjee's novels are all exploring the nature of the assimilation of cultures in foreign countries like North America. Assimilation means transformation and self-innovation. She studied this issue from a female perspective. So far, all the protagonists in her novels are women or Indian women.

Ⅳ. 亚裔美国文学

1. 简介

亚裔美国文学通常细分为华裔美国文学、日裔美国文学、印度裔美国文学、韩裔美国文学和菲律宾裔美国文学。由于这些亚裔美国作家在创作中融入了不同的文化和历史背景，因此亚裔美国文学作品呈现出高度多样化的特点。20世纪70年代，亚裔美国文学才作为美国文学的一个分支开始被关注。那是60年代的民权运动激起了美国各少数民族的民族独立精神。大学校园里的课程变得“民族化”。美国亚裔学术研究项目出现。1965年的《移民法案》带来了新一轮的高学历移民使文化氛围更有导向性，引领亚裔美国作家进一步发展起来。

2. 汤婷婷

汤婷婷出生并成长在一个双重文化环境中：她的成长过程中中美文化冲突与融合非常明显，这也使得身份、种族和民族问题成为她的写作主题。

◆主要作品

《女勇士》

《中国人》

《孙行者》

3. 谭恩美

谭恩美的第一部小说《喜福会》在当代美国文坛掀起了不小的波浪，使读者和评论界对亚裔美国文学进行全面审视。

◆主要作品

《喜福会》

《灶神之妻》

《接骨师的女儿》

4. 巴拉蒂·幕克吉

幕克吉的小说都在探究在北美这样的异乡文化同化的本质。同化意味着变形和自我创新。她从女性的角度研究了这个问题。迄今为止，她小说的所有主人公都是女性，或是印度女性。

◆**Major works**

The Tiger's Daughter

Wife

Jasmine

The Holder of the World

◆**主要作品**

《老虎的女儿》

《妻子》

《贾思敏》

《世界的拥有者》

V. Asian American Poetry

Asian American poetry is a form of literature created by a specific group, with a focus on expressing the identity, cultural experiences, and social issues of Asian Americans. Its content often delves into questions of Asian American identity, including the blending and clashes between ancestral and mainstream cultures, as well as the challenges of self-positioning in a diverse society.

V. 亚裔美国诗歌

亚裔美国诗歌是一种特定群体的文学创作，着重表达亚裔美国人的身份认同、文化体验和社会议题。其内容常常探讨亚裔美国人的身份认同问题，包括对根文化和主流文化的交融与冲突，以及在多元社会中寻找自我定位的挑战。

Garrett Hongo (1951 –)

Hongo is a Japanese American poet. He has won many awards, including the Guggenheim Fellowship, the Hopwood Prize for Poetry, and the Pushcart Prize.

◆**Major works**

The Buddha Bandits Down Highway 99

Yellow Light

The River of Heaven

加勒特·本乡

本乡是一位日裔美国诗人。他获得过多个奖项。他曾荣获古根海姆奖、霍普伍德奖和普士卡奖。

◆**主要作品**

《99 号公路上的佛陀劫匪》

《黄光》

《天堂河》

Ⅵ. Chicano Literature

The term "Chicano" is derived from "Mexicano". Chicano literature is a kind of work about the Mexican-American experience created by American Mexicans and Mexicans in America. For Chicano writers, the sense of nationality is a vital part of their literary perception, portraying the experience of the Chicanos' nation in America and the main issues they are concerned about. This literary tradition dates back to the mid-19th century, but it was not obvious before the mid-1960s. The civil rights movement among Mexican Americans introduced Chicano literature to a new stage. Chicano families, groups and their struggle for civil rights became the subject of Chicano writers. The Chicano Renaissance emerged from the mid-1960s to the early 1980s. The writing theme of Chicano literature is to seek to confirm the national identity and tell the national experience.

Ⅵ. 奇卡诺文学

"奇卡诺"一词衍生自"Mexicano"。奇卡诺文学是美国墨西哥人后裔和在美国的墨西哥人创作的关于美国墨西哥人经历的作品。对卡奇诺作家来说，民族感是他们文学感知至关重要的一部分，刻画卡奇诺民族在美国的经历和他们关注的主要问题。这个文学传统可追溯至 19 世纪中期，但在 20 世纪 60 年代中期以前并不明显。墨西哥裔美国人间的民权运动将卡奇诺文学引入新阶段。卡奇诺家庭、团体和他们为民权而斗争成为卡奇诺作家的创作主题。20 世纪 60 年代中期到 80 年代初期兴起了卡奇诺文艺复兴。卡奇诺文学的写作主题就是寻求印证民族身份，讲述民族经历。

Ⅶ. Chicano Fiction Chicano fiction has grown over the past few decades, and one of the main themes is the exploration and affirmation of Chicano identity by Chicano writers. They struggle to hold on to cultural traditions under the pressure of dominant values and try to resist assimilation.	**Ⅶ. 奇卡诺小说** 奇卡诺小说在过去几十年中得到了发展，其中主要主题之一是奇卡诺作家对奇卡诺身份的探索和肯定。他们努力在主流价值观的压力下坚守文化传统，并试图抵抗同化。
Tomas Rivera (1935 – 1984) Rivera was deeply conscious of the distinctiveness of his culture, with its own way of life and traditions. Simultaneously, he recognized the assimilating forces generated by the mainstream "Anglo" society. ◆**Major works** *Y no se lo trago la tierra* (*And The Earth Did Not Part*)	**托马斯·里维拉** 里维拉对自己文化的独特性非常敏感，深知其独特的生活方式和传统。与此同时，他也非常清楚"英裔"主流社会持续产生的同化力量。 ◆**主要作品** 《大地不会分开》
Ⅷ. Chicano Poetry Chicano poetry has experienced significant growth, expressing the ethnic experience and Chicano heritage while being closely related to politics and sociology. The perspective of Chicano poets differs from mainstream poetry, using images and metaphors drawn from their own lives, and employing a mix of English and Spanish in their poetry.	**Ⅷ. 奇卡诺诗歌** 奇卡诺诗歌经历了显着的发展，表达了种族经验和奇卡诺遗产，同时与政治和社会学密切相关。奇卡诺诗人的视角与主流诗歌不同，他们使用来自自己生活的图像和隐喻，并在诗歌中混合使用英语和西班牙语。
Luis Omar Salinas (1937 – 2008) Luis Omar Salinas is a prominent Chicano poet. There is a significant amount of social criticism in Salinas's poetry, and he possesses a tragic vision in multiple senses. ◆**Major works** *Aztec Angel* *Quixotic Expectations*	**路易斯·奥玛·萨林纳斯** 萨林纳斯是一位著名的墨西哥裔美国诗人，他的诗歌中包含大量的社会批判，在诗歌中表现出多种可能意义上的悲剧视角。 ◆**主要作品** 《阿兹泰克天使》 《狂想》

26.2 考研真题与典型题详解

I. Fill in the blanks.

1. The most famous of the Asian American writers is __________, whose *The Woman Warrior: Memories of a Childhood among Ghosts* won __________ for nonfiction for 1976 and established her as a preeminent contemporary American writer.
2. Another important Asian American writer is Amy Tan, whose first novel, __________, made quite a stir on the contemporary American literary scene and brought Asian American literature to the intensive scrutiny of readers and critics alike.
3. The four parts of *The Joy Luck Club* are: __________, __________, __________ and __________.

Ⅱ. Essay question

1. Analysis of *The Joy Luck Club* by Amy Tan.

参考答案及解析

I. Fill in the blanks.

1. Maxine Hong Kingston, the National Books Critics Circle Award
   (美国最著名的亚裔作家是汤婷婷(Maxine Hong Kingston), 她的第一部作品是回忆录式的小说《女勇士》(*The Woman Warrior* : *memoirs of a girlhood among ghosts*), 此书于1976年出版后, 获当年美国全国书评界奖。这部作品的文学成就和热销的程度在美国文学史上是空前的。她从而蜚声美国文坛。)
2. *The Joy Luck Club*
   (著名华裔美国女作家谭恩美(Amy Tan)的第一部小说《喜福会》一经出版就在美国文坛上引起很大轰动, 并引起读者和评论家们对亚裔美国文学的强烈关注。)
3. "Feathers From a Thousand Li Away", "The Twenty-Six Malignant Gates", "American Translation", "Queen Mother of the Western Skies"
   (谭恩美的小说《喜福会》分为四部分"千里鹅毛"("Feathers From a Thousand Li Away"), "二十六扇凶门"("The Twenty-Six Malignant Gates"), "美国翻译"("American Translation"), "西方天空的母后"("Queen Mother of the Western Skies")。)

Ⅱ. Essay question

1. Amy Tan's first novel *The Joy Luck Club* has set off a lot of waves in contemporary American literary circles, enabling readers and critics to conduct a comprehensive review of Asian American literature.

   It is interesting both in theme and form. Thematically speaking, this is a story about eight two-generation women from four families telling their different stories. These stories share a common connection with each other as connective tissues. It consists of four parts, each of which begins with a vignette or preface, in short italics, and is narrated by one of the four mothers, pointing out the theme of this section. A dividing line can be drawn between the two generations of women. The mothers on one side tell their stories of their experiences in China while the daughters talk about their lives in America. The relationships between the mothers and their daughters are sometimes tense and even confrontational not only because of the generation gap but also mainly due to their different growth and cultural experiences. These stories eventually bridge the gap and represent the efforts of American-born daughters to understand and accept Chinese traditions.

   The format of the book is also very interesting. The sixteen stories are all narrated in the first person. Each of the eight characters has two stories, except Jin Mei, who tells four stories, two of her own and two of her mother. The variety of the voices seems dizzying, but inspires imagination. And there is almost no sense of misalignment between different parts. Everything is in place at the right time and fits well with the overall situation.

